Law of the Sea: The Emerging Regime of the Oceans

Law of the Sea: The Emerging Regime of the Oceans

PROCEEDINGS

Law of the Sea Institute
Eighth Annual Conference
June 18-21, 1973

University of Rhode Island
Kingston, Rhode Island

Edited by John King Gamble, Jr.
and Giulio Pontecorvo

Ballinger Publishing Company • Cambridge, Mass.
A Subsidiary of J.P. Lippincott Company

Funds for the Eighth Annual Conference of the Law of the Sea Institute, held in Kingston, Rhode Island, in June 1973, were provided by the Ford Foundation, the National Sea Grant Program and National Ocean Survey of the National Oceanic and Atmospheric Administration, the United States Coast Guard, and the University of Rhode Island. The continued support of these institutions is gratefully acknowledged by the Law of the Sea Institute.

International Standard Book Number: 0-88410-006-5

Library of Congress Catalog Card Number: 73-18229

Printed in the United States of America

Library of Congress Cataloging in Publication Data

Law of the Sea Institute.
   Law of the sea.

   1. Maritime law. 2. Marine pollution. 3. Marine resources. I. Gamble, John King, ed. II. Pontecorvo, Giulio, ed. III. Rhode Island. University. IV. Title.
   JX4408.L37   1974   341.45   73-18229
   ISBN 0-88410-006-5

Contents

List of Tables

List of Figures

Foreword

Giulio Pontecorvo

We are accustomed to saying that the Law of the Sea Institute is a cottage industry that over the years has outgrown the cottage—but we do not aspire to become a factory. Our aim is to focus on the crucial ocean policy issues and then to maximize the interchange between the speakers and the other participants. It is for this reason that last year we introduced small discussion groups. This experiment enjoyed a favorable response and we will continue it.

In our programs we have tried to anticipate issues as they emerge from the realm of purely academic discussions to the realm of policy issues requiring decision making by nations. Several such items are identified in this book; let me note just two of them. One is the question of mutual assistance in ocean affairs; the second is represented in the person of Senator Edmund Muskie, whose thoughts appear as Chapter 18 of this book.

Historically there has been a strong tendency to conceptualize assistance programs in a simple framework. Two illustrations of this predisposition are the idea held by many in the developed states that assistance programs may be regarded as a market price, a price that has to be paid for a right or privilege that can be supplied by the developing country. Similarly, many in developing states have looked to education and training programs that will provide people with skills as a sufficient condition for economic development.

In this book we will open up these simple conceptualizations to include both ideological and technical considerations, and these will be considered in a case study of how assistance programs are actually working in the Indian Ocean.

The second issue I would call your attention to grows out of the structure of the American political system. Our diplomats representing the executive branch carry on the processes of daily contact and negotiations between nations. But in any significant development, such as a general revision of the law of the sea, the residual power to accept or reject agreements lies in the United States Senate. Senator Edmund Muskie, one of the most powerful voices in the Senate, gives us a clear view of the concerns of the Senate and the criteria by which that body will evaluate the handiwork of our diplomats.

Finally, let me remain in character and conclude by noting one purely academic distinction that may be useful in clarifying issues. Most analyses in the social sciences utilize static models. These models lead men to an understanding of a given system, and once a hard-won understanding is achieved, it is, as Keynes described so well, hard to displace in people's thinking. But the crucial element that must be considered in establishing a stable regime for the oceans is that the system is dynamic. The next decade will see major technological changes in how the oceans may be used and also in the value of ocean space. Accommodation to both these dynamic forces—technological and economic—must be an integral part of the diplomatic process.

Giulio Pontecorvo
Columbia University

Part one

Chapter One

Bloc Thinking About the Oceans: Accelerating Pluralism?

John King Gamble, Jr.
Associate Director, Law of the Sea Institute

In order to make any sense out of the complex situation developing, it is necessary to think in terms of groups of nations willing to act in concert in order to
achieve certain goals. One might call these groups "coalitions," but if coalition is
defined rigorously, the requirements of complete information and conscious
coordination of behavior seem somewhat inapplicable to the rapidly changing
area of international marine affairs.[1] The less restrictive term "blocs" may be
most appropriate, if it is defined as "any political group of states operating as a
unit. . . ."[2] Thus I shall use the word blocs to denote groups of countries which
choose to act together in pursuit of certain results.

Once one has identified the blocs, it is necessary to look for issue
areas about which the blocs are concerned and means, contexts, or fora that can
be used by the blocs in pursuing an acceptable resolution of the issues. There is
even general agreement about what the major blocs and issue areas are. The blocs
would surely include developed states, developing states, landlocked states,
coastal states, naval powers, commercial maritime powers, coastal fishing states,
distant water fishing states, oil exporting states, oil importing states, and so
forth. Issue areas are equally well known and include freedom of scientific research, free transit for military and commercial vessels, freedom of fishing,
claims to economic zones, claims to mineral resources of the seabed, and others.
One could sketch in detail the makeup of a particular bloc as well as how it may
be expected to react to a given issue area; in fact this is exactly what most analyses of the law of the sea attempt to do.

Instead I should like to take a more general, a more prescriptive approach. It is absolutely clear that there is considerable diversity in bloc composition as one moves from one issue area to another. A state may side with a "developing states bloc" on one issue while abandoning most developing states because of a special interest in some other area of marine affairs, e.g., fishing. The result of all this is that there are few blocs with sufficient cohesion to hold together across a wide range of issue areas. Generally speaking, one way to increase intra-bloc cohesion is to reduce the size of blocs. However, this process leads very quickly to extreme positions which have no chance of gaining acceptance by the world community.

I am sure almost everyone would accept the fact that a certain amount of pluralism exists in law of the sea matters. By pluralism I simply mean multiple, constantly changing blocs pursuing a myriad of complex and changing goals. Pluralism is a fact of life at the individual, national, or international level. But international cooperation is possible only when pluralism is kept within certain bounds—this is why the 1958 Geneva Conference was successful. Certainly issues were unresolved—territorial sea width, exact delimitation of continental shelf, etc.—but considerable consensus was left after all pluralistic forces had run their courses.

What then has changed since 1958 to contribute to this increased pluralism? I argue that there are four primary occurrences which have created greater bloc diversity: (1) increase in the number of sovereign states; (2) rapidly expanding technology; (3) significant thaw in the Cold War; and (4) growing environmental concern. These four, or the interaction among them, serve to account for many of the difficulties that will arise.

I look first at the increase in the number of sovereign states. Nearly every commentary remarks that the balance of power has changed dramatically since the 1958 and 1960 conferences. It is no secret that the developing countries now are close to having a 2/3 majority at the 1973-74 conference. However, there is little evidence that any monolithic, cohesive bloc of 2/3 will develop. Quite the contrary, the increase in the number of actors may create added opportunity for divisive forces to operate. But more important are the derivative factors resulting from the increased number of actors.

One of these derivative factors is the fact that a growing number of countries with little intrinsic interest in the law of the sea are participating as equal partners in the international decisionmaking process. This results in a more complicated bargaining process. The marine-related issues themselves are complex enough, but the introduction of actors whose paramount concerns have little to do with the law of the sea can destroy the conference. This lack of intrinsic interest in the oceans is not limited to any group of countries. There are developed countries with little substantive interest in the oceans. There are developing countries whose whole economies depend upon rational management of marine resources. It is ironic indeed that elaborate regimes for control of ocean space have attempted to allocate power according to actual marine interest, while the meetings and conferences that might create such regimes cling to an antiquated one state-one vote scheme that is largely oblivious of reality.

Another result of the predominance of developing countries is a marked tendency to codify international law rather than relying on a customary process developed by and for the developed states. Thus the modal world opinion now favors codification where at all possible. The problem is that the objective situation may make these attempts at codification worthless (i.e., unacceptable) to all but a few states. An argument can be made that excessive reliance on, or anticipation of, codification can impede or even stop the process of customary development. Thus this increase in the number of actors may have created a situation in which international law has no free channel through which to evolve.

The rapid expansion of technology since 1958 has had a profound effect on bloc composition. In the epoch since the Geneva Conventions were drafted there has been little progress toward a more equitable distribution of technological expertise itself or of the benefits produced by technology. At least in relative terms, the rich nations are getting richer while the poor nations get poorer.

Thus there is a marked tendency for the developing countries to view hydrospace as one last arena where the developed world is going to deprive them of a just share of the resources provided by the earth. While the fears expressed by the developing countries may be justifiable, the results of these fears can be detrimental to the world community. Many people feel—I am among them—that the developed world owes the third world a substantially greater commitment in terms of economic development. This commitment has received frequent lip service from the United States and the Soviet Union as well as Western Europe. However, the amount of aid (technology if you wish) actually passed along to the third world has been negligible compared to the need. Thus Ambassador Pardo's 1967 speech struck a responsive note as developing states saw the oceans as a device by which distribution of the world's wealth might be made more equitable.

In recent years many, if not most, developing states have viewed the law of the sea negotiations principally with a view towards maximizing their economic return, usually by means of expanded national jurisdiction. The prospect of increasing technological capability, coupled with the probability of some sort of international control of the seabed beyond national jurisdiction, has raised the hopes of the developing countries. Unfortunately, their hopes are largely false. It is now technologically possible to extract resources from the deep seabed, but it is the economic feasibility that will determine potential benefit to the developing countries. I fear that what has resulted is that the illusion of greater riches from the oceans has impeded the development of workable long-term programs of aid for the developing world.

But the influence of increased technology has had other, more subtle effects on developing issues. While the developing countries may view technology as a panacea for their economic ills, the developed countries often use technology as a way to avoid or delay a limited entry scheme for an overfished region, or to postpone stringent oil pollution regulations on the grounds that the technology is not capable of providing accurate information about the current status of fish stocks or pollutants. There is some validity to claims such as these, but there is a limit to how much one can hide behind the assertion, "the data are not good enough."

I am tempted to offer the hypothesis that ocean science is now at a dangerous juncture. Technology has increased so rapidly that it is possible, if one is so disposed, to get a glimpse of massive stores of wealth to be used for the common good of mankind. On the other hand, technology has not progressed far enough to provide an economically viable way of extracting many of the sea's resources. Thus technology's rapid increase may have served to blur the distinction between scientific possibility and economic viability—an unfortunate occurrence indeed, since this distinction is the most important communications problem between the developed and developing countries.

The third factor contributing to increased bloc diversity is the thaw in the Cold War. At both the 1958 and 1960 law of the sea conferences the world was quite bipolar in nature. The United States and the Soviet Union had considerable influence over the behavior of the rest of the world. This meant that issues on which the two superpowers agreed had a fairly good chance of gaining acceptance. The world of the mid 1970s is decidedly multipolar in nature. There may well be considerable agreement between the United States and the Soviet Union at the 1973-74 Conference, but this agreement probably will not carry along many other countries. Some have even argued that the United States and the Soviet Union may form a bloc of two on some issues.[3] I do not wish to imply that superpower politics should dominate. However, I think it is clear that the diminution of superpower influence in the world will encourage more diversity. The result is likely to be more interest groups taking positions that are difficult to reconcile with one another; in a word, increased pluralism.

The fourth primary factor serving to complicate bloc composition is increasing concern for the marine environment. It would be utterly absurd to contend that ecological considerations should not play a role in the law of the sea negotiations. However, the spectre of irreparable environmental damage casts a new light on almost all law of the sea issues. An already complex situation has been made much more complicated by the introduction of a whole new set of forces.

It is possible that differing positions on environmental issues may make it impossible to reconcile positions between the developed and developing countries. The developed countries are now beginning to concede that economic gains must be sacrificed in order to stop or reverse marine pollution. The less developed countries feel that it is morally unjust and economically impossible for them to make sacrifices to remedy pollution created almost entirely by a small group of highly developed countries.

In this instance attribution of blame is easy—it lies with the developed countries. They have been slow to realize the gravity of the problem; once they discovered it they were naive in expecting the third world to be willing to approach the problem with zeal. Many simplistic solutions have been offered, but few people in the developed countries have realized that it is irrational for most developing countries to make any significant economic sacrifice in order to fight pollution. In fact the developing countries can make a case for the fact that they have a right to pollute, especially if this is the only way they can get an equitable share of the world's resources.

Thus far I have presented a rather gloomy picture. I should like to suggest a few courses of action that may improve the likelihood of achieving solutions that will contribute to a genuine common good of mankind. The first of these involves the perceived interrelatedness of ocean problems. No one would argue that ocean issues form one vast system, i.e., actions affecting one element are bound to influence other elements. However, it does not follow from this that solutions to the problems are best achieved by throwing all problems into the same hopper and trying to draft a single, multilateral treaty capable of resolving all problems. I doubt agreement can be reached on such a treaty. Even if agreement is possible, the resulting treaty would undoubtedly be ratified by too few states and be subjected to so many crippling reservations that it would be relatively useless.

One approach that would help to make a single comprehensive treaty possible is to try to separate all issues that are not necessarily and directly related to the law of the sea. We have learned that there is a limit to how much hydrocarbon pollution the sea can absorb. There is also a limit to how many peripheral issues the oceans can absorb before rational control becomes impossible. I have already touched upon the most important of these peripheral issues, namely the obligation the developed countries have to the third world. As things now stand, the oceans are being perceived as a blank check for meeting this obligation; but technology is incapable of filling in the check's value.

There are a number of issue areas that could be removed from the comprehensive law of the sea negotiations because they are better dealt with by regional arrangements. Many fisheries problems fall into this category. One could argue that most problems of marine pollution could be handled by plurilateral treaty involving relatively few countries.

It is also highly desirable to try to establish more objective ways of measuring national interest in the oceans. The possession of territorial sovereignty may imply some interest in the oceans, but the intensity of that interest varies considerably. It is true that landlocked states should have some rights to ocean utilization. However, it is absurd to assert that landlocked states have in-

terests in the oceans comparable to island states. Neither should landlocked
states have an equal say in how the world's oceans should be controlled. Whether
we like it or not, territorial sovereignty is going to be a dominant force in international affairs for the forseeable future. A direct implication of current patterns
of territorial sovereignty is substantial variation in access to, dependence upon,
and utilization of the oceans.

The three tables that follow (Tables 1-1, 1-2, and 1-3) are intended
to give some indication of a more objective way of assessing countries' dependence on the oceans. Each of the tables considers marine attributes relative to
other characteristics of the country. If blocs developed around objective measures such as these, the chances for resolution of conflicts would be greatly enhanced. It should be pointed out that these tables are designed to be representative, not exhaustive. Obviously other elements of genuine interest in the oceans
would have to be accommodated. Among these are fisheries and military uses of
the oceans.

Table 1-1. Marine Transportation/G.N.P.

Qatar	0.27110	Moroco	0.00530	Thaild	0.00220	Germ. W.	0.00060
Kuwait	0.06230	Senegl	0.00530	U.K.	0.00220	USSR	0.00050
Liberi	0.05700	IvoryC	0.00430	Haiti	0.00210	Romani	0.00040
Mauria	0.05300	Panama	0.00420	Costa	0.00200	U.S.A.	0.00040
Libya	0.05190	Kenya	0.00400	Malags	0.00200	Kore. N	0.00030
Trin. T	0.04940	Somali	0.00400	Cambod	0.00190	Germ. E	0.00020
Saudia	0.03860	Cuba	0.00350	Camron	0.00190	Mexico	0.00020
Gabon	0.03420	U.A.R.	0.00350	Greece	0.00190	China	0.00010
Lebnon	0.03290	Belgim	0.00340	Spain	0.00190	Afghan	0.0
Syria	0.02490	Finlan	0.00330	Israel	0.00180	Andora	0.0
Singap	0.02230	Philip	0.00330	Viet. S	0.00180	Austri	0.0
Tunisa	0.01960	Tanzan	0.00320	Zaire	0.00180	Bhutan	0.0
Venezu	0.01910	Austrl	0.00310	Portugl	0.00150	Bolivi	0.0
Guyana	0.01730	Taiwan	0.00310	Safric	0.00150	Botswa	0.0
Iran	0.01610	Hondur	0.00300	Sudan	0.00150	Burund	0.0
Eqguin	0.01480	Dahome	0.00290	Canada	0.00140	C.A.R.	0.0
Algeri	0.01400	Denmrk	0.00290	Brazil	0.00120	Chad	0.0
Jamaic	0.01200	Indons	0.00290	Bulgar	0.00120	Czechk	0.0
Congo	0.01160	SrInka	0.00280	Ecqadr	0.00110	Hungar	0.0
Sierra	0.00960	Kore. S	0.00270	France	0.00110	Laos	0.0
Maurit	0.00820	Albani	0.00250	Jordan	0.00110	Lesoth	0.0
Nigera	0.00730	NewZea	0.00250	India	0.00100	Luxemb	0.0
Togo	0.00730	Chile	0.00240	Burma	0.00090	Malawi	0.0
Melays	0.00710	Icelan	0.00240	ElSalv	0.00090	Mali	0.0
Nether	0.00700	Japan	0.00240	Ethiop	0.00090	Mongol	0.0
Iraq	0.00690	Sweden	0.00240	Colomb	0.00080	Nepal	0.0
Barbdo	0.00640	DomRep	0.00230	Guatem	0.00080	Paragu	0.0
Fiji	0.00630	Irelan	0.00230	Turkey	0.00080	Rhodsa	0.0
Malta	0.00560	Italy	0.00230	Uruguy	0.00080	Swazil	0.0
Norway	0.00560	Ghana	0.00220	Argent	0.00070	Switzd	0.0
Cyprus	0.00550	Guinea	0.00220	Poland	0.00070	Uganda	0.0
Gambia	0.00550	Peru	0.00220	Yemen	0.00070	Upvolt	0.0
				Yugosl	0.00070	Zambia	0.0

Table 1-2. Shoreline Length/Area

Monaco	5.00000	Albani	0.01409	Yemen	0.00324	Mauria	0.00090
Malta	0.40983	Nether	0.01400	Germ. W	0.00320	Algeri	0.00064
Barbdo	0.33132	Norway	0.01319	Senegl	0.00317	Congo	0.00063
Bahrai	0.29437	Viet. S	0.01288	U.S.A.	0.00316	Sudan	0.00040
Trin. T	0.12828	Kore. N	0.01241	Bulgar	0.00312	Jordan	0.00039
Singap	0.12500	Oman	0.01225	Ghana	0.00309	Iraq	0.00005
Maurit	0.11026	Spain	0.01045	Safric	0.00309	Zaire	0.00002
Cyprus	0.08118	Chile	0.00986	Venezu	0.00306	Afghan	0.0
Jamaic	0.06616	Malags	0.00950	Cambod	0.00300	Andora	0.0
Philip	0.06040	Nicara	0.00886	Belgim	0.00288	Austri	0.0
Haiti	0.05450	Tunisa	0.00875	Canada	0.00288	Bhutan	0.0
Denmrk	0.04125	Gambia	0.00871	Guyana	0.00279	Bolivi	0.0
Cuba	0.03950	Hondur	0.00864	USSR	0.00268	Botswa	0.0
Japan	0.03300	Sierra	0.00790	Peru	0.00253	Burund	0.0
Taiwan	0.03384	Sweden	0.00782	Colomb	0.00232	C.A.R.	0.0
Panama	0.03351	Liberi	0.00674	India	0.00224	Chad	0.0
Greece	0.03229	Thaild	0.00654	IvoryC	0.00220	Czechk	0.0
U.K.	0.02961	France	0.00653	Guinea	0.00200	Hungar	0.0
Icelan	0.02713	Somali	0.00648	Poland	0.00199	Laos	0.0
NewZea	0.02670	Turkey	0.00637	Argent	0.00197	Lesoth	0.0
Lebnon	0.02658	Mexico	0.00636	Tanzan	0.00184	Liecht	0.0
Indons	0.02626	Viet. N	0.00623	Saudia	0.00158	Luxemb	0.0
Srlnka	0.02565	Syemen	0.00588	Iran	0.00155	Malawi	0.0
Irelan	0.02443	Finlan	0.00564	Dahome	0.00149	Mali	0.0
Qatar	0.02400	Bangla	0.00562	Pakist	0.00141	Mongol	0.0
Costa	0.02269	Moroco	0.00519	Libya	0.00133	Nepal	0.0
Italy	0.02107	Austrl	0.00508	Romani	0.00123	Niger	0.0
Portgl	0.02089	Burma	0.00469	Togo	0.00120	Paragu	0.0
ElSalv	0.01985	Germ. E	0.00457	Nigera	0.00116	Rhodsa	0.0
Kore. S	0.01872	Yugosl	0.00431	Ethiop	0.00115	Rwanda	0.0
Kuwait	0.01854	Guatem	0.00423	Syria	0.00114	Sanmar	0.0
DomRep	0.01727	Uruguy	0.00422	Brazil	0.00112	Swazil	0.0
Eqguin	0.01698	Ecuadr	0.00418	Kenya	0.00109	Uganda	0.0
Israel	0.01546	Gabon	0.00386	Camron	0.00101	Upvoit	0.0
Malays	0.01442	U.A.R.	0.00338	China	0.00094	VatCit	0.0
						Zambia	0.0

In conclusion, I think several points should be emphasized. Blocs developing at the next law of the sea conference are likely to be diverse. Diversity is necessary to the degree that it derives from actual marine concerns. However, serious difficulties have been created when negotiations about ocean utilization and control are used as a forum for trying to rectify moral and social ills of the planet. This is not to denigrate the importance of these social ills, especially the gap between the rich and poor nations. If the common heritage of mankind is to be served by the world's oceans, those oceans must be managed so that productivity of living and nonliving resources is maximized along with due regard for both conservation and maritime transit. This simply cannot be achieved by a process that throws together marine interests, general aspirations of the third world, a vague notion of what technology can do, and concern for the environment—and then expects the magic of international negotiation to work miracles.

Table 1-3.   Continental Shelf Area[a]/Land Area

Monaco	158.33299	Italy	0.36100	Senegl	0.12100	Syria	0.01500
Maurit	33.84000	Hondur	0.36000	Guinea	0.11800	Togo	0.01400
Malta	31.14799	Eqguin	0.33200	Yugosl	0.10800	Dahome	0.01100
Maldiv	26.08699	Lebnon	0.32900	India	0.10700	Sudan	0.00700
Tonga	15.55600	Portgl	0.32100	Moroco	0.10500	Jordan	0.00500
Mauru	12.50000	SrInka	0.30800	Yemen	0.09600	Algeri	0.00400
Bahrai	6.49400	Bangla	0.29000	Safric	0.08900	Iraq	0.00100
Trin. T	4.29300	Haiti	0.28900	Guatem	0.08600	Afghan	0.0
Jamaic	2.76500	Kore. N	0.28400	Fiji	0.08500	Andora	0.0
Kore. S	1.87500	DomRep	0.28200	Bulgar	0.08400	Austri	0.0
Nether	1.74700	Sierra	0.27800	Romani	0.07700	Bhutan	0.0
Taiwan	1.69200	Sweden	0.26000	Venezu	0.07300	Bolivi	0.0
U.K.	1.52200	Burma	0.25600	Somali	0.07200	Botswa	0.0
Viet. S	1.42500	Spain	0.25500	Poland	0.06900	Burund	0.0
Irelan	1.35200	Norway	0.24000	Belgim	0.06800	C.A.R.	0.0
Denmrk	1.20800	Costa	0.23400	Brazil	0.06800	Chad	0.0
WSamoa	1.09400	Tunisa	0.23400	Germ. E	0.06700	Czechk	0.0
Indons	1.07500	Cambod	0.23200	Ghana	0.06600	Hungar	0.0
Japan	0.98100	Malags	0.23200	China	0.06200	Laos	0.0
Icelan	0.98000	Uruguy	0.22900	Pakist	0.05500	Lesoth	0.0
Qatar	0.90600	Austrl	0.22300	Iran	0.04900	Liecht	0.0
Malays	0.84800	Canada	0.22000	Peru	0.04900	Luxemb	0.0
NewZea	0.68500	Finlan	0.22000	Turkey	0.04900	Malawi	0.0
ElSalv	0.63000	Argent	0.21700	Colomb	0.04500	Mali	0.0
Barbdo	0.60200	Oman	0.21700	USSR	0.04200	Mongol	0.0
Panama	0.57200	France	0.20500	Nigera	0.03800	Nepal	0.0
Kuwait	0.56500	Guyana	0.17600	Libya	0.03600	Niger	0.0
U.A.E.	0.53600	Mexico	0.16900	Tenzan	0.03300	Paragu	0.0
Cyprus	0.53200	Israel	0.16200	Mauria	0.03200	Rhodsa	0.0
Cuba	0.52700	U.S.A.	0.14800	Ethiop	0.02900	Rwanda	0.0
Philip	0.44900	Albani	0.14500	U.A.R.	0.02800	Sanmar	0.0
Singap	0.44600	Greece	0.14100	Chile	0.02700	Swazil	0.0
Nicara	0.42200	Syemen	0.13500	Saudia	0.02700	Switzd	0.0
Gambia	0.39000	Liberi	0.13300	IvoryC	0.02400	Uganda	0.0
Thaild	0.37800	Gabon	0.13000	Congo	0.02000	UpVolt	0.0
Viet. N	0.36200	Ecuadr	0.12500	Kenya	0.01900	VatCit	0.0
		Germ. W	0.12400	Camron	0.01700	Zaire	0.0
						Zambia	0.0

[a]to 200-meter isobath

* * * * * *

Commentary
Leigh Ratiner[a]

I think one way of beginning the panel discussion today on bloc thinking about the oceans is to take some of the principal ideas which were put forward by Mr.

[a]Office of Ocean Resources, U.S. Department of Interior

Gamble and see where they lead. It seemed to me that there was an implication or a thread running through it that if the Law of the Sea Conference is to succeed, we are obliged as negotiators, and as members of the public who affect the opinions and decisions of negotiators, to limit the number of extraneous subjects and deal only with those that are absolutely essential to a successful conference. That common thread seemed to me to also indicate that what was essential was looking after the varied maritime interests of states and giving as little credence as possible, if you will, to some of the broader interests that developing countries claim to have in these negotiations—and which personally I think they do have. I am forced, now that I have restated his hypothesis, to very thoroughly disagree with Mr. Gamble.

It is quite clear that the law of the sea negotiations are moving in the direction desired by most coastal states with respect to resources. Navigation is not nearly as clear yet, and this may be a problem with people's perceptions of their own interests. Those countries, for example, who favor a pollution zone have fallen into a variety of camps. Some, like Canada, have made some very interesting arguments for pollution zones. Other countries—for example, at the March-April meeting of the U.N. Seabeds Committee—have talked about pollution zones mainly as a place in which they have a right to pollute. Taking the two together you have a bloc, but whose interests are being correctly and rationally perceived? And to what extent are those two different pollution zone proponents really prepared to take into account the interests of lots of other countries—not just the big maritime powers, but developing countries who also use ships to navigate or who depend on other countries' ships to bring goods to their own shores?

So while the Law of the Sea Conference in general may be moving in the direction of accommodating major interests, I think we should ask ourselves what are the real interests that the Law of the Sea Conference can serve. I am not just referring to the failures of the conference to set limits to the territorial sea or to defining the precise outer boundary of the continental shelf. What the world failed to do in 1958 and 1960 (and what it may fail to do in 1973 and 1974) is to establish some kind of sensible world order about the use of ocean space. I am reluctant to use that word, but the fact is that the world had an opportunity in 1958 to create institutional and legal arrangements for the use of ocean space as a model, an experiment, as an opportunity to find out if world cooperation will work and to provide a framework in which world cooperation can work.

Perhaps a better opportunity is available today, since there are now so many more countries in existence than at that time. And yet, I was surprised to read this statement: "Whether we like it or not, territorial sovereignty is going to be a dominant force in international affairs for the foreseeable future." Well, if it is, the world is not going any place. If we are going to take a worldwide conference and use it simply to endorse what is probably the most frightful of all concepts in international law and relations, we will simply make it more and more difficult to act cooperatively when the world's countries need each other—and they need each other every day in thousands of different ways. We will still be making law through a "crazy quilt" of bilateral agreements which are written and negotiated after problems arise. And the most powerful will win in the negotiation.

I think these are the questions that are raised by the law of the sea conference, the really important issues—world order and the settlement of disputes. These are the issues that can be the common thread running through this negotiation. If we can stop talking about the purely selfish interests, either of a maritime power or of a single developing country who wants all the continental shelf possible and will not share revenues with other developing countries, we may avoid a 1958 conference—that is, a conference that confirms what has already been done. A conference that confirms what has already been done seems to me almost useless.

Commentary
Arvid A. Pardo [b]

Basically, I agree with Professor Gamble's assumption that a certain amount of pluralism exists in the law of the sea and that in order to make sense of the complex situation developing at the Conference on the Law of the Sea, it is necessary to think in terms of nations willing to act in concert. I also agree that the four factors mentioned by Professor Gamble will have a significant influence on the manner in which the various nations will decide to act.

The first factor was the increase in the number of sovereign states. This means not only that a number of states with little intrinsic interest in the law of the sea will participate in the formation of a new law of the sea, but also has other possible implications. One of these could be a temptation on the part of a number of states with comparatively small perceived interests in the sea to view their participation in the conference as function of other political interests which they might consider to be more important, and this might give rise to substantial vote bargaining.

A second possible implication of the increase in the number of sovereign states since 1958 could be a situation where a two-thirds majority at the law of the sea conference is obtained by the united action of states which together represent less than 15 percent of the world population.

Should such a situation arise, or should a situation arise where important decisions at the conference are taken by the action of states which, together, represent less than a majority of the world's population and little of the world's maritime technology, there could arise a serious possibility that states

---

[b]Woodrow Wilson International Center for Scholars

which disagree with the decisions taken would reject the decisions of the conference and conclude between themselves a convention relating to the law of the
sea. The conference could thus provide the occasion for the final collapse of a
universally accepted law of the sea and for the appearance of regional laws of the
sea. The consequences would not be pleasant to contemplate.

On the other hand—and here I differ with Professor Gamble—I do
not share his concern with regard to the contemporary trend towards codification of international law of the sea. Reliance on customary practice was per-
fectly acceptable when the seas were used only for a few purposes, but the situation has changed radically. The uses of the seas are multiplying, and a large
number of areas are being intensively used for a number of competing activities.
In these circumstances it becomes essential to codify law. Furthermore, reliance
on customary practice and customary development of the law of the sea means
reliance essentially on the practice of the maritime powers. Such a method of
development of international law of the sea does not appear particularly suited
to a period when the world is striving towards a more equitable international
order.

The second factor mentioned by Professor Gamble is rapidly expanding technology. I certainly agree that this factor will have a great influence
in the type of blocs (if we can call them such) that will develop at the forthcoming Law of the Sea Conference. However, I do disagree with some of Professor Gamble's observations in this connection. First I disagree with the statement
that technology has not progressed far enough to provide an economically viable
way of extracting the resources of the seas, if this sentence is intended to refer
to the extraction of manganese nodules. I think it is now proven that manganese
nodules can be economically exploited.

Second, I disagree with Professor Gamble when he expresses concern
that there might be a serious communications problem arising between developed and developing countries, in connection with a presumed gap between scientific possibility and economic viability of resource exploitation. I do not really
think that this is a serious matter. Professor Gamble may be right in implying
that the relationship between bloc formation at the conference and technological advance concerned with resource development is the only relevant factor.
But if Professor Gamble is right, then the conference is destined to fail. One
should not look at technological advance in the context of resource exploitation
alone, but rather in the context of multiplying uses of the sea and of the increasing power that technology gives to man to use the sea—either for his benefit or
in a manner that will eventually destroy much of the sea's usefulness to man.

The third factor mentioned by Professor Gamble is the thaw in the
cold war. It is true that there has been some decrease in superpower influence
over the past fifteen years, and this circumstance may indeed encourage more
diversity at the conference. However, should both superpowers take similar positions on major issues, this would in all probability impose a heavy political con-

straint on the decisions of the conference. If no more than a dozen or so influential countries were to support an agreed position taken by the superpowers on major issues, this could make possible the creation of an ocean regime alternative to that which might be established by the conference. Small states, therefore, must not only maintain a certain measure of unity but must also exercise realistic political judgment in pressing their interests. This will require a degree of restraint not often seen at the United Nations, and some respect for the vital interests of the major maritime powers.

Finally, I doubt that environmental issues are likely to be as important as Professor Gamble assumes. I believe that most states increasingly realize, firstly, that most ocean pollution derives from land sources and hence should be dealt with within the context of the municipal jurisdictions of states; secondly that less than twenty states are responsible for the bulk of marine pollution; and thirdly that development of ocean space will require some relaxation of more extreme environmental standards.

Development of ocean space and of its mineral resources is absolutely essential. Technologically advanced countries will be unable to sustain the present industrial or postindustrial society without intensive exploitation of the mineral resources of ocean space. Nor will so-called developing countries be able to industrialize easily without developing their offshore resources.

In conclusion, I agree on the whole with Professor Gamble's rather gloomy forecasts. The prospects of a viable law of the sea emerging are virtually nonexistent if the great majority of states continue to negotiate only on the basis of perceived short-term interests, and if these are equated with control of ocean resources at considerable distance from the coast.

I agree with Mr. Ratiner that the conference can only be successful if it creates a new law of the sea. By a new law of the sea I mean an agreed, comprehensive, and flexible legal framework, based on new principles, for the regulation and protection of all major activities that states can undertake in ocean space. This means protection of activities of vital international interest (such as navigation) within national jurisdiction, and international regulation of many activities (for instance the disposal of radioactive or toxic chemical wastes) beyond national jurisdiction. In short, the basic purpose of the new law of the sea should be to permit mankind to continue beneficially to use ocean space in the new circumstances created by advancing technology without serious deleterious effects on the marine environment or depletion of the living resources of the sea.

Discussion

Ratiner: To add another paragraph to your conclusion, I wonder, Ambassador Pardo, if I could ask to what extent you see the negotiators in the Law of the Sea Conference recognizing this major global interest that you have mentioned. If they are not, in fact, beginning to coalesce around an understanding that what the world really needs is a basic legal structure and regime in which to work out its more particular problems in the future, what would your view be of an alternative to such a complex legal system? Might this alternative include the settlement on a compulsory basis of any dispute arising out of the use of ocean space? I mention it only as a possible alternative to the conference's breaking down when it becomes apparent that a complex legal structure and machinery cannot be established because the perceptions that would lead men in that direction have simply not been achieved.

Pardo: You have asked a very difficult question. I do not think that it is possible successfully to graft an effective system of compulsory dispute settlement on the present law of the sea. Such a system could indeed be created, but it would not be credible and it would be certain to fail unless it were a part of strong institutions for ocean space which enjoyed at least the power to administer ocean resources beyond national jurisdiction.

     A treaty-established compulsory dispute settlement machinery, superimposed upon a law of the sea only superficially modified, would be ineffective for a number of reasons. Firstly, the experience of the International Court of Justice has, I believe, proved that states with a doubtful legal case are reluctant to submit it to compulsory adjudication; they usually prefer to maintain an open dispute in the hope of favorable settlement at a politically opportune time. Even normally law-abiding states who had specifically accepted the compulsory jurisdiction of the International Court of Justice have refused to appear in Court to argue their case, when this suited their purpose.

     Secondly, under the present structure of international law there is little incentive for states to submit to binding dispute settlement unless they have an irrefutable case or are the weaker party. Thirdly, there are few means in international law to encourage states to execute a judgment which is not in their favor or which is perceived to endanger even quite minor interests. Fourthly, as you know, there exists no credible means, apart from force or the exercise of overwhelming political pressure, to enforce a binding judgment against a recalcitrant state.

     On the other hand, a treaty-established compulsory dispute settlement system, conceived as an integral part of strong international institutions for ocean space, might have a measure of credibility—at least for certain types of disputes—since the institutions themselves could bring pressure to bear on a state which either refused to accept the jurisdiction of the International Court of Justice or of whatever court might be created for ocean space, or refused to execute an adverse judgment. Pressure could be exerted in various ways, for instance by denying licenses for resource exploitation to refractory states, or even by denying to these states the use of ocean space beyond national jurisdiction. The creation of international institutions for ocean space would, in addition, provide a forum, which now does not exist, both for the discussion of violations of whatever norms were established at the Conference, and opportunity to mobilize opinion against serious violations.

I do not, of course, suggest that a compulsory dispute settlement procedure, even conceived as part of strong international institutions for ocean space, can be effective in all cases. States would probably reject compulsory dispute settlement—particularly in cases which are more political than legal—on those relatively few occasions when they felt that their vital interests were involved. But at least a compulsory dispute settlement procedure conceived, not in vacuo but as part of a much more comprehensive legal structure, would give some assurance of certainty of rights and obligations and perhaps even of justice.

Ratiner: I wonder if the other panelists in their remarks could also address this question, bearing in mind Mr. Gamble's paper which correctly indicated that there are numerous diverse interests and that this is a very pluralistic negotiation, and also bearing in mind what we all know about international treaties, which is that perhaps their single most important characteristic is that they are ambiguous and provide a living for international lawyers for years after they are negotiated.

Perhaps we ought to be thinking as we discuss this question of blocs that the fact that blocs will each be satisfied in this treaty to some extent means that the treaty will have many diverse rules with lots of ambiguities. Is there going to be a useful law of the sea treaty that settles all these issues, if in fact it does not have a section for compulsory settlement of disputes?

Chapter Two

Assessment of the Extension of State Jurisdiction in Terms of the Living Resources of the Sea

Kaldone G. Nweihed
*Institute of Marine Technology and Science
(INTECMAR) Universidad Simon Bolivar,
Caracas, Venezuela*

INTRODUCTION

Bloc thinking about the oceans is a tempting subject and may lead to two different interpretations according to the outlook that is adopted. If we presume the
existence of already established and well defined blocs, irrespective of their response to the manifold ocean problems to be dealt with at the next United Nations conference, our task would be reduced to the analysis of the thinking and
behavior of such blocs in terms of already existing issues, something which I
have not attempted. If, on the other hand, we are able to establish the real economic, political, strategic, or other valid motivations that may lead to the creation of new schools of thought around the specific issues, then the formation of
groups or blocs within the conference would only be the following political step
to be logically expected.

I choose to focus on the process from which such a bloc-forming
tendency may emerge, taking as a vivid example the extension of state jurisdiction in terms of the living resources of the sea. I have tried to illustrate how the
practice has led to a uniform way of thinking; first in Latin America, which by
all means should be treated as a cultural and political bloc already established
before the coming of age of the new tendencies we now observe in the law of the
sea; and second, within the context of what may be already foreseen as a new

bloc in formation, including not only Latin America but probably Iceland (a developed North European country), a number of developing states along the west coast of Africa, Vietnam, and other coastal fishing nations from Southeast Asia, and, most recently—according to a very fresh announcement—a very significant developed country from this hemisphere: Canada.

My endeavor will be to show that the vital issues of the law of the sea, such as the conservation and the exploitation of coastal fisheries, do not necessarily fit within the contexts of already established and traditional political blocs, but rather tend to create new trends of thinking—bloc thinking—that may become transcultural, transoceanic, and probably transcontinental, without prejudice whatsoever to any regional agreements that may be conceived to achieve a better and more practical application of such bloc-building tendencies.

State jurisdiction for the purpose of controlling the living resources of the sea has shown a steady tendency to spread further and further over adjacent waters, with or without connection to the breadth of the territorial sea. The failure of the Geneva Conferences to settle the issue, plus the enormous growth of the fishing industry which all but doubled its output since 1960, may be cited as two causes, but are not the only ones.

There are three main concerns that may prompt a state to seek an extension of its jurisdiction over adjacent sea areas, thus encroaching on what the international community considered as high seas: security and defense, the acquisition of natural resources from the continental shelf, and the exploitation of fisheries. These three objectives do reflect, not to our surprise, the way that nature has chosen to build up the marine universe in three distinct spaces. Thus, the superficial or maritime space is the one most linked with security, navigation, and transportation; the submarine space, or the submerged soil and subsoil, is but the continuation of the emerged territory, while the marine space in between corresponds to the waters themselves as the natural habitat of swimming fish and other living organisms. The ocean bottom, beyond national jurisdiction, though comprising the largest area of the so-called submarine space, is both geologically and legally distinct from the continental shelf. Having been declared a common heritage of mankind, it does not lie within the scope of this chapter.

This threefold outlook upon the spaces of the marine universe and their relationship to the extension of jurisdiction is further enhanced by their different scientific backgrounds. Social sciences such as law, economics, and international studies deal with the maritime space as an essential part of a universal whole, the sea being one great liquid bridge among continents, peoples, and cultures. In the case of the hidden submarine space, however, it is mainly geology that has ushered a new concept into economics and international law—it being the case, as the International Court of Justice has put it, that the soil and subsoil are two words evocative of the land and not of the sea.

When we come to the marine space, theoretically detached from both surface and bottom, an entirely new outlook is at once demanded. Hydrography, oceanology (both physical and chemical), plus marine ecology and biology converge on the liquid space to share in its scientific revelations. Apart from the benefits of general research, a state's main interest in the marine space would be—forgetting about submarine warfare—primarily based on biological concepts and ecological considerations, if the aim is the exploitation of fisheries and living resources in a rational way that permits their protection and conservation.

It is this new approach to the sea that has not won, so far, the full recognition of international law, since the economic factor behind the biological fundamental has not acquired sufficient force to generate a change in positive law on a worldwide scale. But on a regional scale, both in South America and in the Caribbean area, there is another situation to be analyzed. Such is the case, in extreme terms, of Iceland, and in more moderate ones, of Mauritania in Northwest Africa and of Namibia, or Southwest Africa.

This approach cannot be separated from other problems and issues related to the law of the sea. However, we shall not discuss the extension of the territorial sea as such, nor the ever-increasing claims to further depths in the submarine space along the continental terrace, except when any of these concepts disguises a desire to acquire new rights over living resources, or involves a legitimate move towards such an acquisition.

Let us define our terms thus: the *territorial sea* would be the maritime belt around a state, considered in terms of defense, security, and the application of customs, revenue, sanitary, and pollution regulations, whether it is followed by a contiguous zone or not; and the *continental shelf* would be the submarine area as defined under the Geneva Convention and as understood by the International Court of Justice, that is to say, existing as a natural prolongation of the land territory, ipso facto and ab initio.

INTERNATIONAL REGIMES GOVERNING FISHERIES

The living organisms of the sea, being the most precious prize to be found in the immense marine space, have never been subject to a regime of their own within the framework of the law of the sea. No two scholars would disagree on the fact that, prior to the Truman Proclamation on Coastal Fisheries and to other more radical measures such as the Santiago Declaration of 1952, there was no question at all regarding the regime to which the living resources, in general, were submitted. In a nutshell, those within the inland and territorial waters belonged to the coastal state, and those outside the territorial limits belonged to whomsoever came along first and caught them. The classical contiguous zone that came into shape at the 1930 Hague Conference on the law of the sea, thanks to the sponsorship of Gilbert Gidel, was never intended for fishing purposes.

Classic international law, however, has tolerated two exceptions, sometimes confusingly referred to as "sedentary fisheries." They can be readily distinguished once we decide what is being qualified by the adjective: the fish or the gear. Sedentary fisheries as applied to living organisms covers oyster beds, sponges, mussels, seaweed, etc., whose extraction from shallow waters has been an age-old practice along the shores of Ceylon, Bahrein, Burma, and Tunisia, to such an extent that they won the acknowledgement of Vattel, Fulton, and Sir Cecil Hurst. Such organisms, defined as belonging to sedentary species which, at the harvestable stage, either are immobile on the seabed or are unable to move except in constant contact with the seabed or the subsoil, have been recognized as constituting part of the natural resources covered by the Geneva Convention on the Continental Shelf.

Sedentary fisheries as applied to gear implies the fishing of demersed species by means of equipment embedded in the floor of the sea, a practice quite common along the shores of India in shallow waters, and recognized under the Geneva Convention on Fishing and Conservation of the Living Resources of the Sea to fall within the regulating capacity of the coastal state when the practice has been carried out traditionally and without interruption.

Thus, the living resources of the sea have ended up under three separate regimes and all four Geneva Conventions on the Law of the Sea, signed on April 29th, 1958, thus:

1. *Pelagic fisheries* are subject to the freedom of fishing, guaranteed under the Convention on the High Seas (Art. 2) and regulated under the Convention on Fishing and Conservation of the Living Resources of the Sea.
2. *Coastal fisheries* are implicitly recognized, within territorial waters, as part of the state's exclusive sovereignty, under the Convention on the Territorial Sea and the Contiguous Zone, and explicitly under Art. 14, Par. 5.
3. *Sedentary species* are governed by the terms of the Convention on the Continental Shelf (Art. 2, Par. 4). It is quite clear that demersal swimming fish do not fall within this definition, but as far as crustacea are concerned, opposite points of view have led to conflicts, such as the so-called lobster war between France and Brazil in 1963.

Besides these cardinal conventions that did not modify the situation basically, the limit of the territorial sea after Geneva 1958 continued for two more years to be exactly as it was before; that is to say, the only acceptable frontier between the exclusive and the common. The only convention that tried hard to bring about a substantial change was the Convention on Fishing and Conservation of the Living Resources of the Sea. Ironically, though, since the change was enough to disturb some conservatives and not enough to cheer up the liberals, the attempt all but failed.

It may be surprising to find out that since the seventeenth century nearly 223 international agreements relating to fisheries and questions affecting the use and conservation of the living resources of the sea were listed in a special report submitted to the 1958 Geneva Conference. These are, however, agreements to be implemented on the high seas, occasionally in territorial waters when special arrangements had been taken, and even then they have always meant that the enforcement of their provisions fell to each party with respect to its own vessels, an obligation that derives from the general principles that have governed the high seas.

More than 22 conservation and regulation conventions, many of them signed under the auspices of the United Nations Food and Agriculture Organization, cover most of the high seas fishing grounds, and some of them deal with specific species. All of them have led to the establishment of fishing councils whose contribution to the scientific conservation of living organisms has helped to promote production and keep fisheries relatively well stocked. The International Commission for the Northwest Atlantic Fisheries (ICNAF) is a near example, and the Indian Ocean Fisheries Commission (IOFC) is a far-fetched one. Yet nothing has been done to change the rules of the game: each state is responsible for enforcing the law of the team on its own vessels. Such agreements have nothing to do with the extension of coastal jurisdiction, but they do have a lot to do with the common cause: fishing.

THE FIRST MOVES

The Truman Proclamation on Coastal Fisheries was the first announcement to implement unilateral conservation measures outside a state's territorial waters without claiming rights to exclusive fishing. The proclamation did not extend the United States territorial sea, nor did it set up an exclusive fishing zone, a concept then unknown to international law. Its real importance stems from three facts:

First, it concerned itself with coastal high sea fisheries, giving the impression that a coastal state had the obligation of protecting the fisheries nearest to its coast. Thus a distinction was bound to arise between a coastal high sea fishery and an off-shore high sea fishery, though there was no apparent change in their common international status as far as the fishing rights were concerned. The change was embodied in the right of the coastal state to impose conservation measures, with or without the approval of others, depending on who had been fishing those coastal areas and for how long.

Second, Truman's proclamation was a unilateral act, setting the precedent that such acts might generate international norms, at least if their motives (in this case conservation) were morally and scientifically acceptable.

Third, the simultaneous release on September 28, 1945, of the other well-known Proclamation on the Continental Shelf, though painstakingly intended not to mix up one issue with the other, could not stop other nations from issuing their own proclamations or decrees, with both issues probably linked together and the two aspects adroitly or casually combined into one.

The twin American proclamations were destined to tread two different paths right from their birth. Judged by their effect on the process of custom formation that followed, the Coastal Fisheries Proclamation, faced with what Professor Georges Scelle has called an "inflationary process" abroad, dwindled and all but faded away. The Continental Shelf Proclamation, on the other hand, was able to maintain its size and its original attachment to the geological approach to the newly incorporated submarine resources. Its main concepts were adopted, first at the Ciudad Trujillo Conference of the American Nations in 1956, and two years later in Geneva.

Why was it possible to make uniform the legal outlook of the world community on the extension of state jurisdiction to adjacent submarine areas and not to the adjacent waters? Why did the biological approach fail when geology triumphantly added a new base to the law of the sea? Evidently, the answer has nothing to do with freedom of navigation, for under both approaches it would not have been disturbed. A strictly legal answer would definitely claim that the biological approach, as enlarged by many other countries, encroached upon the traditional freedom of fishing on the high seas. Another answer is of a technical nature: It is much easier for a country (or state) to fish beyond the territorial limit of a coastal state than it is for it to drill an offshore oil well without some sort of help from the coast.

Nevertheless, the evolution of the law of the sea in the last quarter-century has shown that freedom of fishing cannot be left undeterred for two principal reasons—of which the first has won worldwide recognition and the second is admitted on a regional scale. By the first we mean the depletion of the living resources, a purely scientific fact that, to our knowledge, was first expounded in Chile by the Venezuelan scholar Andres Bello in 1832. By the second we refer to the right of a state to control, regulate, and rationally exploit the living resources nearest to its coast, by virtue of the principle of preferential rights based on its economic needs and those of its population. This is fundamental to the Santiago Declaration of 1952 and has become the base from which the maritime policies of Iceland and many Latin American countries have evolved.

No dispute could arise regarding the first issue. The second, of course, is still to be settled, so long as the maritime and fishing powers keep challenging it in the name of the freedom of the sea.

LATIN AMERICA'S EARLY STAND:
SPAIN, PORTUGAL, AND THE U.S.A.

It has to be kept in mind that Latin America's aspiration of making better use of the living resources of adjacent seas does not date to the 1952 Santiago Declaration and not even to the series of unilateral acts that followed the Truman proclamations in 1945, but rather to an earlier period when Argentina's scholars like Segundo Storni and José León Suárez wrote books and delivered lectures on the growing importance of the sea and its epicontinental waters during the first quarter of the century. As early as 1925, Suárez called upon the maritime nations of the world to enact conservation measures in the epicontinental sea, down to the 200 meter isobath. In 1927 another Argentine scholar, Nágera, publicly advocated the adopting of a double geological and biological criterion in order to include the continental margin within a nation's full sovereignty.

On the Old Continent, Spain and Portugal had already caught the idea of the biological continental shelf, even before the Argentines did. One of the first acts of the Portuguese Republic was to regulate fishing on its continental shelf, down to the 100 fathom isobath, by virtue of a decree issued in 1910. Six years later, Profesor Odon de Buen, sometimes referred to as the forefather of the continental shelf doctrine, took to the National Congress of Fishing held in Madrid the idea of extending Spain's territorial waters so as to include the whole continental shelf.

To cite another example, here in the United States Senator Copeland submitted a bill to Congress in 1938 calling for the exercise of United States jurisdiction, down to the 100 fathom isobath, over the continental shelf of the Bering Sea. No action was taken on the bill prior to adjournment, reports Mouton. The bill recited the need for protecting mineral deposits, fisheries, and animal life, it being evident, after a slight examination, that fishery interests were predominant.

The overwhelming advantage that petroleum interests in the continental shelf were bound to acquire over fishing concerns since 1942 have given the geological approach the upper hand. The new trend began when Venezuela and Great Britain concluded the Gulf of Paria Treaty, by which the submarine areas of that gulf were divided between Venezuela and Trinidad/Tobago, and was emphasized worldwide by the Truman Proclamation and the forty-odd declarations, decrees, and acts that followed.

It was the biological approach to the continental shelf, already known to Latin America, that was destined to influence the maritime policy of the continent. The Truman proclamations triggered a process that had been long in gestation. Thus Mexico's decree of 1945, a month after Truman's, split the country's announced interests in the shelf almost evenly between the biological and the geological sides, and so did Argentina's a year later. The decrees issued by a number of Middle East kingdoms and sheikdoms were all intended to safeguard oil interests, and thus represented a geological approach, inspired as far as its formal aspect in the Truman unilateral proclamation, and as far as its essence in the Anglo-Venezuelan Treaty of 1942, which claimed sovereignty over the submarine areas and not just control and jurisdiction over the natural (mineral) resources.

When the turn came to the shelfless countries of the South Pacific, there was no shelf to be reckoned with, neither for a geological nor for a biological approach, except for coal mining operations conducted through galleries from Chile's mainland. The alternative was to create a "maritime zone," or a 200-mile belt around the whole area, enriched by the Peru current to incalculable proportions. In fact, that is neither an epicontinental sea in its strict sense nor a territorial zone similar, for example, to the security belt established around the continent, including the United States, by virtue of the 1939 Panama Declaration. In other words, both the geological approach to the continental shelf and the security or navigation factor are completely absent. There is not even a biological approach to a continental shelf concept, simply because there is *no shelf*. Yet there is something more which cannot be denied on any basis: a biological and an ecological reality turned into a great potential, just on the maritime threshold of three South American nations.

In the case of Iceland, the marine zone is indeed related to the shelf and dependent on it, and so it may be in many countries of the world. Epicontinental waters are still the best and most prodigious breeding waters for sea life, as compared to the high seas on one side, or to inland or continental waters on the other. The relationship between epicontinental waters and good fisheries is a prime factor, but not a decisive one. The access of a coastal state to the living resources of the sea could constitute a case by itself, as the South Pacific countries have shown. But with a shelf or without one, the same ethical, political, and economic aspects surround both typical cases; the difference lies in the scientific approach and in the legal framework. Both in Peru, where there is no shelf involved, and in Iceland, where the shelf is the natural support of the island's fisheries, there is the same undeniable link between the living resources of the sea and the economy and welfare of the nation involved.

From the opposite point of view—namely that of high sea fishing nations like Japan, the Soviet Union, or Portugal on a worldwide scale, and probably Cuba, Nigeria, or Thailand on a regional scale—the extension of a state's jurisdiction to cover farther located living resources constitutes a decrease of a hitherto free resource. To such nations, the solutions of fishery problems should be sought on the level of international cooperation, by means of common control, or perhaps allocation. But once a nation has announced an additional jurisdiction, whether it be called maritime zone, exclusive fishing zone, epicontinental sea, patrimonial sea, economic zone, or just territorial sea, they are bound to feel that their fishing interests may be jeopardized.

EVALUATION OF TERMS

All this variety of names, nevertheless, boils down to one main issue and might be summed up under the most objective term of *exclusive fishing zone*. Anyhow, it may be necessary to compare the most usual three terms in connection with the extension of a state's sovereignty over the living resources of the sea.

1. *Exclusive Fishing Zone.* Distinction should be made between any zone set up for exclusive fishing of whatever extension, and the twelve-mile exclusive fishing zone that was born and began expanding just after the 1960 Geneva Conference. Within the first group we may list Argentina's ten-mile zone of 1907, Vietnam's twenty-km. zone of 1936 and even Colombia's twelve-mile zone, set up in 1923 for fishing and oil exploitation purposes, and we may add such recent measures as Morocco's additional zone announced early this year, or Iceland's 50-mile zone effective as of September 1972.

The second group does not only introduce a homogeneous twelve-mile limit but reflects a steady state practice begun by Iceland right after the failure of the first Geneva Conference to set such a limit. For two years it remained as a unilateral measure that Iceland had to defend, barehanded, against British protest; but no sooner did the second Geneva Conference end in 1960 with no agreement either, than other states followed suit at a rhythm that has left no doubt about the development of a new law by custom.

In fact, what most helped this twelve-mile fishing zone become a rule of custom was not what was achieved at Geneva 1960, but what was *not* achieved. It may be remembered that Canada and the United States had tried hard to win approval for their "6+6 formula," that is to say, a six-mile territorial sea plus a six-mile exclusive fishing zone, enabling those states with a three-mile territorial sea to extend their fishing jurisdiction nine more miles. In other words, it was an attempt at separating the territorial sea issue from jurisdiction over the fishing zone, a principle which appeals to Latin America, provided the figures could be adjusted in those marine areas where three or twelve miles mean as little as 50 or 60.

Defeated at the Conference by a single vote, this measure, however, developed into a common state practice soon after. First it was Albania, then a few African nations (Senegal, Mauritania, Morocco, Tunisia); then Denmark stepped in, first in the name of Greenland and then in its own. Ireland followed suit in 1964. That same year, Canada and the United Kingdom adopted the measure. In 1966 the United States came along, then Mexico, France, and Australia. It goes without saying that nations already with a twelve-mile territorial sea, who now comprise the majority, could not afford to oppose it; but neither could the three- or the six-milers. Among the maritime and fishing powers, Japan has maintained a lonely stand against the twelve-mile fishing zone. The European Convention of Fisheries of 1964 was aimed at enlarging the old three-mile limit to six, while keeping the newly acquired belt, the outer six miles, within the exclusive range of the signatory powers.

2. *Maritime Zone.* This is a term designed by the P.E.C. countries (Perú, Ecuador, Chile) to exercise full sovereignty and jurisdiction over a zone 200 nautical miles from their respective coasts, while paying full respect to the freedom of

navigation. These three nations were subsequently joined by six more South and Central American countries, forming what has come to be known as the Montevideo Group, since all of them agree on the extension of the 200 mile limit, whether it be called a maritime zone or territorial sea: Brazil, Uruguay, Argentina, Panama, Nicaragua, and El Salvador.

3. *Territorial Sea.* Some states, in order to safeguard their rights to the resources of the sea adjacent to their coasts, and not satisfied with either aforesaid formula, have gone outright to extend the breadth of their territorial sea. An eloquent explanation can be found in the preamble of the Brazilian decree of March 25, 1970, by virtue of which a nation that four years before had adopted the twelve-mile fishing zone and just eleven months earlier had established a twelve-mile territorial sea, came out for a 200-mile territorial sea. The Brazilian decree said that the interest of a coastal state in maintaining the productivity of the living resources of the sea adjacent to its coasts could only be effectively protected through the exercise of sovereignty underlying the legal concept of the territorial sea.

Looking backwards, it was El Salvador that first declared such a policy in 1950. So far, five Latin American nations claim a 200-mile territorial sea, *strictu sensu*. Along the western coast of Africa, various territorial limits have been registered: Nigeria, 30 miles; Gabon, 50 miles; Gambia, 50 miles; Cameroon, 18 miles; Guinea, 130 miles (probably not for fishing purposes only); Sierra Leone, 200 miles. Archipelagos consider all the waters enclosed between lines connecting the outer points of their islands as national waters, and therefore exclusive fishing grounds. In Southeast Asia, South Viet Nam has gone for 50 miles as from January 1973. The presidential decree announces heavy fines for poaching boats and trespassers.

THE PATRIMONIAL SEA

Strictly speaking, the "patrimonial sea" is not yet positive law for the ten Caribbean nations that signed the declaration of Santo Domingo in June 1972. The idea, inspired in Bello's doctrine and expounded by the Chilean jurist Vargas Carreño, was later developed at a meeting of the Caribbean nations foreign ministers held in Caracas in 1971 at the invitation of the Venezuelan government. After a preparatory meeting in Bogotá, it was agreed to proclaim this new principle for the semienclosed Caribbean and to further cooperation on marine sciences among the riparian nations. The patrimonial sea leaves no doubt whatsoever that its regime will be basically economic and that it will never mean any interference with the territorial sea, whose breadth is set at twelve miles.

The new regime will extend to a belt of 200 miles from the coast, or 188 miles from the maximum territorial limit, for the purpose of exploring and exploiting the natural resources, be they mineral or biological. The new regime is meant to assimilate the state's rights on the continental shelf if they fall within the limits of the new zone and to accept its rights and obligations under the Geneva Convention if this were the case outside the 200 mile patrimonial limit.

In practice, such a situation will not arise in the Caribbean. Since the state's rights to the continental shelf and its resources are already and without any question recognized under the Geneva Convention (to which most of the Caribbean nations are party, except Cuba and the Central American republics not counting Guatemala), there is little doubt that the new regime would only add the living resources of the sea to the national patrimony of the riparian nations. The Caribbean is a semienclosed sea surrounded by more than twenty different sovereignties and it seems very logical that its multiple problems do not allow for new complications derived from overfishing by high sea fishing fleets. If the patrimonial sea becomes the law of the land for the Caribbean, then it will have to be considered as another form of the extension of a state's jurisdiction in terms of the biological resources.

The draft Ocean Space Treaty submitted to the Committee on the Peaceful Uses of the Seabed by Dr. Arvid Pardo on behalf of Malta establishes a national oceanic belt of 200 nautical miles, while the traditional concept of the territorial sea is maintained within the first twelve miles under the right of innocent passage. The Maltese project, in its substance, is another example of the extension of a state's jurisdiction over the resources of the sea into the 200-mile economic limit, besides its valuable contribution to the general development of the law of the sea.

BASES FOR A SOLUTION

What would happen if the Seabed Committee or the 1974 Conference failed to produce a satisfactory deal? In such a case, one of the possibilities would be that the new economic or patrimonial zone—probably called an exclusive fishing zone by nations who prefer this term—might secure its hold and spread among nations in the form of custom establishing state practice, the way the twelve-mile fishing zone made it after 1960.

Meanwhile, it looks as if there may be two bases for a possible approach to the filling of the gap between jurisdiction-extending coastal states and high-sea-fishing states. The first is much nearer to the position of the latter; the second basically goes along with the former.

In the first place, one has to examine the principle called the special interest of the coastal state in the living resources of the high seas in any part adjacent to its shores. Embodied within the original project of the International Law Commission and adopted as Article 6 of the Convention of Fishing and Conservation, this principle, as it stands today in positive law, recognizes this interest as empowering the coastal state to take part, on equal footing, in a system of research and regulation, and even concedes a certain priority to those conservation measures taken by the coastal state; but it does not imply that it could regulate fishing carried out by nationals of other states, and it is absolutely *not* an extension of jurisdiction. As Ambassador Castañeda from México points out, the exercise of this right was surrounded by so many complicated requisites that no coastal state has ever exercised it once. Developing nations, on the other hand, have mainly resorted to the safer practice of extending their jurisdiction.

The other alternative is the principle of the preferential status of the coastal state in offshore adjacent areas when it is scientifically established that special conditions have made exploitation of fisheries in that area of funda-mental importance to the economic development of the coastal state, or to the subsistence of its population. This principle made an impact on the 1960 Geneva Conference, but as it was tied to the unfortunate "6+6 formula" it could never make its way to positive law.

Yet if these two principles, which no doubt reflect the conservative Geneva spirit, cannot be harmonized in order to satisfy the prime needs of devel-oping coastal states within a new international regime, the most probable conse-quence would be the continuation of the status quo and the eventual growth of a tacitly recognized economic zone, until the time comes when it will be consid-ered an integral part of international custom, and therefore, law. The only aspect to be taken care of in a system of coastal jurisdiction would be—as Iceland's ambassador Schram pointed out last year—the necessary exploitation of unused resources in the interest of the international community. As it stands now, it seems that the extension of state jurisdiction over living resources has turned into a precedent that cannot be pushed backwards. The question is whether to institute it immediately as positive international law, or to let it climb its way upwards with the help of state practice and the confirmation obtained through acquiescence. One way or another, it means a deep change for the law of the high seas.

* * * * * *

Commentary
Paul Lapointe [a]

Not having had a chance to prepare myself for this panel, I find that we have a good example right here of doing something like what is mentioned in the last line of the first page of Mr. Gamble's paper—that is, we are pursuing a myriad of complex and changing goals, and if that is pluralism, I think we are demonstrat-ing that there is pluralism in this. Mr. Chairman, I find that I am generally in agreement with you. It is just unfortunate, I suppose, that we end up with differ-

[a]Legal Operations Division, Department of External Affairs, Canada

ent conclusions, but what I found difficult to understand is that on the one hand everybody seems to be keen in arguing against selfish interests, but at the same time, I think that everybody is trying to promote these selfish interests, be it as a major power or as a minor one. What we fail to realize is that the world has been accustomed over centuries to tackling this problem in a very free manner. Everything was permitted outside of a very small limit; and now because of rapidly changing technology we are faced with a completely new set of circumstances that forces us to imagine a new system, a new regime. I do not think that a solution can be found simply by saying that we should not be selfish. I think international law is still based on the fact that sovereign states are sovereign, and by definition, as you say, perhaps selfish also. I do not think that you can change that. I think that you have to invent a new regime that will satisfy the largest number of countries possible and at the same time link all this together so that you have a new world order.

You will not have a dispute settlement procedure that will work unless you have a majority of states agreeing with a certain order that exists. It is all right to say that we are not selfish; but when Canada (to take my own country) decided that international law was not sufficiently developed to protect its environment, it moved to protect its own interests. When the United Kingdom, which criticized our action, decided that it needed extraterritorial jurisdiction to protect itself against disasters at sea, for instance, it moved also. It now has extraterritorial powers. When the Netherlands decided that it needed protection to cover certain offshore operations, it moved also.

This means that international law as it presently exists is not sufficient. What we are now trying to develop is not a system of unilateral declarations of interest or protection, but something that will satisfy these selfish interests and at the same time link them together into a new system. And once you have that—I am not like Professor Pardo, I am not all that optimistic—but if you do have that, then you might think of a settlement of dispute procedure. As of now, for instance, the United States has the Connally amendment. If the United States decides that this is a national matter, it does not let itself be taken to court. These are facts of life. When France is testing nuclear weapons in the atmosphere it has already withdrawn from the court for that purpose. Certain countries are trying, in a roundabout way, to take France to court anyway, but that may or may not succeed.

So I think that we need a different approach to the entire problem. To say, simply, "Let's not be selfish" will not resolve anything, because we all are to some extent. What I think Professor Pardo tried to propose was that we have a new worldwide agency that would do everything for everybody and satisfy everyone. If he will forgive me (he knows my views on this), I think this is a bit too utopian. Who can be that agency? We have thought, and we have been promoting this idea, that the states themselves should be the agents for the international community and contribute altogether to a general system. If you want to avoid unilateralism, I think that you need a better system. You will not get a better system if you simply hang on to an outdated sort of philosophy which may have been excellent for 300 years, but is now passing.

Discussion

Ratiner: Paul, you have just said that it makes no difference and does no good to appeal to the unselfish instincts of men or states. Let us just assume that the Law of the Sea Conference concluded with a treaty article in its chapter on marine pollution which simply said that coastal states have an important interest in the preservation of the marine environment in waters adjacent to their coasts and that this interest should be protected by the coastal state in cooperation with maritime states whose shipping passes near to their shores. I assume from the position of Canada on the law of the sea negotiations that that would simply not be an acceptable resolution to Canada. Yet looking at some of the other countries' positions, it might be as far as some countries were willing to go in connection with marine pollution, simply a recognition of the special interest of the coastal states—perhaps adjacent to the territorial sea, if we could make the treaty article more specific.

Now would Canada—not in an act of unselfishness but in an act of accommodation—be prepared to allow a tribunal of judges in the future to decide what it could lawfully do in that area of its special interests and what other nations could lawfully do when they used that area of special interest? Or would Canada be so afraid of compulsory dispute settlement and the judges on the tribunal that it would leave the Law of the Sea Conference without signing the treaty, unless the nature of Canada's rights were made much more specific?

The same question can be asked for any of the issues. My fear is that on many important issues the law of the sea treaty will of necessity be ambiguous. Will nations be prepared to take a chance on a new way of resolving disputes, or are we going to write a treaty that will give rise to disputes and force us to negotiate another silly exercise in Geneva five, six, seven, ten, fifteen years from now after a few more years of conflict?

Lapointe: It depends, to some extent, on what you mean by "in cooperation with other states." If you mean that any coastal state would simply, as has been the case before, bow and salute the flag flying on the mast of the supertanker and forget about doing anything about it because it belongs to somebody else, I think that my answer is No, if that is what you mean by cooperation. I think cooperation works both ways. I think the United States itself realizes this. The United States, I think, has been saying in certain quarters that if within two or three years the international system does not produce sufficiently high standards for, say, the hull construction of a ship or the manning of a ship, the United

States itself will pass legislation to make sure that within its own waters, whatever its waters may be, certain standards will be respected by all.

I think there is an element of protection of certain interests, and I think that Canada is as prepared as anybody else to cooperate in this sense: let us try to define high standards, which will be of worldwide application. We are all for that. It is just that in the face of certain special situations, like ice-infested waters such as we have in the north of Canada, we think that special standards have got to be established. And they cannot be the same standards that apply to the Caribbean Sea. I think that no captain would be stupid enough to enter Arctic waters without having a ship that is properly built. The only thing we want to do is to ensure that it is so. Cooperation, yes; but if you mean simply again bowing to the pressures of certain maritime states which have primarily their own interests at heart, I would say, No. This is exactly the system that we are trying to change. This is the new world order that we are going after.

Ratiner: I think what you have said, Paul, has opened up a third alternative between naked compulsory dispute settlement and a general law of the sea treaty, which I think we can all anticipate. The third alternative is what you might call living rule making—a congress or a parliament for certain ocean uses. The fact is that we seem now to be talking about three ways of controlling ocean uses well into the future in order to make ocean law living law. This could be achieved by establishing a treaty with general principles and regulatory machinery, which would have substantial control and regulatory authority over specified uses, and compulsory dispute settlement. I am sure that to the many Americans sitting in this audience, and to the representatives of other countries, this sounds like a familiar system—the executive, congress, and the judiciary—applied to the ocean. And they probably feel that the Law of the Sea Conference at this point is past considering that kind of arrangement. I know Ambassador Pardo's Ocean Space Treaty has not met with wide favor and support, but I wonder if, as the negotiations proceed, we are not (on a very piecemeal basis) inevitably working toward a modest recreation of what was Ambassador Pardo's dream so many years ago.

Nweihed: Mr. Ratiner emphasizes quite a lot the importance of compulsory settlements of disputes with respect to the success of the future law of the sea treaty, but I am afraid I must take the opposite point of view. In this sense I should like to pose a question to Mr. Ratiner. If you all remember, in 1958 there were four conventions drawn and signed in Geneva. Two of them dealt with already established norms that were codified; two of them dealt with the new spaces, namely the marine space and the submarine space. I refer to the Convention on Fishing and the Living Resources of the Sea on one hand, and to the Convention on the Continental Shelf on the other.

Now as it came out, the first of the two above-mentioned conventions, the Fishing and Living Resources, was provided with a mechanism under its Article 9 to settle disputes that might ensue from its enforcement, and the other convention was not. Thirteen years afterwards, if we review the success of these two conventions, we find out that the convention that was not provided with such a mechanism is a success. It has already been established in international law, not only by convention, but its custom-establishing process has been recognized by the International Court of Justice. In other words, it has become a success with no mechanism attached to it, while the other one was not resorted to once. So, in other words, that mechanism was not a success. So, I should like to know how could we attach such an importance when we do have these contrasting examples?

Ratiner: Perhaps we should look at one of the other treaties, the Treaty on the Territorial Sea and Contiguous Zones. I do not know whether you would characterize that one as a success or a failure. I characterize it as a failure. Were it not for the absence of compulsory dispute settlement and some decent rules in the Territorial Sea and Contiguous Zones Convention we might not today be having a Law of the Sea Conference.

The Declaration of Santiago, for example, and the failure in many of the Latin American countries to adhere to the Territorial Sea and Contiguous Zones Convention are not, from their point of view, the result of the lack of compulsory settlement of disputes, but the lack of a decent treaty. As Paul Lapointe observed, what you first need is a treaty which, in fact, accommodates the prevailing interests of the world community. That means some sacrifices on everybody's part. The point is that a treaty has to be written that leaves those things which cannot now be resolved with clarity and precision to the later decision of wise men with an interest in making objective decisions and not to the use of force, which is the way we now seem to be settling our law of the sea problems.

Killefer: It seems to me that Dr. Gamble did a service to us when he tried to describe that which exists right now and some of the reasons for our present situation in the international environment. Although I do not totally agree with his many points, at least he tried to focus some of our attention on the way things have developed and how they exist at the present time. Mr. Ratiner seemed to disagree with him and say that that is all well and good, but we should focus on that which should be. That seemed to me also important, but you cannot deny the many basic points that Dr. Gamble made. I wish I could show a little bit of my thinking on this because I think I share both gentlemen's focus here. I tried first of all to think and describe that which is, then tried to look and see if we can reach some sort of cohesive hold as to that which should be, and then try to define the mechanisms or the organizations or the modes of thought that will help us facilitate the transition between the two.

Lapointe: I was just about to ask you if you thought that you could agree that the one question that is not resolved, and that will be most difficult to resolve, is the expected confrontation between the interests of those who want free passage in straits as opposed to those who want certain pollution controls, for instance. Is this not one of the major areas that is likely to remain with us until the very end? It involves, of course, most of the other aspects, but I see a very definite confrontation on this point between the interests of commercial and military fleets and the kinds of control that are desired by most coastal states; and the new relationship that pollution control involves—this redefinition of innocence as part of the innocent passage concept. So far we have only heard two positions: one, there will be free passage—that is, without control; and the other, that there will be controls over passage.

Ratiner: Paul, I think there are really two answers to your question. First, you have not really accurately stated what is on the table in the U.N. The United States' position, for example, on free transit through and over international straits, has been elaborated upon in several statements made by the head of our delegation which indicate a willingness to subject passage through straits to reasonable pollution and safety controls of different types. I do not think the United States or the Soviet position on transit through straits is inconsistent with genuine safeguards for the coastal state in straits.

Second, I think there is a question of perception here. The question is, "when do we start to negotiate about the problems of navigation through straits and solve them in a rational way?" Right now the issue on straits is, "it is my strait, and I want to control it and tell you what to do." That is the perception of a straits country. As long as Spain and Malaysia and others continue to hold that view, then it will continue to appear in these negotiations that there are diametrically opposite views on the question of transit through straits. We will probably be on the road to a solution when Spain and Malaysia are prepared to say, "We have the following problems with respect to transit through straits, and these problems involve pollution and safety in navigation. We want to find ways of accommodating the interests of all states in getting through our straits safely, and we are not going to insist that we, and only we, are capable of determining what safe transit is and how safe transit should be accommodated."

However, I am not anticipating that that solution will come at an early stage in the negotiations, but rather at a much later stage. I think we have to bear in mind that the Ministry of Maritime Affairs in a straits country does not know that much more about the safety of navigation through straits than an international organization like IMCO. I imagine that they could benefit from discussing genuine questions of navigational safety and pollution control with other countries with a view toward establishing objective and rational rules so that Spain, for example, would not sit at the Strait of Gibraltar, controlling the world's maritime transport between the Mediterranean Sea and the Atlantic Ocean.

Labastida: I wish to comment on the propriety of using the expression "peripheral issues" in relation to any of the problems or questions to be dealt with by the United Nations Conference on the Law of the Sea. I respectfully submit that no issue can really be termed peripheral so long as any given group of countries attach any importance to such issue. One must remember that in convening the Conference, the General Assembly decided that the Conference would not be limited to a few important issues but that it should be ample and comprehensive of all related issues of the law of the sea. This should not be forgotten in formulating negotiating tactics on the basis of only certain questions.

By way of example I would like to refer to the question of marine pollution, to say that one should resist the temptation to call this issue peripheral. In the light of the increasing concern for the protection of the marine environment, it is most important for all countries, in particular the developing countries, to be fully equipped in terms of scientific knowledge and technological means to be able to recognize and honor their international responsibilities to prevent pollution.

Can these matters be considered a peripheral issue? Considering the grave implications for the marine environment that could result from a failure to successfully resolve these questions, one has to conclude that they are very important indeed and very central to the main concerns of the conference on the law of the sea.

Bailey: I should like to comment on the point made by Mr. Ratiner that without a dispute system there will be a dead law of the sea because unlike national law, international law does not change simply by the judicial process or by acts of the law-making body. A disputes system is only one of the ways other than treaties and the work of the International Law Commission embodied in treaties of contributing to the progressive development of international law. One of the paradoxes of international law is that a new rule of law can often be established by the very breach of an old rule. If the old law does not keep up with the changing needs of the international society, a new rule of law may emerge by a unilateral act accepted by a sufficient number of states, and nowadays this process could be a rather rapid one with a multistate consensus obtained through such bodies as the General Assembly of the United Nations. But on the other hand, I agree with Mr. Ratiner that such a process has the danger of leading to chaos.

Ratiner: I think that is what we have already in the law of the sea, and I do not see any reason to expect it to change without compulsory settlement of disputes. All I have tried to do is identify what may in fact be at the core of the problem in the law of the sea—the need for a permanent system of abandoning the way in which international law is made. International law is a nice discipline to study. It is a very difficult one to practice because what it basically does is give rise to conflict. If the United States does not like Canada's pollution zone, our job in international law is to violate it, and then it is Canada's job to come up and say, "We are going to shoot you if you violate our pollution zone." That is not a good way to make laws, but that is the way international law develops in this world. Those countries that are most responsible about the use of force— that is, who do not use force or are unwilling to use force—make customary law by allowing others to enforce their claims. Now is that the way we want to live in the world in the future? It seems to me that this is the only question for the Law of the Sea Institute.

Knauss: I think we probably would all agree with John Gamble's major point, which is that we see accelerating pluralism; and I guess we would probably all agree with you, Leigh, that because of this, the Law of the Sea Conference will produce a treaty with a certain amount of vagueness to it. It will be left to the international lawyers of the future to interpret.

I admire your rather missionary zeal in pushing compulsory dispute settlement, but I wonder. The U.S. has not had a very good history in the past, as best as I can remember, with respect to taking issues to the International Court. Certain other major nations in the world have not had a good record on this matter either. I would be interested in your views, or the views of anyone else for that matter, as to whether or not you really believe that the U.S. would agree to international dispute settlement on issues of major importance and whether other major nations would either.

Ratiner: The answer to your question is a simple yes. I think we will agree to it if the Law of the Sea Conference produces a generally satisfactory settlement of issues. We will have in the United States presumably the United States fisheries industry, the United States petroleum industry, the Department of Defense, and other major organizations, all of which will strongly favor the outcome of the Law of the Sea Conference and want to see that treaty ratified, including its provisions on compulsory dispute settlement. I find it very difficult to imagine how such a diverse group of special interests in the United States, if they are all satisfied with the law of the sea treaty and believe it to be better than anarchy and chaos on the oceans, would not be able to persuade two-thirds of the United States Senate to ratify a treaty with a compulsory dispute settlement. I think the United States has come a long way since the Connally Amendment; at least I hope we have.

Gamble: Since World War II, the United States has been party to a couple thousand treaties, but has not been willing to go before the International Court of Justice on any major issue. I wish I could accept Mr. Ratiner's optimism, but I don't see what has changed in recent years to make the United States willing to accept compulsory dispute settlement. It seems to me that talk of flexibility in treaty provisions is merely a subtle way of ignoring hard-to-reconcile positions. In pragmatic terms, the Conference may well have to choose between a vague treaty that will not work and a strong treaty that does not get ratified by major marine states.

Clingan:　I am really quite startled and delighted to learn that compulsory dispute settlement is the difference between a dead and a live law of the sea. It does concern me a little, however. I think it can be pressed a little too far. If the principle is accurate, then I suggest we might test it at home by disbanding the Congress and allowing those nine grand men in their white mausoleum on the Hill to evolve our law for us.

　　　　Now, they do that to some extent; but we do find from that experience that it is necessary from time to time for the Congress to take another look at a law that the Supreme Court says is bad; so that if we are working toward an international mechanism where we can just forget about future conferences and writing down in codification, and leave it to some sort of dispute mechanism, and find a way to eliminate the politics from that mechanism, I would be delighted.

Herrington:　It seems to me what is being discussed has mainly settled down to an issue of what kind of convention we wish to have come out of the conference. Do we wish a philosophical conference that sets high ideals for mankind and the world order, or do we wish a convention that is pragmatic, realistic, that recognizes human nature for what it is and that its sovereign states are still sovereign?

　　　　As I belong to the second category, I would like to see something come out of the conference that will be a factor in saving the resources of the oceans for the future of mankind; I go along pretty much with what Dr. Gamble has stated. I could dispute with him a number of points he has made, but I agree with most of his conclusions. I believe the Chairman must belong to the league of order of the Napoleonic law and not to the order of Anglo-Saxon law. In the 1958 Conference there was an example of one with primarily Anglo-Saxon background. The other was a mixture of Anglo-Saxon and Napoleonic law. The Continental Shelf Convention was primarily Anglo-Saxon. It was based primarily on codification of principles and practices that the nations had come to accept, and there was some compromise. But in each case, to get a compromise, both parties must achieve something they consider more valuable than what they give up. The Fisheries Convention was a combination. A large part of that was the progressive development of law; and although it was the result of compromises, i.e., the getting together or narrowing down of blocs, well over a two-thirds agreement was reached on the final convention, which included such things as obligatory settlement of disputes. It included a number of other very highly desirable things; but having gotten well over two-thirds vote in the conference, it never was ratified by more than a few countries, including only a couple of major fishing powers. So, it may have set some good ideas for the world to follow, and most countries have practiced many of the things that were set forth in the convention, but it never has become an active part of international law.

I think that one thing to consider very seriously is if you want to get a convention out of the conference coming up, and if you want to get the support of nations, and have them observe this convention, you have got to think very much in pragmatic terms. In the way of pragmatic negotiations, one of those that has been carried on recently by Dr. Kissinger was, I thought, a beautiful example of pragmatic negotiation. I think only in that way can we get the nations to accept things that at present they do not.

Pardo: There is no opposition between pragmatism and idealism. I do not think that many people realize the implications of the extraordinarily rapid revolution now taking place in our use of ocean space. In the past the oceans were used essentially for navigation and fishing—and not for intensive fishing at that. Now, for the first time in history, ocean space is beginning to be used for the same wide range of purposes and as intensively as land. Ocean space is being incorporated in our living space; it is being industrialized; it is being militarized.

Under these circumstances the two basic concepts of traditional law of the sea—that is, the sovereignty of the coastal state within national jurisdiction and freedom beyond national jurisdiction—are no longer sustainable. It is not a question of idealism or pragmatism, but of common sense. The two traditional concepts just will not work in the new circumstances that are arising.

We need, for instance, management of living resources both within and outside national jurisdiction, not for pragmatic or idealistic reasons but because pressure on many stocks of fish is increasing to such an extent that management is essential if we are to avoid the destruction of most desirable fish stocks. We need norms for the abatement of pollution in the oceans, not for pragmatic or idealistic reasons, but because of the enormous increase in the dangerous byproducts of industrialization that make their way to, or are disposed of in, ocean space; activities in the oceans—oil exploitation, supertanker traffic, and so on—increase the dangers of serious contamination. We need agreed-on standards for the use of technology because technology is now becoming so powerful that we may soon be able to use the oceans to change the climate of half the globe. And I could comment on a number of other uses of the seas.

In this situation we need an authority to regulate and harmonize uses and activities and to prevent abuses. This authority can be either national or international. In recent years, we have seen an extension of national authority in ocean space and an explosion of national claims, largely prompted on the one hand by improved accessibility of off-shore hydrocarbons and on the other by the increasing dangers of marine pollution and by abuses in the exploitation of living resources. Should present international law remain substantially unchanged we may expect a rather rapid extension of coastal state jurisdiction for one purpose or another over virtually the entire oceans. The extension of national jurisdiction solves the problem of the present lack of authority in the oceans, but the consequences of a national solution to ocean problems are serious: International intercourse and navigation would be obstructed and scientific research would be crippled. Exclusively national management of fisheries would in all probability bring about a deterioration in the state of fish stocks and would render rational management of nearly all species of fish virtually impossible because of the fragmentation of ocean space into more than one hundred different jurisdictional areas, in each of which different standards of conservation and harvesting would be applied.

Should there, then, be a comprehensive international organization which, among its many duties, would regulate and harmonize uses and activities in ocean space, manage international fisheries, and in general act like a superstate? The idea could be attractive to theorists, but such a concept ignores the fact that we are living in a world of national states extremely jealous of their sovereignty. What *is* essential if we are to avoid the division of the oceans among coastal states is an international organization that can provide both a forum with regard to any serious problem which arises in ocean space and a mechanism through which international rules and standards can be negotiated with regard to the conduct of the more important activities that take place in the oceans. Finally, the international organization should administer seabed resources beyond national jurisdiction and provide a mechanism within which management standards can be elaborated with respect to fisheries. Basically, we need an international system for ocean space that is parallel to the United Nations system. I feel that unless such a system is created, conflict is bound to increase in ocean space.

Nweihed: I have a very brief remark on what I thought was the impression that I could define as the predictability or the ponderability of the attitude to be assumed by nations or their delegates at the United Nations. I thought that Dr. Ratiner wanted to say that the attitude of any country—he mentioned Venezuela, but it might be any other country—towards the law of the sea would be easily predicted because you know exactly what the motivations are behind it, and I should like just to throw a little doubt on this. For instance, France in 1970-71 was on the side of nations who favored three miles, and then within a few months jumped to the twelve-mile side. Brazil is another example; in less than 28 months it changed from a six-mile to a twelve-mile limit, and then within eleven months between the second decision and the third, went over to a 200-mile limit. Then we have the case of Canada. Who could have told—and I hope in this case Mr. Lapointe might be able to give the answer—the future in 1970 when Canada issued a set of regulations against pollution which were based on a scientific examination of the situation? (In arctic waters pollution causes disastrous effects, and the bacterial oxidization of petroleum slicks takes more than 50 years which is not the case in other waters and therefore justifies scientifically what Canada has done.) So, who was able to predict at that time that within two years, Canada would take an attitude based upon protecting her fisheries to a 200-mile limit?

Actually Dr. Pardo's last observations are really valuable concerning the philosophy on which the law of the sea is developing, due to the fact that multiple uses are being incorporated into the mechanisms of the law of the sea, and the growth of the uses to which the sea is committed. That is why we really cannot talk so simply of being able to predict what nations might have to say at the next forum.

Rebagliate: I address myself to the points Mr. Ratiner made. The latter one referred to who might benefit from the Conference on the Law of the Sea, and the previous referred to the question of compulsory settlement of disputes. (Personally speaking, I think that besides some hotels and restaurants of New York and Santiago, all the states in the international community will benefit from the Conference on the Law of the Sea!)

Certainly everybody is concerned about what is going to be developed at that conference, taking into account the wide participation of countries in the negotiations that are going on now and the anticipated participation of other countries who are members of this Seabed Committee of the United Nations. There is a clear picture of this concern and interest.

The international community is supposed to be the beneficiary of this conference, and of course the international community as such and all its members, namely the states. Talking about the question of force, I think many times international law, unfortunately, was made through force. Slavery and colonialism were international law institutions, and under international law were legal up to some time ago—not too long ago, unfortunately; and then international law developed in a different way. Of course, talking about the example you made about the question of refraining from the use of force as a means to allow international law to be developed by other countries, the example you made in relation to Canada or Peru, I think that that would not create international law so far as the U.S. is concerned, provided that in a peaceful way the U.S. does not recognize the unilateral acts of Peru or Canada. But if many other countries follow the path of Peru and Canada, and it becomes a widely recognized procedure by the international community—despite the nonrecognition by two or three states—this will necessarily become international law for all states. Disregarding the use of force or the nonuse of force or the nonrecognition by one, two, or three states, the unilateral, coordinated, and widely recognized measures will become international law even for that small number of states. I think the use of force or the nonuse of force is irrelevant to this point. Apart from that in the present state of international relations I think the use of force has no place, and more specifically, it has no place in this context.

The use of force for preventing a country from dictating or enforcing its national law with regard to the law of the sea is illegal. Verbal notes and protest are the legal means directed to avoid recognition of such unilateral measures. Politically, it will also be advisable to continue using this civilized means of protesting and not recognizing the unilateral measure by the other countries which do not share those claims.

I do not imagine a situation in which three or four or five countries will embark themselves, fighting against a number of the international community members. I could not imagine a situation, if I may, in which the U.S. and the Soviet Union and Japan would fight against China or Brazil, Senegal, Argentina, Chile, and so forth. I really cannot imagine that situation at all. I think that we have to be optimistic and think that the future law of the sea will be settled. I think the international community has already proved that these kinds of efforts can be made successfully.

In reference to the question of the settlement of disputes, I think that this question should not have to be emphasized so much, especially as a possible alternative to the lack of a broad agreement on the law of the sea. I think that one point is that the agreement be as broad as possible and as detailed as possible, and the other is the compulsory settlement of disputes. This question of the settlement of disputes can be a complement of such an agreement, but it cannot be substituted. I think that if countries cannot agree upon substantive matters, they will not be able to agree upon a procedural way to deal with something that is not clear, is not recognized. What would be the worth of the law of the sea without a compulsory settlement of dispute system? I think it would be of the same worth as the other parts of the international law. I think that international law in many fields has its own way of peaceful means of settlement of disputes and they are not necessarily compulsory.

I do not exclude the possibility of having compulsory settlement of disputes for the law of the sea—or perhaps more likely for some specific matters related to the law of the sea—but theoretically speaking it is possible to have a living law of the sea, as a living outer space law, as a living diplomatic and consular relations law without having a compulsory settlement of disputes. States can behave, and there are peaceful means of settlement of disputes without necessarily being compulsory.

I think that this last possibility can be explored theoretically. Politically it is quite a different problem, but theoretically it can be a complement to the law of the sea, although not an alternative. I do not think that by drafting a very general and deliberately ambiguous treaty we can go home successfully from the conference. I think we will be betraying ourselves if we deliberately try to bypass the responsibility of drafting a new, widely recognized law of the sea by coming up with a very ambiguous and nonclear treaty or treaties. I think that no states will rely on wise judges' opinions because they will in advance know that this law is just as uncertain as was the situation before the conference on the law of the sea.

Lee: I just wanted to pick up what the previous speaker said about the question of your emphasis on the compulsory settlement of disputes. I really feel this is putting the cart before the horse. I was pleased to note that the majority of the panel, particularly with respect to marine pollution, were not in agreement with Mr. Gamble's comment that we should combat this on a regional basis, rather than via the means of a comprehensive international legal framework. Surely if we have a comprehensive international legal framework, and if we have effective enforcement of jurisdiction, and if we have provisions for compensation for damages, we are going to have very few disputes—and we will not have to worry so much about the compulsory settlement of disputes.

The other point I wanted to make pertains to your references to the development of international law via the use of force. I know that one has to be a little dramatic in order to generate discussion, but certainly in the case of Canada with regard to the Arctic Waters Pollution Prevention Act, yes, it was a unilateral act, but also it was very firm government policy to pursue a multilateral solution to this problem. Indeed, we spent much time and energy trying to get some multilateral action in this field. We were caught on the horns of a dilemma. The U.S. seemed to favor multilateral action but did not really like what we did. The USSR, our other major neighbor to the north, seemed to favor the unilateral action per se but did not like multilateral action. So, our legal advisers are still working on that, but I think to say that this was development of international law by use of force was a bit overcolorful, perhaps.

Chapter Three

How Will the Future Deep Seabed Regime be Organized?

Andres Aguilar
Ambassador of Venezuela to the
United States

The organization of the deep seabed regime is a very difficult and complex matter. Thus, instead of exploring it in full, I have selected only those issues which I feel are most crucial to the success of the negotiations that are being carried out by the U.N. Seabed Committee.

The international regime covering the area of the seabed and the ocean floor beyond the limits of national jurisdiction is the first and without doubt one of the most important items on the list of subjects and issues relating to the law of the sea prepared in compliance with Resolution 2750 (XXV), of the General Assembly of the United Nations by the Committee on the Peaceful Uses of the Seabed and the Ocean Floor Beyond the Limits of National Jurisdiction, hereafter referred to as the U.N. Seabed Committee.

As agreed on by the Committee, this list ". . . establishes no order of priorities for the examination of these various subjects and issues." Nevertheless, the fact that this topic is first on the list reflects an agreement to give it a certain priority, which priority has in effect been formalized by the creation of Subcommittee I. This body is dedicated exclusively to this subject, even though the responsibility for making recommendations to the Committee on the very important question of the precise limits of the area rests with Subcommittee II, and the question of peaceful utilization was assigned to the Committee, according to the organizational agreements arrived at in the meetings of March and August 1971. On the other hand, both Subcommittee I and the Working Group of 33 nations, established in March 1972, have had the time to achieve a certain degree of progress in examining this subject and drafting alternative recommendations.

If greater progress has not been achieved it is certainly due neither to lack of sufficient time nor to defects in scheduling the work load. Subcommittee I and the Working Group have actually been engaged in a very serious and constructive effort and their working methods could hardly be improved upon. The problem lies elsewhere. The international regime covering the seabed beyond the limits of national jurisdiction is but one of the many subjects being studied by the Committee that will have to be resolved by the United Nations Conference on the Law of the Sea.

It should not be forgotten that the problems of ocean space are closely interrelated and should be considered as a whole. Progress in the efforts of the Committee in this field depend upon the progress achieved in other areas and on other basic questions. The truth is that it is not possible to reach an agreement on the rules to cover the deep seabed as long as the question of the limits of the area is not resolved and as long as there is no basic agreement on the regime covering other maritime spaces.

In spite of the priority which has been accorded to the regime for the seabed beyond the limits of national jurisdiction, the attention of most of the members of the U.N. Seabed Committee has dwelt upon those areas which are or would be under some form of national jurisdiction; that is to say, territorial sea, patrimonial sea or exclusive economic zone, continental shelf, issues relating to straits used for international navigation, and archipelagoes—to mention just a few of the topics which have recently caused much debate. The truth is that the enthusiasm and hope that the subject of the regime of the seabed originally inspired has waned somewhat, and even though work on this issue has continued without interruption since 1967, some of the initial impetus has been lost.

Clearly the resistance of certain developed nations to accepting the fundamental principle that the seabed and the ocean floor and its resources are the common heritage of mankind and the proposals made by other developed nations to weaken or make this principle practically meaningless have contributed to an impression in the developing nations that the real objective of both groups is to establish an international regime whereby in fact, though if not by law, they would control the resources of this area.

Likewise, the opposition of some of the more highly developed nations to democratic machinery invested with the powers required to give real meaning to the Declaration of Principles adopted by the General Assembly in its Resolution 2749 (XXV), leads one to believe that some of the powerful nations seek to dominate the seabed and its resources through an international agency and enjoy, with the support and security offered by an international treaty, universal in character, the advantages afforded them by their capital and technology.

It has been said, perhaps with a certain degree of exaggeration, that the true motivation of some nations has been to secure acceptance by the developing countries of a law of the sea cut to the measure of their needs and interests in exchange for an unspecified income and under such conditions that little or nothing would be contributed to diminish the gap between the rich and poor nations. In spite of all these doubts and apprehensions, there are still many nations who maintain the hope that, one way or another, an agreement will be reached on this matter. It would be truly unfortunate if we lost this opportunity to preserve for mankind this last frontier on our planet and to rationally utilize its resources for the benefit of all our peoples.

It is timely to recall at this point the very incisive words of the late President Johnson when on July 13, 1966, he stated:

> . . . under no circumstances, we believe, must we ever allow the prospects of rich harvests and mineral wealth to create a new form of colonial competition among maritime nations. We must be careful to avoid a race to grab and to hold the lands under the high seas. We must insure that the deep seas and the ocean bottoms are, and remain, the legacy of all human beings.

Let us now proceed from a general consideration of these matters to deal with some of the most important and controversial issues concerning the seabed regime. One fundamental point is the need to base all our work, both in the U.N. Seabed Committee and later on at the conference, on the Declaration of Principles, particularly its vital concept that the area and its resources are the common heritage of mankind. In this connection I would like to quote from a very appropriate statement made by Mr. Hambro, former Norwegian Ambassador to the United Nations and former President of the General Assembly. In a paper he presented at the last Annual Conference of the Law of the Sea Institute he stressed the importance of the concept of the common heritage of mankind, saying:

> Some of the articles of this Declaration are of great importance. First of all, it is now settled—I hope and trust finally settled—in solemn words and in a most authoritative way that the riches on and under the seabed are the common heritage of mankind. This is a new term in "international law" and met with opposition from many quarters. Lawyers were apt to say that the term has no strict legal significance and was unknown in legal terminology. That is probably true, but that is why it was deemed important to use it and to give it a new significance. It is a new term, and it denotes something new in international relations. It is also a term which speaks to the imagination of ordinary people like the term in the outer space treaty that astronauts are "envoys of mankind." I believe that terms such as these are of great significance in international life just because they are

"loaded" terms, because they express a program and an aspiration. They appeal directly to people and convey an idea which no elaborate legal terminology could ever do. They counteract the inherent danger in international law of becoming so esoteric that only the initiated few understand what it is all about.

It is well to remember that the Declaration of Principles is the result of a compromise, reached after prolonged and laborious negotiations. Without attempting to resolve the question of whether this Declaration is legally binding, there is no doubt that it has moral and political value due not only to the high principles it enunciates but also to the support it received from the General Assembly. It is a matter of record that the Declaration was adopted by 108 votes, with no negative votes and only 14 abstentions.

Having said this, I am going to address myself to the issue of the limits of the area. This is a very important issue as you all know since the position of many countries on other matters will depend on the actual area to be covered by the international regime. To this effect I should begin by saying that according to international law, the coastal states have acquired rights to their respective continental shelves, and it is quite unlikely that they would renounce these rights unless they had very good reasons to do so. There is a general agreement, of course, on the need to define precise limits to the continental shelf, as the second criterion adopted at the 1958 Geneva Convention, the exploitability criterion, is not appropriate. In fact, a number of concrete proposals have already been submitted to the Committee as to what these limits should be.

No one disputes these facts, and yet somehow some people have come to believe that the deep seabeds, with the exception of those covered by territorial waters, have overnight become a common heritage of all mankind. The Declaration of Principles clearly refers to the area of the seabed and the ocean floor and the subsoil thereof *beyond the limits of national jurisdiction.* I emphasize these words, for the coastal states do exercise sovereign rights over their respective continental shelves, although up to limits which have as yet to be determined precisely. In other words, by definition, the continental shelf—subject as it is to the national jurisdiction of one or another of the coastal states—is *not* a part of the international area unless these coastal nations renounce their rights.

I sincerely believe, in the light of the work done by the U.N. Seabed Committee, that at the present time there is no reason for us to think that any of the nations interested in maintaining these rights are going to modify their positions now, or later at the conference. The reception given to the proposal of the United States on an intermediate area is very eloquent in this respect. It is quite probable that the international area of the seabed will be located beyond 200 miles, and this on the very hypothetical supposition that the nations which have a continental shelf that extends beyond this limit would consent to accept this distance as the only criterion to define the limits of the continental shelf. That is why I feel that one of the most realistic proposals made to the U.N. Seabed Committee has been a Maltese proposal. (I am pleased to be able to say this in the presence of its author, Ambassador Pardo.) Perhaps one of the simplest ways of settling this question is to make a distinction between the area of national jurisdiction, the national maritime space up to 200 miles, and the international area beyond 200 miles as proposed in the Maltese draft.

In any case there would still remain a considerable area of seabed and ocean floor regarded as the common heritage of all mankind in which there are ample proven resources. I was reading an article on the subject by one of the members of the U.N. staff, Mr. Branco of Brazil, in which he states that the metal-rich manganese nodules ". . . are found over large areas of the seabed and even in some lakes, but only those lying on the deep ocean floor seem to be of economic interest." He further notes how important those resources may be for our present situation and for the future. So the argument that the area beyond the continental margin will be worthless is not really well founded.

An issue of equal importance to the one we have been discussing is the question of the functions of the authority which has been proposed to deal with this area; that is to say, the scope and nature of the functions that it will be called upon to discharge.

Everybody recognizes that this is one of the most controversial issues. While some nations wish to hold the powers of this authority to a minimum and limit its functions to the issuing or registration of licenses, or at most to the coordination of the activities carried out by states or persons natural or juridical sponsored by them, other nations favor the granting of broad powers, foremost among them the right of the authority to conduct on its own the exploration and exploitation of resources in this area.

A very important issue is at stake here. To developing nations the concept of common heritage implies not only sharing in the benefits to be obtained from the exploitation of the resources of the area but also, and above all, an effective and total participation in all aspects of the management of this common heritage. To be more precise, the developing nations seek to participate in all the activities to be carried out in this area: in scientific research, in exploration and exploitation, and in management and distribution of the benefits to be derived.

As I said at a meeting of Subcommittee I of the U.N. Seabed Committee in August 1971:

> . . . were the developing nations to take a purely passive position as beneficiaries, this in my view would condemn them to a situation of perpetual minority or dependence. The rights and interests in the common heritage would for an extended period be administered by the more developed nations, and the developing nations would be relegated to the role of mere marginal spectators in the development

process of the area's resources. It is evident that this state of affairs will also not be favorable, in the long run, to the interests of the international community as a whole. Just as in the domestic affairs of any given nation it is not a very healthy situation to have any relatively important group alienated from the decision-making process and programs, it is unsound for international society to permit the gap between the highly developed and lesser developed nations to persist and grow even wider.

The thesis supporting the concept of granting the authority the powers to carry out, on its own, exploration and exploitation activities—not to mention other equally controversial powers—has run into tenacious opposition from the great powers. It has been sustained that the authority would become a supernational entity, to which the supporters of this thesis have responded that the authority would have jurisdiction over an area which, by definition, would be international, and it would, therefore, not have any power or jurisdiction over individual states.

It has also been said that it is contrary to the principles of common law that this authority should simultaneously regulate the mining activities in this area while it participates in these activities, as this would place the states who engage in similar activities at a disadvantage and would arouse doubts as to the observance of due legal process. I am not really qualified to judge whether this is really true in common law, but I can affirm that in many nations there seems to be no problem about having a governmental enterprise conduct activities parallel to those of private enterprises. Rather, it is a common practice in several nations to do so in order to maintain a reasonable level of prices for basic goods and services.

In any case, this problem would not exist if the proposal made by several Latin American nations to the Committee were accepted, since according to Article 15 of this draft proposal, the authority would engage in its own activities of exploration and exploitation in this area, but would be able to use for these purposes either natural or juridical persons, be they public or private, national or international, through a system of contracts or the creation of mixed enterprises. It is obvious that within this framework, individual states could carry out these activities only in association with the authority.

This concept certainly is neither as novel nor as revolutionary as it would appear at first sight. In many countries certain economic activities, such as the exploration and exploitation of hydrocarbons, or the production and distribution of electrical power, for example, are reserved to the state itself, which usually then creates for this purpose an enterprise to which it grants the exclusive rights to carry out these activities and gives it authorization, in most cases, to sign service contracts or to participate in different forms of association with other domestic or foreign firms.

In keeping with this format, according to the proposal presented by several Latin American nations to which I have been referring, the authority would include among its organs an enterprise which would be responsible for carrying out all of the technical, industrial, and commercial activities relating to the exploration and exploitation of the resources of the area, on its own or through mixed companies duly sponsored by the states.

Another alternative is the proposal by Tanzania in its draft statutes for an International Seabed Agency, according to which the authority (which in this proposal is called the International Seabed Agency) would be empowered to explore the international areas of the seabeds and exploit the resources for peaceful purposes with its own means, equipment, and services, or through those means which it obtains for these purposes. It could also issue licenses to contracting parties, individuals or to groups, natural or juridical persons, under the sponsorship of these contracting parties.

It is worthwhile to mention at this point that at the Organization of African Unity meeting of experts on the law of the sea, held in Addis Ababa last April, this concept was endorsed, and one of the recommendations on the regime of the seabed, reads as follows:

> The machinery shall be invested with strong and comprehensive powers. Among others it shall have right to explore and exploit the area, to regulate activities in the area, to handle equitable distribution of benefits and to minimize any adverse economic effects by the fluctuation of prices of raw materials resulting from activities carried out in the Area; to distribute equitably among all developing countries the proceeds from any tax (fiscal imposition) levied in connection with activities relating to the exploitation of the Area; to protect the marine environment; to regulate and conduct Scientific Research and in this way give full meaning to the concept of the common heritage of mankind.

It is really difficult to understand why some states have no objection to different forms of association with other states or state-owned enterprises for the exploitation of resources belonging to those very same states while, in turn, they have difficulties in accepting the idea of a similar association with an international entity of which they would form a part and in whose administration they would participate under equal conditions with other nations.

It must be remembered by the way that in practice, and for a long time to come, private or public companies of developed nations will, because of the resources and technology they possess, be in an advantageous position to enter into this type of mixed company or to be awarded service contracts by the authority.

Let me now make a few comments about another very important aspect of this problem, one which is very closely related to the one we have been discussing. That is the question of the powers of the authority to reduce to a minimum the fluctuation in the prices of relevant minerals. On this point I share the view that the authority should have broad powers to prevent the negative effects which, according to studies carried out by the United Nations, the exploitation of the resources of the seabed areas might have upon the prices of certain raw materials. It would be inconceivable if we permitted utilization of these resources to ruin some countries which produce these raw materials and which are almost all in the developing process and highly dependent on the prices paid for one or another of these products.

The Declaration of Principles is quite clear in this respect. In the last paragraph of the preamble it states that the development and use of the seabed area and its resources shall be undertaken in such a manner as to foster the healthy development of the world economy and minimize any adverse economic effects stemming from the fluctuation of prices of raw materials resulting from these activities.

The same declaration in its operative part states that "The regime shall, *inter alia*, provide for the orderly and safe development and rational management of the area and its resources. . . ."

In order to apply these principles effectively it would be necessary to grant the authority adequate powers to take all of the necessary steps, including, as was proposed in the previously mentioned working paper prepared by several Latin American nations, the right to control, reduce, or suspend the production, or set the prices for the products obtained through the exploitation of these areas, whenever this production might have adverse economic effects on the developing countries which export these raw materials. A provision very similar to this appears in other drafts in the Tanzanian draft and also in the recommendations of the OAU meeting of experts.

Without these or similar provisions, the consumer nations (generally the highly developed nations) would have in their hands a powerful instrument for applying pressure, which they would not hesitate to use against the producing nations (generally the developing nations) to get them to consent to ridiculously low prices or to obtain concessions for the exploitation of the land-based raw materials under outrageous conditions.

But these are not the only reasons that justify the creation of a powerful authority. The transfer of science and technology, which without doubt is one of the most important tools for accelerating the pace of development, calls for an agency endowed with sufficient powers to plan and to implement these goals. And it is not enough that the authority be strong. Its organization and functions should be inspired by genuinely democratic principles. The principle of each state having one vote should be applied in all its collective bodies. Nor should there be either single or plural vetoes, nor systems of weighted votes that give certain states, individually or in groups, a greater voice than others in the decision-making process.

The regime, including the international machinery governing the seabed and the ocean floor, cannot be formulated with myopic vision on the basis of current conditions or those to prevail in the near future, and they should certainly not have as an objective the preservation of the present and passing power structure. History teaches us that with time, and for different reasons, the ranking and position of the great powers is subject to change. As some are eclipsed or fade away, others rise to the heights of power. All the discussions, for instance, about the composition of the Security Council and who should be on it, proves that you cannot freeze forever certain power structures.

To conclude, I should like to comment briefly on the pressure which has been exercised by certain circles to begin the commercial exploitation of the deep seabed even before there is any agreement, and on the basis of standards to be established unilaterally. I am not going to analyze the bills before the U.S. Congress dealing with this matter. I was pleased to learn, of course, that the Administration opposes these bills for rather good reasons. As Charles N. Brower, the State Department's Acting Legal Adviser, very aptly said when speaking about the Metcalf-Downing Bill, the measure ". . . . has become a symbol to many countries of what they regard as defiance of the multilateral negotiating process. . . . It is necessary to achieve timely, widespread international agreement on outstanding law of the sea issues in order to preserve and save over two-thirds of the earth's surface from national conflict and rivalry."

And Mr. Ratiner, Director of the Interior Department's Ocean Resources Office and one of the members of the U.S. Seabed Task Force, put it very forcefully when he stated that if the U.S. Congress should go ahead and pass the industry's seabed mining bill ". . . it would be the functional equivalent of preempting the Law of the Sea Conference on this issue. The U.S. has committed itself to the proposition that the regulations and use of the deep ocean mineral resources should be accomplished under an international agreement which in particular would be of benefit to the developing countries."

There is no doubt really that the unilateral establishment of such arrangements, in the midst of an international negotiation, is not the most appropriate way to reach an agreement. I would even venture to say that its value as a means of applying pressure for achieving a prompt agreement is very relative. Rather, in many cases this pressure would have the effect of making other positions more rigid and the negotiations more difficult.

In turn, I would regard the proposal made by the United States at the spring session of the U.N. Seabed Committee inviting support for the idea of provisional entry into force of aspects of the regime and machinery at such time as the new treaty relating to the law of the sea was opened for signature as very interesting and worthy of close examination. The study requested by the Committee from the Secretary General on precedents of the provisional entry into force of multilateral treaties, in whole or in part, would provide a good basis for making a decision on this issue.

Part Two

Chapter Four

Technological Dependence of Developing Countries: A Survey of Issues and Lines of Action

Surendra J. Patel
Chief, Transfer of Technology
Branch, United Nations

INTRODUCTION[1]

In less than two centuries the process of industrialization has spread from a tiny triangle in Britain to nearly 25 percent of the world population. But it has so far largely bypassed the developing countries, including China and other socialist countries in East Asia, as well as the countries from Portugal to Bulgaria lying on the southern periphery of Europe. These developing countries account for almost 75 percent of the world population, but for only 20 percent of the world income. On the other hand, the developed countries, with only 25 percent of the population, account for as much as 80 percent of the real world output. Their average per capita income is around ten times higher than in the developing countries. This, in brief, is the image of our unequal world. To bridge the gap between the two partners in the unequal world is the main task of the twentieth century.

The economic and social development of the poor countries is now no longer conditional upon the development of new scientific and technological knowledge, as was the case until the middle of the last century. The world storehouse of technological knowledge, accumulated in the developed countries since the Industrial Revolution, was responsible for raising their real per capita income nearly ten times over the last century. But most of mankind continues to remain ill-fed, ill-clad, ill-housed, and illiterate. If the available technological knowledge

can be transferred to them, their economic and social transformation can be
carried out rapidly.

As was pointed out by Lord Snow:[2]

> We cannot avoid the realization that science has made it possible to
> remove unnecessary suffering from a billion individual lives—to re-
> move suffering of a kind which, in our privileged society, we have
> largely forgotten. . . . It does not require one additional scientific
> discovery, though new scientific discoveries must help us. It depends
> on the spread of the scientific revolution over the world. There is no
> other way.

This is why crucial significance attaches to creating the proper conditions for a very rapid transfer of technology to the developing countries. But
such transfer is handicapped by a large number of constraints. This chapter dis-
cusses the background of the technological gap among nations in the first section
and the position of developing countries in the world market for technology in
the second. It then takes up a brief survey of the major problems arising from
the technological dependence of the developing countries and indicates a few
major lines for action.

TECHNOLOGICAL GAP AMONG NATIONS
AND THE TRANSFER OF TECHNOLOGY

Origin of the Technological Gap

Over the long span of history, technological and social innovations
have taken place at various places in the world. Before the Industrial Revolution,
countries considered underdeveloped now were responsible for contributing
most of the advanced technological and social innovations.[3] For instance, the
use of fire, the taming and domestication of animals, the evolution of agriculture
and the development of irrigation, the invention of pottery, the art of weaving,
the smelting of ores and exploitation of metals, the invention of script, paper,
and later the art of printing; the decimal system of numerals and the art of calculations; the use of gunpowder, the development of the marine compass and the
stern-post rudder of ships, the use of crankshaft and the windmill. All these innovations originated from countries now called "developing." Medieval Europe
borrowed both science and technology from them. The technological superiority
of the "developed" countries over the "developing" ones is thus very recent in
origin. Only a few centuries ago, the flow of technology was the other way
around.

The present economic distance between the developed and developing countries, which is mainly a reflection of the technological gap, is even more
recent in origin. Even as late as 1850, only five countries—the United States, the
United Kingdom, Switzerland, Canada, and the Netherlands—had attained an

average per capita income of about $200 (in 1954-58 prices). This was only slightly higher than the current average for the developing countries.

Main Features of Modern Technical Knowledge

The precise definition of technology or technical knowledge may be subject to considerable debate.[4] But four of its main features may be singled out for their contemporary relevance to economic growth.[5] First, major additions to the stock of useful knowledge and the extension of its applicability have been cumulative in character. As a result, the world's storehouse of useful knowledge has expanded immensely.[6]

There is no satisfactory way of measuring the quantity and the growth of technical knowledge. But an impression of these magnitudes may be obtained from the growth of per capita output—which is, after all, a result of technical progress in the developed countries since 1850. The combined population of the developed countries has since the middle of the last century tripled (at one percent per year). But their real national product has grown 33-fold (at about three percent per year). The per capita level of real income has thus multiplied ten-fold in 120 years since 1850 (at about two percent per year). In sharp contrast, the real per capita income of these countries could have hardly doubled in the 4,000 years prior to 1850.[7] These magnitudes give a measure of the speed of the spread of economic growth—and of the distance the developing countries have to cover to close the gap.

Second, the evolution of such knowledge has not been restricted to any single geographical territory or racial stock. In the cumulative addition to knowledge, no single nation or race has remained pioneer for long. The technical knowledge has thus been transnational in character. Its sources over time have been many, and its emulation, adoption, and adaptation very wide indeed. Moreover, an important feature of the transnational and cumulative stock of world technical knowledge is its relatively easy transmissibility. Once it has been proved to be useful, it is, as Professor Kuznets pointed out, usually "invariant to personal traits or talents and to institutional vagaries." In this sense, it is different from the technical knowledge of traditional societies, including the skills used in pastoral operations, peasant agriculture, and handicrafts.

Finally, the development of a particular facet of technical knowledge may have involved economic cost; but its transfer is singularly different from that of individual commodities. Once the tested addition to the knowledge has been made, its use anywhere else does not in any way diminish its supply to the originator or to others. Technical knowledge is thus cumulative in growth, transnational in origin, transmissible across frontiers, and irreducible in supply upon transfer.

Transfer of Technology and Economic Growth

One facet of the economic advance of the developed countries has contemporary relevance. This concerns the spread of economic growth and the speed of that spread. The pioneer country in industrialization was Great Britain, with a population of a little over nine million in 1781, or slightly more than one percent of world population at that time. Since then, industrialization has spread to most of Europe, North America, Australia and Japan, altogether accounting for some 900 million persons, or one-fourth of the world's population.

In the process of the spread of industrialization from the pioneer to the others, there was a steady rise in the growth rate of per capita output for each new entrant into the process of modern economic growth. For instance, it has been estimated that the long-term annual per capita growth rate during the period of industrial transformation in England and France ranged from 1.2 to 1.4 percent; that for Germany, Denmark, Switzerland, United States, and Canada from 1.6 to 1.8 percent; that for Norway, Sweden, and Japan from 2.1 to 2.8 percent; and that for the Soviet Union was at least 4 percent or higher.[8] Each new entrant to industrialization has thus benefited from the widening of its perspective by others who had already industrialized earlier.[9] This is the main source of the now famous "advantage of the latecomers."

Economic development is thus dependent on technological progress. And the growth of the world's stock of transmissible knowledge furnishes the basis for the progressive rise in the rate of growth for each new entrant. Transmissibility of such knowledge increases the interdependence of countries. Technical progress is not merely a result of indigenous evolution, but one of significant transfers across geographical, political, and cultural frontiers.[10]

Developing Countries in the Market for Technology

If technology followed the laws of fluids, it would simply flow from a high to a low point. Technological and income gaps would be transient phenomena. All countries would eventually become economically equal and those that are a bit behind need not spend sleepless nights over it, for the force of gravitational pull will draw technology to the low points. But technology does not seem to flow that way. Its transfer is faced with a number of obstacles. Particularly serious are the limitations on the market for it and the weak bargaining position of the developing countries. Before these are taken up, it will be useful to review the ways in which such transfer takes place.

Ways of Transferring Technology

Technology is transferred in numerous ways. Among them, the following are the most important.[11]

1. Flow of books, journals, and other published information
2. The movement of people between countries, including immigration, study visits, and other travel
3. Knowledge of goods produced elsewhere
4. Training of students, technical staff, and employment of external experts

5. Exchanges of information and personnel through technical cooperation programs
6. Import of machinery and equipment and related literature
7. Agreements on patents, licensing, and knowhow
8. Direct foreign investment and operation of multinational corporations

The developing countries use simultaneously almost all these ways, either singly or in combination, to obtain the elements of technological knowledge needed for setting up required production facilities.[12] The choice of one or several of these ways is usually dictated by the nature of the technology desired and the technological capabilities already existing in the developing country. Some of the knowledge is obtained through the free flow of information. Some of it is embodied in imported machinery and external consultants. The older and easier the knowledge, the more likely it is to be available through one or several of the first six ways listed above.

The more modern the knowledge, the more likely that it will be in the possession of external enterprises or persons. And this will have to be obtained, usually through agreements on patents, licensing, and knowhow, and direct investment and operation of multinational corporations. It is mainly the last two of the ways listed above, which are discussed under the heading of the commercial transfer of technology.

Several organizational forms for the transfer process have evolved in the developing countries. At the one end of the spectrum, it takes the form of direct investment by foreign enterprise, establishing in the developing countries subsidiaries or affiliates with various degrees of autonomy. This arrangement requires minimum form of participation by the developing countries in supplying any of the various elements of technical knowledge. On the other hand, they have practically no control over the operations of the foreign subsidiaries or affiliates. This was the classic form nearly universally used by external enterprises in former colonies or even independent countries.

At the other end of the spectrum is the latest newcomer on the stage: the public enterprise in the developing country attempting to obtain, under the most advantageous terms, various elements of knowledge from different external sources. As is to be expected, several other mixed forms have evolved between these two extremes. They consist mainly of various varieties of joint ventures in which the public and private sectors of the technology supplying and receiving countries participate in varying degrees in capital, supply of skills, and control of management.

Limitations of the Market for Technology
The inadequacy of the market mechanism for guiding the less advanced countries in their development has now been widely recognized.[13] In consequence, planning in some form has been accepted as an instrument of

achieving a more rapid economic and social transformation of these countries. But the market for technology—if it can at all be called a market—is even more imperfect than for other commodities. Some of the more important limitations[14] of this market are described here.

One deficiency of the market mechanism is that the fixing of a price for technological information is a difficult exercise, because one really needs the information to decide what price one is ready to pay. This is an inherent impossibility in the market for technological knowledge, which is even more imperfect than that for products.

Second, an enterprise in a developing country will look for a new production technology and the details of its operation only if it has the basic information that such technology can be found somewhere on reasonable terms. But such primary information in the field of modern technology is often lacking in the developing countries; this may block the prospect of a later transfer of the most suitable technology on best possible terms.

Moreover, in a situation where competition is not perfect and there are elements of monopoly, technical information may be the most closely guarded aspect of modern production, because emulation by others may cut out markets. This is not to say that the private firm will not part with the information no matter how large a price is paid for it, but only that the price will have to be relatively high for it to be worthwhile for the private firm to sell its technological information.

Finally, private profit calculations of a firm in a developing country cannot take complete account of the social benefits that a nation can derive from the formation of skills as a consequence of an investment involving the transfer of modern technology. Skill acquired by working in a technologically advanced firm is partly a gain for the firm itself, but in addition there are benefits to the persons who acquire the skill and also to the nation as a whole, which may obtain the benefits of his services in other productive enterprises. Thus private profit calculations of the firm tend to underestimate the total social gains (nonmarketable outputs) or "externalities" as they are classified in economic literature.

As a result of these serious limitations, there is really neither a world market, nor world exchange, nor world prices for technology. It is more like the tourists buying souvenirs in foreign lands, with the important difference that the developing countries' need for technology is far more pressing.

BARGAINING WEAKNESS OF THE DEVELOPING COUNTRIES

The developing countries suffer from a special weakness in the transfer process. In the exchange of technology among the developed countries, technology usually proceeds in both directions. In consequence, any particular country is at the same time a receiver and a supplier of technology. This two-way flow generally tends to correct some of the weaknesses of the market mechanism mentioned above. In the transfer of technology from the developed to the developing countries, however, the flow of technology is usually only a one-way flow. In consequence, the limitations of the market mechanism are compounded against, rather than cancelled out in favor of, the developing countries.

Apart from this, the economic position and technical capabilities of enterprises in a developing country are, as is now widely recognized, considerably weaker than those of the technology-supplying enterprises of the developed country. Moreover, the developing countries are faced with serious shortages of foreign exchange. As a result of these factors, the developing countries are inherently in the position of unequal partners in this process. It is not surprising if, under these circumstances, the external suppliers of technology have often acted as what Tawney called "virtuosos in unscrupulous profiteering." Hence, the need for concerted action at the national, regional, and international levels.

MAJOR PROBLEMS ARISING FROM THE TECHNOLOGICAL DEPENDENCE OF DEVELOPING COUNTRIES

Technological dependence is a relatively new subject for both governments and international organizations. Understandably, therefore, there is a serious lack of empirical evidence. Agreed coverage and definitions of the items to be included in the foreign exchange costs of the transfer remain to be worked out. As a result, whatever data are available vary widely in coverage and comparability.

An attempt is made here to use the available information for a brief assessment of the major issues arising from such dependence. As a more detailed understanding of the working of the process of transfer of technology to developing countries is obtained, the actual shape of the issues and the size of the problems they have created will obviously have to be redefined with greater precision. Only then will a real basis be created for viable policies at the national, regional and international levels. Recent work in UNCTAD has pointed to the following as the chief among the major issues.[15]

Technological Intensities of Industry

UNCTAD secretariat has analyzed over 7,500 contracts concerning transfer of technology to the developing countries. Data for thirteen developing countries showed that 57 percent of the numbers of contractual agreements in manufacturing were in the modern sector (which includes petroleum refining, all chemicals, instruments, and all machinery and equipment), 26 percent were in the traditional sector (food, tobacco, textiles, clothing, leather, wood products, paper and printing, stone, clay and glass, and fabricated metal parts), and 17 percent were in "other manufacturing" (cosmetics, rubber goods, ferrous and nonferrous metals, and miscellaneous manufacturing).

The share of the modern sector in total contracts is much smaller (only 20 percent) for Dahomey, which is one of the least developed in the developing countries; but it is as high as 81 percent in the Republic of Korea, a major developing country and exporter of manufacturing goods. The high concentration of contractual agreements in the modern sector does not necessarily indicate an extensive utilization of advanced technology. In many of them—particularly pharmaceutical, electrical appliances, and automobiles—the degree of technological sophistication is often very low; most of the operations consist of the assembly, mixing, or combining of imported components. On the other hand, the widespread prevalence of such agreements in the traditional industries, using relatively simple standardized technologies, suggests the scope for the reduction of such technological dependence.

Organizational Forms for the Transfer of Technology

Three major organizational forms for the transfer process may be distinguished: majority foreign-owned equity, majority domestic equity, and wholly nationally-owned enterprises. The predominance of one or other organizational form in different countries depends upon their particular economic circumstances and political and social conditions and on the nature of legislation governing the ownership of enterprises. A complex combination of organizational forms for the transfer has thus emerged in each particular country.

The distribution of contracts by type of ownership of the enterprises purchasing technology varies widely from country to country. In Cyprus, Colombia, and Brazil, between one-third and one-half of the contractual arrangements involving some form of transfer of technology were made by enterprises with majority foreign equity. For the Republic of Korea, Pakistan, India, and Yugoslavia this proportion ranges from one-seventh to nil.

The forms of transfer to developing countries have changed over the years. In the early phase of industrialization most of the undertakings using modern technology were completely owned and controlled by foreign interests. The development of domestic capital resources, the training of skilled indigenous manpower, and the growth of a new class of entrepreneurs on the one hand, as well as the formulation of national policies for industrialization and development on the other, appear to have strengthened national participation in enterprises. Thus the more developed a poor country becomes, the greater is the scope for reducing its technological dependence.

The Direct Cost of Technological Dependence

The sale of technology is an especially complex transaction in which the ways of charging for it are rarely, if ever, clearly stated. In the case of subsidiaries of multinational corporations, most of the arrangements for the transfer of technology are implicit; they do not usually form part of explicit agreements for the transfer. On the other hand, transfer of technology through licensing arrangements, entered into by joint ventures or independent enterprise in the developing countries, is usually effected through explicit agreements for the transfer; but even here, there are instances of implicit arrangements. For these reasons, only limited progress has been made in estimating the direct cost of the transfer.

The direct costs consist of the payment for the right to use patents, licenses, process knowhow and trademarks, and for technical services needed at all levels from the preinvestment phase to the full operation of the enterprise. The information available on direct costs is very inadequate. Provisional estimates by UNCTAD Secretariat indicate the costs paid by the developing countries in foreign exchange to be about $1,500 million in 1968. They are estimated to rise at about 20 percent per year, or to increase some six-fold—i.e., to $9,000 million—by the end of the 1970s.

The relative burden of the current direct costs would be better appreciated if they are compared with some other magnitudes in the developing countries. They were equal to:

1. 5 percent of net investments
2. 8 percent of imports of machinery and equipment (excluding passenger vehicles) and chemicals
3. 37 percent of service payments on external public debt
4. 56 percent of annual flow of direct private foreign investment (including reinvested earnings)
5. Two-and-one-half times the domestic expenditure on research and development (R & D)

These are indeed very high burdens. They arise from the weak bargaining position of most of the developing countries. The external enterprises succeed in obtaining effective royalty payments which range to as high as 10 to 30 percent of the value of sales, and salaries for their consultants which in some cases were as much as 50 times those paid to local personnel undertaking similar work. A strengthening of the negotiating position of the developing countries has usually led to considerable lowering of the range in both these cases.

There is one more point about direct costs of technological dependence which may merit some discussion. As pointed out above, these costs amounted to some two- and one-half times the domestic expenditures on R & D. These two together were responsible for 0.7 percent of the GDP of the developing countries. Considerable attention is currently being paid to the need for raising the R & D expenditures of the developing countries. It is well to keep in mind, as pointed out by Professor Bernal, that these amounted to less than 0.1 percent of the GNP of even the most advanced country up to the end of the nineteenth century.[16] The sums the developing countries currently spend on these two—imported technology and R & D—are thus relatively so large that assuring their most efficient utilization plainly assumes major significance.

Indirect Costs

The direct costs, however, have to be treated only as the tip of the iceberg. The hidden portion, or indirect costs, form a much larger part of the total. The indirect costs are paid for in various ways. Chief among them are payments through

1. Overpricing of imports of intermediate products and equipment ("price markups")
2. Profits on capitalization of knowhow
3. A portion of repatriated profits of the wholly-owned subsidiaries or joint ventures
4. Price markup for technology included in the cost of imported capital goods and equipment

Most of the indirect costs are indeed difficult to measure in absolute amounts. Much more systematic work needs to be initiated before definitive evidence can be produced. In the meantime, illustrative data have recently been developed on the first item in the list of indirect costs. This deals with "hidden" costs, or overpricing of imported inputs of intermediate products, equipment, and spare parts. The practice of including, in transfer of technology agreements, specific clauses limiting the purchase of such inputs to technology suppliers themselves, or to sources specifically designated for this purpose, is very widespread. Such specific tie-in purchase clauses are not even necessary in the case of direct private investment.

Evidence on hidden costs or overpricing has recently become available. In a study prepared for the Third UNCTAD,[17] the Junta del Acuerdo de Cartageña showed that in the Colombian pharmaceutical industry the absolute amount of hidden costs, incurred through overpricing of intermediate products, was equivalent to six times the royalties and 24 times the declared profits of foreign firms; in the same industry, the absolute amount of the hidden costs did not exceed one-fifth of declared profits of national firms.

A sample of firms in the same industry in Chile indicated overpricing of imported products in excess of 500 percent, while in Peru the range was between 20 and 300 percent. In every case, the overpricing of imports by foreign firms was much greater than that by nationally owned ones.

Similar evidence is available in other industries in the Andean Pact countries, e.g., electronics, rubber, and chemicals. The phenomenon of overpricing is not confined to the Andean Pact countries alone. Preliminary research in Mexico, India, Ethiopia, and Spain, to name just a few countries, shows that the same kind of practice is occurring there also. It should be clear that wherever it is possible for foreign firms to use this channel of collecting returns, and wherever it is in their interest to do so, then there is a priori presumption that it will be used as far as possible.

It is impossible to generalize on the basis of such limited evidence. In any future attempt at making such an estimate, it is obviously important to keep in mind the following facts: Imports of developing countries of crude materials and machinery and equipment amounted to nearly $30 billion in 1969. Even if the minimum level of overpricing indicated above were to apply to only a part of this grand total, the costs incurred by developing countries through "overpricing" could indeed be quite substantial.

Other Costs (Including Cost of "Nontransfer")

Beyond the direct and indirect costs there are other, not easily perceived but qualitatively of major significance for national policies, real costs or benefits foregone, of the transfer. They result from

1. Limitations imposed in transfer arrangements
2. The transfer of wrong or inappropriate technology
3. Inadequate or delayed transfer
4. The "nontransfer" of technology
5. The long-term influence of imported technology on deflecting national policy away from a sound development of national technological capabilities

These are areas to which very little serious consideration has been given so far. As a result, we are far from even exploring the range of implications of these areas, let alone getting precise quantitative measurements. Therefore, the thoughts presented below on some of these issues are meant merely to initiate the discussion. Apart from the limitation in transfer agreements concerning tied-in purchases, these agreements also contain various types of restrictions.

1. Restriction of exports (total prohibition, partial limitations, or geographical restraint)
2. Demand of guarantees against changes in taxes, tariffs, and exchange rates affecting profits, royalties, and remittances
3. Limitations of competing supplies by restriction of competing exports, preventing competition for local resources, and obtaining local patents to eliminate competitors
4. Constraints limiting the dynamic effects of the transfer through excessive use of expatriate personnel and discouragement of the development of local technical and R & D capabilities

Recent studies in UNCTAD throw considerable light on the degree of the incidence of these limiting clauses. They also take up an analysis of the current patent system through which foreign enterprises hold nearly 90 percent of the patents in the developing countries, which are taken out to discourage rather than encourage their use in the production processes.

Quite clearly, these limitations impose severe burdens on the developing countries. Some of them, by limiting export possibilities, constrain the efforts of regional economic cooperation and the benefits to be gained from the introduction of the Generalized System of Preferences. Others adversely affect the formation of skilled personnel, domestic R & D, and the emergence of integrated national policies on key questions. Methods remain to be devised whereby at least the order of magnitude of their costs could be given. It is also important that steps be taken at the national, regional, and international levels to ensure that the adverse effects of these limitations are alleviated or removed as soon as possible.

Considerable work has already been done on the subject of transfer of wrong or inappropriate technology and of inadequate or delayed transfer. It needs no emphasis that each of these also involves major costs or benefits foregone.

Perhaps a word may be said about the costs of the "nontransfer" of technology. This is a sensitive area, which is usually overlooked through what Professor Myrdahl has aptly termed "diplomacy by definition." Once a plant is located in a developing country, it is generally believed that a transfer of technology has taken place. But in many cases the location of the plant in a developing country is solely based on the fact that that country possesses a particular resource endowment for it—e.g., mineral deposits, climatic conditions, etc. The basic elements of the technology connected with the operation of the plant are not at all transferred to the nationals of the country concerned. There is in reality no transfer of technology in these cases.

The petroleum industry is a classic example of such a practice—but not the only one. For instance, most of the mineral ore processing and metal producing plants, plantations, and quite often even plants employing such traditional and well-known technology as textile manufacturing located in the developing countries fit this classification.

In all these cases what is euphemistically called payments for the transfer of technology are instead payments for the nontransfer. This is yet another area awaiting careful research.

MAIN LINES OF ACTION

As reviewed above, the costs of technological dependence of the developing countries are very heavy indeed. Much remains to be done to measure them more accurately. And even then, some of the items involved may never be fully satisfactorily estimated. A guess (submitted here as an as-yet-unverified hypothesis) would place these costs at an annual figure of some $6,000 to $12,000 million or somewhere between 2 and 4 percent of the national income of the developing countries, (excluding the socialist countries of East Asia). In comparison, the sums these countries spend at home on research and development—about $600 million—are only one-tenth to one-twentieth of these costs.

The choice between absolute external dependence and mainly doing it oneself is thus neither an empty argument among irritable academics nor a silly self-glorification by foolish politicians. It is plainly a crucial choice to be guided mostly by common sense, some simple arithmetic, and perhaps a bit of economics. It is not surprising, therefore, that the clearer the issues have become, the stronger have been the pressures for action at the national, regional, and international levels. It is not necessary to review here in detail the developments toward such action. But the presentation of a few selected points may help give an impression of the main direction of these changes.

Action in the Developing Countries
at the National Level

In the postwar period the developing countries have attempted to deal with these problems through the adoption of special laws, regulations, executive policies, administrative directives, general guidelines, etc. These steps have often covered a very wide field including industrial property laws (specifically, patent laws), regulations dealing with foreign investment, foreign exchange control acts, import controls, implementation of development plans, and so on. Understandably, this mosaic of regulatory provisions and machinery for implementing them has not always proved very successful. Most of these measures have been taken more or less on an ad hoc basis. Their implementation is usually handed over to separate ministries or administrative organs, which more often than not have operated in a spirit of total noncommunication with each other.

It is only recently that consciousness has been growing concerning the need for a coordinated implementation of these policies in the framework of national development plans. Some of the recent attempts specifically dealing with problems connected with the transfer of technology may therefore be indicated. India enacted in 1970 a new patent law; its policies on transfer of technology are now being implemented through guidelines issued on the subject. Colombia adopted a new Commercial Code in March 1971. Through its adoption of Law 19,231 in September 1971, Argentina created a national registry on licensing and knowhow agreements; in December 1971 Brazil adopted a new industrial property code.

The countries in the Andean Pact—Bolivia, Chile, Colombia, Ecuador, and Peru—generally follow the statute adopted by the Junta del Acuerdo de Cartageña towards the end of 1970 concerning a common policy in these countries toward foreign investments, trademarks, patents, licensing and royalties, known as Decision 24. Venezuela is joining the Pact and may soon also be accepting Decision 24 as some kind of a guideline.

Mexico appears also to have taken a step of even greater significance. Its "Law on the transfer of technology and the use and exploitation of patents and trademarks," adopted in December 1972, may well be considered the world's first special law on the transfer of technology. In the history of evolution of national laws, Mexico has thus initiated what may soon become an important field of national legislation in most developing countries. This law, as stated by the Mexican Government in its foreward to it, "is in keeping with resolutions adopted at the third UNCTAD held in Santiago de Chile in April/May 1972."

The law is of such significance that some of its provisions may be spelled out.

> The law establishes a Registry in which all contracts for the transfer of technology must be registered. This will provide a record of the terms on which technology is sold to Mexican businessmen, as well as permit the authorities to examine contracts and reject the registration of those containing clauses that could be damaging to Mexico's development.
>
> Contracts shall not be approved when they refer to technology freely available in the country; when the price or counterservice is out of proportion to the technology acquired or constitutes an unwarranted or excessive burden on the country's economy; when they restrict the research or technological development of the purchaser; when they permit the technology supplies to interfere in the management of the purchaser company or oblige it to use, on a permanent basis, the personnel appointed by the supplier; when they establish the obligation to purchase inputs from the supplier only or to sell the goods produced by the technology importer exclusively to the supplier company; when they prohibit or restrict the export of goods in a way contrary to the country's interest; when they limit the size of production or impose prices on domestic production or on exports by the purchaser; when they prohibit the use of complementary technology; when they oblige the importer to sign exclusive sales or representation contracts with the supplier company covering the national territory; when they establish excessively long terms of enforcement, which in no case may exceed a 10-year obligation on the importer company; or when they provide that claims arising from the interpretation or fulfillment of such contracts are to be submitted to the jurisdiction of foreign courts.

Apart from Mexico, a number of other countries have taken or are in the process of taking important steps toward the establishment of some form of special institutions and policies dealing with the problems connected with the transfer of technology. These countries include Argentina, Bolivia, Brazil, Chile,

Colombia, Ecuador, Ethiopia, India, Iraq, Mexico, Pakistan, Peru, Spain, Sri Lanka, Venezuela, and Yugoslavia.

Moreover, the developing socialist countries of East Asia (China, North Korea, and North Vietnam) have, for quite a number of years, been actively following policies of eliminating (or controlling severally) foreign investment and promoting national capabilities for scientific and technological development. Another set of countries—Algeria, Cuba, Egypt, Guinea, Iraq, Sudan, Syria, etc.—where some form of planning of the national economies is being introduced, have also circumscribed very severely the limits within which external enterprises are allowed to operate, and are working towards unpackaging foreign investments and transfer of technology.

Such defensive actions of one or another type in a large number of developing countries have fundamentally altered the setting for foreign investment and the transfer of technology. In the early years of the postwar period, the field was virtually open. In sharp contrast, some form of regulatory action has now become the dominant feature of policy in nearly all of the developing countries, irrespective of the shade or the color in which they appear on the world political spectrum. The problem has moved away from political rhetoric of the Right or the Left to formulation of technical blueprints. Even a cursory reading of the names of countries listed in the preceding paragraphs would prove this beyond dispute.

It may be suggested that the countries mentioned above number less than 30, and there are after all nearly 100 developing countries. But this will be falling a victim to misinterpreting statistical significance. These thirty-odd developing countries are among the more populous, and relatively more advanced in the degree of their industrialization and scientific and technical progress. Together they account for over 2,000 million persons, or some 80 percent of the population of all the developing countries. Their share in the industrial output of the developing countries is even greater—around 95 percent of the total. Thus they constitute not only the dominant practice at present, but what they have done can only be taken as a foretaste of what other developing countries will undoubtedly do.

The nature of the laws, policies, directives, and the institutional machinery for regulating the transfer varies from country to country. This is to be expected, for each country has its own special background to be taken into account. But one facet is beyond dispute: the setting in which foreign investment and transfer of technology took place a quarter-century ago is now decisively altered. No return to the early position is even conceivable.

An International Code of Conduct

Quite clearly, a new network of laws, regulations, and special institutions has begun to be established in the developing countries. All these by and large are in line with the decisions in UNCTAD, particularly with resolution 39

(III) adopted at the third conference. This resolution may well be called the "Santiago Charter" for improving the access of the developing countries to technology. This new setting has now created a situation that could be more conducive to an intensification of conflicts concerning interpretation of terms and conditions of contractual arrangements and regarding the settlement of disputes. An internationally coordinated approach aimed at establishing an orderly way of dealing with these complex problems therefore assumes crucial significance for avoiding an intensification of conflicts.

It appears that the steps taken in the developing countries are having their effect on the other end of the spectrum—that is, the technology-supplying enterprises in the developed countries. Two developments may be singled out here. In the first place, there has been quite some discussion in recent years on arrangements which have come to be known as "fadeout" policies. These require a slow but systematic reduction in the share of foreign-owned equity in enterprises in the developing countries. Such a policy would work toward ensuring an increasing participation of developing countries in the conception, inception, construction, organization, and management of their enterprises. The greater the success in this direction, the larger the "unpackaging" of foreign investment from essentially needed technology.

Another development of some significance was the publication of the "Guidelines for International Investment" issued by the International Chamber of Commerce on November 29, 1973. In his foreward to the Guidelines, the Secretary-General of the ICC recognized "the essential interdependence of investors, of governments in the investors' as well as in the host countries." These Guidelines deal not only with foreign investment, but also specifically with "technology, including inventions and knowhow skills" (section VII), and also with the related problems such as ownership and management, finance, fiscal policies, legal framework, commercial policies, and so on.

The Guidelines of the ICC could be taken as the first response of the business community as represented in the International Chamber of Commerce. Two points about it deserve particular attention. In the first place, the introduction to the ICC Guidelines makes it quite clear that they are meant only for further discussion in the United Nations forums. It is stated, for instance

> . . . that these Guidelines will be helpful to the United Nations and other intergovernmental organizations in their efforts to promote constructive discussions on the relationships between international investors, the governments of host countries, and the investors' governments.

Another point in the Introduction also underlines the nature of the further discussion that is envisaged. Both host and capital-exporting countries are expected to participate in it. The Introduction to the Guidelines states, for instance, "Efforts will be made to foster better understanding of the rights and obligations of both host and capital-exporting countries, as well as of individual investors."

The preceding discussion may be briefly summarized as follows: (1) Some 30 developing countries, accounting for around 80 percent of the population and over 95 percent of the industrial output of the developing countries, have now adopted some form of laws, regulations, or policies concerning transfer of technology. They have also created, or are in the process of creating, special institutions for implementing these decisions. (2) ICC on its part has put forward its own views on the subject. It has recognized the importance of further discussion in the United Nations. It also recognized the need for a better understanding of the rights and obligations of "both host and capital-exporting countries."

These developments seem to have set the stage for moving quickly towards discussions of establishing a truly international Code of Conduct in the field of transfer of technology. This recognition forms the background of paragraph 17 of Resolution I (II) of the second session of UNCTAD's Intergovernmental Group on the Transfer of Technology (TD/B/424/Annex 1), in which the developing countries asked the Board of UNCTAD to consider the question of promoting the preparation of such a Code.

These developments on a world scale were carefully considered by the Secretary-General of UNCTAD in his "Review and Appraisal of the Implementation of the International Development Strategy" (TD/B/429). He concluded his Review by affirming that

> The time would appear to be ripe for the international community to distil the lessons of this experience and to work towards designing an international code of conduct in this field which might benefit all countries, particularly the developing countries.

Appendix to Chapter 4

Document No.	Title of Document
TD/28 and Supp. 1 and Supp. 1/Corr. 1	The transfer of technology to developing countries, with special reference to licensing and know-how agreements; study prepared by C.H.G. Oldham, C. Freeman and E. Turkean, Science Policy Research Unit of the University of Sussex, England.
TD/106 and Corr. 1	Transfer of Technology: report by the UNCTAD secretariat. See Proceedings of the United Nations Conference on Trade and Development, Third Session, vol. III, Financing and Invisibles (to be issued as a United Nations Publication), part two.
TD/107 and Corr. 1	"Policies relating to the transfer of technology of the countries of the Andean Pact: their foundations; A study by the Junta del Acuerdo de Cartagena." (Ibid.)
TD/122/and Corr. 1 and Supp. 1 and Corr. 1	Restrictive business practices: report by the UNCTAD secretariat. See Proceedings of the United Nations Conference on Trade and Development, Third Session, vol. II, Merchandise trade (to be issued as a United Nations Publication), part two.

Document No.	*Title of Document*
TD/164 and Add. 1 and 2	Report of Working Group; III. See Proceedings of the United Nations Conference on Trade and Development, Third Session, vol. I, Report and Annexes (to be issued as a United Nations publication), annex VI, I.
TD/168 and Add. 1	Report of the Second Committee. See Proceedings of the United Nations Conference on Trade and Development, Third Session, vol. I, Report and Annexes, . . . annex VI, B.
TD/B/255	Restrictive business practices: progress report by the UNCTAD secretariat. See Official Records of the Trade and Development Board, Ninth Session first and second parts, Annexes, agenda item 10.
TD/B/310 and Corr. 1	Elements of a Programme of Work for UNCTAD: study by the UNCTAD secretariat. See Official Records of the Trade and Development Board; Tenth Session first, second and third parts, Annexes, agenda item 14. Parts of the document dealing with the substantive issues involved were also published as "UNCTAD: The transfer of technology" in Journal of World Trade Law, vol. 4, No. 5 (Twickenham, Middlesex, England, Vincent Press), September/October 1970.
TD/B/327 and Add. 1	Report of the Trade and Development Board on the first part of its tenth session. For final text, see Official Records of the General Assembly, Twenty-fifth Session, Supplement No. 15, part two. For the account of the Board's debate on transfer of technology, see chap. VI, sect. D. For the text of Trade and Development Board resolution 74 (X), see Official Records of the Trade and Development Board, Tenth Session, Supplement No. 1, p. 4.
TD/B/365	Report of the Intergovernmental Group on Transfer of Technology on its organizational (first) session. See Official Records of the Trade and Development Board, Eleventh Session, Annexes, agenda item 7.
TD/B/Ac. 11/1	Provisional agenda, annotations to the provisional agenda and suggestions for the organization of

	work of the Group: note by the UNCTAD secretariat.
TD/B/AC. 11/2 and Add. 1	Scope of activities of bodies within and outside the United Nations system in the field of transfer of technology: note by the UNCTAD secretariat.
TD/B/AC. 11/3 and Add. 1	Work relevant to the transfer of technology being done by the main Committees of the Board and other subsidiary organs of UNCTAD: note by the UNCTAD secretariat.
TD/B/AC. 11/4	Questionnaire on the transfer of technology, including knowhow and patents: note by the UNCTAD secretariat.
TD/B/AC. 11/5	The channels and mechanisms for the transfer of technology from developed to developing countries. A study by Charles Cooper with the collaboration of Francisco Sercovitch: note by the secretariat. (This study was jointly commissioned by the Office for Science and Technology of the Department of Economic and Social Affairs of the United Nations and the UNCTAD secretariat, in response to the request of the United Nations Advisory Committee on the Application of Science and Technology to Development made at its Thirteenth Session.)
TD/B/AC. 11/6	Suggestions for a possible programme of work: note by the UNCTAD secretariat.
TD/B/AC. 11/9	Guidelines for the study of the transfer of technology to developing countries.
TD/B/AC. 11/10 and Add. 1 and Corr. 1	Major issues in transfer of technology to developing countries: a study by the UNCTAD secretariat.
TD/B/AC. 11/12	Progress report on the implementation of Conference resolution 39 (III).
TD/B/AC. 11/13 and Corr. 1	Mexico: Bill concerning registration of the transfer of technology and the use and working of patents, tradenames and trademarks.
TD/B/AC. 11/L. 1	General Assembly resolution 2726 (XXV) and views of the Advisory Committee on the Application of Science and Technology to Development on the proposed work programme for UNCTAD: note by the UNCTAD secretariat.

TD/B/AC. 11/L. 8   Methodology for studying the transfer of technology. Major issues arising from the transfer of technology. Progress in implementing Conference Resolution 39 (III).

TD/B/424   Report of the Intergovernmental Group on the transfer of technology on its second session (see annex 1 of Resolution 1 [II] adopted by the Group).

TD/B/C. 2/54 and Corr. 1 and Add. 1 and 2   Restrictive business practices: report by the UNCTAD secretariat.

TD/B/C. 93 and Add. 1   Restrictive business practices: report by the UNCTAD secretariat.

TD/B/L. 224/Add. 1 and Corr. 1   Elements of a programme of work for UNCTAD: texts adopted or being considered by UNCTAD bodies on transfer of technology and other material relevant to a consideration of this subject.

TD/B/L. 224/Add. 1   Action taken by the Economic and Social Council at its forty-ninth session on questions relating to science and technology: note by the secretariat.

Conference resolution 39 (III), "Transfer of Technology" (see annex 1 above).

Conference resolution 73 (III), "Restrictive business practices."

Discussion

Krause: Dr. Patel mentioned the gradual phasing out of an investment. How shall we put it: a phasing out of the technology coming in and then the gradual replacement of investment from that within the country? I will ask, How is it possible, then, to prevent the parent company from allowing that company just to deteriorate without putting in the funds necessary to maintain the investment and to maintain the long-term health of an establishment of that kind?

Pontecorvo: The deliberate destruction of capital by allowing the deterioration of industrial properties is a serious problem. I think that all I can say is that Dr. Patel speaks here of the development of an international code of conduct, and such behavior would obviously be in violation of this code. I think there is no way out of this particular problem. It will depend upon the skill of the developing country to protect its own interests. You are dealing in the market here where there is a rule of caveat emptor. I would think that this rule would probably prevail in defiance of such a code, although clear violation of such code over extended periods might well result in a systematic process of dispute settlement at some international level; but you are really, it seems to me, taking quite a chance.

Wolf: Could we ask you to give a definition of transfer of technology as Dr. Patel uses the phrase? Does it simply mean investment abroad, or does it simply mean the establishment of a technologically oriented plant, or does it mean instruction—or does it mean all of these?

Pontecorvo: The question really should not be answered within a narrow context. Personally, as an economist, I look upon the problem of technology as one of the vital aspects of what you would define as an industrialized society. So what you are really talking about in a larger sense is the transfer of the whole industrial complex. This really relates to the whole complex matrix of how goods are produced, transferred, bought and sold in the market, and so forth and so on, and the skills associated therewith. These skills may be thought of as the ability to run a machine, for example. They also may be thought of as the ability to run a bank, or to conduct a money market, or even run a stock exchange firm. The skills are widespread.

     My feeling about the transfer of technology is that it applies to all aspects of an industrialized society and to all the aspects of the skills associated with that, right on up from the basic skill of literacy, through the ability to construct and utilize a computer, if you will.

Brittin: I do not think that technology transfer must necessarily cut across the entire spectrum of an industry. Senegal is a good example of this, where through an aid-related program, as I recall, their canoe fishery off their coast was motorized, and it was motorized in a very simple way. The United States sent over something like 200 outboard motors, and that was it. Of course, they sent somebody skilled in repair to teach them how to repair these motors. What this program did was abruptly change the mode of operation of their canoe fishery so that these boats now go out much further and are much more effective in their work. That certainly does not fit the definition of technological transfer that you are speaking about. It is a much more limited thing—and, as far as I know, quite successful. I think you see this kind of thing happen in many different places in the world, and it certainly does not encompass the entire industry.

Pontecorvo: I would quite agree that it is possible, in a partial equilibrium sense, to look at any aspect of the technological transfer process. One can, in fact, pick out an example such as you have given and look at a specific technological capability and assume also that the skill required to run an outboard motor is not significantly greater than the skill required to paddle a canoe, and assume that this is the process and leave it there.

However, I would ask one further question in this connection. Who is supplying the gasoline, the spark plugs, and the other hardware necessary to keep those outboard motors going, plus the mechanical skills required to repair them after they arrived in their nice shiny boxes on Christmas Day from the rich uncle? I think the process should be thought about in a larger context—but you may of course examine any specific aspect of this proposition. The danger you run when you do that is that the second order questions may eat you alive. That is what Patel referred to here, and I digressed and spoke a little bit about the market for this technology, because any change in the production function—any change you introduce such as that—really raises other questions. For example, how many fish can be caught? Is the population sufficient to sustain the more intensive fishery?

Branco: I would like to ask a sort of devil's advocate question. I noticed that Mr. Patel talked about the financial costs to the developing countries of their technology transfer; but from an economist's point sometimes it is far more important to know the opportunity cost. What would have been the alternative to developing countries had they *not* imported the technology, regardless of the cost that they had to pay for it? What would the opportunity cost? Could you expand a bit on that?

Pontecorvo: The answer is that I do not begin to know what those opportunity costs are. By opportunity costs we mean the alternatives that were foregone. I would point out that that is an extremely complex question. It really asks whether or not you introduce a technology because this technology has been utilized elsewhere in the world, and because this technology has proved useful in certain kinds of functions for which there is a market in the developed states. I mean the fact that Ghana grows cocoa, for instance, is because the Englishman enjoys his cup of cocoa; and whether Ghana is in fact paying a very high opportunity cost instead of growing something else, and should historically have been growing something else for which it is much better suited than the growing of cocoa, is the question you are asking—and I cannot begin to answer that.

What appears to be true is that the developing states, without reference to the opportunity cost question, may never really ask themselves the question, What should we be doing and what is it appropriate for us to be doing? They instead address the question by saying, "What is the United States doing? They are all rich. Therefore they must be doing what is right, and how can we, in fact, opt for that particular technology?" This process is one of imitation, of course, and is inadequate.

Bates: I am new to this definition of developing nations. Since Patel is with the United Nations, what is the definition of Mainland China? Is that a developing nation? You know, it develops nuclear weapons and rockets, and yet in its consumer goods it has a long way to go.

Pontecorvo: I would not attempt to speak for Mainland China. I will not ask the representatives of Mainland China here to speak to the question unless they wish, but it is possible to have a country in which the average level of income is low, which still has a very capital-intensive infrastructure that it acquired somehow or other. India is a good example of this; a railroad system, major cities with major port facilities and all the other capital-intensive activity, a steel industry, and so forth and so on—and yet the average level of income is quite low. This is a contradiction which in part has to do with the population side of the equation with respect to per capita income.

Chapter Five

Technology Transfer
and the Oceans

Charles Weiss
Science and Technology Advisor
International Bank for Reconstruction
and Development

From the point of view of the developing countries, improvements in the system of technology transfer may turn out to be an attractive bargaining point in negotiations concerning ocean policy issues. In other words, the promise of increased technical assistance and of improvements in the technology transfer system might induce developing countries to compromise on political, legal, and economic issues that are important to developed countries.

These questions of technology transfer originally came to the attention of the oceans policy community largely because the scientific community wanted continued or increased access to the coastal waters of developing countries for purposes of fundamental research. But the needs of developing countries for technology transfer and technical assistance go far beyond what scientists can offer with their own resources, and indeed beyond what developed countries would be willing to exchange for the assurance of freedom to conduct offshore research. For this reason I would like to put forward the proposition that the issue of technology transfer to developing countries, as it affects the debate over the law of the sea, goes far beyond the issue of marine science.

Technology transfer, in marine as in other areas, typically takes place through investment, and must be considered in the context of commercial

The opinions expressed in this paper are those of the author, and do not necessarily reflect the position of the World Bank.

relations between developed and developing countries. If the interests of the developing countries are to be served, any attempt to incorporate considerations of technology transfer into the negotiations over the law of the sea will necessarily involve a sophisticated blend of the academic and the commercial, including careful attention to the role of the private sector.

As a scientist, I sympathize with the belief that scientific research is, ultimately, for the benefit of all mankind. On the other hand, it is clear that freedom of research is at the very least not as high a priority to developing countries as it is to developed countries. Therefore it will inevitably appear in any negotiations as a concession from the developing to the developed countries.

The developing countries want not only an increased share of the revenues coming from the exploitation of their marine resources. They want to participate more and more in the enterprises exploiting these resources in a way that will lead to autonomy of management and of technological decision making, and to better protection against the kinds of abuses that Dr. Patel has discussed here and in other forums. In other words, they want a piece of the action. By marine resources I mean primarily offshore oil, gas, and minerals; coastal and, to a lesser extent, distant water fishing; and undersea mining. Each of these is a complicated subject in its own right, involving as it does political, institutional, legal, and commercial issues. When a particular developing country decides to take part in any of these activities (especially in undersea mining, a capital-intensive technology, carried out far from the borders of any country), that country must consider policy issues that will depend on each detailed situation.

The major source of modern technology for exploiting these three kinds of marine resources is in the developed countries—frequently in the multinational corporations. If developing countries are to benefit from participating in this exploitation, they must learn about the technology, the economics, and the practical management problems solved. Only in this way can they hope to hold up their end of international bargaining situations, and to take an increasingly responsible role in the management of the enterprises involved.

How are these skills obtained in the real world? Some of them are available in universities[a] and in research programs based in developed countries; through university fellowships in marine science and economics; through invitations to developing country fisheries experts, petroleum geologists, and the like to participate in oceanographic exploration and research; and through technical assistance and bilateral links to marine laboratories in developing countries. All these have great value, and are the kinds of programs ocean scientists naturally propose when asked to make their activities more valuable to the developing countries off whose shores they wish to do research.

But a developing country needs not only marine scientists and economists. It needs plant managers, fishing boat masters, experienced exploration geologists, and petroleum economists. It also needs access to proprietary tech-

[a]See Chapter 6.

nologies available only through the international private sector. Some of these skills and technologies are available through the hiring of experienced people as expatriate employees or as consultants, or of developing country nationals who have worked in multinational corporations or in other companies involved in these fields. Others are available by purchase or through participation in joint ventures.

For countries at the very first stage in the development of their marine industry, the first need is for an impartial source of advice on where to get the right kind of technology. Dr. Patel has already discussed some of the restrictions often written into joint venture agreements and other technology transfer instruments. The first need of the developing country is for a man who knows enough about the subject to negotiate a joint venture agreement which will protect that country's interests. He will learn only a limited amount of this on a scientific research vessel.

I understand that several international agencies are now willing to advise on these matters, and are tooling up to provide guidelines on such matters as the proper provisions of joint venture agreements. This kind of work involves commercial secrets that are not readily fitted into the traditional operations of international organizations. Moreover, the experts they hire come from developed countries, are in short supply, and are therefore hard to recruit. Ultimately, there is no substitute for a developing country's having its own expertise.

The story of how the oil exporting countries learned enough about the technological, economic, and management end of the oil industry to gain some measure of control over their most important resource, is one of the most important cases of successful technology transfer from a developing country's point of view. I feel that this deserves a good deal of study. For example, let us look at the Organization of Petroleum Exporting Countries (OPEC). OPEC illustrates the complex of skills that the developing countries are seeking and which they will demand that developed countries help them to gain. This is a controversial subject, and I do not intend to touch on the larger issues dealing with OPEC and the energy crisis. Whatever else may be said about OPEC, the international oil market is one place where developing countries have achieved a certain degree of autonomy of technological and managerial decision making, and where they do hold up their end of a bargaining situation with developed countries and with multinational corporations.

This ability to bargain on the international marketplace depends first on the unique position of oil in world markets. It also depends on a sophisticated understanding of the technology and economics of oil exploration, exploitation, refining, and distribution. In OPEC this understanding was gained by a combination of experience and education. According to Dr. Mikdashi's book on the subject, one of the tasks of the OPEC Secretariat is to see that new, less sophisticated member countries gain this information from their more advanced colleagues more rapidly and efficiently than they would through the ordinary learning process of trial and error at the negotiating table.

Technical assistance should in some way improve the bargaining position of developing countries vis-à-vis the international technology market, the international fishing fleets, the oil companies, or the undersea mining consortia. If assistance does not clearly have this aim, I suspect that it will not be an attractive quid pro quo in any international negotiations that are supposed to elicit concessions from developing countries on freedom of transit, on definitions of territorial waters and/or resource zones, and on the other issues that are important to the developed countries and to the ocean policy community.

I do not have ready answers to how these broader ocean policy issues might be linked to the technology transfer problem. I think this question will take a great deal of study. It could start with a critical analysis of existing public and private sector efforts at technical assistance in fishing industries in several developing countries, viewed against the criteria described before. It will need to consider private sector policies towards the hiring and training of personnel from developing countries for responsible positions, towards the licensing of technology, and towards the drawing up of joint ventures. These are commercial matters that go to the heart of international trade relations. It is safe to predict that the recommendations of any such study will go beyond codes of practice, and beyond traditional programs of fellowships, laboratories, and technical assistance in pollution control or resource survey.

Thus the issues of technology transfer in the oceans have a lot more to do with international trade and politics than with freedom of scientific research. Furthermore, the responsibility for effective technology transfer is shared by developing and developed countries alike. A developing country can scarcely complain of its inability to negotiate with foreign companies and to judge the legitimacy of ocean-going research ships if it, itself, is not making use of the trained personnel already within its borders. On the other hand, as Professor Pontecorvo has pointed out, a developing country has every right to decide, on the basis of its own priorities, that it does not wish to devote scarce financial and personnel resources to build up competence in marine science. Such countries might find it possible to call on some international body to certify, well in advance, that a particular expedition is indeed purely scientific and has no immediate commercial value. These certification techniques might be worked out in advance, with maximum input from representatives of the developing countries, and would, I hope, be subject to continuing improvement.

This puts scientific oceanographers in an awkward position. One may hope that they will accept the thesis propounded by Dr. Knauss and others that the long-term health of the profession requires a commitment to a major program of training of, and collaboration with, developing country colleagues in areas of highest priority to the developing countries—even if this requires some inconvenience and expense. The success of such a program of enlightened scientific collaboration, however, may depend on a substantial program of technical assistance in the more commercial aspects of ocean resource management. My hope is that an agreement can be worked out and a reasonable set of regulations, acceptable both to developing countries and to scientists, can be negotiated to minimize the involvement of basic scientists in the thornier and more delicate problems of technology transfer.

We are left with the conclusion that if technical assistance is to be an attractive bargain to developing countries, the package offered must be a rather sophisticated blend of the academic and the commercial, one carefully tailored to the needs of the particular developing country, and one which may sooner or later have an effect on relations between developing countries and multinational corporations in ocean matters.

Depending on the choices and priorities of the developing countries, one may hope that it may also lead to more of a concern for the small fisher-man—the man who needs an outboard motor for his canoe. It is this traditional fishing sector that offers the most hope of exploiting the resources of the sea to alleviate in some measure the employment crisis gripping the developing countries. The World Bank and other development assistance agencies are turning increasing attention to the problem of increasing the income of the rural fisherman and giving him the benefit of direct access to international markets and to adequate credit facilities. The problem of technology transfer and technical assistance to this rural fishing sector presents a crucial challenge.

In conclusion, if technology transfer is really to play an important role in resolving the controversies regarding the oceans, I suspect that it will have to be substantially redirected toward the commercial as well as to the scientific needs of the developing countries. It need hardly be added that in order for it to be attractive to developing countries, any increase in marine technical assistance will have to represent an increase in overall development assistance, and not a mere diversion of resources from some other form of aid.

Discussion

Herrington: You and the others have stressed the desire of the developing countries to have their own experts to assist in evaluating projects and seeing that proper terms are arranged. Over past years many students from developing countries have attended universities and colleges in developed countries and have attained a good deal of technology, but when they return home, if they really become experts in the field, more often than not they are offered positions either in foreign countries or in their own country outside the field of fisheries. So this acquired expertise is not brought to bear on the fisheries problems. Would you care to comment on that and what possible solution there is to this problem?

Weiss: This certainly happens. We and other aid agencies are prepared to help with technical assistance to countries that have decided that fisheries are a priority to themselves; but if this policy decision is not taken, there is not a great deal that we or anybody else can or should do to tell a country that it should be more active in fisheries.

Johnson: I would like to hear you develop a little more this relationship between technical assistance as you have discussed it and your main subject of technology transfer, because there are some steps involved which I think are important for us to know. Could you either enlighten us now or else in the later discussion go into a little more detail on this?

Weiss: By technical assistance I mean steps taken consciously, by a developed country or by a company based in a developed country, to impart a technology to a developing country through provision of experts or what have you; and by technology transfer I mean the general process of implanting a technology in the developing country.

My main thesis today has been that from the point of view of a developing country, the aim of technology transfer is not only to get the technology working in the developing country in the same way that it has worked elsewhere, except with developing country nationals pushing the buttons; rather it is, ideally at least, to enable the developing country to achieve a certain amount of technological autonomy so that it can make its own technological decisions with a full awareness of what the world has to offer.

From this point of view, the aid program or private investor providing technical assistance is an agent of technology transfer, and what you are asking is: How can agents of technology transfer contribute to the developing country's presumed goal of technological autonomy?

This is a tough problem and has not been fully explored in the marine context. We [the World Bank] and the FAO have a certain amount of experience and I think this should be explored and evaluated. We can say at this point that developing countries will need technical assistance in the negotiations leading to joint ventures or to licensing and patenting agreements. It may extend to help in working out new sets of relationships—not just a code but a real, new pattern of behavior—by private investors, which would include emphasis on such things as training and upgrading developing country personnel, either as company employees or perhaps on the basis of a service contract.

This is an area where people with more field experience in marine industries than I should—and, I believe, are—taking an active interest in types of technical assistance that can assist the developing countries. My purpose is to raise areas for increased study rather than to suggest detailed solutions.

Uchegbu: I want to make a small point. I think this has been extremely stimulating, but I wonder if it was not high time for topics of this nature to be given by those from the developing countries themselves. The absence of this, drains this of its scientific basis from the point of view that we talk about "the priorities they have," "the priorities they need," "what they do." Maybe if the people from the developing countries who are engaged in decision making were to give this lecture, then it would probably have a more scientific basis in the sense that we will have been in a position to know exactly what they actually need and what their priorities are.

Weiss:　　I am in no disagreement.

* * * * * *

Commentary
Warren S. Wooster [b]

The great discrepancy in economic development among countries, the almost discontinuous distribution of wealth between the handful of industrial powers and all of the rest of the world, is one of the most troublesome problems of our time. Some discussions of the resource potential of the deep seabed of the high seas have implied that this region of so-called "common heritage" can serve to eliminate the development gap. This seems highly unlikely to me, particularly as I watch the heritage being eroded by the steady expansion of national control over resources of the adjacent sea.

On the other hand, individual countries along the ocean shore are clearly in a position to use the ocean and its resources for their own economic benefit. To what extent would a marine science capability improve the odds of obtaining such benefits? And if the answer is positive, how can the transfer of this capability be accomplished? Although much of the discussion of the ocean research issue has implied that such research leads to immediate benefits, the facts are that these benefits are not usually realized for many years.

On the other hand, applied research, related, say, to the discovery of new resources or improved methods for their harvest, can often lead to early payoffs. It is not surprising, therefore, that applied research is usually considered of higher priority than more fundamental investigation especially in the developing countries, but increasingly so also in places like the United States and the United Kingdom.

Thus we see numerous fishery development projects under the United Nations development program—more than 60 were administered by FAO a year or so ago—which were devoted to various aspects of applied research and contain only minor elements of what a critical observer would consider oceanography. Perhaps, then, marine science should be considered a luxury for developing countries. I consider this an incorrect conclusion for a number of reasons.

[b]Rosensteiel School of Marine and Atmospheric Science, University of Miami

For example, foreign technology may not always, or even often, be directly applicable or the effects of its application be fully appreciated without an adequate knowledge of the conditions or the environment where the application is to be made. The gathering of this environmental knowledge could perhaps be left in foreign hands but scientific colonialism is presumably no more attractive than any other kind. There are lots of decisions that must be made in a coastal state relating to its resources and environment.

The judgments that have a science base should derive from an indigenous review and evaluation of the available facts. It could even be argued that training and experience in scientific research (in this case oceanographic research) is a most valuable preparation for solution of the variety of multidisciplinary problems that face modern society.

The question of a native science capability was discussed in a much broader context by the great Indian leader of scientific and technological development, Homi Bhaba, in a speech just before his death in early 1966. Bhaba said,

> What the developed countries have and the underdeveloped lack is modern science and an economy based on modern technology. The problem of developing the underdeveloped countries is therefore the problem of establishing modern science in them and transforming their economy to one based on modern science and technology.
>
> An important question which we must consider is whether it is possible to transform the economy of a country to one based on modern technology developed elsewhere without at the same time establishing modern science in the country as a live and vital force. If the answer to this important question is in the negative, and I believe our experience will show that it is, then the problem of establishing science as a live and vital force in society is an inseparable part of the problem of transforming an industrially underdeveloped to a developed country.

Much of Bhaba's speech was devoted to the Indian experience in acquiring a capability in modern science. Bhaba contrasts the conventional method of designing an elaborate program, recruiting scientific staff, and constructing facilities—all before any real work is done—with a method he calls "growing science," where research programs are built around a few able people, these programs being used for training additional scientists and giving them research experience. Only when the growing of scientists is under control are the more elaborate institutional and facility problems resolved.

As he states, in summary,

> . . . of the two ways of establishing science as a national activity in an underdeveloped country, the standard method on the one hand and the alternative method of what I have called growing science on

the other, the second seems to lead to better results in the end with greater potential for continuous growth. While it may seem much slower and harder at the beginning, it has the capacity for continuous growth and for developing the people it needs, and its faster growth rate in later years more than compensates for the slow beginning. Moreover, it may lead to concrete results sooner than the other method in developing countries in which there is not a large pool of mature scientists to draw from.

If one were to apply this reasoning to the development of marine science capability in a developing country, he would first identify several imaginative and mature scientists (in almost any field) who could be interested in ocean problems, and would then build a program of research and education around them, almost without regard to the short-term applicability of their work.

Once this farm for growing marine-oriented scientific talent was in production, the resulting group of scientists would be in a position to identify and to tackle intelligently the oceanographic problems of greatest importance to their country. Needless to say, this is not the approach being followed in any developing country that I know of.

Commentary
Herman T. Franssen [c]

Addressing oneself to the question of transfer of technology from advanced industrial societies to developing, primary-product-producing countries, one must first define the terms "developing countries" and "transfer of technology." Although developing countries are rather diverse, they share certain common characteristics. Most are poor in terms of per capita income and are technologically unsophisticated. Their populations tend to grow rapidly, and the majority of their people depend on subsistence agriculture for survival. The industrial sector is relatively small, and exports are dominated by agricultural commodities and raw materials. Science and technology in developing countries are usually poorly developed in terms of both resources allocations and institutionalization.

Depending on the criteria one employs, different countries can be included in the group of developing countries. To avoid unnecessary confusion, references made to developing countries made in this commentary are to members of the Group of 77 (now totalling 97) who consider themselves "developing countries." This group was formed prior to the first United Nations Conference on Trade and Development.

Technology can be defined as the totality of means employed to provide objects necessary to human sustenance and comfort, or, in the narrower

[c]Woods Hole Oceanographic Institution

sense of the word, as the knowledge of the industrial arts. Therefore, transfer of technology could merely consist of transferring technical knowhow to major industrial and service sectors in the economy, or could be defined as to include the total process of transferring scientific and technical knowhow, including training of scientific, technical, managerial, and administrative personnel, the development of science policy institutions, etc., to other nations.

If one employs the narrow definition, it should be pointed out that although there is some relationship between technological inputs (such as scientists and engineers and R&D expenditures) and economic growth, the relationship has often been exaggerated and is by no means automatic. Fritz Machlup, a well-known international economist at Princeton University, once compared R&D managers and science policy makers with farmers, who believe that when they increase R&D resources, they would get higher output and when they diminish them, output would fall. A few examples may illustrate the difficulties involved in applying input-output analysis to prove the existence of a close automatic relationship between input of technological resources and economic growth.

The United States and Great Britain both spent far more on R&D and employed more scientists and engineers throughout the 1950s than any other industrial country. However, both countries experienced considerably less economic growth than the countries of continental Western Europe or Japan. The United States also employed considerably more resources on R&D in the 1950s than in the 1920s, but growth rates during the 1920s were considerably higher than in the period following the Second World War.

Contributions to economic growth other than labor and capital are frequently referred to as the "residual." Attempts to separate technological change from other factors that contribute to the residual have not yet been refined to the point whereby individual contributions can be weighed accurately. For example, a great deal of technological change is brought about by improved capital equipment or by a better trained labor force. The technology factor cannot be separated out easily from capital or labor. Attempts to oversell the need for more science and technology inputs without simultaneously changing other factors that have contributed to technological backwardness could have disappointing results.

As it goes beyond the scope of our discussion to enter into detail of any of those contributing factors that bring about technological change in society, it suffices to briefly list the more important ones: educational infrastructure; governmental science policy; general attitudes towards science and technology; managerial capabilities; capital markets, including availability of risk capital; differences in the size of markets and individual firms; and international cooperation, particularly in the big sciences.

Several studies on the subject of the contribution of science and technology to economic growth have indicated that scientific and technological knowledge cannot in the long run generate any additions to output at all, if not combined with complementary inputs. Indeed, the most advanced scientific laboratories are of little importance to economic growth, if the knowledge generated in such institutions cannot and is not put to practical use.

However, it should also be recognized that the desire to achieve rapid economic growth is not the only criterion in the quest for an independent scientific and technological capability by nation states. Even the nations of Western Europe that were growing faster than the United States throughout most of the 1960s were wary of their growing dependence on the United States in certain areas of advanced technology considered to be of vital importance for the independence of the state. While the issue is no longer of political importance in Europe, due to altered political and economic circumstances, developing countries have in recent years let no opportunity go by to discuss the problems of the growing technological gap between the developed and developing nations of the world.

Policy makers from developing countries fear that if no progress is made toward narrowing the gap between the technological haves and have nots, the latter will continue to be primary product producers, while remaining dependent on Western business for sophisticated industrial products. Some degree of scientific and technological independence is regarded as a must for complete political independence. Most developing countries would therefore agree with the Deputy Director of UNESCO at the 1964 Lagos Conference on Science and Technology, who said that "political independence without scientific knowledge and competence is as contradictory as the concept of a vegetarian tiger."

Whereas the discrepancy between the R&D efforts of the developed and developing countries will continue to be considerable in the near and medium future, efforts could be made to redress the situation. Today, more than 90 percent of the world's R&D inputs are employed in developed countries (10 countries account for 80 percent of the more than $50 billion spent on R&D throughout the world), and only about 2 percent of these resources are spent on problems that are of particular importance to developing countries. In the field of oceanography, Japan (the world's third largest oceanographic power) spends more on oceanic research than all of Asia, Africa, and Latin America together; it has approximately twice as many marine scientists and an equal number of research ships of over 15 meters. Efforts are presently being made to enhance the capabilities of the developing countries by increasing both the amounts spent on R&D by the developing countries themselves and the percentage of nonmilitary R&D of the developed countries to be devoted to problems of primary interest to the developing countries.

In various statements presented in Subcommittee III of the Seabed Committee, meeting in Geneva and New York since 1971, delegates from developing countries have argued that in order for them to participate fully in the exploration and exploitation of ocean resources, developed countries should share their technical knowhow with the developing countries. And they succeeded in having the issue put on the official agenda of the pending Law of the Sea Conference.

In view of the different definitions of "transfer of technology," it is not entirely clear at this point whether the debate on technology transfer will be limited to transfer of technical knowledge only, or will include discussions on the entire process of modernization. Even the limited definition of technology transfer could include both proprietary and nonproprietary technology, and ranges from the acquisition of simple labor-intensive fishing techniques to advanced capital-intensive technology of offshore mining. While aid programs could include acquisition of modern fishing vessels equipped with the latest navigational and fishing gear, many developing nations would still need technical assistance to utilize and maintain this equipment.

Moreover, growing supplies of fish brought ashore by modern trawlers would require refrigeration, canning and marketing techniques, onshore storage and docking facilities, and training courses for those who have to work with the new equipment. Technology to explore and exploit seabed minerals is even costlier and will require more advanced skills. To enter the manganese nodule mining industry may require initial investments of $100 to $200 million, and capital outlays for offshore oil drilling platforms are between $6 and $12 million each. Assuming a developing nation will purchase the advanced mining equipment, it would still need highly trained people to operate, inspect and maintain these complicated systems. Offshore mining requires a technological infrastructure that few nations have. Moreover, offshore mining technology is proprietary and controlled by a few advanced industrial nations only. Difficulties related to the transfer of proprietary technology are extensively discussed in Dr. Patel's excellent paper and need no further elaboration.

National Science Policy Bodies

I would like to address myself to the need to assist developing countries in building up a marine science capability and the necessary science policy bodies to facilitate the application of knowledge to practical needs. In order to make the best use of sciences and technology in their development plans, nations need to establish a network of institutions at the public and private level.

Science and technology are integral elements of overall national development plans in most developed and some developing countries, but a large number of developing countries have not yet recognized the need to integrate planning with sciences and technology. Due to past colonial experiences, there is often no coordination of science policy at the highest governmental level. Prior to independence, science policy was determined in the mother country and science advice came from research establishments in the mother country.

For successful coordination of the research programs of each government department, a ministry of science or a national science policy committee is required. Formulation and planning of research could be undertaken in national councils for science policy attached to the highest office, assisted by the science advisory committee, a part of the national planning authority. Coordination, promotion and financing of scientific research at the national level can be exercised by National Academies of Sciences for basic science and National Councils for Industrial Research for Applied Sciences. In addition to supporting their particular activities, these organizations provide the necessary liaison between the central science policy bodies and the institutions performing research and development.

A national science policy is needed to organize, direct, and apply scientific and technological resources and to achieve certain national objectives that are part of an overall development plan. Without such high level science policy bodies one can expect only haphazard development of national capabilities. National science policy institutions also act as a channel for receiving and adapting existing knowledge from other countries. They are equipped to deal with registration, deposit, and approval of technology transfer agreements in both the private and public sector; to assist in negotiations of technology transfer contracts; to review, evaluate, and negotiate such contracts; and to review royalties and technical services.

Finally, national science policy institutions can promote higher education, help to create an environment conducive to research, assess future needs of scientists, engineers, and technicians, establish research priorities, evaluate research results, and act as agents to bring about international cooperation in science and technology.

On the basis of past experiences, developed countries can assist developing countries in establishing science policy bodies at various functional levels. Building an independent research and development capability and successful transfer of foreign technology are both dependent on the development of national science policy bodies in developing countries.

Imported Technology vs. Development of Domestic Capabilities

It has frequently been argued that instead of investing scarce resources to acquire a basic scientific and technological capability, developing countries should instead concentrate on importing existing foreign knowhow. This way, the argument goes, countries can make substantial savings which could be invested elsewhere in the economy. There are several fallacies in this argument. In the first place, factor allocations usually differ considerably in developed and developing nations. The latter tend to suffer from serious unemployment, wages are generally low, and capital is the scarcest factor of production.

In the developed countries labor is scarce and consequently industries pay higher wages. Thus the primary function of industrial technology in the developed countries is to find labor-saving production methods. To transfer labor-saving, capital-intensive technology to developing countries has frequently been wasteful or even socially damaging. Ghana's development of a capital-intensive fishing fleet during the 1960s is a good example. Of the 18 private and state-owned trawlers purchased during the 60s, ten Russian-built side trawlers are not at all used, two tuna purse seiners were uneconomic and sold, and two Japanese stern trawlers proved efficient but too costly to finance. The investment was not merely a drain on foreign currency and involved high social opportunity costs, but it did not make any major contribution to solving unemployment problems, nor did the modern fleet replace dependence on foreign imports of fish.

Transfer of capital-intensive technology can also lead to dislocations of labor in other sectors of the economy, causing serious social problems. Thus the development of a modern fishing fleet in southern Brazil resulted in serious unemployment in traditional fishing villages in northern Brazil. Traditional fishermen in the North can no longer compete on local markets with cheap frozen fish imported from the South. Economic and social hardship as a result of serious underemployment was an immediate result of the transfer of modern fishing technology to other sectors of the fishing industry. Other fallacies of the argument that developing countries should primarily rely on imported technology are related to high costs and other restrictions imposed on developing countries' purchasing of foreign technology.

To be able to reduce long-term dependence on foreign technology and to enhance their bargaining position vis-à-vis industries in the advanced countries, developing countries need to develop an indigenous scientific and technological infrastructure. There are a number of arguments to support the desire of developing countries to develop an independent scientific capability. In the first place, a limited scientific capability is required in order to make a rational choice among various alternative foreign technologies and to adapt those technologies to local conditions. Even in those cases where foreign technology is appropriate to the needs of a particular developing country, it is frequently not available in ready-made form.

For the development of an indigenous research and development capability, developing countries must first improve their overall scientific education. To train future generations of successful R&D personnel, developing countries should not specialize in applied science only, but should develop a capability in the basic sciences. It is difficult to achieve a viable capability in applied sciences without also acquiring a basic science capability, and we know from past experiences that most technologically advanced countries are also strong in the basic sciences. Modern science and technology undergo rapid changes that make it necessary for scientists to conduct their own research in order not to create a future generation of scientists and engineers who are not well acquainted with the fundamentals of current science. Scientists who have little contact with the forefront of science will soon become out of date and their effectiveness will be reduced to next to nothing.

Complete specialization in one field of science without acquiring a sufficiently broad general background can lead to overspecialization in a narrow area of research and make it difficult for researchers to shift to other projects. Particularly in developing countries, where highly trained manpower is scarce and frequent access to specialists in other related fields is usually not available, a broad scientific background is preferable to overspecialization. Moreover, in order to train future R&D specialists, a more general technical education based on a general science education is needed.

In the marine sciences, for example, the important phenomenon of coastal upwelling (which is related to high biological productivity) is not too well understood and requires a great deal more research. Both the biological and physical aspects of upwelling need to be studied extensively and systematically in order to utilize and maintain the fishing resources that are dependent on this phenomenon. Also construction of offshore platforms have to be proceeded by interdisciplinary research. Geological and geophysical surveys can locate favorable areas for oil and gas development, but studies of surface and deep sea currents, waves, tides, etc., are required to determine the construction of the platforms.

A first step in the direction toward an independent ocean science capability is the creation of a critical mass of scientists in the main subdivisions of the marine sciences: physical, chemical, geological, and biological oceanography. In addition to training scientists in these four fields, an ocean science institution would need ocean engineers, technicians, and science administrators. The latter should be experienced researchers with managerial talents to manage the institution and provide planning and direction for research activities.

To build up a viable independent research capability will take time. The first generation of marine scientists is likely to devote most of its time to teaching, building up of the institution and consulting. However, in order to keep in touch with their field and to head off a possible brain drain, they should be given sufficient time to conduct research. The second generation will have more time available for research, but they too are not likely to achieve a broad and substantial degree of scientific excellence. The third generation will have the opportunity to achieve progress in science.

Some success in the basic sciences can be achieved earlier, with limited resources, and if it does occur it will contribute to the moral and social consciousness in developing societies. Today, many developing countries lack the confidence to participate in international scientific programs. A success in one area of science could be accomplished without the vast investments needed for big science, and would strengthen the feeling of achievement, cohesion, and perseverance in a developing nation. Once feelings of inferiority are replaced by self-confidence, human resources can be channelled into cooperative and constructive international ventures.

Each coastal state will have to decide for itself whether the development of an ocean science capability is a priority need. Such decisions will be influenced by overall development needs, availability of resources, practical applicability of research findings, geographical location, domestic popularity, and by existing knowledge of offshore resources. Countries with little potential for offshore resources are not likely to invest heavily in building up a marine science capability. It therefore seems essential to first undertake a general resources survey in cooperation with UNESCO, FAO, and ocean sciences institutions of the maritime nations.

Developed countries can assist in establishing and financing national and regional ocean science institutions in accordance with proposals made by the United States at the 1972 preparatory conference on the law of the sea in Geneva. If financial resources are forthcoming, ocean science institutions in the maritime countries could perform a very important role, helping institutions in developing coastal states with training scientists and technicians, problem identification, cooperative research projects, common use of facilities, research management, and by exchanging scientists and supplying those institutions with surplus equipment. Several such cooperative programs between institutions in the United States and sister institutions abroad have been very successful and contributed significantly to enhancing marine capabilities in various developing countries. Additional public aid could broaden the scope of these cooperative efforts and include a larger number of developing countries.

A great deal of completed and partially completed projects that could make contributions to economic development are presently shelved at institutions at home and abroad. One of the reasons for this is the lack of information, dissemination, and communication of research findings. On the basis of an earlier successful A.I.D. experiment, which involved transfer of technology developed under NASA auspices to developing countries, the government could finance a study to determine to what extent selected types of marine technology developed with public support in the past are relevant to specific marine problems in developing countries.

The A.I.D. project involved an American university and the Korean Institute of Science and Technology. American specialists assisted the Koreans in searching NASA technical data banks and in developing a methodology for relating the data to specific industrial problems. The Korean specialists were responsible for adopting the most promising technologies to specific Korean needs, with particular emphasis on industrial opportunities for generating employment, developing export opportunities, and utilizing indigenous raw materials and local skills. The success of the program, and the belief that a great deal of existing marine technology could be adapted to local needs, might warrant a similar effort between an American ocean science institution and a national or regional center of excellence in a developing region of the world.

**National and Regional Centers of Excellence
in the Marine Sciences and Technology**

To alleviate serious shortages of trained ocean scientists and engineers in developing countries will require national and international action. Rather than spreading available resources over a number of small coastal states, research efforts could be concentrated in a few large centers in each coastal region. Such centers would not necessarily replace national activities, but would instead complement the work done at national universities and institutions. At the national level, technical assistance could emphasize the creation of a critical mass of ocean scientists needed to form the basis of future national and regional research efforts. But whereas scientists from national institutions would conduct some research in addition to teaching responsibilities, regional centers of excellence would draw large numbers of postgraduate students and other researchers from the region and possibly from other parts of the world. Such centers could concentrate on a few particular marine problems of interest to the region and should include projects with expected short-term social or economic returns.

Centers of excellence in the marine sciences could become partially self-sufficient through contract research. The Asian Institute of Technology in Bangkok is a good example of benefits accruing to the region by bringing together scientists, engineers, and technicians in one major institution, supported in part by contract research. UNESCO support is presently being awarded to three marine centers of excellence in South and Southeast Asia (Indonesia, Thailand, and India), each specializing in a different area. Regional centers have the advantage of combining regional resources, initiating research programs of interest to the entire region, and offering opportunities for scientists from the regions to exchange ideas and remain up to date in their field. National and regional centers of excellence could take part in coastal resources surveys, develop new technologies to exploit ocean resources, adapt foreign technology to local and regional needs, and so forth. One area of overriding importance would be research leading to rapid increases in harvesting ocean-based protein resources.

In view of limitations on the overall increase of ocean fishing, and the considerable inequality of distribution of general productivity in the oceans, developing coastal states (particularly in the tropical zones) will have to turn increasingly to mariculture as a means to meet growing protein demands. Today, some 4 million metric tons of fish are produced annually through aquaculture in fresh and brackish waters. However, in contrast to fresh-water aquaculture, mariculture is still in its infancy. There is a possibility for vast expansion in many parts of the world. It has been estimated that if 10 percent of the unutilized brackish swamps in the archipelagoes of Southeast Asia were developed for mariculture, an additional 10 million metric tons (i.e., one-seventh of the present total world catch of ocean fish) of fish and shellfish could be produced. However, various problems of engineering, nutrition, control over reproductive biology, and disease will have to be solved first.

Recent research at the Woods Hole Oceanographic Institution, where treated sewage is used to enhance the natural productivity of the sea, provides hope to find ways to pay for expensive secondary sewage treatment by controlled use of sewage for the growth of phytoplankton, the basis of the marine food chain. Particularly in unproductive parts of tropical seas, artificial nutrients could vastly increase productivity in coastal swamps, for example.

In many parts of the world, output of fish by mariculture is limited by the number of young animals that can be caught locally. Researchers from developed countries could do more research at centers of excellence in developing countries on artificial spawning of brackish water fish. If this could be done successfully, and small hatcheries were built, fairly large numbers of young animals would be available every year to increase the stocks in coastal swamps.

Permanent linkages between national research institutions and regional centers of excellence would facilitate the move toward independent scientific capabilities, improve regional cooperation in the marine sciences, save on scarce national resources, and reduce the danger of a continuing brain drain.

Chapter Six

Planning Workshops on the Development of University Marine Programs

Nelson Marshall
Director, International Center
for Marine Resource Development
University of Rhode Island

The following prospectus represents an approach to technological transfer being promoted by the International Center for Marine Resource Development at the University of Rhode Island. Two such workshops are now provisionally scheduled in countries which are oceans apart and equally different as to the current status of their technological capability. As anticipated, neither workshop is being formulated with strict adherence to the blueprint of the prospectus, especially inasmuch as special circumstances and wishes of the host universities are taken into account.

Our provisional schedule is obviously ambitious and, with desired follow-up, we may not be able to add appreciably to these undertakings. We will, however, be pleased to explore the possibility with those who might be interested. We also hope that other universities expanding their advisory services will accept our prospectus as an invitation to exchange views as to optimum procedures. Obviously we do not, at this stage, know how our concepts will unfold in practice. In another year I should be in a position to offer an informative evaluation report.

THE AREA OF CONCERN

Just what are the marine resources of your country or region? What is their value? What is their potential? What is being done to realize, to develop, and to manage

99

this resource potential? For those of us concerned with education and research, these questions must be asked in terms of the role of higher education in support of marine interests. We must ask just how education is and should be responding to these needs. How can university education and research programs interact most effectively with both government and commercial enterprises bearing on the marine resource potential?

In the United States these questions have been probed intensively over the past decade. As a result, university marine resources efforts have expanded substantially beyond the marine science, fisheries biology, and oceanographic work of earlier years. Several universities have developed a total marine resources outlook that involves a comprehensive approach to marine problems, interrelating the input from the social sciences with the more familiar contributions of the natural sciences. In addition, engineering, technology, and vocational training, as well as law, policy, and advisory services collectively play a substantial role in modern university marine resource programs.

The University of Rhode Island, starting with its Marine Resources Program in 1960, subsequently building its capabilities with support from the federal Sea Grant Program, and more recently with funding from the U.S. Agency for International Development, has been the pioneering U.S. institution developing this broader approach to marine resources. A sense of the University's overall involvement in marine work can be gained from Table 6-1 below. For countries or regional organizations wishing to share the insights gained through this experience, the International Center for Marine Resource Development of the University of Rhode Island can arrange for a team to make an advanced study of the country or region, to visit the area, and to join in a workshop focussing on developing an integrated university marine program. Topics to be covered in the lectures, panels, discussion sessions, and illustrated presentations of such a workshop include:

1. The scope and nature of the marine resources—What is meant by marine affairs?
2. The scope of a comprehensive university marine resources program—What can be done in programs of lesser scope, through division of effort, through interinstitutional cooperation?
3. The harvested fisheries as a marine resource
4. Mariculture as a marine resource
5. Technology and engineering in relation to marine resources development
6. University interaction with industry concerned with marine resources, including liaison with the fishery
7. University relationships with other government agencies concerned with marine resources. Faculty, students, and research in the following fields in support of marine resource interests: oceanography, biological sciences, fisheries, engineering, resource economics, geography and law of the sea, food and nutrition, sociology, political science, and planning.
8. Levels and kind of education: graduate, undergraduate, vocational

Table 6-1. Faculty Participation in Marine Programs

	Faculty	*Graduate Students*
Biological oceanography including estuarine, coastal, and reef ecology	9	50
Physical, chemical, and geological oceanography	16	65
Fisheries biology and aquaculture	4	15
Supporting biological disciplines	5	20
Ocean engineering and allied engineering fields	10	85
Vocational education for fisheries and marine technology	5	N.A.[a]
Food chemistry and nutrition	5	15
Resource economics	9	31
Geography, marine affairs, law of the sea, community planning, and public administration	5	25
Sociology applied to fisheries and marine enterprises	4	10
Marine advisory services	8[b]	N.A.[a]

[a]Not applicable
[b]Chiefly staff, nonfaculty appointments

9. Overseas visiting student arrangements in relation to the development of a university program
10. Marine advisory or extension services
11. Education in marine subjects for children and for teachers of children
12. University administration provisions for a marine resources program
13. Funding a university marine resources program

Preferably such a workshop would be only the first step in a series of contacts with educational programs in your region. Later steps could include more prolonged advisory visits by personnel from the University of Rhode Island dealing with selected disciplines. Other follow-up steps might include short or extended visits to the University of Rhode Island by personnel from your country who wish to study or do research here. Still other patterns might unfold, but follow-up, as important as it is, can best be handled after an initial workshop.

PARTICIPANTS IN A PLANNING WORKSHOP

The planning workshop would be designed to aid decision makers who are responsible for government and national educational planning and to provide background information for those responsible for program planning within universities. Personnel with such responsibilities are selected for participation in such workshops, together with the team from the University of Rhode Island. Leaders representing economic interests in marine resources may be added to the roster of participants.

The visiting team from the University of Rhode Island would represent the entire scope of the University interests and more specifically, the following areas: oceanography and ocean engineering, resource economics, nutrition, vocational education, law, and marine advisory work. On each team there would be at least one contributor well versed in matters of academic administration and funding, and one having firsthand experience with ties between universities, industry, and government agencies. For a broadened perspective we would select one or two representatives from other U.S. universities having comparable programs. Selected additional observers from the United States or from the world community (United Nations Development Program or World Bank, for example) would be encouraged to attend. Before travelling to your country the visiting team from the University of Rhode Island would spend the equivalent of one week studying source materials to acquire an introductory familiarity with the area. The first week in your area would involve further study and observation before the final comprehensive workshop session ending with the preparation of summation information.

THE SCOPE OF FACULTY PARTICIPATION IN MARINE PROGRAMS

Table 6-1 shows the multidisciplinary setting that exists at the University of Rhode Island for the study of marine resource problems. Numbers represent full-time equivalent faculty members and graduate students active in marine oriented programs. (Technical assistants and supporting administrative staff are not included.)

* * * * * *

Commentary
Emmanuel G. Bello

I speak entirely as one from a developing nation, and I share their point of view on this question of transfer of science and technology. It is very easy to presume that the subject of discussion borders too much on the grandiose side. Each time the phrase "transfer of science and technology" is mentioned it almost always conjures up high philosophical thinking, generalities, and a diversity of inconsistent views. If one is a cynic one might go so far as to describe it as a panorama of a distant landscape. The trouble is that if it had been otherwise, we would have no reason to be here at all, nor would we have been emphasizing the point. On the other hand, it might be rather dull and boring to praise collectively those brilliant schemes and programs which have changed the picture of the world in technology and scientific achievement. Unfortunately, such is yet not the case. So, we must continue to propose ideas, whether limited or grandiose in perspective.

There are those who hold tenaciously to those rigid and calculated views on how transfer of science and technology to the developing nations should be effected. Anything not consonant with those traditional methods is alien and totally without substance. The upsurge of independent states in Asia and Africa since the 1960s has brought the subjects to the limelight. The frequency of conferences and meetings on the topic underlines the importance attached to it.

Apparently the Committee on Science and Technology for Development met only recently in New York in March to deal with the same problem, and here we are again dealing with it. If we narrow down the scope of this subject to marine sciences and marine environment, we find that the events of the last years show that the less developed countries have been trying sufficiently reasonably to keep up and develop the different sectors connected with ocean management.

I suppose they realize that any breakdown in their attempts to avail themselves of the opportunities provided by the potentials of modern technology in oceanography is not only a future threat and disaster to their development but a present reality. In many cases, either the measures taken are widely dispersed or they are inefficiently coordinated. One good reason for this is the fact that oceanography is relatively new to most developing nations. Yet it appears to be a fertile ground for promoting or eliminating those differences and misunderstandings between the abundance and scarcity nations of the world.

Experience shows that many governments of the less developed countries will only give their support to international cooperative projects if the sum total of scientific, political, and economic benefits exceeds the cost; but the big question is whether those benefits can really easily be separated in practice. Quite clearly only a policy maker who is knowledgeable in the issues involved can present a logically discernible pattern of events that can persuade his government to take a positive stand.

Our attention is always directed to training the professionals who actually do the job when they think of transfer of science and technology to a developing nation. Yet the man who dominates the activities of the trained professionals is the government administrator. It is not uncommon to see many people from the third world who get training, end up doing something totally unrelated to what they learned when they go back to their home countries. Some have no jobs to go to because governments did nothing beyond training to assimilate and use their talents. Many of the trained professionals in certain cases get so frustrated that they change to a completely new field. The result is that many years of education and training is wasted. There is the recent case of a physical oceanographer who joined a bank because he had not enough work to do. He is not the only one by any means. I hear there is another marine biologist who became an estate agent because of the same reason.

I wish to submit, therefore, that in order to tackle the problems of the less developed countries effectively, it is of primordial importance to begin our training program not from the beginning but from the top. By this, I mean the top administrators, those who are in control. A training program should be devised for an influential group of representatives from the developing nations. The aim would be to paint a broad picture of the sea so that they could at least be aware of the problems and of the assets which may be within their grasp. This would help them share, understand, and accept the necessity of fundamental structural changes that are now taking place. It will show them that they need to create new forms of planning that will permit them to evaluate the directions in which they should move.

One of the prime considerations would be to create a good standard of understanding of oceanographic problems with the top echelon of government. The knowledge of those whose deliberations and decisions affect the development in marine affairs will consequently be upgraded. It is hoped that this familiarization will accelerate governmental incentives in furthering schemes and programs dealing with research investigations and marine affairs in general.

Training such an influential group may lead to a full and dispassionate inquiry into the working conditions and the best utilization of the trained professionals. Not only will this uplift the status of oceanography and marine affairs, but it will also better their image in a different society. Governmental support could help in the creation of an infrastructure and other facilities necessary for the management of marine environment. It may be good for the policy makers to know that it is useless to train a man in sophisticated equipment where simple types could suffice. For these and other reasons I suggest that there is a justification for embarking on a training and education program that will cater to the needs of men and women who will take a stronger lead in formulating marine policies and development programs in the third world.

The Intergovernmental Oceanographic Commission of UNESCO is interested in promoting such a training program under the direction of its present and able secretary, Commander Desmond Scott. Before going any further I wish to draw attention to the danger of the constant use of the phrase "the transfer of science and technology" for research and development. Our sweeping generalizations create a great deal of confusion in the minds of those responsible for government policy. To some it simply means embarking on all branches of scientific and technological development, whether it relates to the immediate needs of the country or not. To others it is a matter of prestige to have people training in technologies which may never be valuable to their government, even in the future. It is always clearer to specify what branch of science and technology is contemplated and to what area of development it refers.

I contend that there cannot be a global approach to the totality of the problems of science and technology, to promote research and development. Hence, I am concentrating on transfer of technology within the field of marine research and development. We must be pragmatic and systematic. We must be careful to lay down each stone one by one in a tempo that is conducive to each country's needs and priorities. Governments are not always frank about what is going on after training a candidate. Perhaps it is human nature for them not to say, "We could not do something right away." Usually they paint a rosy picture of a nonexisting situation.

To carry out the sort of training and education program which I referred to earlier, the strategy would require all the resources of the specialized agencies. These would be mobilized and enlisted through coordinated efforts of the IOC and UNESCO. I should take three specific directions: (1) assist in training and education in all problems of the marine environment; (2) build up a structure of science of technology in the less developed countries which are member states of the IOC; and (3) attack specific problems to avoid the waste of manpower and resources that has characterized past activities in many cases.

Personally, I would like to see the IOC continue to attribute to science, technology, and research the importance which is their due. A training program such as the one envisaged will begin with the original workshop. This may tally with the suggestion made by Professor Marshall with regard to exchange programs which his university may have with other universities in the developing countries.

Be that as it may, I consider it to be of vital importance for developing nations to evaluate their marine resources and to capitalize on the worldwide program that is unfolding. Here, a country's marine policy should be considered in regard to its overall science policy. An assessment of existing priorities of institutions for formulating and implementing marine policy can be made. It would also be necessary to develop a knowledge base about the relation of marine science development to overall economic, social, and political development. The extent of the effect of marine resources on economic development will also be determined and the ability of technology to develop mineral resources will be dealt with.

The workshop will seriously consider the distinction between pure research and applied science. All these would be a prerequisite to developing a course in ocean science and methods for administrators. A compendium of lectures will then be compiled for the general course. Content materials selected should be those in most common use for this purpose.

The first will be for two months. Various university facilities will be considered. The selected university will be a place where participants can live together, talk together, and know one another. The general course will familiar-ize the participants with what oceanography can do towards their country's problems, treat individuals' mutual problems, and would bear relevance to the overall program of development. It may be necessary for the participants to go to sea and get their feet wet, get to know the difficulties involved generally. I propose that there would be a period or a "break" of one month in which the participants will return to their own countries to discuss with the governments. At this stage, discussion will cover a broad spectrum of marine affairs programs, but the important question is to determine the country's needs and priorities in science, technology, and research.

The second general course would be divided into two parts of specialization in the area of immediate interest to each country participating. Institutions and universities dealing in those particular areas would be requested to accept them for a period of three to four weeks. They will be acquainted with all the necessary and important areas which they have chosen.

The final stage will be of two or three weeks' duration and will deal with the experiences of the participants. They will discuss and lecture one another, write an evaluation of the course from a strictly personal point of view, and show how their training would help them in their own countries. They will return to their own countries to act as subsequent liaison and focal points for marine programs.

It is expected that a participant, as a policy maker, will endeavor to inculcate among his own people an appreciation of this approach which will influence their development. There is no doubt that individuals who can contribute towards developing ideas on their country's need in marine sciences, would play a key role for subsequent liaison and contact.

The funding of the program is a very important question. Here we have to ask for the general support of foundations, such as Ford and Rockefeller, voluntary assistance agencies, governments, multinational corporations, oil companies to try to carry out this worthwhile educational program. The IOC would be pleased to have the support of bodies and organizations which would be interested. I hope it will be possible to develop a specific mechanism for working out this program.

In conclusion, therefore, the less developed countries must realize that scientific development is a slow and painful learning process. There are no miracles. There is only one, which is necessary in order to gain support and broad participation of as many countries as possible. The oceans are the last frontiers that man must conquer. The developed world is determined to realize this goal. It is also the responsibility of the less developed countries to join in and conquer it.

Discussion

Royce: It has seemed to me, as I have followed the discussion about the transfer of technology in the marine area, that we have really been looking at the easy problems of moving information, of moving people, of training scientists, of moving hardware from one country to another—but neglecting some of the rather basic social issues that I think are the principal restraints on this, especially in the area of fishery development.

One needs only to look at the range of productivity in fisheries to gain some comprehension of the problems that are generated. We have several tens of millions of fishermen in the coastal countries of the world who are producing only about one ton per man per year. Now the modern fishermen, using first-rate equipment, are producing on the general level of 100 tons per man per year, in countries like Iceland or the distant water fisheries of Poland. In countries like Peru where the fishermen are fishing on very low-valued species such as anchovy, or in the United States fishery for menhaden, production runs to about 1,000 tons per man per year.

Along with this there is a very important time problem. We have been looking, I think, in terms of years with respect to developing marine resources where we should probably be looking in terms of decades. Let me comment briefly on what I see as the two major issues that we have been dodging. First is the educational one—not that of training scientists, but of the education of the people whose lives are affected by the shifting technology. It means a changing way of life for many of these people. It means moving, commonly, to other occupations and other locations. Let us start with an example of introducing outboard motors. Let us assume a coastal village with a production level of about one ton per man per year, and that the introduction of outboards raises this to perhaps five tons per man per year.

This means that people must learn the technique of managing outboards and bringing ashore an increased catch. It means learning to handle credit. It means learning to operate marketing systems without getting lost in the hands of middlemen who grab all of the money. It means learning to process the catch. It means responding to a rather consistent schedule so that the transportation system is always there ready to take the catch, and so on. It means both change in a way of life and the requirement for a significant increase in the educational level of the people of that village.

Looking more broadly at the development of a fishery that begins to compete with world fisheries, the fishermen must move to an urban base where vessels can be maintained and serviced and where they can dispose of their catch. It is important to realize that most fishermen have been rural people, living in isolated villages where one of their principal forms of subsistence is the catch of fish itself and not merely the sale of fish.

The second major point that I want to make is the need for political structure in the resource agency, the fishery agency, or whatever it is called. We have seen examples in the last few years in Latin America in the reorganizations that have followed the changes of government. All scientific personnel in fishery agencies have been changed, frequently without being replaced by scientific personnel. It just seems to me mandatory that any sensible system of development of the resources of a country must require the development of an effective government agency, one that is not changed radically with the changes of government, one that has scientific expertise of the kind that we have been discussing, and one that is clearly responsible to the needs of the people whose lives are being changed, not merely to the problems of the science.

McKnight: The discussion has left me very confused and puzzled with respect to one particular area, and that was alluded to by Mr. Franssen when he mentioned the work of Subcommittee III of the Seabed Committee which, supplemental to marine pollution and scientific research, added to its mandate the matter of drafting articles in connection with the transfer of technology. What confuses me is how Subcommittee III is going to discharge that assignment. What sorts of factors will be considered that could be translated into treaty language that may emerge from the Seabed Committee or the Law of the Sea Conference transferring technology from developed to developing countries? Fortunately we have several members who are actually participating directly in the work of the Seabed Committee. I do not know whether the panel would want to address themselves to this, but we might get some further enlightenment from those who are actually faced with the responsibility of coping with this problem.

Bello: The problem is not really one of writing treaty language but one of accommodating the interests of the nations or individuals concerned. You have to consider what is involved. Subcommittee III is not really writing articles of treaties that will be automatically binding before the conference proper is held in 1974. So, whatever they do is only an expression of a declaration of intention, or what they believe to be the proper way of approaching the problem or treating the particular point, and this will be left open to the legal experts or draftsmen who will later incorporate the various interests accommodated in the final conference into the treaty in question.

Uchegbu: In the first place, may I say I was lured to this conference in the belief that we were going to discuss the law of the sea, but what I have seen here is that I am being entertained by what one might call "high politics." By this I mean political economy. Somehow, for one reason or the other, we have talked much about developing countries, but nobody has been able to give a precise definition of who constitutes these developing countries.

This particular phrase "developing countries" has been a burning question of terminology, as some people may know, in the General Agreement on Tariffs and Trade (GATT) and in UNCTAD as well. I would therefore have thought that a discussion on technological transfer to developing countries would have attempted, at any rate, to identify exactly who constitutes the developing countries, and what criteria (one might ask) we should use in identifying these developing countries. Are we using GNP, for instance? Are we using density of industries? Are we using geographical location? Are we using, indeed, racial criteria? Also, the expression "the third world" has been used merely to add confusion to what is already a confused situation, and this self-negating phrase, "the third world," begs the question, I must say, because I do not know who is the first world and who is the second.

Now I move to the second problem, and that is the question of the definition of "technology transfer." I will say that we in the developing countries need *ownership* of transferred technology and not technology transfer as it has been defined in this place. I think there is a danger, which one must emphasize in this conference, that when we talk of technology transfer *simpliciter* (more so if we define the phrase to include education), then we are on the borderline of what one might call "cultural imperialism." I use this phrase quite deliberately because it is common knowledge that education is an expression of the culture of a given people, and when you transfer education from A to B, you transfer with it all the culture that goes with it. What we need in the developing countries is not, I emphasize, technology transfer *as defined*. We need, besides ownership of technology, capital to develop our own universities, which then will have to carry out studies on this marine technological innovation that seems to be going on these days.

We have also been entertained by this profuse technological advancement all over the world. Can I stand here and say that this technological development has not reached the people in developing countries? It seems to me that we appear to be imposing technological advancement in one country or in one region onto the world scene and then attempting to universalize it, whereas more than half of the people of the world are still maintaining bare minimum subsistence.

Then there was the talk about organizing a workshop. This equally well goes with what I am talking about, meaning to say that we need to feed the people. This is basic, you see, and the so-called technological transfer must be symbolized in terms and in the form of capital in order for us to explore our own natural resources to feed our people. If, therefore, we talk about university training, we have got our universities, and they need capital for research and development. These universities are there to study the culture and the social problems which confront us. In this connection, I think one speaker has made reference to the social impact of this technological transfer, and this, for one reason or the other, has been ignored in this conference. I maintain that this is the fundamental question that one has to focus on in talking about technological transfer.

Wooster: I would just like to comment on your first point. Knowing this group and people like them, I know that they love to get wrapped up in semantics, and I am afraid if we got into a discussion of what is the definition of a developing country, what is the definition of the third world, or what is the definition even of technological transfer, we would not get beyond the defining stage and into any substantial arguments.

It seems to me we must accept that there are various artificial definitions which have been made of developing countries of the third world. We cannot refine them at this meeting. We just assume that there are some countries that are more developed than others, and we are looking at whether or not there are ways whereby—or whether, indeed, it is useful to transfer technology, and if so how one might go about it in a way that reflects the realities rather than the theoretical concepts that people in countries who some have called "overdeveloped" may have in mind. So I think the debate on whether this is a good thing to do and how you go about it *is* a useful one, regardless of whether we all agree on who is developed or who is not. I remember hearing Roger Revelle refer to the United States as a developing country. That was a year or so ago; I am not sure what he would say today.

Lapointe: I am prompted to ask a question in light of Mr. McKnight's question and the answer given by our colleague from UNESCO. I have had the great pleasure of participating in the Seabed Committee, and I have just heard that we lawyers are now expected to draft something that will implement this transfer of technology idea.

I am not too sure exactly what is expected of the Law of the Sea Conference in this respect. We have so far, within the draft articles on the seabed regime, a very vague formulation related to transfer of technology (which is sort of put in terms of motherhood more than anything else), and I have yet to hear, either within the Seabed Committee or even here, apart from certain bilateral programs that already exist or may exist later or some of the work that is already being done by some already existing institution, exactly how this is supposed to be done. Is the new seabed agency, which will look at only one aspect of the technological picture expected to do it all, and if so, how? Or are we going to create new agencies; or are we simply going to develop our bilateral programs? Whatever the answer is, I would like an indication as to how I am supposed to help draft it.

Brittin: Like my good friend Paul Lapointe, I am a little bemused about the question of just how we are to go about drafting transfer of technology in Subcommittee III. I would point out, however, that there have been several constant themes not only in Subcommittee III but in all three subcommittees, and that is a general expression that transfer of technology must take place. There is going to be an obligation of some sort.

So I would expect, speaking as an individual here, perhaps in response to Max McKnight, that we might well end up with the general obligation on the part of developed states to transfer technology of a marine character. I agree with what Paul has said. The issue is very complex indeed, and I should point out in the first part of my comment that these have been generalized statements. We have not yet got to the point in the working group on scientific research as to what we are specifically talking about, and I think that this summer, when we get into that, perhaps some of the drives, some understanding will emerge that will make it a little bit easier for the so-called "lawyers" to put things together.

One brief comment on the question of developing countries. As I see it, there is no logic to the broad picture of what constitutes a developing country. It certainly is not just an economic base, because there are some developing countries which have a larger per capita income than a lot of developed countries. I think that we use the expression because it is a fact of life in our work in the law of the sea. It is present, and you have to deal with it.

Let me make two further comments to the panel as a whole, which struck me when you all finished speaking. One is that I believe that you all struck a note of pessimism for a variety of reasons, one being that marine science is very, very complicated, very sophisticated. In the developing countries do they have the right kind of people? Mr. Bello put his finger on something I thought was very important, and that is that the decision makers, the policy people—are they attuned to what their own national interests are? If you look back over the past ten years, I believe we are now in a situation in the world where there is now more information and more understanding about the oceans than there has been over the past ten or twenty years. The reason for this, in my estimation, is the fact that we are so deeply engaged in preparations for the law of the sea conference. In the delegations of countries from all over the world we do have policy makers; thus I am inclined not to be quite so pessimistic as the panel is, because I feel that this period is a period of opportunity; that with this increased knowledge on the part of all the countries in the world there will be a greater understanding of the needs, the requirements, and the desirability of moving in the direction of doing something about the oceans off their coasts.

The second theme I observed was that your comments in general were addressed to **resource-related** marine science. I would just like to suggest that while I certainly recognize that resources are of primary interest to all countries in the world—particularly developing countries—there are also other interests I believe I hear in the law of the sea forum. One would be the question of protection of the marine environment, or pollution controls. In a way, this question is quite divorced from resources, and requires different kinds of technology and different kinds of interests. I do not know whether it is as sophisticated as the pursuit of resources in general, but I would suspect that there would be need to enter into this facet of marine science in addition to **resource-oriented** marine science. In this connection, when we talk about highly sophisticated activities at sea (and this is a query) is there not an opportunity for follow-up projects to a research cruise? For example, monitoring after a research cruise is finished could be conducted by personnel of developing countries in their area, perhaps in con-

junction with a developed country. The research would perhaps be pursued on a
much lower level, but would certainly still be very important to the overall pros-
ecution of the project.

Weiss: I hope that these remarks have exposed the oceans policy community
to a set of very broad science policy questions about which there is still very
considerable ignorance. We need a lot more information about how marine technology is transferred to developing countries—both in the modern sector, where
technology is typically transferred through investments by multinational corporations, and in the traditional sector, which aims to raise the income of traditional rural fisherman, as has been discussed. While there is a certain amount of
conventional wisdom on the subject, and a fair number of studies, we need hard
data and careful study of how industries actually develop and how developing
country nationals actually learn how to get hold of their own affairs and to run
things for themselves.

   As one lawyer has suggested, these problems do not get incorporated
into treaty language except in grand generalities that express everyone's joint
purposes. But they do get incorporated into the hard bargaining that precedes
and follows the signing of the treaty, and so they do have their place in policy
discussions.

   Whether the transfer of fisheries technology to developing countries
is going to aim at the modern sector or the small fisherman is basically a policy
question taken up by the developing country. I want only to add that the success of technical assistance to the traditional sector depends not only on technology but, as was mentioned, on credit, marketing, and distribution facilities—and
on an economic policy that gives the small guy a chance. This, in turn, has to do
with very fundamental questions of the distribution of income within developing
countries. This is a delicate political issue in many developing countries; it
touches on the attitudes of developed countries as well as those of technical
assistance and financial assistance agencies.

   I hope very much that these discussions will be the start of deeper
and more detailed discussions within the oceans policy community that will
illuminate a neglected area.

Chapter Seven

The Transfer of Technology and the Role of the Indian Ocean Fishery Survey and Development Programme

Ivan J. Silva
Senior Fishery Officer
Indian Ocean Fishery Survey and
Development Programme
FAO of the United Nations

As the title implies, the scope of this chapter is limited (1) to the Indian Ocean, and (2) to the role of the Indian Ocean Fishery Survey and Development Programme. In particular, this paper will deal with how this Programme assists the developing countries in resource exploitation, in dealing with more advanced countries or in dealing with each other on a joint basis, the range of services provided by the Programme, and how these are utilized.

The questions connected with the transfer of technology to developing countries—such as whether technology should be imitative or innovative, the degree of adaptability and ability of the recipient countries to absorb such technology, the costs of transfer, the factors affecting transfer, the need for training, etc.—have been exhaustively dealt with by various U.N. Advisory Committees on Science and Technology and in many publications.[a]

While I do not wish to tread the same ground, it will be obvious that some of the questions dealt with in these publications will figure overtly or im-

---

[a]Hamlisch,—"The Influence of Social and Economic Factors on Technological Change in the Fishery Sector," in Fishing Boats of the World, Vol. 3; Robin Clarke,—"The Great Experiment—Science and Technology in the Second U.N. Decade," U.N. 1971; Jones,—"The Role of Science and Technology in Developing Countries," OUP 1971; R.S. Eckaus,—"Technological Change in the Less Developed Countries in Development of the Emerging Countries," Washington, D.C.: Brookings Institution.

plicitly as I attempt to portray the role of the Indian Ocean Programme as an instrument of change and modernization in the field of fisheries. It will also be obvious that the Indian Ocean Programme is one among many agencies of change. The private sector, bi- and multilateral arrangements also play a significant role in the transfer of technology. Technology as interpreted by me is not being used in purely the primary sense of applied science but also in the wider sense, which is one of its meanings, as the totality of the means employed by a people to provide itself with the objects of a material culture. The concept therefore includes machinery, the ability to use it, training, new management methods, organization, changes in tools, techniques, methods, and attitudes—in short, the total modernization process.

The countries of the Indian Ocean region are inhabited by almost one-third of the world's population. The large majority of this population is poor and ill-fed. They have an annual protein deficit of three million tons, but scientists believe that protein supplies can be increased by about six times with existing technology. While the larger share of the fisheries is in the hands of the peoples of the region, and is mainly subsistence in nature, the more lucrative fisheries such as tuna are heavily exploited by outsiders, notably Japan, Korea, and Taiwan. The share of non-Indian Ocean countries as of 1971 was about 8 percent and is expected to increase in the future. With large areas of the other oceans reaching almost the maximum exploitable level, there has been a tremendous surge of activity in the Indian Ocean. One of the functions of the Programme, therefore, particularly at this stage, is to help ensure that the countries bordering the Indian Ocean also benefit from this activity.

The entire region suffers from all the classic characteristics of underdevelopment—low nutritional levels, low levels of skills, unemployment, low purchasing power, lack of capital, underdeveloped infrastructure and high rates of population growth. Unless development in any field is seen in relation to the total problem of underdevelopment, attempts made in isolation will have only a marginal effect at best. As the Plan for Fishery Development in the Indian Ocean states, "Fishery development should be viewed first and foremost as part of general economic development leading to generally increasing standards of living, and to the diffusion of economic well-being (including the ability to acquire needed amounts of protein) throughout the population." Fishery development in this sense, therefore, includes the following objectives: (1) to contribute to general economic development, including especially the stimulation of investment from international as well as national sources in the fisheries sector; (2) to provide a source of foreign exchange; (3) to contribute to various socioeconomic needs; and (4) to provide a needed source of protein.

The Indian Ocean Fishery Survey and Development Programme, an interregional project, funded by the UNDP and executed by FAO, commenced operations in 1972, after two years of preparatory work. The Programme is primarily investment oriented and is meant to help the countries of the region help themselves. This special emphasis is a sign of the awareness of the FAO that we are fast approaching the stage where the activities of the Department of Fisheries in the region are moving away from the fundamental ones of research and re- source surveys to the more complicated ones of exploitation and utilization of such resources with all their attendant problems of capital, expertise, choice of techniques, skills, infrastructure, markets, and so on. In this context, the types of technology that should be transferred or developed and the means of such transfer have to be carefully evaluated. This is not to say that there has been no transfer of technology before the Programme was instituted. The process of technological change is a continuous one and the FAO among others has been an active instrument of transfer. One only states that there has been an intensifica- tion and concentration of effort with the inauguration of the Programme. The Programme has become one of the main channels through which the expertise, skills, capital, and knowhow are sought to be transferred.

In meeting this challenge, the Programme has spelled out the follow- ing particular objectives:

1. To facilitate the flow of information in order to make projects more effec- tive and to avoid duplication of effort
2. To identify and assist in development of country and regional preinvestment projects
3. To prepare investment feasibility studies and to make liaison with potential investors such as private industry, government, and development banks
4. To train personnel
5. To monitor and assess work done by various projects developed under the Programme
6. To supervise and generally coordinate resource surveys, which will mainly be implemented by mobilizing resources (particularly vessels and technical staff) through voluntary contributions from member countries of the Com- mission and by coordinating relevant activities of existing projects, as well as those of new projects to be developed; to conduct surveys under UNDP funding.

The underlying assumption of the Indian Ocean Programme in its work is that there must be a recognition of geographic, ethnic, and cultural fac- tors, changing environmental demands, the opinions of national decision makers, and changes in the economic environment. There is also an awareness that tech- nologies found successful in Western developed nations cannot be transferred indiscriminately or nonselectively either, because they do not meet the urgent problems, are too expensive, are not suitable, or will result in unnecessary social and economic dislocation. We try to avoid, therefore, the situation such as oc- curred in one Asian country where the installation of expensive automatic signal- ling equipment was advised by foreign experts to improve rail transport when the major problem was an acute shortage of rolling stock and locomotives, and not delayed trains. In this context too the emphasis of the Programme as I see it is not to push the modern to the ultramodern but to concentrate on such activities that will help the large number of traditional fishermen to move from subsistence fisheries to commercial operations.

Technology can be purchased in the marketplace but this can be very expensive and, for a technologically backward country, can be wasteful in that, lacking experience and proper guidance, unsuitable technology may be imported. A particular Asian country desirous of venturing into fish canning bought machinery suitable for tuna when what was required was machinery for sardine and other small fish. Although the initial price for the machinery was very attractive (a factor influencing the purchase), the costs of adaptation and the fact that to date the machinery has not been able to operate at full capacity has made the investment a very expensive one. In another country a fishmeal factory has been constructed and is lying unused because no proper study was made of the availability of the raw material in sufficient quantities. Obviously, the machinery salesman had been very persuasive.

Neither is technical autarchy possible, and if fishery development is to take place there is a need for inputs in the forms of skills, techniques, and capital from the developed world as well as accessibility to the markets of the developed world.

Interesting questions arise at this point: What is the best method for transfer, excluding the institutional one? Is it from the top downwards—that is, is it to be through elites who will be the leaders of change? If so, will we not help to create privileged groups and perpetuate unhealthy and socially undesirable distinctions? Will this process be a slow one? On the other hand, there is the Chinese experience where training of the large mass of people was considered essential so that the obstacles to change in the form of ignorant masses were virtually eliminated.

The other aim of the Indian Ocean Programme in assisting in the introduction of technology and facilitation of change is to reduce a country's dependence on imported technology in the form of experts. It therefore encourages and assists fishery scientists and administrators, apart from taking up training in the developed world and attending seminars, etc., to work with the Programme as short-term consultants on specific subjects or problems in areas relevant to their countries. We have had in the recent past a scientist from Sri Lanka to work on a proposal for small boat tuna long-lining and another from Indonesia on shrimp fisheries. This activity will continue.

The staff of the Programme consists of six professional members representing various disciplines who are expected to work as a team and bring a multidisciplinary approach to the problems. In addition, consultants are engaged in specific fields where the Programme feels the need for special skills and knowledge, either from within the Department of Fisheries or from outside. The services of the technical staff are also available as time and money permit to the member countries on request. In this connection, staff members have visited the United Arab Emirates, Thailand, Indonesia, Burma, and Ethiopia to prepare specific proposals or to conduct preinvestment studies.

Inclusive of "A Plan for Fishery Development in the Indian Ocean," on which all the major activities are based, the Programme has published 27 papers on various aspects of fishery development in the region, ranging from resources, fishery harbors, and landing places to marketing and economic planning for fisheries. (A detailed list of publications is given in Appendix 7-1.) Two more papers are in press on the fishery resources of the Upper Bay of Bengal and on the economic feasibility of small boat tuna long-lining in the Indian Ocean. These publications contain much information on the status of fisheries, possible lines of development, and also indicate investment opportunities. They are therefore of particular value to the countries of the region as well as to potential investors. Copies have been circulated to international fishing companies, investment institutions, and regional banks. The Programme thus serves as a clearinghouse of information, filling a vital communication gap.

As stated earlier, the Programme has also undertaken a number of individual studies on request. This service is being increasingly resorted to by member countries, and at the end of 1972 it had identified and formulated development proposals which, if acted upon, involve a total investment of approximately $37 million. Broken down roughly into categories, the proposed investment envisages about $11 million in private or government funds, $6 million in government contribution in kind, $11 million from bilateral sources, and about $8 million from the UNDP.

Among the activities of special interest is the study undertaken by the Programme to examine the best possible vehicle to transfer technology in keeping with the social, cultural, and political situations of the countries of the region. A large majority of these countries have just emerged from a colonial status and quite naturally are eager to ensure that their financial and economic destinies are in their own hands. At the same time there are pressing needs and urgent development problems, all of which cannot be handled unilaterally by the countries concerned as they not only lack capital but also the technology and the managerial skills. Some mechanism has to be found which, while providing for the import of these vitally necessary inputs, will preserve the economic integrity and independence of the countries concerned. Direct foreign investment through wholly-owned subsidiaries of international corporations is not always the most welcome. Apart from the suspicion and fear of such large international organizations, it can be said that they have not generally taken too active a role in the development of local skills, both technical and managerial, and there is in fact very little transfer of technology to the locals.

A common form of technology transfer is through patents and licenses, but as experience has shown, this has become very expensive due to excessive royalty payments demanded by the transferor and excessive prices charged for components and materials and for the services of technicians. It has been estimated that one country in the region paid out as much as $100 million per annum for patents and licences. The whole question of patents and licenses and their costs has been dealt with at length in various U.N. publications and other literature; one of the remedies suggested is the establishment of national technology transfer centers linked to planning bodies, industries, and particularly the universities to assist the smaller firms which cannot afford the costs of transfer.

Perhaps the best means of affecting such transfers would be through international bodies, but while transfers do take place through them, the ability to do so is limited by their very nature. They are not the custodians of technology and are not always in possession of the latest information and knowledge. Rightly or wrongly, technology—particularly in the forms of machinery and equipment—belongs to individual corporations or organizations; the patent system precludes their use by others. The only way to obtain such technology would therefore be through some joint arrangement. The type of technology in the fishing industry would include machinery and equipment, techniques, and managerial and technical expertise. A few countries have taken the more difficult road of shutting themselves off completely from the rest of the world and developing their own methods—an attitude of autarchy. But this is possible only in countries which have both the resources and the determination to do it. This could also mean a greater time lag, though not necessarily so. The Indian Ocean Programme's approach is based on the conviction that time is running out for these countries—the problems are urgent and time is therefore of the essence.

Against this background a special study is in progress of the mechanism of joint ventures in the field of fisheries. There are a large number of joint ventures in the region, and in fisheries this has been a favorite mechanism for the exploitation of high value fishery products, notably shrimp and lobster where the resources are within national jurisdiction and the skills and expertise of the foreign partner are combined with the labor and other inputs of the local partner. Not all joint ventures, however, have been successful or satisfactory. It is the view of some that joint capital participation is not necessarily more favorable to developing countries because of the short life span of such ventures, the conditions that are stipulated in the agreements for early transfer of complete ownership and control to the local partner, and the withholding of certain critical elements by the foreign partner—all of which are not conducive to developing a healthy relationship. Consequently, it has been suggested that it may be more useful to engage the services of industrial and management consultants under special terms and conditions such as responsibility to the local directorate and the retention of part of the remuneration for payment at a later date in order to ensure that a viable concern has been established that could operate even after the departure of the foreign experts. Closely allied to this study is a study already in progress on government-operated cooperatives and fishery enterprises and a review of currency evaluation problems in the region. We believe that the joint venture study, together with the two other studies referred to, will be of practical use to the countries of the region, not only in deciding on the institutional arrangements for development where foreign capital, expertise, and markets are involved but also in deciding what kinds of pitfalls should be avoided.

One of the assumptions underlying the Programme is the importance of building institutions. Institutions are comprised of the men who make them, and their usefulness depends largely on the quality of such men. Emphasis has, therefore, been given to special manpower training programs, updating the training of existing staffs of fisheries administrations and managements in private firms, on-the-job training, etc. Training has long been recognized as a vital element in all development programs by the FAO, and the Indian Ocean Programme is continuing this practice with perhaps a change in emphasis from administrators and biologists to business managers and technicians.

A further important activity is the promotion of joint mutually beneficial proposals such as the Cooperative Fishery Survey and Development Project in the Gulf lying between Iran and the Arabian Peninsula and in the Gulf of Oman. The project, which is to be carried out cooperatively by the countries bordering the Gulfs with assistance in the form of experts, is intended to (1) provide information on the kinds, distribution, and abundance of commercially important (or potentially so) demersal and pelagic fishes; (2) provide assistance in the introduction and demonstration of appropriate kinds of gear and in the solution of handling, processing, distribution, and marketing problems; (3) provide assistance in the resource management with initial attention on shrimp; and (4) provide assistance in the establishment of statistical systems to supply information for the development of economically viable fisheries. Five of the countries have agreed to participate in the project and steps are being taken to appoint a project manager who will commence the preproject activities.

In the course of our examination of the fisheries situations in many countries, we have found that a major constraint on the development of fisheries is the lack of knowledge of proper handling, processing, and marketing of fish. A considerable increase in income could be ensured without increasing production by observing certain basic principles of fish handling and preservation so that the value added could be increased. To meet this shortcoming, the Programme has prepared a proposal entitled "A Fishery Product-Identification Processing Marketing Vessel." This multipurpose operation would not only introduce techniques, it would also train fishermen and assist in the preparation of marketable products, particularly for exports markets. The interesting feature of this proposal is that the training vessel will visit countries in the region and attempt to serve a wider cross-section of the fishing populations.

What has been stated above is, in the main, a rather broad outline of the activities of the Programme in the light of the topic under discussion. The Programme carries out its work acutely conscious of the sociological and economic problems that are encountered in the process of introducing technological change. The main thrust of the Programme's effort is to identify the critical areas and attempt to provide or suggest the type of technology most suited to the situation and which, hopefully, can produce the best results. Whether technological change should be introduced from the top downwards through existing elites or whether, like the Chinese model, technological change should be introduced to the vast masses of society are questions of methodology, which, though agitating our minds, cannot be taken up at this stage.

As Guy Hunter(3) put it,

> At present, countries try to give some technical elements to developing societies, sometimes even a whole package—techniques, banks, trade unions, democracy, cooperatives, country council, and modern (Western) business management. But in the strange soil of Africa or Asia these transplants behave most strangely; some die, some grow gigantically, some become diseased; some sweet-fruited here give bitter fruit in their new home. It was painfully obvious that this was to be expected. Society is not made up of discrete factors—social, political, economic, religious; these are our own analytical abstractions. Society is a whole in which these elements are almost totally fused in a pattern of daily activities, values, and relationships in which all elements are simultaneously present and interacting. They cannot all be swept away at a blow or changed one by one.

The role of the Indian Ocean Programme is that of a catalytic agent. It cannot, with its limited funds and staff, hope to bring about major changes by itself. However, through its intensive study and knowledge of the fisheries situation and the economic, social, and political framework within which fisheries can develop, it is in a position to identify critical areas and critical needs, to influence change, to help create the conditions for change, and also to assist in bringing together inputs from the West and the factors in the region in order to develop fisheries in an orderly, economic, and rational manner for the benefit of the countries of the region.

Finally, one question of a speculative nature remains to be asked. I have not at any stage attempted to discuss the validity of the concept that technological change *is* necessary, as that is outside the scope of this paper and this is not the place or time to discuss it. Whether we like it or not, the dominant culture today which pervades the world is the Western materialist one and every society is striving to attain the goals of this ethic. Technology as I see it is an essential part of this culture and in the process of introducing technological change we are in fact introducing alien culture as well. This is a major reason for the difficulties encountered in introducing this kind of change. I am not making out a case for preserving what might appear to be idyllic, pastoral societies—the reality is harshly different. I am only posing a question which I am not attempting to answer.

Changes have to be introduced with great care and understanding (the need for empathy), with the realization, as Steinbeck and Ricketts(7) have said in their profoundly moving human document *The Sea of Cortez*, that "there [are] material prices for material things, but one cannot buy kindness with money." Five hundred years ago, in the wake of the white man's invasions of the third world, came Christianity, also considered a liberating and modernizing agent at that time. Most of these countries are now politically independent but the cross on which these societies have been impaled remains.

BIBLIOGRAPHY FOR CHAPTER 7

1. Clarke, R., The Great Experiment—Science and Technology in the Second United Nations Decade (U.N., 1971).

2. Eckaus, R.S., Technological Change in the Less Developed Areas in Development of the Emerging Countries (Washington, D.C.: Brookings Institution).

3. Hunter, G., Some Western Transplants Yield Strange Fruits, FAO, *Ceres*, Vol. 5 No. 1, 1972.

4. Jones, G., The Role of Science and Technology in Developing Countries (OUP, 1971).

5. Marr, J.C., Management and Development of Fisheries in the Indian Ocean (FAO, 1972).

6. Marr, J.C., *et al.*, A Plan for Fishery Development in the Indian Ocean (FAO, 1971).

7. Steinbeck, J. and E.F. Rickets, *The Sea of Cortez*, (New York: Viking Press, 1941).

Appendix to Chapter 7

PUBLICATIONS OF THE INDIAN OCEAN PROGRAMME

1. A plan for fishery development in the Indian Ocean. Marr, John C., D.K. Ghosh, Giulio Pontecorvo, Brian J. Rothschild and Arlon R. Tussing. IOFC/DEV/71/1, 78 p. FAO, Rome.
2. Survey of Resources in the Indian Ocean and Indonesian area. Cushing, D.H. IOFC/DEV/71/2, 123 p. FAO, Rome.
3. Stock assessment. Hayasi, S. IOFC/DEV/71/3, 34 p. FAO, Rome.
4. Management. Gulland, J.A. IOFC/DEV/71/4, 8 p. FAO, Rome.
5. Fishery statistics. Banerji, S.K. IOFC/DEV/71/5, 15 p. FAO, Rome.
6. Field surveys and the survey and charting of resources. Alverson, Dayton L. IOFC/DEV/71/6, 22 p. FAO, Rome.
7. Harvesting: Experimental fishing and introduction of alternative techniques. Hiebert, Robin Ann and Dayton L. Alverson. IOFC/DEV/71/7, 30 p. FAO, Rome.
8. Existing fishing vessels and future development possibilities. Guckian, W.J., N.W. van den Hazel, N.F. Fujinami and L.O. Engvall. IOFC/DEV/71/8, 20 p. FAO, Rome.
9. Reconnaissance survey of fishery harbours and landing places. W.J. Guckian and N.W. van den Hazel. IOFC/DEV/71/9, 35 p. FAO, Rome.
10. Reconnaissance survey of fishing vessel construction and repair facilities. Guckian, W.J., N.W. van den Hazel, N.F. Fujinami and L.O. Engvall. IOFC/DEV/71/10, 31 p. FAO, Rome.
11. Storage, processing, and distribution of fish. Moal, R.A. IOFC/DEV/71/11, 137 p. FAO, Rome.

12. Economic development of the Indian Ocean countries: problems, policies, prospects. Clement, M.O. IOFC/DEV/71/12, 20 p. FAO, Rome.
13. Fishery economics. Tussing, Arlon R. IOFC/DEV/71/13, 41 p. FAO, Rome.
14. International trade-tuna. Broadhead, Gordon C. IOFC/DEV/71/14, 27 p. FAO, Rome.
15. International trade-shrimp. Peckham, Charles J. IOFC/DEV/71/15, 19 p. FAO, Rome.
16. International trade-crab. Alverson, Franklin G. IOFC/DEV/71/16, 20 p. FAO, Rome.
17. International trade-fish meal. Franklin G. Alverson and Gordon C. Broadhead. IOFC/DEV/71/17, 42 p. FAO, Rome.
18. International trade-groundfish. Lanier, Barry V. IOFC/DEV/71/18, 32 p. FAO, Rome.
19. Economic planning for fishery development. Tussing, Arlon R. IOFC/DEV/71/19, 26 p. FAO, Rome.
20. Assessment of stocks of demersal fish off the west coasts of Thailand and Malaysia. Isarankura, Andhi P. IOFC/DEV/71/20, 20 p. FAO, Rome.
21. Crustacean fisheries of the west coast of India. Joseph, K.M. IOFC/DEV/71/21, 23 p. FAO, Rome.
22. UNDP/FAO fishery projects in the Indian Ocean region. Silva, L.I.J. IOFC/DEV/72/22, 41 p. FAO, Rome.
23. An economic feasibility study of a trawl fishery in the gulf lying between Iran and the Arabian Peninsula. Bromiley, Peter S. IOFC/DEV/72/23, 64 p. FAO, Rome.
24. Some introductory guidelines to management of shrimp fisheries. Gulland, J.A. IOFC/DEV/72/24, 12 p. FAO, Rome.
25. Plan for a pelagic fish assessment survey North Arabian Sea. Midttun, L., O. Nakken, G. Saetersdal and O.J. Østvedt. IOFC/DEV/72/25, 23 p. FAO, Rome.
26. Marketing of Red Sea demersal fish. Bromiley, Peter S. IOFC/DEV/72/26, 23 p. FAO, Rome.
27. A review of the Indonesian shrimp fishery and its present developments. Unar, M. IOFC/DEV/72/27, 20 p. FAO, Rome.
28. Fishery resources of the upper Bay of Bengal. West, W.Q.B. IOFC/DEV/72/28, ... p. FAO, Rome. (in press)
29. Economic feasibility of small boat tuna longlining in the Indian Ocean. Sivasubramaniam, K. IOFC/DEV/72/29, ... p. FAO, Rome. (in press)

Discussion

Nweihed: I have one question for Dr. Silva. I understand there are two fishing councils that regulate fishing activities in the Indian Ocean. One of them, I believe, was created in the wake of World War II, the Indo-Pacific Fishing Council, and the other was recently formed under the auspices of FAO, which is the IOFCC, the Indian Ocean Fishing Council Commission. May I know, please, if there is any overlapping in the functions and the jurisdictions of each, and if there is none, how do they divide their functions?

Silva: Yes, there are two councils. One is the IPFC, Indo-Pacific Fisheries Council and the other is the Indian Ocean Fishery Commission. Now, the Indian Ocean Fishery Commission was set up by the FAO under Article VI of the FAO Constitution in 1968, and the area of its activity was demarcated to be the entire Indian Ocean. The Indo-Pacific Fisheries Council has now confined its activities to a large extent outside the Indian Ocean region, though of course there is a very close link between the two. There is no conflict as such because both are interested in fisheries development, and there is very much of a correspondence between the two. I am sorry I cannot clarify the legal aspects of these things, but this is the position as it now stands.

Esterly: Mr. Silva's paper was very good in recognizing the social, economic, and political problems which are involved in introducing a new technology and also attempting to bring about technological change, but we had only a few examples of the political problems involved, and I was wondering whether you might just comment on that briefly.

There are many different countries which border the Indian Ocean area. There are those which are African and Arab, as well as India and now Pakistan and Bangladesh, and then of course we have Malaysia and the countries along the eastern edge of the Indian Ocean. Could you comment on their attitudes to the receipt of this assistance and its political acceptability by the various countries?

Just one more point. Has there been a conflict over the prospect of other countries coming in unilaterally and trying to assist individual countries in the area? I have in mind the attempts by the Japanese to furnish aid and training, and to provide various forms of technical assistance on an individual basis, perhaps to India.

Silva: The position is, as mentioned, that 26 countries have joined this interregional project, they have subscribed to the objectives of the project and they are participating in it actively. Since we cannot possibly, of course, supervise everything that is going on, we try to act as a kind of umbrella. We are aware of all the activities that are taking place, and we try to ensure that even bilateral aid and assistance are either channeled through the Programme or, if not channeled through the Programme, that we are consulted before such aid or proposals are implemented. Of course, we have this problem that some countries or companies make direct contact and we find that the recipient country, in its ignorance, accepts these offers made by outsiders, sometimes to their detriment, which they do not realize until a few years later.

So, we have that problem, certainly. We also find certain banking institutions going to the same region to promote fishery development, to which we do not object, but we have had to point out that if you want to promote fishery development in the region in an international way then you should make use of this Programme, because it is now best equipped to understand and appreciate the problems of the region and to advise whoever is going to provide funds of the best places and the best methods of investing that money for the mutual benefit of both sides. Have I answered you adequately or would you require further elaboration?

Esterly: In my first question, Mr. Silva, I was wondering whether you could make any comment on the public attitude from the various countries in the area towards this kind of assistance and help? In other words, have you overcome most opposition, namely of the political type?

Silva: I think that we are in a more favorable position than an individual country going to give aid to a particular country, because there is no suspicion on the part of the recipient country that there are any strings attached. As you know, there is a kind of phobia in our part of the world, maybe sometimes justified, sometimes unjustified, but there is a phobia that whatever aid that comes is always tied, and that one's independence of action is curtailed. They consequently prefer to deal with an organization which is ostensibly cut off from all this kind of thing.

I know, for instance, that staff members from the Programme are in a better position to visit countries which do not permit certain individual aid agencies entry. We do get entry, and we are in a better position to help those countries since we have this kind of access and contact. I think on the whole it is a most welcome project, and I have found in the course of our activities in the last one and a half years that apart from what we had planned to do ourselves, we have had many requests from the fisheries departments or the governments of the countries of the region to help them to assess certain aid proposals that have come, to help them to evaluate offers made by foreign companies for joint ventures, and so forth. This gives you an idea of the kind of faith they seem to have in the Programme, which I think is a good sign.

Bates: The point was made earlier that it is very difficult to obtain a critical mass of marine technical skills in some of the countries coming out of colonialism. Has FAO given any thought to utilizing the maritime academies of these various parts of the world? Here in the United States our own maritime academies have been wondering whether they shouldn't teach much more than just ship handling. It might be feasible—since operating the ship is probably the single largest cost in fishing—for some of these two million seafaring people of the world who already to down to the sea in ships to be "retreaded" (retrained or reoriented) from just simply moving ships from point A to point B, to using them as marine technology platforms. All the uses of ships could be taught to these people, from the time they are young, by training them in the maritime academy system operated by many of the smaller nations for their naval forces.

One extra statistic: 78 countries now belong to the United Nation's Intergovernmental Maritime Consultative Organization (IMCO) in London. I do not know how many countries are interested in marine fisheries; perhaps not quite so many as that. I do point out, however, that 78 countries already consider themselves seafaring enough to belong to IMCO.

Silva: I think that use could be made of such academies, but there certainly has to be a change in the curricula to reflect the needs of the region, and that would be also an area for study.

Galey: I am interested in the impact of the Programme on the participating countries. Have there been departments of fisheries or natural resources established in the countries bordering on the Indian Ocean that did not exist prior to the Programme's coming into being? Second, could you comment on the increase in skilled manpower—what percentage over, let us say, the last couple of years has been brought about as a result of the Programme—and have there been any significant effects on the social and economic structure: for example, unemployment costs, dislocation of people working formerly with some kind of very simple techniques and then learning how to use other techniques to catch fish? In other words, have there been unemployment problem costs as a result of the Programme?

Silva: I could not quite catch the first question, but I think what you meant was whether there were institutions, whether there was any kind of structure for fisheries existing in certain countries or regions or not.

Galey: Has the Programme helped establish institutions that did not previously exist?

Silva: On that question I can say, "Yes, we have." For instance, in the countries around the gulf lying between Iran and the Arabian peninsula (more familiarly known as the Persian Gulf) there are certain countries there which have had no fisheries administrations or any kinds of structures or institutions, or else very rudimentary ones, and the Programme is now going into that area and is helping to establish or strengthen fisheries administrations. Of course, do not get the impression that this had not been done earlier. This is being done all the time by FAO, Department of Fisheries. What FAO is doing through the Indian Ocean Programme is to concentrate these activities in a particular group of people so that they can pay greater attention to these problems.

Then on the question of the impact on employment. It is very difficult to assess this, but we have been preparing various proposals, and in certain areas—Indonesia for example—we are preparing a number of proposals for development of their fisheries, fish production, etc., which will have an impact on employment; but I am not able to quantify this at this stage. As you know, it all depends on the kind of fisheries you try to bring in. If, for instance, you bring a rather modern type of fishery into an area, the impact on employment is limited in the immediate fishery, but there will be a multiplier effect somewhere else. There is employment that will arise, possibly in some processing industry, in transport, in ice making, and so many other areas. This is very difficult to assess, but I am sure there is some impact.

Certainly there is an improvement in the economic levels of the people and consequently also on employment. I do not think there are unemployment cost problems surfacing at this stage, but this will certainly be a problem and a consequence that will have to be kept in mind in formulating development plans. As I explained in my paper, while we cannot foresee every eventuality, the Programme, in the formulation of proposals, seeks inter alia both to create more employment and minimize social and economic dislocation.

Johnson: I think, Mr. Silva, you have made really a marvelous contribution here because the things you are talking about help us to see better the significant role which these law of the sea meetings are performing. In other words, at one end of the spectrum we can say that the lawyers are concerned about international matters, but at another end of the spectrum, you, Mr. Silva, are pointing out the various economic development aspects and suggesting ways that these two can come together. As I see it, there is a definite coming together on these. I would suggest, in the form of a question to you, Have you looked into other aspects of scientific and technical efforts related to the problems that you get into when you go out further into the water? Here I am talking about the making and use of bathymetric maps, for example, which use the sciences of hydrography and geodesy, and which help to lay out boundaries. These boundaries become extremely important with respect to law of the sea. Thus I would ask if your organization is making efforts along these lines?

Silva: Quite frankly, no—I mean from that angle. But we are certainly interested in certain problems that arise. I was remarking to some of my colleagues here, that in the gulf lying between Iran and the Arabian peninsula, where we intend to start a cooperative fishery survey and development project, there is a shrimp resource which has been overfished. The problem is to bring the countries together to conserve the resources, to prevent a waste of capital there, and to ensure that the fishermen have a certain standard of living. Demarcations of areas of fishing, areas of national jurisdiction, will become important in this context.

From our angle—the angle of economics and biology—there are certain definite steps that can be taken. But we have the more intricate legal and political problem of trying to get these countries together to define what their areas of interest are, how much they should contribute to the project, how much they should get out of it; some of these have to be legally defined now. To that extent we have a certain interest in the legal aspects, but your specific interest— the demarcation of boundaries and things like that—while we are interested in what is happening and will use the results of such work, we are really not involved right now.

* * * * * *

REPORT OF DISCUSSION GROUP LEADERS

One of the most valuable aspects of the Law of the Sea Institute's annual conference is the period of informal discussion and debate that follows the formal presentation of papers and panels. There is never time enough for all of the many participants who wish to ask questions, raise issues, or express viewpoints. In an effort to allow more time for free and open discussion, an experiment was tried last year at the Seventh Annual Conference whereby one afternoon was set aside to be devoted entirely to small discussion groups.

This year the concept was expanded somewhat to allow additional time and to provide, through the formal presentations, substantive bases for discussion. Participants in the Eighth Annual Conference were divided into eight groups of about 25 persons each. An attempt was made to balance the groups by equally distributing the visitors from foreign countries, representatives of various disciplines, occupations, special interests, etc., wherever feasible. The groups met following the presentation of a lead-off paper. They were provided with a suggested list of questions for discussion topics. In order to encourage free expression of ideas and opinions, no record was kept of what transpired in these meetings. The leaders of the eight discussion groups were:

> Francis Cameron, University of Rhode Island
> Henry Esterly, CUNY-NYC Community College
> Margaret Galey, Purdue University
> Albert Koers, University of Utrecht

John Logue, Villanova University
Roger Mesznik, Columbia University
Joseph Nye, Harvard University
Giulio Pontecorvo, Columbia University
Atwood C. Wolf, Attorney, New York City

After the convening of the discussion groups on two afternoons, all group leaders met to evaluate the effectiveness of this type of conference activity. Following is a summary of some of the comments made by the leaders during this meeting.

There are several purposes for having small discussion groups. One of these is to increase participation; another is to provide a change of pace enabling people to face each other and talk freely rather than sit in the auditorium and be lectured at continuously. One of the principal purposes is to give people a chance to speak without having their words taken down for the record, since the rest of the conference is recorded.

The arithmetic of participation through the groups is interesting. If an average of six persons in each of the eight groups say a fair amount, this means some 50 people have participated in the discussions. On the other hand, in the regular sessions there may be only five or six questions asked from the floor. The discussion groups are thus expanding the chance for individuals to talk about a subject without having to make a speech on the floor. Still, there are many who do not participate; getting them to talk is another matter. It might help to prepare participants for discussion by giving them a small piece of homework, such as a reprint of an essay to read and focus on as a takeoff point. This might assure a certain amount of general background and add self-confidence among participants for discussion.

One of the things that conference planners are concerned about is the use made of the foreign participants who are brought here as guests of the institute. Why not be both pragmatic and substantive by asking some of the foreign participants if they would be prepared to speak for five minutes and comment on an article being sent out? Use an article which is readable, has some good points and some controversial points, and have the foreign guest speak informally from notes for a few minutes at the beginning of each discussion group. This would add interest, get the discussion rolling, and possibly provide something for the transcript.

Some participants did not feel competent enough to discuss technical subjects such as transfer of technology, and were not willing to contribute. There were only a few with very much real knowledge of the problems of technology in the marine field. When the conversation turned to political aspects, several other persons developed a participating interest; even those who remained silent seemed more interested in this area than in, for example, the economics of fishing out of a stern trawler.

In discussing the complex problems of the general Law of the Sea Conference, one person suggested that not everyone should be allowed to vote; this statement became the basis for a lively discussion. The following day another participant asked, "How did the mutual assistance issue ever get into the law of the sea question anyway? I mean, it really does not belong." This also made a very interesting discussion, which involved a lot of people.

There seemed to be general agreement that the potential for revenue from the deep seabed is not so great, and that sometimes it has been purposely exaggerated, perhaps to influence the acceptance of a regime for the seabed. On the other hand, if it is not as important financially, the nations of the world might be persuaded to adopt a regime for this one part of the entire ocean space area—a step toward what many nations, maybe the majority of nations, want; this might also be acceptable to the larger powers, and so on. In other words, if we can get an agreement on this one area—even if not much is gained by it or even if it is not the solution to the whole ocean problem—it is a step in the direction of the world community's having some kind of say in what happens there.

One group discussed the functional approach to the seabed regime, and also the idea of tying in zone definition with the international seabed regime. Whatever definition is chosen, countries which tend to lose from such a definition or to gain less than other countries should be compensated proportionally in whatever kind of international regime might be developed for the seabed.

In discussing technology transfer to LDC's, it was argued that the technology of the deep seabed is held by only about four countries, that it is not a sensible or practical technology to transfer intergovernmentally, and that therefore the demands for transfer of technology in this area are probably bargaining ploys. It was felt that marketing controls are undesirable and infeasible, that the threat of driving some minerals out of their markets is probably greatly exaggerated, and that there is not a huge resource which will come in all of a sudden.

One point discussed at length from Dr. Aguilar's paper was the role of the authority: whether it would be involved in exploitation directly, or involved in joint ventures with governments, or should it be an organization for holding options or collecting royalties; and should it do this directly or by governments as intermediaries? There were comparisons to joint ventures in technology by governments in other areas, with generally pessimistic conclusions. The roles of the authority were felt to be (1) to hold options, (2) consider externalities—the pollution effects of the option principle—and (3) to provide information to perfect the option process so that governments would have some idea of what they are doing. There were differences of opinion on the voting and representation within the authority and on the principle of one state, one vote.

One group felt that in technology transfer there are certain areas in which the state could be more effective, and other areas in which international organizations could be more effective. While many participants took a dim view with respect to the capabilities of international organizations, there were felt to be two areas where the latter could play an important role. The first is initiating the process of building up initial capabilities, identifying initial needs. The second is the elimination of certain suspicion, which could exist on the interstate level. The question of technology transfer was felt to be somewhat outside the law of the sea debate proper, having crept in just as a quid pro quo deal for the freedom of scientific research. For that reason the United Nations, and all people, should be reluctant to deal with technology transfer problems because this is a new issue, while on the other hand there is an established body of knowledge in other areas in all United Nations committees. The United Nations Seabeds Committee, for example, may not be using all available expertise.

Why is transfer of technology being discussed in the law of the sea context? Many felt that it is essentially for political purposes—a way for states to stake a claim when they do not know quite what is there or what they have. The claim would be staked in vague terms and would have very little effect on the major form of transfer of technology. It is necessary to distinguish between proprietary technology and technology that is readily available for intergovernmental transfer; it seems that intergovernmental organizations could affect the terms on which proprietary technology is transferred, but could not affect the transfer itself very much.

There may be some forms of transfer of technology that would be entered into for political bargaining reasons but that might be suboptimal from a long-term local point of view. There is a possibility of perverse effects on the receiving country in which there is a net loss because the opportunity costs of the capital and high level manpower tied up are very high. For example, if a number of developing countries turned to increased distant water fishing capacity, it might turn out to be a source of conflict, and thus suboptimal from a local point of view over a ten-year period.

There was an interesting reaction to the oft-mentioned statement that "if the LDC's would develop a good plan for this or that, we would raise the money for it and give it to them." It was pointed out that in a way this is a very unjust request, because the LDC's are expected to have much better long-range social plans for their own economic development than any European or North American country has. They are expected to have plans for different industries, etc., ranging over ten or fifteen years! Yet nobody expects the United States or European countries to have such plans for different segments of their own. This point makes an important impact on the outlook of different help programs.

An American lawyer in one group stated that decisions about technology transfer would ultimately be made by lawyers; an American engineer countered that scientists would be the ones to decide what technology was to be transferred. There seemed to be little concern here with social responsibility, spinoffs, or what the impact would be on groups of people.

Should we assume that technology transfer is a good thing—or is it, as was mentioned in one paper, a harsh reality? Consensus seemed to be that if the developing countries choose it, it is their decision. In the field of marine technology specifically, we are concerned with what technology is available to be transferred, and what the needs are of the developing countries. We are also concerned with where marine technology transfer fits into the law of the sea and into the seabed authority, for example. Perhaps there could be a revenue sharing plan with an arrangement whereby developing countries make their own decisions as far as what projects they want, and set their own priorities. There was a real effort on the part of many discussants to try to determine what the needs of developing countries were. Unfortunately there seem to be too few representatives of developing countries who could respond in terms of defining what those needs would be.

Part Three

Chapter Eight

Islands: Normal and Special Circumstances

Robert D. Hodgson[1]
The Geographer
Bureau of Intelligence and Research
U.S. Department of State

INTRODUCTION

Since the Geneva conventions on the sea and the shelf were signed in 1958, world states have directed much of their attention to the uses of the sea and the seabed. In the past five years, political leaders, diplomats, and lawyers have debated widely on the establishment of a limit between national and international jurisdictions for the peaceful exploitation of ocean resources. While this grand design of maritime jurisdiction continues to be discussed freely, boundary experts grapple with the language of the Geneva conventions while groping for solutions for the limits between national sovereignties or jurisdictions.

The conventions left many unanswered questions. While a precise seaward limit of national jurisdiction on the seabed remains one of the more important of these, the rational development of potentially the most fruitful area—the shelf—has been limited by questions concerning the sovereign and jurisdictional limits between adjacent and near opposite states. Germany, the Netherlands, and Denmark had to refer their insoluble differences to the International Court of Justice for adjudication. The Court's judgment, while troublesome in that it raised almost as many questions as it answered, served to settle the immediate dispute. The solution, however, was not detailed by the Court. Rather it

---

[1] This paper does not represent the official position of the United States government.

laid down general ground rules and left the states to delimit the precise boundaries through good sense and cooperation.

Progress toward the solution of maritime boundary issues requires the rationalization of many vexing technical questions. Basically, these topics involve the vagaries of geographic, geologic, and hydrographic realities, which often appear to favor one state over another. The German-Danish-Dutch problem rested on the shape of the German coastline. While both the Danish and Dutch shores faced the North Sea convexly, the German shore fell away concavely. As a consequence, reliance on the equidistant principle developed from these differing baselines would have been most disadvantageous to Germany. Feeling that an inequity existed, the Federal Republic refused to negotiate, and shelf resource development languished for the three states.

Other technical questions involve the value of ocean "deeps" as natural limits. Does a particular area 300 meters deep represent a local aberration in the shelf which should be ignored, or does it mark the natural limit to the prolongation of a particular state's continental shelf? The resolution of the issue will require time and delay development. However, the single most troublesome natural feature to cloud the maritime limits field has proven to be islands—islands as basepoints, islands and maritime boundaries, islands as atoll, islands as archipelagos, islands as islands. The issues are pervasive and troublesome.

Unfortunately, conventions and other diplomatic accords negotiated between opposing points of view tend to reflect the least common denominator of compromise. Specific language is diluted to avoid dispute; technical points are not discussed. The Geneva conventions do not deviate from the norm. The International Law Commission and others perceived even before the final agreement on the conventions that islands would raise thorny questions. In the bodies of the agreements, islands have received general references as normal circumstances of geographic reality. In the lack of specific references, islands have been viewed as special circumstances to be treated uniquely as each situation dictates. From these two views come the problems of the present. Are islands normal or special circumstances? Should they be examined everywhere the same or each as a unique occurrence?

Just as no two individuals are identical, each geographic occurrence is unique. Nevertheless, elements of commonality prevail through all phenomena. To achieve a peaceful and rational use of the sea and the seabed, islands as maritime realities must be examined objectively to determine how they should be regarded or, if necessary, disregarded. Sovereign interests of the near-shore should be examined first, not necessarily because their solutions will be easier, but because they must be established as the bases for the more distant lines and limits. Without a solid foundation, the peaceful uses of the sea cannot prevail. Disputes may embitter nations and peoples and lead to conflict at worst or to delay in needed economic development at best.

GEOGRAPHICAL FACTORS

Conventionally, men view the world as comprising a limited number of continental land masses, variously numbered and grouped. Little argument may be found with the concept of North and South America and Afro-Eurasia as continents. Usually, Australia and Antarctica are included in the general continental category, but certain purists define them as subcontinental in nature. There is no doubt, due to their immense size and extensive configuration, that they may be conceived as "mainlands" of the earth. Mainland areas, grouped in the conventional concept of seven continents, are as shown in Table 8-1.

Smaller in size than continents but situated above mean high water at all times are more than one half million pieces of distinctly subcontinental land territory defined generically as islands. With a combined area exceeding 3,823,000 square miles, they range in size from mere dots or pinnacles, virtually without measurable surface, to extensive masses, such as Greenland, possessing an area of more than 840,000 square miles, greater in size than all but eleven countries of the world. In fact, 61 islands have areas in excess of 4,000 square miles (approximately the area of the independent states of Jamaica, Cyprus, and Lebanon); and at least 123 are larger than 1,000 square miles (approximately the area of Western Samoa and Luxembourg). Table 8-2 follows.

Islands are situated in varied and dissimilar patterns throughout the world. In reality, no two insular arrangements may be considered identical. Islands, nevertheless, are associated with all continents as well as with the open oceans. Insular areas, by the closest continental associations, are as shown in Table 8-3. Approximately 7 percent of the land area of the earth is encompassed by oceanic islands. (The figure would be greater if one were to consider islands in lakes and rivers, but these are essentially beyond the scope of this paper.) Virtually every coastal country possesses islands to a greater or lesser degree, and many countries are totally insular in geography.

Table 8-1. Mainland Areas

Africa	11,732,532 sq. mi.[a]
Antarctica	5,165,000 sq. mi. (ice covered)
Asia	18,506,328 sq. mi.
Europe	2,718,087 sq. mi.
North America	9,362,021 sq. mi.
South America	6,879,450 sq. mi.
Australia	3,302,400 sq. mi.
Total	57,665,818 sq. mi.

aThe areas are in square statute miles: 1 sq. statute miles: 1 sq. statute mile = .755 sq. nautical mile.

Table 8-2. Islands

Area	Size (sq. mi.)
Greenland, Arctic Region	840,000
New Guinea, Oceania	316,856
Borneo, Indonesia	286,967
Madagascar, Indian Ocean	227,800
Baffin, Canadian Arctic	183,810
Sumatra, Indonesia	182,860
Honshu, Japan	88,930
Great Britain, North Atlantic Ocean	88,756
Ellesmere, Canadian Arctic	82,119
Victoria, Canadian Arctic	81,930
Celebes, Indonesia	72,986
South Island, New Zealand	58,093
Java, Indonesia	50,745
North Island, New Zealand	44,281
Cuba, West Indies	44,218
Newfoundland, North Atlantic Ocean	43,359
Luzon, Philippines	40,814
Iceland, North Atlantic Ocean	39,800
Mindanao, Philippines	36,906
Ireland, North Atlantic Ocean	32,596
Novaya Zemlya, Soviet Arctic	31,390
Hokkaido, Japan	29,950
Hispaniola, West Indies	29,530
Sakhalin, Soviet Union	29,344
Tasmania, Australia	26,383
Ceylon, Indian Ocean	25,332
Banks, Canadian Arctic	23,230
Devon, Canadian Arctic	20,861
Tierra del Fuego, South America	18,600
Axel Heiberg, Canadian Arctic	16,671
Kyūshū, Japan	16,215
Melville, Canadian Arctic	16,141
Southampton, Canadian Arctic	15,700
West Spitsbergen, Arctic Region	15,260
New Britain, Oceania	14,592
Formosa, China Sea	13,885
Hainan, South China Sea	13,127
Timor, Indonesia	13,094
Prince of Wales, Canadian Arctic	12,830
Vancouver, Canada	12,408
Sicily, Mediterranean Sea	9,926
Somerset, Canadian Arctic	9,370
Sardinia, Mediterranean Sea	9,301
Shikoku, Japan	7,245
Halmahera, Indonesia	6,870
Prince Patrick, Canadian Arctic	6,696
North East Land, Svalbard	6,350
Bathurst, Canadian Arctic	6,193
Ceram, Indonesia	6,046
Sumbawa, Indonesia	5,965
New Caledonia, Oceania	5,671
Flores, Indonesia	5,513
Samar, Philippines	5,124
King William, Canada	5,062

Table 8-2. (cont.)

Area	Size (sq. mi.)
Bylot, Canadian Arctic	4,968
Negros, Philippines	4,903
Palawan, Philippines	4,500
Panay, Philippines	4,448
Sumba, Indonesia	4,306
Ellef Ringnes, Canadian Arctic	4,266
Jamaica, West Indies	4,232
Hawaii, Oceania	4,030
Cape Breton, Canada	3,970
Bougainville, Solomons	3,880
Mindoro, Philippines	3,794
Prince Charlos, Canada	3,676
Cyprus, Mediterranean Sea	3,572
Komsomolets, Soviet Arctic	3,570
Kodiak, Gulf of Alaska	3,569
Puerto Rico, West Indies	3,435
Corsica, Mediterranean Sea	3,352
Disko, Greenland	3,312
Crete, Mediterranean Sea	3,217
New Ireland, Oceania	3,205
Leyte, Philippines	3,090
Anticosti, Canada	3,066
Wrangel, Soviet Arctic	2,819
Sjaelland, Denmark	2,709
Cornwallis, Canadian Arctic	2,592
Iturup, Kurils	2,587
East Falkland, South Atlantic	2,580
Guadalcanal, Solomons	2,500
Graham, Canada	2,485
Isabella, Galapagos	2,249
Bali, Indonesia	2,243
Prince of Wales, Alaska	2,231
Prince Edward, Canada	2,184
Vanua Levu, Fiji	2,137
Chichagof, Alaska	2,104
West Falkland, South Atlantic	2,038
MacKenzie King, Canadian Arctic	1,949
Edge, Svalbard	1,942
Billiton, Indonesia	1,866
Trinidad, West Indies	1,869
Lombok, Indonesia	1,826
Unimak, Alaska	1,800
Santa Isabel, Solomons	1,800
Amund Ringnes, Canadian Arctic	1,764
Madura, Indonesia	1,762
Buton, Indonesia	1,759
Nunivak, Alaska	1,750 est.
Cebu, Philippines	1,702
Admiralty, Alaska	1,664
Long Island, United States	1,620
San Cristobal, Solomons	1,600
Andros, Bahamas	1,600
Malaita, Solomons	1,572
Kunashir, Kurils	1,548
Coats, Canadian Arctic	1,544

Table 8-2.   (cont.)

Area	Size (sq. mi.)
Bohol, Philippines	1,491
Espiritu Santo, Solomons	1,485
Euboea, Aegean	1,457
South Georgia, South Atlantic	1,450
Majorca, Balearics	1,405
Wetar, Indonesia	1,400
Socotra, Africa	1,400
Kolguyev, Soviet Arctic	1,350
Masbate, Philippines	1,262
Wellington, Chile	1,200
Pines, Cuba	1,182
Gotland, Sweden	1,167
Fyn, Denmark	1,149
Revillagigedo, Alaska	1,120
Moresby, Canada	1,060
Saaremaa, Gulf of Finland	1,046
Zanzibar, East Africa	1,020
Choiseul, Solomons	1,000
Reunion, Indian Ocean	970

Table 8-3.   Insular Areas

Africa	241,782 sq. mi.
Antarctica	7,669 sq. mi.
Asia	1,243,732 sq. mi.
Europe	350,657 sq. mi.
North America	1,569,759 sq. mi.
South America	53,505 sq. mi.
Australia/Oceania	356,206 sq. mi.
Total	3,823,310 sq. mi.

Islands may be situated in all manners and patterns. They may perch immediately adjacent to the continental masses or be dispersed in midocean. They may be found in singular isolation or grouped by dozens, hundreds, or even thousands. They may be arranged in quasigeometric patterns—arc, quadrangles, triangles, polyhedrons, etc.—or randomly strewn across the water surface. Although each island group remains virtually unique, certain generalizations may be made for the sake of simplification and classification. Along the eastern shores of Asia and North America arcuate island chains rim the continents. Although the chains may commence or terminate in near shore areas, they often extend for hundreds of miles seaward from the continental mainlands. In the central and southern Pacific Ocean, islands are randomly but quite regularly scattered in a belt extending from north of the Equator in the northwest to about 30° south latitude in the southeast. The belt does not reach the South American continent.

The Indian Ocean possesses a similar insular dispersion, although in linear rather than arcuate patterns, south of India and adjacent to Burma and Thailand. The Arctic Ocean is virtually ringed with islands, including many of the largest in the world. Little rational arrangement may be found in the remaining areas of the world.

The dispersed and isolated islands, due to their detachment from the evolutionary biologic processes which took place on the continents, tend to have primitive and delicate biotic patterns; their flora and fauna lack the richness and diversity found on the continents. The ecological balance, as a consequence, tends to be finely adapted to climate and soil and readily subject to being damaged or placed into a status of imbalance. In contrast, islands close to the continental shores do not exhibit the same brittleness or spareness of the environmental balance. But islands of the polar regions provide an exception: there, harsh physical factors and conditions prevail to induce precariousness of the biotic balance.

POLITICAL STATUS OF ISLANDS

Just as islands range in geographic and biologic diversity, so do they also encompass the full range of the political spectrum, extending from complete independence to virtually total political dependence. A review of the varied political status of islands is necessary, for certain political polemics on dependent territories, and the degrees of independence or autonomy, have tended to cloud a rational analysis of islands within the law of the sea context. It has been advanced, for example, that certain islands should be considered of lesser importance as base points since they are "colonial" in administration. Abstract and subjective criteria of this nature need not—and should not—be applied to the analysis of islands and their effects. The sword of such an analysis may cut in different ways. It may be argued with equal logic, and perhaps a greater sense of equity, that "colonial" insular territories should have a greater influence to compensate for their low political status.

The colonial argument is obviously based on the premise that most dependent islands are situated offshore from independent, "developing" nations. These islands could be detrimental to the hopes of these nations. The French Comoro Islands, for example, could mask Tanzania from certain seabed areas under an extensive distance boundary criterion. An opposite situation prevails just as commonly. The "colonial" but "developing" Bahama Islands flank the United States, a developed, independent state. Should the Bahama Islands be restricted in their value as base points in any shelf negotiations with the United States?

Moreover, a question of degree of dependence might have to be entered into any formula for the solution of ultimate values. The Comoros are locally autonomous. Should they receive a greater value than islands whose political status inclines more toward a greater dependency on another state? If so, how may we measure the degrees of "independence" and of "dependence" enjoyed by each territory to insure a truly equitable allocation? Can an equitable scale of values really be determined when each political status is, in fact, both unique and dynamic? Political status does not remain constant; laws are continuously modified to increase local independence. If a maritime boundary were to be negotiated with a dependency in which the value of the dependency's base points was reduced, what does equity demand if the territory wins a greater degree of autonomy or achieves independence as a developing state? The constitutional instrument of the French Community, for example, provides for the independence of the Comoros should the local government request it.

Logic indicates that this type of approach to jurisdictional boundaries is fraught with difficulties and would make successful boundary negotiations virtually impossible to attain; litigation could be endless. The dynamics of political development further mitigate against such proposals. A developing state might claim that an inequity would exist only if the revenues from the seabed of a dependency passed entirely, or nearly so, to the administering developed state. This possibility appears unlikely; political justice, the dynamics of political developments, and local autonomy oppose such an arrangement.

Independent Insular States

More than 18 percent of the world's independent states are completely insular in their geography. These states are:

Bahrain	Madagascar
Barbados	Maldives
Republic of China	Malta
Cuba	Mauritius
Cyprus	Nauru
Dominican Republic	New Zealand
Fiji	Philippines
Haiti	Singapore
Indonesia	Sri Lanka (Ceylon)
Iceland	Tonga
Ireland	Trinidad and Tobago
Jamaica	United Kingdom
Japan	Western Samoa

(The Bahamas will enlarge this list on July 10, 1973.)

Moreover, many more—probably a great majority—of the world's islands constitute integral parts of independent states. Some, such as Hawaii (USA), Sicily (Italy), and Corsica (France), form primary administrative divisions of the "mother country," while others, such as the Azores (Portugal), Sjaelland (Denmark), and the Canary Islands (Spain), comprise multiple administrative divisions of the continental states. Most nearshore islands, however, form parts of the primary administrative divisions situated on the adjacent independent mainland, e.g., Long Island (New York, USA), Novaya Zemlya (RSFSR, USSR), Ko Kut (Koh Kong, Cambodia).

Special Relations

Because of geographic separation, special regimes of administration have evolved in recent years to incorporate overseas entities into the standard administrative pattern of the metropole while granting certain exceptions to recognize the unique local character of the territory. France, for example, has created "overseas departments" and "overseas territories." The former include the insular areas of Guadeloupe, Martinique, and Reunion. These overseas departments, in effect, are administered in a manner nearly identical to, and on an equal footing with, the metropolitan departments of France. The overseas territories, which include the insular possessions of St. Pierre and Miquelon, French Polynesia, the Comoros, Wallis and Futuna, and New Caledonia have a unique status because of local conditions. They elect representatives to the French parliament, however, as do the departments. Inhabitants of both the departments and the territories are French citizens and enjoy local representative government.

A second type of special relationship has been developed by Denmark and the Netherlands. In each instance the overseas areas and the "motherland" constitute a "realm." The territories, as integral parts of the realm, are partners in the processes of government; laws of the motherland do not normally apply, however, to the overseas parts of the realm unless approved by local bodies or representatives. Thus a large measure of national autonomy exists, with elected local legislatures or bodies providing for enactments of a specific, local nature or competence. The Faeroes (virtually independent) and Greenland constitute insular parts of the Danish realm, while the six main islands of the Netherlands Antilles form part of the Dutch realm.

Autonomous States

There is a significant group of insular entities which have individual and complete autonomy or local self-government. Normally this category includes detached islands, which have relatively dense, indigenous (and distinct) local populations. They have full jurisdiction over internal affairs although postage, coinage, foreign affairs, and defense normally remain within the domain of the motherland. Puerto Rico (USA), the Cook Islands (NZ), and St. Christopher-Nevis (UK) are examples of locally autonomous states.

Trust Territories

The United Nations trusteeship system, while considerably reduced in number of participants from the immediate postwar years, continues to apply to the completely insular areas of the Trust Territory of the Pacific Islands (USA

administration) and to the Trust Territory of New Guinea. The latter is administered as part of the territory of Papua New Guinea by Australia.

Centrally Administered or Dependent Territories

A large number of small and/or isolated islands is administered cen-
trally from metropole states. Wide variations exist in the form and degree of
government or local self-government, and it is not possible, or useful, to generalize to any great degree on these islands and their institutional arrangements.
However, almost every coastal state possesses islands that fit into the general
category. Certain states administer the territories from the central government,
e.g., Andaman and Nicobar Islands (India), the Northwest Territory (Canada),
and Fernando de Noronha (Brazil). The links with the motherland are direct,
and the indigenous population of the islands is often related to groups found
within the continental parts of the state. In other instances, the territory is administered by a major administrative component of the national state. Such an
insular territory still retains a dependency characteristic, but often the relationship to the national state may be closer than that in the previous category.

Uninhabited and Disputed Islands

Many of the detached or isolated islands of the world are either uninhabited or are populated by nonindigenous populations. Howland, Baker, and
Jarvis Islands (USA), for example, cannot sustain a permanent population due to
the lack of potable water, fertile soils, and/or other physical necessities. The
French Southern and Antarctic Lands (France), Prince Edward and Marion Islands (South Africa), and Midway Islands (USA) are inhabited by scientific,
usually meteorologic, administrative or service personnel. The people, normally,
are rotated periodically from the motherland and are generally citizens of that
country. Some personnel, however, may be drawn from indigenous populations
of adjacent islands. The earnings of these "native" people often represent a significant increment to local earnings.

Finally, certain islands or island groups have obscure titles to ownership or are claimed by more than one nation. Most of the disputed islands are
situated in the Pacific Ocean, but they also are found elsewhere in the world,
e.g., the Red Sea, Persian Gulf, South and East China Seas, etc. Normally, the
disputed islands do not contain indigenous populations, but exceptions—e.g.,
Abu Musa and Big Tumb—do exist.

Countless additional small islands, located near the seaward termini
of international land boundaries, may also be involved in disputes. These prevail
either where numerous islands exist offshore and the boundary delimitation is
terminated at the shore, or they may occur where the international boundaries
are situated in rivers whose mouths are subject to deposition and, as a result, to

seasonal or annual alterations in their beds. Unless boundary surveys are maintained continuously or have been carried seaward to envelop all islands, disputes automatically develop, e.g., Cambodia-Vietnam, Canada-USA, Argentina-Chile. With the exception of the shores of the unclaimed sector of the Antarctic, all islands of the world have been claimed by one or more coastal or insular states.

Summary
As political entities, or parts of entities, islands assume the entire range of political levels of administration from independence to total dependence. Political status, it is strongly believed, should contribute to the value of islands as basepoints; it should not positively detract. To reduce value as basepoints because of political "dependence" would be inequitable and disruptive of good order, due to the transitory nature of political dependence. An exception would involve unoccupied (by an indigenous population) islands that are known to be in dispute. Disputes raised by the delimitation of boundaries based upon insular basepoints should be examined most carefully in the light of historical evidence of the dispute.

ISLANDS AND THE TERRITORIAL SEA

In examining oceanic islands as ingredients in marine boundary determination, we see that they will or may affect (1) the seaward limit of a nation or territory, (2) territorial sea boundaries between adjacent or opposite states, and (3) the limits of jurisdiction on the seabed beyond sovereign territory. There does not appear to be an overriding reason for islands to be treated in precisely the same manner within the two contexts, i.e., sovereign territorial sea and jurisdictional continental shelf/seabed limits. Looking at the issue positively, there may be very good reasons for the differentiation. The territorial sea issue is security oriented, and security applies to all national territory. The shelf and seabed claims, in contrast, are resource oriented. Not all national territory has the same value for resource potential.

For example, a small island may be used as a basepoint for the measurement of the territorial sea but may have no value (beyond the previously stated limit) in the determination of a continental shelf boundary with an adjacent or an opposite state. The Iranian-Saudi Arabian treatment of the islands of Farsi and Arabi illustrates this situation.[1] Each islet has a 12-mile territorial sea except where the distance between them is less than 24 miles. Under these circumstances the "boundary" is the equidistant line; each island is a basepoint for the territorial sea of the two states. However, for the seabed limit of national jurisdiction, the two have no value beyond their own territorial seas. Many examples abound of similar treatment. Certain values, however, may remain constant within both general categories, as will be shown later.

ISLANDS IN THE LAW OF THE SEA CONTEXT—
GEOGRAPHICAL FACTORS

In the Geneva Convention on the Territorial Sea and the Contiguous Zone, islands are defined, cited, or inferred in various articles. Article 10 defines, in paragraph 1, an island as follows: (1) An island is a naturally formed area of land, surrounded by water, which is above water at high tide.[2] The article suggests no size criterion, locational requirement in relation to mainland, or other particular geographical or special condition. The island does need to be *naturally formed*. The use of "formed" rather than "created" raises distinct or potential questions of interpretation. Obviously, the island must be land—dirt, rock, organic matter, or a combination thereof.

However, to maintain navigation channels, states and individuals dredge certain earth materials from the subsoil of rivers, harbors, and other coastal areas. Such material, or spoil, creates problems of disposal; and dredgers, motivated by cost factors, seek a local place in which to dump the spoil. This site often occupies nearby shallow waters. Currents, tides, and other natural forces act upon these man-made dumps of earth. When dumping ceases, most often they disappear, transported and redistributed over the bottom from which they were dredged by the restless environment of coastal waters. Occasionally these spoil dumps remain above sea level, but their external shapes and dimensions are altered markedly or "formed" by the actions of tides, waves, currents, and wind. A "naturally formed island" is born. However, should it be considered to be an island under the terms of the Convention?

The language of the Convention and the labors of the legal and technical experts who assisted in the preliminary drafts emphasize the chart representation of geographic features—the external, two-dimensional forms. Genesis of the landforms, difficult and expensive to establish or prove, was not a major factor in the proceedings. Charted forms dominate in the geographic-legal definitions of bays, river mouths, etc. As a consequence, man-created spoil banks may become, through the forces of nature, islands in the legal-political, as well as geographical, sense of the Convention. The U.S. Supreme Court acknowledges that spoil, when attached directly to the mainland, becomes a part of the mainland for purposes of the base line. The parallel to a "naturally formed" island would follow.

However, if dumping of spoil continues, the artificial nature of the spoil bank will be maintained. The shape of the "island" will continue to be artificially formed and the definition in the Convention will be negated. This fact would be reinforced if the coastal state continued to mark the "island" as "spoil" on official charts. The "island" would then remain "an artificially formed" node above sea level and should have no effect on the extension of the territorial sea. Geographically an island, the spoil bank does not legally exist as a base point. It should be noted that the effects of such islands on the extension of the territorial sea are normally limited. To survive, they must be in relatively shallow water close to land.

Nevertheless, the definition in the Article presently excludes man-made objects, which do not constitute "land." Within the 1958 context, petroleum platforms, derricks, rigs, and "Texas tower" types of platforms did not, in the minds of the Convention drafters, warrant being designated as base points for the territorial sea. While many of these installations have been constructed, they have normally been considered transitory features related to the exploration or exploitation of the shelf rather than to sovereignty over the sea. Safety zones were deemed sufficient to protect the rigs; freedom of the seas remained unencumbered as a result.

Times and technology, however, have changed and will continue to change. The rate of change, in fact, accelerates. Consequently, a revised or new convention must face novel uses, not necessarily related to the seabed, which may or may not require sovereignty or sovereign rights: (1) offshore loading and unloading ports; (2) floating airports; (3) atomic power plants situated offshore to minimize environmental damage; (4) permanent storage structures for gas, petroleum and other products, etc.

Many other similar but nonconventional uses of the ocean surface will be made as man's occupation of the planet intensifies. They may prove that existing regulations, only slightly amended, can satisfy the political-legal requirements of these structures. On the other hand, new rules may be required. Since the bases for the ultimate decision will be predominantly political, rather than geographical, detailed analyses have not been attempted here. Geographic factors, will be strong however, and they should be considered in any ultimate solution. If these "islands" receive territorial sea, for example, should they be considered for the establishment of lateral or median line boundaries? Points made in the following sections may be applicable to man-made islands as well as to natural ones.

ISLANDS AND THE TERRITORIAL SEA BASEPOINTS

Paragraph 2 of Article 10 establishes the bases for islands when it states: (2) The territorial sea of an island is measured in accordance with the provisions of these articles.[3] Thus an island, regardless of size and other physical attributes, is entitled to a territorial sea. However, logic based on geography shows that not all islands will be allocated the full territorial sea claimed by the administering state. To receive a full territorial sea each island would have to be situated so as to be twice, or more than twice, the breadth of the territorial sea from all other islands, from the mainland baseline, from low tide elevations, and from closure lines of rivers, bays, historic bays, and straight baseline systems. Certainly the most seaward islands will extend the territorial sea, outward at least, for the claimed breadth. Elsewhere, the degree of allocation relates to the proximity of other basepoints.

If geographic factors can limit the extent of the territorial sea about islands, so may the factors of "special circumstances." They represent, in effect, nonphysical limitations of position and proximity. A territorial sea boundary between adjacent or opposite states will, under certain circumstances, affect this limitation. Objections to these circumscribings of effects are rarely voiced except when one state feels that they produce an inequitable result.

It is difficult to define precisely the conditions of inequity in boundary delimitations. Obviously, certain conditions predominate: (1) State A possesses many offshore islands, while State B has few or none; (2) State A's islands are situated immediately adjacent to and offshore of the mainland of State B; and (3) State A controls islands relatively distant from its shore which affect the territorial sea of State B. (Of note, the Anglo-Chinese treaty concerning Hong Kong appears to deny the island of Lan Tao a territorial sea on its western shore.[4] The international boundary between China and Hong Kong follows a meridian that intersects the shore of Lan Tao (island). The boundary then follows the shore until the meridian is rejoined. As a result, the island is British; the adjacent waters to the west are Chinese.)

Rationally, beyond the natural composition of islands, as specified in Article 10, geographic analyses of islands as boundary factors must consider: size, location, relationships to the mainland or to other islands, number, and configuration. These analyses must be related to the provisions of the Convention on the Territorial Sea and the Contiguous Zone and to those of the Convention on the Continental Shelf.

ISLAND SIZE—THE REASONABLE BASIS FOR DIFFERENTIATION

As noted, islands vary immensely in size. They constitute the smallest integral marine-geographic feature, often too small to be shown accurately on even the largest-scale maps and charts. Symbols, e.g., asterisks or dots, often must be used to denote the situation of an island, if not its physical dimensions; for it must be kept in mind that the smallest rock which lies above mean high water is geographically and legally an island. The primary source of difficulty in the delimitation of maritime boundaries has stemmed from islands. A state quickly claims that an island or islands of another state grant an inadmissible advantage to the possessor. These islands, it is claimed, produce an inequitable boundary. The basis of these claims is that, under particular circumstances, certain islands should not be granted a full value in the delimitation, to avoid inequity. A categorization of islands by size, as a result, becomes imperative if differing values are to be assigned under factors of special circumstances. For this purpose, islands may be classified as follows: (1) *rocks*, less than .001 square mile in area;

(2) *islets*, between .001 and 1 square mile; (3) *isles*, greater than 1 square mile but not more than 1,000 square miles; and (4) *islands*, larger than 1,000 square miles.

Islands, in a sense, are abstractions. They have little or no value merely because of their existence. Their utility to the state and in particular to the inhabitants of the state (for it is for the people that the state has been established) creates their value. Size relates to value, for surface area is necessary for habitation and for sustenance. Other factors may enter into the equation, but they tend to be difficult to measure without detailed and costly study.

Rocks, by these definitions, constitute high tide elevations which, due to their small size, would be unfit for human habitation. The value of rocks, as a result, would be negligible or nonexistent. They might conceivably be used as sites for navigational lights, but this form of occupation is both artificial and transitory, depending entirely on external support for its continuance.

Islets, in contrast, could under certain select circumstances support human habitation on a limited scale. Due to their restricted area, they could not be expected to sustain a sizable element of the state's population, even of the smallest of nation states.

Isles, with favorable physical conditions of soil, climate, landforms, etc., could maintain significant populations. Under certain conditions, they could and do form the major core area of small insular states, e.g., Western Samoa, Nauru, Tonga.

Finally, due to their large size, *islands* can and should be conceived of as mainlands which have all legal-geographic attributes of continents. Obviously, the United Kingdom believes Great Britain has all the endowments, for purposes of territorial sea and marine boundary determination, of continental territory. Iceland, Sjaelland, Cuba, Sumatra, Corsica and many other islands should possess the same legal-geographic nature as mainlands. The administering states have assumed this status in the creation of straight baseline systems.

LOCATION AND RELATIONSHIPS

Obviously, all four categories of islands have territorial seas according to Article 10 (2) of the Convention on the Territorial Sea and the Contiguous Zone. Depending on their geographic relationships to other islands and to adjacent and opposite states, they may have full or partial effects on the breadth of the territorial sea claimed by the parent state. Value as base points, however, becomes a critical issue only with the correlation of the islands to the territory of another state. Thus, the factors of special circumstances as they relate to islands increase with the islands' proximity to the adjacent or opposite state.

The breadth of the territorial sea has not been standardized. However, to avoid awkward problems of discussion, it is assumed here that the territorial sea breadth of all states is 12 nautical miles. All mileage figures, other than square mileages, refer to nautical miles. The statement refers only to the international aspects of islands. They could, of course, assume great importance within a nation which has a federal system. As the proximity factor decreases from 24 miles, islands begin to assume an effect, both on the territorial sea and the development of maritime boundaries, which may cause real or apparent inequity to a second state. The degree of inequity relates directly to (1) the proximity of the islands to the adjacent or opposite state; (2) their physical relationships to the second state; and (3) to a degree, the coastal length of the second state in question.

Obviously, if the island(s) of State A extends up to or along the shores of State B, a basis for a claim of inequity may exist; at a distance of 24 miles a balance of forces occurs. As the distances between base lines decreases, the threat perception to the territorial sea extension increases. However, if State B possesses an identical or similar pattern of islands, a balance will develop as the two island groups relate to each other and to their respective states. The problem of inequity pertains directly to the excess insularity of one state and the proximity of placement of these islands to the baseline of another state. Thus, two islands situated 12 miles from the shores of their respective states and 24 miles from each other would not, in themselves, lead to inequity. Difficulties arise when a state appears to gain a large relative advantage due to the size, number, and/or location of its islands as they affect another state.

The inequity becomes particularly important to states with narrow coastlines; the island(s) of second states may deprive them of large percentages of the territorial seas they might otherwise enjoy. It is difficult, for example, to perceive a great threat of a reduction or expansion of the national territorial sea induced by, for example, the Mexican Coronado islands. Both Mexico and the United States are large coastal countries; the effects of these islands on the total territorial seas of the two states would be minimal. A small islet, such as North Coronado, would have a normal territorial sea of approximately 450 square miles ($12 \times 12 \times 3.1416$). Assuming that half the sea could, as a maximum, lead to a reduction in the U.S. territorial sea, the area of concern involves less than 225 square miles. The U.S. territorial sea (at 12 miles) measures approximately 150,000 square nautical miles, and Mexico's about 55,000; the areal significance of the islands, as a result, can be seen to be minimal.

Except for narrow coastal countries, this fact is of paramount importance for all islands as they concern the territorial sea of another state. Islands as special circumstances can scarcely affect decisively territorial sea delimitations in an areal sense. (The individual island could have an immense strategic or economic importance, but the area, nevertheless, will be small.) Few detached islands of one sovereignty are situated immediately offshore of other states. Exceptions occur in the case of Macao, Hong Kong, Portuguese Timor, Kamaran, Perim, Corisco and the Elobeys, the Dodecanese and possibly certain other Aegean islands, the Spanish islands off Morocco, the Channel Islands, Los Monjes, Aurba-Bonaire-Curaçao, St. Pierre and Miquelon, and the Australian islands south of Papua. A few other islands, which fall in the disputed category, have similar relationships.

STRAIGHT BASELINES

Within the concept of islands as they affect baselines, the Convention further recognizes that islands may serve in a more complex manner as a basis for the measurement of the territorial sea. Following on the International Court of Justice's famous *Anglo-Norwegian Fisheries Case*, the Convention states in Article 4 that:[5]

1. In localities where the coastline is deeply indented and cut into, or if there is a fringe of islands along the coast in its immediate vicinity, the method of straight baselines joining appropriate points may be employed in drawing the baseline from which the breadth of the territorial sea is measured.
2. The drawing of such baselines must not depart to any appreciable extent from the general direction of the coast, and the sea areas lying within the lines must be sufficiently closely linked to the land domain to be subject to the regime of internal waters.
3. Baselines shall not be drawn to and from low tide elevations, unless lighthouses or similar installations which are permanently above sea level have been built on them.
4. Where the method of straight baselines is applicable under the provisions of paragraph 1, account may be taken, in determining particular baselines, of economic interests peculiar to the region concerned, the reality and importance of which are clearly evidenced by a long usage.
5. The system of straight baselines may not be applied by a State in such a manner as to cut off from the high seas the territorial sea of another State.
6. The coastal State must clearly indicate straight baselines on charts, to which due publicity must be given.

Probably no other article of the Convention based on islands has been so used and perhaps misused by the states of the world. More than 60 coastal nations have employed straight baselines or have enabling legislation that permits their use. National practice varies from the most conservative Finnish model, in which no baseline segment exceeds twice the breadth of the territorial sea claim of four miles,[6] to extreme and indefensible violations of the intent of the Convention. Many states have segments that measure over 100 nautical miles in length. The Burmese example contains a line segment measuring over 222 miles in length.

     While a restriction of segment length, in general, could be the single most important factor to prevent abuses of the system inherent in the article's vague language, length alone is insufficient. The Convention, of course, does not specify any maximum to line length. As a result, a long, straight baseline in itself need not be inadmissible. However, the longer the length of the line, the greater the possibility of including water areas in violation of the intent of the Article. A detailed analysis of the elements of straight baselines is contained in *Towards an Objective Analysis of Special Circumstances* (Law of the Sea Institute Occasional Paper No. 13); the salient factors, which have been demonstrated to determine the applicability of a system, are as follows:

General Direction of the Coast
     Single segments of a straight baseline system should not depart more than 15° from the general direction of the coastline. The latter should be determined, for a reasonably extensive coastal length, by an analysis of small-scale charts, i.e., c. 1:1,000,000. Should local departure from the norm be dictated by special conditions, large-scale charts of the locality should be consulted. However, the concept of the "outermost points of the outermost islands," as a determinant of the general direction of the coast, is patently ridiculous. By this criterion, any line connecting any two islands would follow the general direction of the coast. One need only to examine certain national systems to see the abuses to which such a criterion may lead.

Length of Line
     While not specified in the Convention, the maximum length of line concept becomes essential. Generally speaking, the longer the length, the greater the chance for manifest abuse. In the *Anglo-Norwegian Fisheries Case,*[7] the longest geographical line measured slightly more than 40 nautical miles in length. In the Lopphavet sector, where historic-economic factors were determinants, the length of line was greater—45 miles. Except in these isolated instances, provisions should be made to limit the length in relation to its distance from enclosed islands on mainland. A 100-mile-long line segment, for example, which "skims" a fringe of islands at distances of a few miles, would be far more acceptable, within the provisions of the *Fisheries Case*, than a line of 60 miles in length that in certain areas might be tens of miles from the nearest intervening base point.

Fringing Islands
     Next to length of line, the concept of "fringing islands" has been the factor most subject to abuse. In certain national systems, a small island every 20 or 30 miles has been deemed "fringing." In others, reefs and shoals, both sub-

merged or drying features, have been utilized in national law as parts of the systems. By contrast, in the Norwegian example, islands masked the mainland on the average for nearly two-thirds of the length of the coastline. In many areas the mainland was totally obscured from the sea by continuous and overlapping lines of islands. The Norwegian guide should be paramount. Furthermore, where fringing islands cease to exist, the system of straight baselines, in the absence of a deeply indented coastline, should return to the mainland and terminate. A second system obviously may be established when proper conditions again dominate.

Subject to the Regime of Internal Waters

Due to the complexity of potential land/water relationships (i.e., islands may be situated in numberless arrangements), an ideal measurement relates to the land/water ratio contained within the straight baseline system and the normal baseline of the coastline. The Norwegian ratio was determined to be 1/3.5. In combination with length of line, the ratio forms the best basis for evaluating a system of straight baselines to determine its conformity with the spirit of the Convention's Article 4 and the Norwegian example.

These determinants, of course, mark norms. States may establish more restricted systems which meet their national demands for security and for the protection of economic, historic, environmental, and social interests. The entire Article, in fact, is not self-executing; the coastal state need not employ straight baselines even where favorable geographic conditions occur.

OPEN ELEMENTS ON ISLANDS

The Convention on the Territorial Sea and the Contiguous Zone did not address two elemental types of islands: archipelagos and atolls. The latter were discussed within the Group of Experts and the former entered into many discussions prior to and during the Conference's sessions, but no final articles were approved concerning either. Nevertheless, archipelagos and atolls from significant insular geographic elements, and certain arrangements should be enacted to permit orderly development in marine jurisdictions.

On the Problem of Archipelagos

A geographic analysis of archipelagos should be based on three premises: (1) archipelagos exist as important (or significant) and cohesive geographic, historical, or political entities; (2) archipelagos may warrant a special regime within the law of the seas and/or seabeds context; and (3) the community of states must determine acceptable limits within which an archipelago principle may be applied. To accomplish this third premise or objective, the definition of the archipelagic feature and the rules to be applied therein should be relatively precisely delimited to protect universal requirements for freedom of navigation.

At the same time the approach must be sufficiently pragmatic to meet the legitimate demands of the claimant states.

To understand the basic problem of archipelagos, it is helpful to recall that the "principle" has been extended to these island types in three different manners.

1. The first archipelago system has been applied to coastal islands, which conventionally have been integrated with the mainland territory of the same state. The Norwegian straight baselines system is the classic example of this type; the language of the International Court of Justice's *Anglo-Norwegian Fisheries Case* has, to a large measure, been incorporated into the Geneva Convention on the Territorial Sea and the Contiguous Zone. The provisions, although very general and subject to abuse, have generally provided a basic system to integrate coastal archipelagos into the maritime regimes of the continental territory of states.

2. A second method of dealing with the problem has been adopted by states which are entirely insular in geography. This system accepts in principle that one (or several) large islands constitute mainland in a manner similar to that permitted by the Convention on the Territorial Sea and the Contiguous Zone. Smaller, fringing islands are "tied" to the mainland by a system of straight baselines. The United Kingdom, France (Corsica), Iceland, Denmark (Sjaelland), Greenland, Ireland, Cuba, Dominican Republic, Canada (Newfoundland), Haiti, and many other states have utilized this concept without undue protest from the international community. (The Icelandic system, of course, drew many protests, including one from the United States; however, these protests were not publicly based on the use of the archipelago principle but were tied to the extent of the lines and their effects on the local cod fishing of distant water fleets.)

3. The third type of archipelago principle involves the consolidation of oceanic archipelagos into a single unit by a system of straight baselines. Normally, this insular type varies from the second system in the scale of the archipelago—it invariably covers a larger area than the second category—and in that no single island dominates, in its dimensions, the total land area of the archipelago. Here the islands are nearly all of an equal size—e.g., Galapagos Islands and Svalbard—or several are equally large but dispersed.

Insular states, particularly in the early stages of their political development, encounter difficulties in establishing administrative control over outer islands. Communications along the water routes tend to be poor and, as a result, central control is weakened. Where large islands with substantial populations and resources exist, they develop as important regional centers of power in conflict with the capital. Regionalism of this type is typical of developing states with poor infrastructure, but the problems become more critical in insular states because of the difficulties of communication (both physical and electronic).

Local foci of power conflict with the central state's desire to unite the nation, weakening the concept of a single nation. Indonesia and the Philippines are the principal example of this latter type. In the former, Borneo, Sumatra, the Celebes, Java, and western New Guinea (Irian Barat) have offered potentially divisive "mainlands." In the Philippines, the islands of Mindanao, Palawan, and Luzon all form large, regional centers. No one island geographically dominates the archipelagos. Furthermore, the great dispersion of these islands restricts the use of the mainland option.

The oceanic archipelago states, which have adopted the third form of straight baseline system, cite the practices of the first two types of states as precedents for their activities. Implicit in this approach is the view that a totally insular state, which may normally face greater political problems of divisive geographic forces than states in the first two categories, should not be denied the advantages which accrue, through conventional international law, to their more favored continental neighbors.

Geographically speaking, it is hard to deny that comparative inequities may exist. However, as a consequence of the strategic positions of the Philippines, and in particular Indonesia, the strict employment of the archipelago principle has severe effects on the interests of the maritime states. If allowed to proliferate to less justifiable conditions, much of the world's oceans should be encompassed by archipelago straight baseline systems.

What is an archipelago? The standard dictionary definition of the generic term "archipelago" provides little aid to the delineation of the problem. Originally, archipelago referred to a *sea* studded with many islands. In particular, the designation applied to the Aegean Sea. By transposition, however, the generic term has universally come to designate the studding *islands* within the sea. An analysis of the Aegean reveals that the islands are scattered randomly but widely throughout the Sea. In fact no point in the Aegean is situated more than 35 nautical miles from an island. The islands in general are large in the sense that their average size would encompass several hundred square miles. The total land area of the islands probably exceeds 6,500 square miles.

Generalizing from these characteristics, an archipelago should rationally contain the following characteristics:

1. There must be a substantial number of relatively large islands scattered throughout a sea in an areal and not a linear pattern.
2. The islands should be situated so as to relate geographically (adjacency) to each other and to others in the group.
3. They should be perceived as a unitary whole because of political administration.

By these definitions, archipelagos would be restricted to a limited number of major island groups that are relatively concentrated and interrelated. Moreover, by definition, the islands should constitute a state (independent or dependent) in themselves—they should be excluded from the mainland, where normal straight baseline provisions would apply.

The above definitions are general and would be subject to many interpretations and to certain abuse. To come to grips with this problem, archipelagos could be treated as "special circumstances" of straight baseline systems. Due to the special circumstance of total insularity, the parameters developed in the *Anglo-Norwegian Fisheries Case* should be modified to reflect objective criteria which would suit political and geographical realities. The most useful objective criterion adopted in international law to measure a geographic condition is the semicircular one for a bay. While not perfect, the rule combines simplicity of application with apparent logic and ease of comprehension on the part of the user. The latter is most vital.

The most important characteristics of an archipelago would be:

1. Areal dispersion of many islands over two or more axes (longitudinal and lateral)
2. Adjacency of islands among themselves with special reference to the length of the line about the perimeter
3. A land/water or territorial sea/insular sea ratio contained within the ultimate archipelagic baselines system

Why a special circumstance?   The principal oceanic archipelago claimants have been Indonesia, the Philippines, and Fiji. These three have met to formulate a nearly common position concerning the "principle," but they have now embarked on a concerted campaign to convince the less developed states, in particular, of the soundness of the principle.

As McLoughlin of Fiji stated: "It is important to such [archipelago] countries, and of vital concern to Fiji, to control the development of their marine environments in order to ensure that such development is in their best interests and to prevent any form of depredation or pollution that may endanger that environment or deplete its resources."[8]

Prof. Mochtar Kusumaatmadja (Indonesia) elaborated on the bases for the claims when he said

". . . in an archipelago there exists a very close relationship between the *land* (island) and the surrounding sea (water). The existence and distribution of natural resources throughout an archipelago—both living and nonliving (or mineral)—are the result of or dependent upon the geophysical and ecological unity and interdependence of the island and the intervening waters. Secondly, where the people inhabiting the islands are technologically underdeveloped, free competition with technologically more advanced outsiders would be disastrous."[9]

He further stated that the dangers to the environment "seems to further strengthen the case for considering an archipelago as one unit." Finally, almost as an aside, he mentioned the problems of security faced by an underdeveloped and insular state in which the naval forces of a stronger power may "maneuver" uncurbed and immune. While the Philippines have objected strenuously to derogation from full internal waters status within the archipelagos, Prof. Kusumaatmadja has implied strongly that "innocent passage" should be guaranteed.

Thus it appears that the archipelago principle, at its roots, is resource or resource-protection oriented. If so, control over resources could be granted within the archipelago system to the state; and, if carefully negotiated, a form of transit (perhaps along specified corridors) through a limited number of "international transit straits" or corridors could be correlated with the otherwise resource-oriented archipelagic system. Such a solution could appear to accommodate both the world's and the archipelagic states' basic objectives.

Proposed archipelagic system. Hodgson and Alexander have proposed a system of archipelago baselines.[10] At the time of writing, their principles had not been applied to Indonesia or to the Philippines, although they could have been. Certain modifications in their suggested approach would be required, however, if these principles were to be applied to these two vital stages.

1. *Adjacency.* The proposal required that, as a maximum, 40 to 48 nautical mile closing lines be used as a measure of adjacency. These lines have since been applied to Indonesia, the Philippines, Fiji, the Galapagos, Tonga, and the Bahamas. The effects are minimal: in Indonesia, the islands of Sumatra, Borneo, Java, and the Celebes become a unit, if a narrow connection may be declared unitized. The eastern area remains detached and broken. Nevertheless, the system works effectively for the remainder of the states, although the Philippines straight baselines would not enclose the Sulu Sea.

Pragmatically, neither the Philippines nor Indonesia is likely to accept the results of these lines unless other economic resource zone limits would allocate the residual areas. Furthermore, these countries probably would want to hold that the waters within the baselines were internal waters, which would effectively close all Philippine and Indonesian straits except the Molucca-Ceram passage to Australia. The continuation of the route to East Asia would, nevertheless, be denied by the Philippine limits.

To find a realistic solution, the proposed absolute limit should be amended to permit the construction of a limited number of lines (this may be expressed as an absolute figure, i.e., ten lines of this length, or as a percentage of the total number of baseline segments) to tie together the major geographic segments of the archipelago, which may be defined as a percentage of the total area or as an absolute area. The change in the original position is justified on the basis of state practice in the drawing of straight baselines. The original concepts proposed by Hodgson and Alexander evolved from the Norwegian example. The longest geographic baseline was 40 nautical miles, although "historic waters" were enclosed by longer segments (approximately 45 n.m.).

Of the 30 states employing straight baseline systems that the Office of the Geographer has studied to date, nearly 50 percent have employed one or more lines in excess of the 40 nautical mile limit of the Norwegian example. These are shown in Table 8-4. It can be argued that selected limits in excess of the Norwegian example maximum have become standard state practice. The logic, as applied to archipelagos, is relatively simple; if the parts are to be joined, geography determines the length of line. Of course, "good" geography and "bad" geography coexist in any system of straight baselines. "Geography" can be as bad an excuse as "history" or any other ill-defined reason. To keep "good" geography from being overwhelmed, an additional test in the form of integration is proposed.

2. *Perception of geographic integration.* The essential measure of the relationship between land and water in an archipelago is not only a factor of distance, i.e., adjacency. Of equal importance is the proportion of land to water within the system, which may logically be expressed in two ways. In the cited paper, Hodgson and Alexander suggested that the territorial sea, measured from the normal base points, should relate to the total area of insular waters. These latter were defined as the jurisdictional waters beyond the normal territorial sea gained by the use of the construction lines. It was stated that insular waters

Table 8-4.

State	N.M.
Dominican Republic	45.0
Faeroes	60.8
Burma	222.3
Madagascar	123.0
Venezuela	98.9
United Kingdom	40.25
Mozambique	60.4
Portuguese Guinea	79.0
Thailand	59.15
Philippines	140.05
Iceland	74.0
Indonesia	124.0
Guinea	120.0
Mauritania	89.0
Ecuador	136.0

". . . may not exceed the aggregate of areas contained within circles twelve miles in radius calculated about each basepoint used."[11] In the case of atolls, it was strongly recommended that the limit of the coral reef be used as base points rather than the normal "island" shoreline. The reefs and lagoons should also be measured as land in the land/water ratios mentioned below.

These ratios have not been fully developed for the island archipelagos under study. Before this proposal is discussed in depth, it would be wise to examine the effects of a proportion of territorial to insular waters on the larger archipelagos. The smaller island aggregations, such as Fiji and the Galapagos, however, would meet the insular/territorial water criterion because of their size and configuration.

A second possibility would be to establish a maximum permissible land/water ratio contained within the baselines. In the Norwegian example this ratio is 1:3.5; for archipelagos the limit should be eased to 1:5 due to the basic maritime character of archipelago. The examples have been measured from the specific baseline system to determine the following ratios:

Indonesia	1:1
Philippines	1:2.14
Galapagos	1:4.59
Fiji	1:4.88
Tonga	1:25
Bahamas	1:10+
Faeroes	1:3.5

Although 40 n.m. "construction" lines may be drawn, Tonga and the Bahamas could not qualify under this criterion as archipelagos, nor could French Polynesia, the Trust Territory of the Pacific Island, the Cook Islands, and other oceanic atoll groups. The exercise has not been applied to the Maldives, but they probably would not meet the land/water ratio criterion.

3. *Areal distribution.* If this characteristic needs to be quantified— and it may not—one need only say that the maximum transverse axis length must be at least 1/10 of the length of the longitudinal axis. The purpose of this requirement is to prohibit the drawing of archipelago limits about line islands. Such chains of islands—e.g., the Aleutians, Kurils, Lesser Antilles, and Marianas— extend across vast areas of the oceans and seas in narrow chains, often only one island wide. These islands should not be considered as archipelagos. Their problems do not relate to interisland waters; in fact, the only waters of this nature are situated between two islands in the string.

The twelve-mile territorial sea provides for the major problems associated with most of these islands. To permit the drawing of construction lines would add little to the economic well-being of the states, for little integration would be gained. The lines, however, would lead to security problems for the world maritime states; each connecting line cuts through a potential strait. In certain instances, limited problems of these arcuate or line islands may be solved by the "mainland" concept of straight baselines, i.e., by localized grouping.

4. *The status of waters.*   As stated in Hodgson and Alexander's original proposal:[12]

> *Rationale for the proposal.*   The system suggested here is designed to afford archipelago areas an opportunity, under certain prescribed conditions, to assert [economic] competence over their interisland waters. The construction lines are in a sense artificial baselines. From them the seaward limits of insular waters are measured, and all areas of insular waters must be within 24 miles of these seaward limits, or the base points themselves. Thus, if adjacency in archipelagos can be taken as less than, or equal to, twice the breadth of the territorial sea (measured as twelve miles) then the principle of adjacency is not violated in this proposed scheme.
>
> Waters within twelve miles of the base points would be subject only to the normal regime of territorial waters, and not to the additional restrictions of "insular" regimes, so far as freedom of transit and overflight are concerned. The system suggested here implies also that territorial waters may be delimited in the case of coral reefs, as suggested in the Addendum of the Second Report on the Regime of the Territorial Sea in preparation for the 1958 Geneva Conference. Many of the island groups of the world, such as the Maldives, Truk Islands, and the Palau group, have extensive coral formations which themselves form a part of the geographic whole. It would hardly make sense to exclude these features in the delimitation process.
>
> The various restrictions noted here would apply only in the case of delimitations based on the principle of adjacency. If special circumstances exist, either on the ground of history or of economic need, some adjustments in delimitation restrictions may be necessary. There are many situations in which special competence of the coastal country over activities well away from its coast can, in theory at least, be justified. But under no conditions should the freedom of navigation and overflight for purposes of transit beyond the twelve-mile territorial limits be compromised. Like the regime for straight baselines, this archipelago system should require delineation on officially recognized large-scale charts to which due publicity should be given.

Discarded Concepts.   Several alternatives for archipelago determination have not been pursued for the stated reasons.

1. *Minimum area of land.*   Most underdeveloped countries are small and they resent the developed "giants." To deny that a small archipelago cannot

have a system which a large archipelago may have would be offensive and unproductive.

2. *General direction of an archipelago.* To say that the baselines must follow the "general direction of an archipelago" (similar to the straight baseline concept) would require further quantification and complication of criteria or the acceptance of lines joining outermost points of the outermost islands as determining the "general direction." The concept is at best foggy ashore, but it is intolerable offshore because of the nature of the comparison. In the straight baseline proposal, the comparison is between the trending directions of offshore islands and a mainland.

In the case of a midoceanic archipelago, the comparison would be between the trend of the islands qua islands and the islands qua a group of islands. The distinction would be so slight that the effect of such an argument would be to permit lines to be drawn about the outermost points of all islands that politically may be conceived as part of an archipelagic state. In reality, certain islands do not constitute integral parts of the archipelagos based on adjacency, and they should not be joined to the remainder of the islands.

3. *Geological/geophysical basis.* Two objections to this thesis become immediately apparent: (1) If one goes deep enough in the ocean, one can find a geologic or geophysical continuum for any given area. This fact would apply to atolls, for example, wherever they might be in the same ocean. (2) If one does not go deep enough in the water, archipelagos such as Indonesia become divided. Geologically, Sumatra, Borneo, and Java are one entity; the eastern islands a second one. Consequently, the idea is difficult to support without a comprehensive determination of scientific facts, which could be difficult and expensive to prove or disprove. Geological and geophysical criteria alone are insufficient; furthermore, they are very complex to apply to tectonics, geomorphology, seismology, sedimentation, structure, geologic age, etc., and difficult to determine without extensive and costly research.

4. *Historical/economic factors.* Any state may point to historical or economic reasons for unity and/or control of communication lanes, etc. The same reasoning could be applied by the U.S. (or any divided country) to explain why it should control, for example, the area between the U.S. and Hawaii. Worse still, it is the ultimate reason for claiming all intervening areas in any insular state. The argument parallels the national wish to attain "defensible frontiers." These "defensible" positions are *always* outside the existing boundaries, even though equally useful lines may be within present state limits.

5. *Perceptional factors.* As with the previous concept, "perceptional" factors must be greeted with skepticism. Americans perceived the occupation of the west as their "manifest destiny," which led to the indefensible

slaughter of native Indians and the needless destruction of animals. The nationalistic leaders of any emerging nation cannot be expected to avoid the pitfalls into
which we ourselves fell. They are bound to perceive interisland water areas as
vital to their national development, or at least to see the need to exclude all foreign activity from them.

Summary

In order to maintain law of the sea objectives, the world community of nations must find a means to adapt the Convention to the problems
engendered by the application of the archipelago principle. While it is not
entirely clear that the proponents of the concept can obtain the adoption
of the principle in a future conventi)n, the prospect of a confrontation between
the major maritime states and these developing insular states looms. The reper-
cussions could be most damaging to peace with the third world states.

Any solution, however, must not compromise general maritime objectives—yet it must be pragmatic enough to satisfy the requirements of certain
of the archipelago states. Moreover, it must establish limitations to prevent a
proliferation of claims by less qualified island states. A solution may lie in the
strict, objective definition of an archipelago based on the following principles:

1. *Areal dispersion* along two or more major axes which would relate to each
   other by a ratio of 1:10 or larger.
2. *Adjacency*, as determined by construction lines of 48 nautical miles or less,
   drawn along the perimeter of the archipelago, which would join islands together; where required, a limited number of construction lines, up to 80
   nautical miles in length, could then be drawn to unite major insular components.
3. *Geographic integration*, as expressed by either a territorial sea/insular waters
   ratio or a land/water ratio within the baseline system. In the former case, a
   ratio of 1:1 could mark the limit while in the latter a 1:5 ratio could apply.

Transit of the insular waters could be free as on the high seas. Corridors should
be designated for a limited number of international straits; at least two should be
defined across the longitudinal axis and one along the lateral.

The Choice of Baselines About Atolls

Atolls primarily comprise chains of tiny, low limestone islets
("motus") that partially crown a circular or oval coral reef. The reef normally is
completely submerged at high tide but heads dry at low water. Geomorphically,
atolls present several external forms, dependent on the stage of development or
on genesis. They may be characterized as true atolls, almost atolls, partly raised
atolls, and raised atolls. Basically, the major difference in the external, two-
dimensional character affects the nature and extent of the lagoon contained

within the reef. In a true atoll, the reef is virtually continuous; islands are limited, and the lagoon is expansive and completely marine. In the raised atoll the lagoon has become a saucerlike depression completely above sea level. The two remaining categories form immediate steps.

The true atolls and raised atolls represent the major problem area in the development of an equitable and logical baseline for the measurement of the territorial sea. The reefs are almost entirely formed by coral skeletal structures that live in a restricted environment. The skeleton of the coral polyp develops by cells on its bottom and sides which excrete calcium to protect the otherwise defenseless marine organism. The coral builds upward upon the skeletons of its dead ancestors. While live coral may be found in water depths to 1,000 feet, most exist between 20 feet and 160 feet below sea level. The reef becomes a cemented mass of skeletal material, modified by dissolution and recrystalization through the actions of sea water. Wave action will break off hugh chunks of reef, which eventually may be pulverized and reduced to sand. The top surface of the reef is covered with this debris in all sizes and forms.

Reef corals live only under restricted geographic conditions. They cannot survive except within the temperature range of 65°-96°F, with ideal water temperature being about 80°F. Consequently, atoll development is restricted to the tropical and warm subtropical waters of the Pacific, Indian, and Caribbean seas. Moreover, major coral concentrations are situated in the central and western portions of these bodies. The coral reef has a characteristic profile. The outer or seaward edge of the reef drops steeply to the sea floor. The inner or lagoon side shades gradually to a flat, shallow basin, the atoll lagoon. These bodies of water are clear, beautifully blue, and teeming with marine life. Coral fundamentally cannot survive in silty or polluted waters, hence the purity and richness of the lagoon flora and fauna.

In virtually every instance the rim of the coral reef is nearly continuous; perimeter coverage is generally greater than 75 percent and usually averages about 90 percent. Lagoon openings are situated normally on the lee side of the motus. Motus, in the true atoll, are limited in number and in linear extent. Rarely do they attain 50 percent of the total perimeter; normally they total much less. In certain atolls the motus may constitute less than 10 percent of the total perimeter.

An atoll forms a geographic and ecologic unity. The lagoon, which constitutes the center of life in the atoll, has the definition character of land-locked waters. The lagoon is generally calm, exceedingly clear, and of a characteristic color distinct from the general ocean. Wind-induced wave action is broken by the seaward extent of the reef. Other physical factors such as temperature, salinity, etc., show marked differences from the oceanic norm. However, the most important feature of the lagoon is the rich and varied biota; most atoll lagoons generally teem with fish and other marine life.

The economic well-being of the indigenous population depends to a very large measure on the harvest of the lagoon fishery. This fact relates to the absolute lack of land surface and the even greater restrictions for cultivation in the normal atoll; the sterility of the limestone soils and the lack of indigenous animal life on the motus are other factors to be considered. Coconuts constitute the primary agricultural products, although some root crops are also grown. Vital protein comes primarily from the lagoon. (On some near atolls and raised atolls, pigs and other domesticated animals are raised in limited numbers, but they are generally insufficient to meet the requirements of the population.)

The reef not only forms the lagoon that sustains the population but its existence is essential for the maintenance of the motus themselves. Without the reefs, the motus would soon be destroyed by wind and wave action. Thus the reef gives the motus both life and survival. The recent threat of reef-destroy-ing crown-of-thorns starfish represents an unusual danger to the inhabitants of these atolls because the destruction of the coral eventually means the end to the islets through erosion.

For survival, the inhabitants require all three: reef, lagoon, and motus. As a result, it is impossible, geographically, to separate the three interre-lated elements. While man may be destined to live his life on the motus, to main-tain his existence he must harvest the lagoon formed and nurtured by the reef. This need, which is basically one of economic survival, must be reflected politi-cally. To protect the resource upon which life depends, the inhabitants must be in a position to control the lagoon. To accomplish this fact, the territorial sea of an atoll should be measured from a baseline formed by the seaward side of the reef. From this concept, the following should develop:

1. The lagoon forms internal, landlocked waters of the state or the atoll as part of a state.
2. The territorial sea should be measured seaward from the outer limit of the reef, even where it is submerged at mean low water as shown on official charts.
3. The contiguous zone should be measured from the same baseline as the terri-torial sea.
4. If geographic conditions permit, a system of straight baselines may be drawn so as to use the reefs rather than the motus as turning points.
5. Where openings in the reef are greater than twice the claimed territorial sea, the openings may be closed at the natural entrance points of the reef, in a manner similar to bays on a mainland shore. This provision is vital to pre-serve the internal waters nature of certain lagoons.

ISLANDS AND BAYS

Article 7(3) of the Convention on the Territorial Sea and the Contiguous Zone concerns islands in the mouth of the bays insofar as the islands affect the length of bay-closing lines. However, islands may relate to the bay-closing lines in three distinct manners: (1) those situated within the mouth of a bay; (2) those which screen the mouth of a bay; and (3) those which form the headland of a bay.

In the first of these situations, the method of drawing the bay-closing lines is relatively simple. If the selected closing line intersects an island within the mouth of the bay, that island will be used to form a part of the closing line. Natural entrance points should be determined. Should these closing lines, or their continuations, intersect other islands, such islands too will form a part of the closure line. Obviously, islands not intersected by the line segments will not be used (see Figure 8-1).

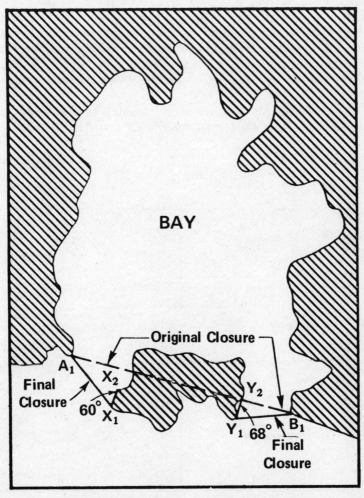

Figure 8-1. Bay Closure: Island in Mouth of Bay

The purpose of a bay-closing line is to enclose a natural feature—the bay—where a line does not normally exist in nature. Under certain circumstances, however, a series of islands may exist which naturally "screen" the mouth of a bay. If the islands serve to block more than one-half of the opening of a bay, they may be judged to screen the mouth of the bay from the sea. Since the greater condition, i.e., more than one-half of the mouth, is represented by islands, they should be deemed to form the dominant geographic characteristic of the mouth and serve to enclose the water within the bay; these islands screen the bay from the sea. Under this condition, the islands may be considered to form the natural closure for the bay even if they are not situated directly in the mouth of the bay. Since the islands are the natural line which terminates the conditions of landlocked waters, the bay-closing line must be drawn by using the screening islands. The string of islands may, however, project landward or seaward of the line joining the natural entrance points of the bay (see Figure 8-2).

The screening islands may occasionally continue beyond one or both natural entrance points of the bay. In this instance, the bay-closing line would not be continued along the line of islands unless they form a part of a straight baseline system. The bay-closure line should terminate at the natural headland of the bay.

Finally, islands themselves may constitute headlands of a bay under certain conditions. These islands must closely relate to, and be associated with,

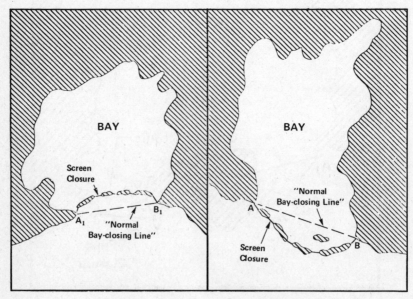

Figure 8-2. Bay Closure: Screening Islands

the adjacent mainland. To be used as headlands, however, they should also form a natural extension of the two-dimensional coastline formation as viewed on a nautical chart. Moreover, the area of the island should be greater than the area of the intervening water between it and the true mainland. A matter of scale is also involved, which relates directly to the nature of the feature. Under normal conditions, the islands used as headlands will be relatively small so as not to dwarf the true proportions of the original bay feature and, hence, change its entire character. The enclosed water area should ideally resemble a channel in configuration.

ISLANDS AND TERRITORIAL SEA BOUNDARIES

Article 12 of the Convention on the Territorial Sea and the Contiguous Zone defines negatively the procedures for territorial waters delimitation.[13]

1. Where the coasts of two States are opposite or adjacent to each other, neither of the two states is entitled, failing agreement between them to the contrary, to extend its territorial sea beyond the median line every point of which is equidistant from the nearest points on the baseline from which the breadth of the territorial sea is measured. The provisions of this paragraph shall not apply, however, where it is necessary by reason of historic title or other special circumstances to delimit the territorial seas of the two States in a way which is at variance with this provision.
2. The line of delimitation between the territorial waters of two States lying opposite or adjacent to each other shall be marked on large-scale charts officially recognized by the coastal States.

In general practice, coastal states have seized on the provision of equidistance in the article (which is merely a maximum limit of unilateral action where agreement does not exist) to make it a law of territorial waters delimitation. While time has not been sufficient to enshrine the principle as a "conventional wisdom," belief in the principle has become widespread. The result, however, is to place islands in a position where they may cause inequities.

The best boundary between states is one that both states accept peacefully. This limit may be based on equidistance or on any other logical precept that appears to result in equity. The presence of a significant geographic feature, such as a navigation channel which could be of benefit to both states, may be of far greater consequence than an enshrined principle of equal area sharing.

Furthermore, where many islands exist randomly in the territorial sea boundary region, an equidistant line will by definition be tortuous, and may be so complex as to be meaningless. Alternatives to the principle can result in an

equal distribution of the sea without the associated complexity of equidistance.
In view of the limited amount of territory that results from the normal island
and a twelve-mile territorial sea, these alternatives should be considered seriously
in order to reduce, in effect, the problem of boundary delimitation involving
offshore islands. Certain of these alternatives, which may have to be modified
depending on the locations of the islands, include: (1) straight line azimuths,
(2) parallels of latitude or meridians of longitude of the land boundary termini,
(3) continuation of existing land frontier line, (4) continuation of river median
lines or thalweg channels.[14]

Should equidistance be preferred, or be easier to accept as a basis for
negotiation, a simplified line may still be delimited. In the Mexico-U.S. maritime
boundary for the Pacific, a more easily administrable line was produced by an
equal exchange of territorial sea.[15] A further refinement of this procedure
would require the states to negotiate the general directions which they desired a
lateral boundary to follow in its extension from the land to the sea limit. The
line could then divide equally the least distance, measured perpendicularly to the
selected general azimuth, between their adjacent islands.

This concept is illustrated in Figure 8-3. Islands 1, 3, and 5 belong to
State A, while 2, 4, and 6 belong to State B. The distance between selected pairs
is divided in half to determine the precise position of the boundary. The resulting line constitutes a modified form of equidistance but, being simpler, is easier
to administer. However, if the equidistance principle is to be used for the continuation of the boundary on the shelf, the terminal point of the territorial sea
should be selected close to or at equidistance to avoid unnecessary complications
in prolonging the delimitation. The number of azimuths to be chosen will relate
to the complexity of boundary delimitation desired.

Notwithstanding, certain adjacent or opposite states will find equidistant boundaries easier to negotiate due to the international acceptance of the
principle. Islands will come to the fore and may lead to problems of inequity
and the demand for an application of special circumstances. To meet some of
these difficulties it is proposed, where inequities may arise, that,

1. Rocks, as defined, should have no effect on the equidistant line,
but they should not, unless situated more than twelve miles from the resulting
maritime boundary, become enclaves within the territorial sea of another state.
They may be accorded a sea breadth sufficient to remain contiguous to the territorial sea of the parent state. The line of contact, however, must be sufficiently
wide to permit easy and free access. (See Figure 8-4 for an example.)

2. Islets should be granted a partial effect in the construction of an
equidistance boundary. The value should be one-half or more, in view of the

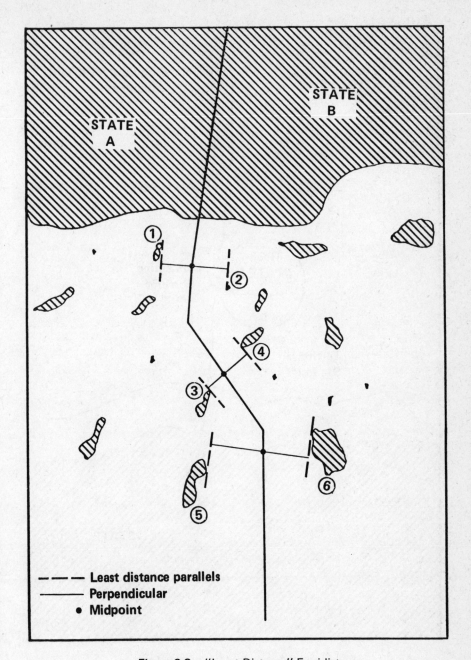

Figure 8-3. "Least Distance" Equidistance

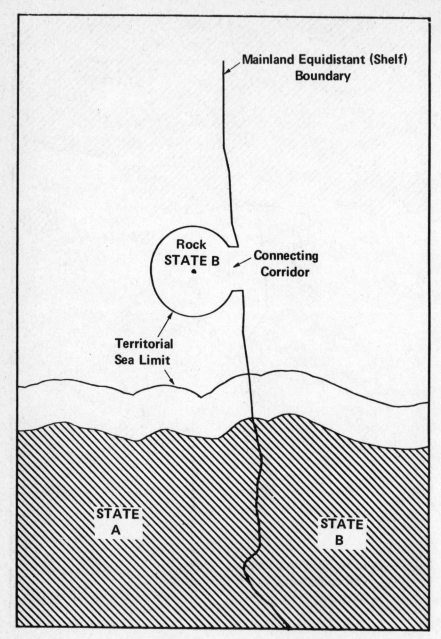

Figure 8-4.   Enclave Connecting Corridor

small areas involved in the territorial sea. The precise value to be assigned will derive from the relationship of the islet to the adjacent or opposite state. As a measure of the effect of an islet, the equidistant line should be constructed with and without the islet as a base point. If the islet remains within the territorial sea of its parent state while not serving as a base point, the islet should receive a value greater than the half-effect. Obviously, the inequity which might be caused is not an extensive one. However, if nonuse of the islet as a base point would separate it from the national territorial sea, the base point value of the islet should be reduced. Where feasible, the factor of contiguity should determine the precise value so as to avoid difficult-to-administer enclaves.

3. Isles should receive full effect on an equidistant boundary unless they are so situated, in relation to a narrow coastal state, as to affect a sizable proportion of the area of territorial sea that the coastal state might otherwise receive. A loss of one-third or more of the area would represent a potent threat. This type of situation, however, would be very rare. Two potential cases come to mind:

a. Three disputed islands lie offshore from Kuwait and Saudi Arabia. If all three of these islets/isles were to come under Saudi sovereignty, the resulting effect of an equidistant boundary would be most inequitable to Kuwait. As stated, the sovereignty over the isles remains clouded and the question is theoretical (see Figure 8-5).

b. The coastal islands south of Papua (Papua New Guinea) have been reserved to Australia. Due to the positions of these islands and their effects, they would (or could) deprive Papua New Guinea of virtually all territorial sea south of the main state area. The results could be very inequitable for this particular area. Although the percentage of the total territorial sea of the "state" may not be excessive, a condition of relative inequity would prevail. In these two situations, special regimes might be considered to protect the interests of masked coastal states.

4. Islands, as defined, should receive full effect on equidistant boundaries because of their size and importance. They are mainland in the legal-geographical sense.

As noted earlier, the grossest inequities will develop with those islands detached from the parent state which lie close onshore to a second state. The reality of the inequity, however, may be only local. It should be measured in relation to the category of the island(s) and to the effect it (they) will have on the total territorial sea of the second state. Examples of such islands are: the Channel Islands (U.K., adjacent to France); St. Pierre and Miquelon (France,

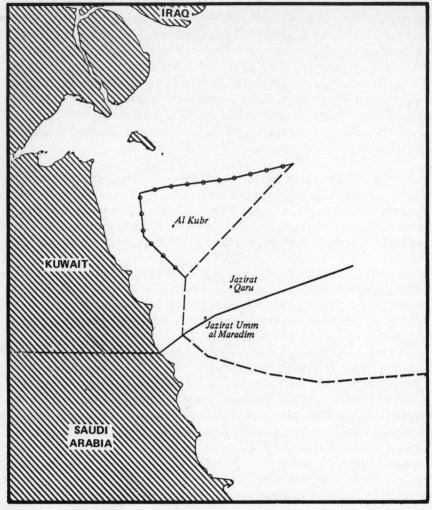

Figure 8-5. Theoretical Kuwait-Saudi Arabia Equidistant Lines

adjacent to Canada); Los Monges (Venezuela, adjacent to Colombia); Aruba-
Bonaire-Curaçao (Netherlands realm, adjacent to Venezuela). These examples
were chosen to illustrate that the conditions may prevail to the advantage and/or
disadvantage of the same states. However, other examples can be found throughout the world, e.g., Macao, Portuguese Timor, Kamaran, etc. In a sense each of
these islands is unique, but they have much in common. With the exception of
Los Monges, all are inhabited and possess a large degree of local governmental
autonomy. In addition, they are all situated within 24 miles of adjacent main-

lands. With the possible exception of Aruba-Bonaire-Curaçao, none of the islands affects a sizable portion of the territorial sea of the other state. The Dutch islands, due to their linear alignment parallel to the Venezuelan coast, negate an important but relatively small segment of Venezuela's potential territorial sea. The remaining islands scarcely affect the total seas of France, Canada, and Colombia. They and similar detached islands should not be denied full value as base points except where isolated low tide elevations, rocks, or islets (as defined) may lead to local gross inequities, also as defined.

SUMMARY

1. Assuming a uniform twelve-mile territorial sea, islands have only a minor effect on the extension of the territorial sea of a state. Under certain circumstances a condition of inequity may develop, but it will be relatively limited in scope. Generally, each island is entitled to a territorial sea, although under certain geographic and political circumstances it may be less than the full national claim. In at least one situation, China and the United Kingdom appear to have agreed that a sector of one island of Hong Kong would have no territorial sea.

2. Islands may, according to certain criteria, be used as headlands for bays and as parts of bay-closing lines. If a nearly continuous band exists across the mouth of a bay, the islands may even form the closing line as a consequence of their linear alignment and percentage of cover of the bay mouth.

3. Where islands form a screen of the mainland, a system of straight baselines may be drawn following the general direction of the mainland coast. The system forms the new baseline independent of the mainland of the state. The prime effect of a justifiable system is to greatly increase the internal waters of a state but to have only a limited effect on the extension of the territorial sea. Exceptions may occur where certain geographic or historic conditions dominate. These conditions should be limited in scope and be justified by the state through evidence of continuous occupation.

4. Mid-ocean archipelagos, if they meet specific criteria, may be enclosed by a system of construction lines to preserve the political-geographic unity of the insular groups. Waters beyond the normal sea limits should be categorized as insular waters under national jurisdiction but not sovereignty. Transit routes must be designated across the longitudinal and transverse axes to protect the maritime interests of the world community.

5. The seaward limit of the coral reef about atolls should constitute the national baseline for the measurement of the territorial sea and contiguous

zone. Closing lines may be drawn where openings in the reef are greater than 24 miles to maintain the basic internal waters characteristics of the atoll lagoons.

6. Islands may be categorized according to their size and habitation as (a) rocks; (b) islets; (c) isles; and (d) islands. The last-named category possesses all political-legal characteristics of continental mainlands.

7. Due to the limited extent of the territorial sea breadth, inequities caused by islands on the territorial limits of other states will be limited. Many simpler and perhaps better territorial sea boundaries—as opposed to those based on the principle of equidistance—may be negotiated. These limits may preserve the concept of equity and be easier to administer. A "least-distance perpendicular" boundary offers a logical alternative to equidistant lines in an insular area.

8. If equidistance is chosen as the basic principle for a maritime boundary delimitation, islands may be assigned varying values based upon size if inequities develop. Generally, inequities either will not occur or will be limited in extent due to the narrow breadth of the territorial sea.

9. The greater political inequities may develop with islands detached from the parent state that lie immediately adjacent to the shores of another state. Even under these conditions, gross inequities will be rare and generally local. In certain instances, access may become a greater problem than area lost.

ISLANDS: THE CONTINENTAL SHELF AND THE SEABED

While the legal definition of the continental shelf is currently elastic, the term in this discussion refers to the 200-meter depth unless otherwise indicated. Generally, the continental shelf of maritime states extends farther seaward than the territorial sea. While in certain areas, such as the western shores of the Americas, the 200-meter limit may lie within twelve miles of the baseline, on the average the shelf edge is situated more than 35 miles seaward. When the seabed is considered as an area of national jurisdiction, the distance becomes even greater. In spite of the lack of general agreement on the national limit of jurisdiction on the ocean floor, it is relatively safe to assume that the ultimate boundary will not be landward of the 200-meter isobath but probably will be seaward of it, i.e., between the 200-meter isobath and 200 nautical miles.

Islands constitute the most seaward limit of the national baseline for many coastal states. As a consequence, these bits of territory will be the last significant points for the delimitation of a boundary based upon equidistance. Since the breadths of the shelf and seabed are greater, island base points assume a greater relative importance. In addition, the random distribution of isolated, midoceanic islands may allocate thousands of square miles of seabed to states if a distance criterion is adopted. A 200-mile seabed boundary could grant an isolated rock a 125,000-square-mile seabed area (200 × 200 × 3.1416). Generally, insular inequities will be least with the territorial sea, greater with the shelf, and greatest with the seabed. Since in most areas of the world, the toe of the slope is within 200 miles of the baseline, islands could cause the greatest inequities under a 200-mile national jurisdiction parameter.

The basic instrument on the relations of islands to the ocean floor is the Geneva Convention on the Continental Shelf. The shelf convention does not, however, repeat the conditions specified in the territorial sea convention but relies on the definitions and principles contained therein. Article 1 of the shelf convention allocates a continental shelf to islands.[16]

> For the purpose of these Articles, the term continental shelf is used as referring (a) to the seabed and subsoil of the submarine areas adjacent to the coast but outside the area of the territorial sea, to a depth of 200 meters or, beyond that limit, to where the depth of the superjacent waters admits of the exploitation of the natural resources of the said areas; to the seabed and subsoil adjacent to the coasts of islands.

It would appear that every island has a legal continental shelf and, by projection, a seabed contiguous to the shelf. In the former instance, the continental shelf areas of small, isolated islands are usually minimal. Islands, when grouped, however, may be situated upon extensive shelves. One need only examine a bathymetric chart of western Indonesia to see the extent of these areas.

If the seabed relates to the depth criterion, the area adjacent to isolated islands remains restricted. With a distance boundary, the seabed becomes most expansive, being limited only by the selected breadth and by the geographic relationships of adjacency. Other factors, which will be discussed later, could be deemed to prevail.

GEOGRAPHIC RELATIONSHIPS

Most of the provisions of the Convention on the Continental Shelf are very general and were drafted without a deep or acute examination of existing physical situations. The conference appeared to conceive of the world as relatively uncomplicated and regulated in its physical relationships. Unfortunately, even a brief examination of conditions shows that simplifications do not prevail in the three-dimensional world of the shelf and the seabed. Islands and bathymetry combine to produce a myriad of potential combinations each of which may defy solution on the general principles of the Convention. These geographic relationships are far more complicated than those involved in the territorial sea, in scope as well as in dimension. As a consequence, states may more quickly resort to the "special circumstances" clause to claim that inequities exist.

Two islands of differing sovereignty, for example, may be located upon the same oceanic ridge. The "shelf" area of one island may be more extensive than the other (see Figure 8-6). The prolongation of the 200-meter isobath of Island A obviously extends closer in certain areas to the land territory of Island B than to its own baseline. Should the boundary be an equidistant line? Can one say that the shelf area about Island A should adhere to Island B, from which it is physically separated according to one criterion? How may one determine equity or, for that matter, really define it under the terms of the Convention? One may question if equity relates to the resulting areal allocations, which are fairly equal, or to the justice of the unity of the prolongation of the feature. How may the boundary expert balance parameters involving depth (200 meters), distance (adjacency) and technology (exploitability) in a rational and equitable manner? Boundary criteria must be altered—simplified or clarified—to clear the current jungle. If a depth criterion is used to determine seabed limit, boundary relationships between states should not relate, under all circumstances, to mileage, i.e., an equally distant line. Conversely, if the relationships are based on distance, bathymetry need not be deemed relevant.

However, the Convention remains valid and will prevail until replaced, revised or expanded. Solutions to maritime boundary problems must relate to all aspects of the conventions on the territorial sea and the continental shelf as well as to developing customary practices of states and of the courts, e.g., the ICJ North Sea Cases. In the latter, however, many of the seemingly rele-

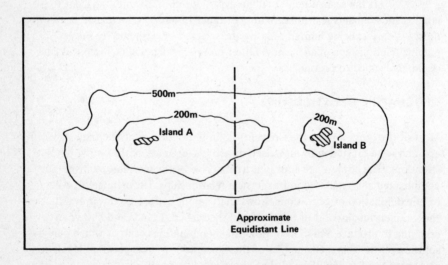

Figure 8-6. Islands: Equidistance vs. Depth

vant points may prove geographically irrelevant. For example, under certain conditions, it may be impossible to delimit "natural prolongations" in conditions of natural adjacency. How may one determine the limit between Dutch and German prolongations in the North Sea when nearly identical geographical conditions exist on land? In addition, the Court stated that the resulting division of the shelf, to be equitable, should relate to the respective coastal lengths of the adjacent states. The litigants—Germany vs. Denmark and the Netherlands—have virtually identical coastal morphology: low tidal flats fringed by islands aligned parallel to the coastline. A constant factor prevails. What would the relationships be if one state possessed many islands and the other few or none? Should the coastal lengths of the islands be added to that of the mainland? Should both the seaward and the landward coasts of the islands be included in the measurements?

It would appear just that the bases for settlement should rest not only on seeming equity but also on equity based on relevant geographic facts. To include the total perimeter of an island or islands could lead to excesses and injustice. The comparison of coastal lengths should relate only to those portions of the coastline that directly affect the measurement of the territorial sea. These might be determined by the construction of special systems of straight baselines for the purpose, or by a direct comparison of the areas of the territorial sea involved (assuming, of course, identical breadth of claims). The latter probably would produce the greatest equity for it would remove from influence areas of internal and tidal waters that do not directly relate to the territorial sea. Many irrelevancies would be eliminated as a result.

While the North Sea Cases applied to adjacent states, the same conditions may prevail when state positions are opposite. (See Figure 8-7 for an illustration of a similar problem.) One may argue, on depth alone, that Island B, separated by deeper water, should receive only the circular shelf area immediately about it. Adjacency begs the issue and would assign to B a portion of the shelf which "prolongs" from A. Of greater complexity is the situation where B sits astride the same shelf areas but is separated from its parent state by deeper water. To a degree, the answers to these questions concern (a) the relationships of islands to each other and/or to the mainlands, (b) their size, as previously discussed, and (c) their status.

These illustrations, however, focus on certain of the issues which have been raised and on which the language of the Convention and of the North Sea Cases do not assist. The Court cannot be expected to ajudicate the many maritime boundary problems which are evolving unless certain objective and specific criteria are created to assist in problems of delimitation for all jurisdictions: sovereignty, sovereign rights, economic resource zones, fisheries zones, etc. It should be recognized that most current maritime boundary discussions have related to seabed resource allocations. However, if a fisheries convention is drafted, whether based on species or on a zonal approach, limits will be required between adjacent states and even, under certain conditions, between opposite states.

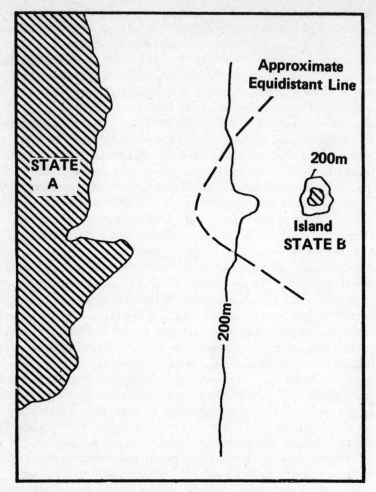

Figure 8-7. Islands and Mainland Shelf: Equidistance vs. Depth

The only alternative is a regional zone of common usage, but limits between zones will still be necessary. For example, how may one define the limits between the United States and Canada—species or zonal—for the allocation of fisheries rights or conservation? Will the same boundary for fisheries apply also to the shelf? Would two noncoextensive limits be acceptable? Do the same parameters prevail? Will additional "special circumstances" become issues?

ISLANDS AND SHELF BOUNDARIES: NORMAL
OR SPECIAL CIRCUMSTANCE?

The language of the shelf convention pertaining to limits is similar to that of the territorial sea convention. Curious differences in language occur that may or may not have meaning.

Article 6[17]

1. Where the same continental shelf is adjacent to the territories of two or more States whose coasts are opposite each other, the boundary of the continental shelf appertaining to such States shall be determined by agreement between them. In the absence of agreement, and unless another boundary line is justified by special circumstances, the boundary is the median line, every point of which is equidistant from the nearest points of the baselines from which the breadth of the territorial sea of each State is measured.

2. Where the same continental shelf is adjacent to the territories of two adjacent States, the boundary of the continental shelf shall be determined by agreement between them. In the absence of agreement, and unless another boundary line is justified by special circumstances, the boundary shall be determined by application of the principle of equidistance from the nearest points of the baselines from which the breadth of the territorial sea of each State is measured.

3. In delimiting the boundaries of the continental shelf, any lines which are drawn in accordance with the principles set out in paragraphs 1 and 2 of this article should be defined with reference to charts and geographical features as they exist at a particular date, and reference should be made to fixed permanent identifiable points on the land.

Both conventions specify that boundaries should be determined by agreement between the states concerned. Both acknowledge the influence of (undefined) "special circumstances." Note that the territorial sea convention states that "failing agreement to the contrary" neither state is "entitled to extend its territorial sea beyond the median [equidistant] line. . . ." The strange difference in the language of the shelf convention's paragraph 1–"in the absence of agreement . . . , the boundary *is* the median line"–appears to place a much greater emphasis on the mandatory use of equidistance.

While this language may have been intended to establish a more secure tenure for exploitation in the absence of agreement, it also appears to lead directly, as a result of the influence of islands, to a greater potential for special circumstances to question the validity of the principle involved. This action would be the direct result of the increasing chances of inequity induced by islands, which develop as distances from the baseline increase.

One perceives that islands may have, on the basis of equidistance, a full effect as basepoints equal to any continental or mainland base point for the construction of a continental shelf boundary under certain conditions. Under differing conditions, islands may also be disregarded completely in the construction of an equidistant shelf boundary as sources of gross inequity. In between these two obvious extremes, there exist gray areas where the use of an island or a type of an island as base points might be assigned a partial value. The precise degree of utilization of the island will relate to the particular factors which are involved in the specific case. Finally, unique conditions may prevail, as a result of insular treatment, to warrant very unusual determinations or arrangements. These last-named conditions presumably will be most limited in application, for exceptions normally prove the rule.

Islands: Full Effect on Shelf Boundaries

In the categorization of islands by size under the discussion of the territorial sea, it was hypothesized that certain islands constitute mainland as a consequence of their size and importance. By definition, these islands were larger than 1,000 square miles in area and were inhabited by a particular population. While the political status of the islands was not deemed determinative, nearly all were found to be independent, either in themselves or as constituent and integral parts of an independent state, or they had attained an autonomous status which conferred many of the attributes of self-government.

There does not appear to be any logical combination of circumstances that would justify denying these islands full effect as well on the delimitation of a continental shelf or of a seabed boundary. These islands constitute major and significant geographic entities of a magnitude to warrant their particular status. As such, shelf and seabed would devolve to them as "mainland." Cuba, Greenland, Borneo, et al., possess all of the attributes of mainland in themselves, and they should not be denied rights associated with their nature.

The problem will always be raised under any absolute scale of values, and perhaps rightly: If 1,000 square miles would constitute mainland, why not 999? Or 998? Or 997? In any categorization of scientific phenomena, certain specific parameters are chosen to delineate each species. Most examples will meet the limits handily, but occasionally unusual circumstances may lead to deviations. One may only recommend that the individual cases be examined on their merits to determine exceptions to the rule. It is suspected that few exceptions will occur.

A second group of islands that should have full effect on continental shelf boundaries are those which relate geographically to the mainland in such a way as to constitute a cohesive part thereof. Regardless of size, these islands are situated so as to be linked geographically to the land. Two tests may be used to determine this interrelationship: Boggs[18] recommended that lines be drawn tangent to the ends of the island axis that relates to the mainland coastal direction. The parallel lines should be constructed to enclose the minimum area of low water surface between the island and the mainland. If the area of the island exceeds the water surface, the island should be treated as mainland and used as full-effect base points on the national baseline for adjacent or opposite equidistant determinations. Conversely, if the water area is greater than the area of the island, it should not receive a full effect depending on other circumstances. Generally the land-water relationships are obvious; in certain cases, however, the areas will require multiple measurements to assure the minimum water area selection and the proper land-water relationship. The identical system may be used, of course, to relate smaller islands to mainland islands or to group smaller islands and to obtain greater and more significant relationships (see Figure 8-8).

The second test[19] has been developed to validate the use of islands as headlands to bays, but the same general conditions prevail for the mainland/island relationship. In effect, the goals and associations are identical. The island should not be situated at a significant distance from the mainland shore, and

> . . . the area of the island should be greater than the intervening water body. The latter, in configuration, should ideally be channel-like. . . . The character of a channel may be easily established by relating the length of the water course to its average width. Closing lines may be drawn at the natural entrance points. These would, of course, be determined by the application of the 45° test as in the bay situation. The average width, assuming nearly parallel banks for the channels, may be determined by averaging the lengths of the two closing lines. The length of the channel may be measured along the line connecting the mid-points of the two closing lines. To be truly channel-like the ratio of the length to the average width should be 3:1 or greater. A lesser ratio would not exhibit the true riverine characteristics of a channel. . . . Rather, the feature would be more bay-like in its two dimensional configuration.[20] (See Figure 8-9.)

The latter test may be utilized to relate an island of any category to continental mainland—or an island of any category to a mainland island. In this manner, islands smaller than 1,000 square miles in area may be entitled to full effect if they have the proper areal associations with "mainlands."

It should be noted that the two tests are likely to have differing effects, and they may prove to be useful under diverse conditions. Boggs's proposal, for example, would be particularly useful for islands whose long axes are perpendicular to the coastline while the Hodgson-Alexander test favors those exhibiting parallel relationships. Logic may indicate, as islands become "unitized," that the area of the "unit," i.e., land and water, be used to further extend

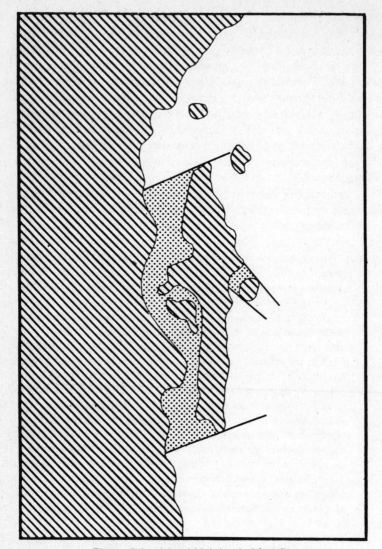

Figure 8-8.   Island-Mainland, After Boggs

the unit as full-effect base points for the shelf determination of linear insular units, e.g., the Kurils, Aleutians, the Ryukyus.

A third group of islands would also call for full effect as equidistance base points, i.e., where the insular geography is identical or nearly identical. In these situations, which normally will prevail for adjacent states but may also for opposite states, the presence of many offshore islands along the coasts of two

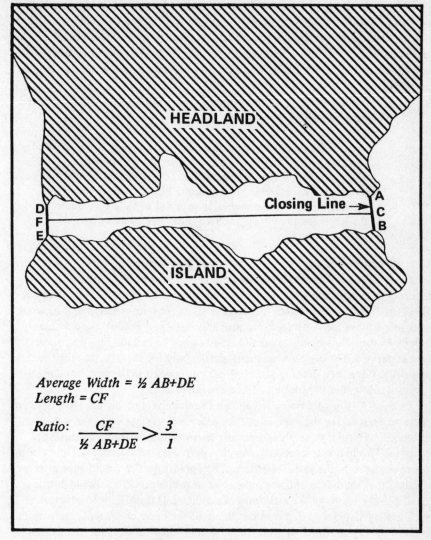

Figure 8-9. Channel: Ratio of Length to Width

states will tend to equalize the effects on equidistance. Since no single state will appear to gain a marked advantage, the islands should be granted their normal influence on the construction of the median or lateral boundaries. A practical application of the effect of the islands would involve the construction of equidistance lines using the islands (with full effect) and not using them. If the practical deviations in total areal allocations are relatively minor, the islands should be granted their total value.

Many states have followed this criterion in their delimitation of shelf boundaries. Norway and Sweden have granted full effect[21] to their respective islands, as have the principal states in the delimitation of the shelf boundaries in the North Sea.[22] No appreciable advantage accrues to the coastal state if it refuses value to the islands of the second state while also denying value to its own insularity.

Northcutt Ely[23] has suggested a fourth situation in which an island might be granted full effect. He wrote

> . . . an islet should be *prima facie* entitled to recognition of its coasts as a component of a baseline for demarcation of seabed boundaries if any portion of the islet lies within 24 nautical miles of the coast of its owner's mainland or major island. This is because the island's 12-mile contiguous zone merges with the 12-mile contiguous zone of the larger land territory, the two thus forming an envelope encompassing both.

It would appear that the author conceived of the situation of opposite states in a relatively large semienclosed sea situation. His rule could, for example, lead to inequity in an adjacent situation or in a narrow sea. While Ely chose not to define "islet" and "major island," it seems obvious from his remarks that he would probably equate islet with rock and probably with islet as previously defined herein. In turn, "major island" could be presumed to include isles and islands, also as defined. The concept has merit, particularly for the situation for which it appears to have been developed. It may also be applied in the negative sense as the author intended. This point will be expanded later.

A fifth situation also calls for the full effect of islands, although care must be exercised in the application. An independent state, or perhaps even an autonomous insular state, should possess territory that warrants treatment as mainland. While it was stressed earlier that political status should not exercise a negative effect on the value of islands as basepoints, justice would appear to demand that the status of independence or near-independence should entitle a small island state to all the attributes of mainland. It is difficult to conceive of such a small state being deprived justifiably of shelf and/or seabed merely on the basis of size. While few independent and small insular states are situated in close proximity to other states, the potential exists. With the increasing trend for independence on the part of small areas, the world may well see in the near future many of these entities, which will be limited in territory. Equity should logically demand a maritime domain undiminished by the special circumstance of small-area insularity.

It is difficult to assess how far the premise should be extended. While the need for independent states would be obvious, the requirements of the autonomous state could be equally as great. Problems then arise, as pointed out before, of degree of autonomy and of the dynamics of political change. The answer is by no means clear.

Nevertheless, we should not assume that since an independent small island group is entitled to full effect, all rocks, islets, and isles of the state should have full effect. The general premises established before should dominate once the "mainland" territory has been identified.

The sixth and final condition that should lead to full effect for islands stems from mutual agreement of the parties concerned. Reasons beyond those directly concerned with the law of the sea and the seabeds may affect a state's perception of the issues at stake. As a consequence, the factor of island-induced inequity may not be relevant to national problems. Within the framework of marine jurisdiction, however, both states will probably have considered the previously enumerated situations and have determined to disregard the consequences of islands on boundary delimitations.

Islands: No Effect on Shelf Boundaries

At the other extreme in the delineation of shelf limits, we perceived situations where islands would be totally disregarded as base points. Generally, the elimination of these islands stems from the negotiating process, and hence the factor of mutual agreement enters into the arrangement. Without dwelling on the obvious factor, there are certain geographical situations where islands should clearly be disregarded as base points.

The first example would include islands which are in dispute. More properly, the issue should involve the establishment and recognition of national jurisdiction over insular territories. If the mere criterion of "dispute" is used, a nation wishing to disclaim the effect of an island need only to establish a contrary claim to sovereignty. As a consequence, a need exists to clarify the status of the dispute in relation to the time of negotiation for the shelf boundary; most of the islands in dispute are currently known, although perhaps not universally acknowledged.

As cited earlier, most disputed islands are situated in the immediate vicinity of the seaward termini of international land boundaries or are in the middle of seas or oceans relatively distant from land. In the former instance, which will affect lateral limits, the presence of a single island in dispute will cause considerable diplomatic problems. If the island happens to be situated in the mouth of a river or stream which is the land boundary, the influence of the island will be very small. In fact, it may and perhaps should be disregarded in the delimitation of the boundary, for at shelf and seabed distances from the baseline, the effects of these nearshore islands will be minimal.

If the island is situated reasonably distant—e.g., twelve miles offshore—however, a serious problem in delimitation may occur. Since most of these islands will prove to be rocks or islets, they should reasonably be eliminated as factors. Pending the solution of the dispute, a twelve-nautical-mile area could be assigned to the disputed island(s) and the resources allocated equally to the claimant states. Since the area will most probably be small, the equal allocation would appear reasonable. The proposed solution, however, may be a nonsolution. If the states can agree on the allocation of the revenues they can also agree on the allocation of the territory. Furthermore, the oil companies may not be interested in making the necessary heavy investment when it could pass to another state or to another company.

The second category of islands to be disregarded in the construction of equidistant boundaries are those situated in the middle of restricted water bodies, i.e., semienclosed or enclosed seas. Generally, these islands will be small and uninhabited, falling in the rock and islet categories previously defined. Many of these troublesome "dots" of real estate are found within twelve miles of the equidistant line constructed without their use as basepoints. These islands have the effect of displacing (assuming a position near midpoint on an opposite situation) the boundary approximately a quarter of the width of the body of water; they may continue to influence a displacement along the water body's length for a maximum distance equal to the width of the body. The inequity would be obvious.

Many states have adopted this principle or practice. Italy and Yugoslavia,[24] Iran and Saudi Arabia,[25] and Abu Dhabi and Qatar,[26] to name a few, have agreed to eliminate as base points the troublesome islets in midsea or even along the midline of adjacent coasts. In the first two negotiations, the islets received twelve-mile "seas" in their general vicinities but did not displace the median lines at greater distances. In the last-named agreement, the island in question received a three-mile sea, equal to the claimed territorial seas of both states. Of interest, however, the Yugoslav islands in the middle Adriatic receive twelve-mile limits although Yugoslavia only claims a ten-mile sea and Italy a six-mile sea. The acceptance of twelve miles appears to relate to the contiguous zone breadth of the territorial sea convention.

The third category of islands to be disregarded stems from the Ely proposal noted earlier. Ely states ". . . we would disqualify isolated islands which are not only too distant to be in contact with the contiguous zone envelope of their owner's territories, but which are also uninhabited or support only caretakers or other tokens of the owner's sovereignty, such as lighthouses or communications facilities."[27] The premise is excellent, again within the framework of opposite states in enclosed or semienclosed seas. Difficulties, however, may be encountered with the concept as distances increase. For example, an islet may be situated upon a tongue of continental platform, a sub-200-meter shelf plateau, which is isolated from the territory of two other states to the north and to the south by relatively significant trenches. The same plateau may extend continuously eastward to territory of the administering state. The uninhabited islet is obviously more than 24 miles from all other land area. Should the islet have only a twelve-mile zone with the division of the plateau to be made from the "mainland" of other territory? Or is it to be given an effect on a seabed boundary? On shelf allocations, in the restricted sense, the value of the islet on the allocations of the adjacent states would of course be negligible.

Equity, based on area or concentration of land considerations, would appear to demand that these isolated geographic phenomena be discounted if adjacency and depth continue as dominant criteria for maritime boundaries.

The fourth and final condition whereby islands would be discounted as base points involves agreement of states. For the Italo-Yugoslav shelf boundary delimitation previously discussed, the Italian Tremiti island group, which is situated approximately twelve miles from the mainland, has not been used as base points for the boundary delimitation. The effect of these islands on the boundary would have been limited in any event due to their proximity to the mid-sea Yugoslav islets. A similar situation developed between Bahrain and Saudi Arabia, on a lateral boundary development, where selected points chosen for the construction of the boundary ignored rocks, islets, and low tide elevations. A simpler boundary resulted. Thus the ignoring of small islands may involve the desire for simplification of alignment or the perception of equity. In either instance, developing state practice does acknowledge a case for the elimination of certain insular base points. The islands so involved have generally been allocated a territorial sea (and associated shelf) equal to the claimed territorial sea or to a twelve-mile contiguous zone. Certain low tide elevations have not been granted equivalent rights.

Islands: Partial Effect on Shelf Boundaries

The vast gray area of shelf boundary delimitation occurs with islands which, because of size and/or population combined with geographic position, can neither be ignored nor granted a full value for the construction of equidistant lines. The prime example of partial use stems from the Saudi Arabia-Iran shelf negotiations in the Persian Gulf. In the original negotiations, which were later modified,[28] the Iranian island of Kharg caused disagreement. Kharg occupies about eight square miles and at the time was sparsely inhabited. Situated approximately seventeen miles from the Iranian shore, the use of the island as a baseline element caused Saudi apprehensions. Its displacement of the boundary was critical in its effects on known petroleum fields situated near the center of the Gulf. By agreement, the isle received a half-effect, i.e., the boundary was to be delimited halfway between the lines constructed with Kharg as national baseline and lines constructed without it.

The treatment of Kharg conflicts with Ely's suggestion of full value for all inhabited islands within 24 miles of the national baseline. Nevertheless, the underlying logic of the negotiators remains valid. Kharg is an isolated isle, a solitary phenomenon only lightly inhabited. Full effect would have displaced the boundary approximately eight miles towards Saudi Arabia in an area of known petroleum deposits. The results of half-effect reduces the displacement, on the average, to approximately four miles. Kharg most probably received this special allocation because the general outlines of the mid-Gulf oil fields were known and concessions had been granted. In effect, the solution confirmed the existing situation as conforming with "reality" although minor modifications had to be made later.

The question arises, Would the agreement have been made in the same manner if the resources were suspected but their exact location not known? Or would the agreement have been the same if the oil deposits were farther to the west so that a half-effect line would have placed them entirely in Saudi Arabia? While the question is essentially academic, the answer would probably be negative. Prof. H. Gary Knight has suggested that a procedural device might be devised whereby part of the negotiations would involve a study of the potential resources of the disputed area. The study could be made by the countries or an impartial arbiter. The knowledge of the resource location, or nonlocation, could contribute to the equitable solution of the dispute.

Kharg has since grown in importance with offshore petroleum development and is now a major transshipment point. An offshore loading zone, connected with the island by the world's largest submarine pipeline (56-inch diameter), will service 300,000-500,000 DWT tankers from a steel "island," 1,800 by 310 feet, situated 4,500 feet offshore.

A second group of islands deserves a partial effect—islands situated near the median zone but inhabited by sizable populations of indigenous peoples. Reports have been received that Italy and Tunisia have agreed, in principle, on a median line boundary between the two states. The negotiations were complicated by the presence of several small Italian islands—Pantelleria and the Pelagie group.[29] Tunisia demanded that the islands be discounted while Italy's claim called for their use as base points. The agreement in principle gives to each island a thirteen-mile zone of Italian jurisdiction; the final delimitation has not been accomplished, however.

The choice of thirteen miles is curious. The shortest distance between Pantelleria (Italy) and the Tunisian baseline is approximately 38 miles. Full effect would have displaced the boundary about 19 miles; half effect, 9.5 miles. In contrast, Lampione lies approximately 60 miles distant and the relationships would be 30 and 15 miles, respectively. Thirteen miles represents, hypothetically, nearly the average of the half-effects of the two islands. While the bases for the negotiation are not known, the agreement assigns to Italy a seabed zone of jurisdiction greater than the claimed territorial sea and contiguous zone which, accidentally or by design, allocates to the islands an average half-effect. The thirteen-mile zone does little violence to the unity of the shelf that prolongs from the Tunisian coast. Lampione lies on that shelf; the other islands are separated by narrow stretches of water deeper than 200 meters.

A second arrangement occurs in the Indonesia-Malaysia shelf boundary; here lateral limits are involved. The Malaysian baseline comprises the coast of Borneo, which is virtually without offshore islands. In contrast, Indonesia possesses two island groups that extend northward roughly perpendicular to the

Malaysian baseline (a true equidistant boundary would extend northeastward). The Natuna island groups, however, have not been assigned full value as base points on the boundary.[30] The boundary, defined seaward by points 22-25, extends as shown in Table 8-5.

As the boundary projects farther seaward the islands have been granted lesser values, even though the more seaward islands are larger in size than those closer onshore. The boundary effect gives islands a decreasing importance, which averages almost three-quarters value. The terminal point, 25, has approximately half-effect. Consequently, partial effect ranges from approximately half at the terminus to nearly full value (86%) onshore, to produce a boundary of apparent equity in a condition where islands greatly favored one state.

Detached islands constitute a third group that could or should be assigned less than full value as base point. (The choice of examples does not necessarily indicate that they should have reduced values.) The islands assume two different geographic characters: (1) those which lie in a position that may connect with the jurisdictional area of the homeland under certain criteria; and (2) those totally removed from any direct connection with the state. Examples of these would be the Channel Islands and St. Pierre and Miquelon.

The heavily populated and quasi-independent Channel Islands, situated adjacent to France, lie more than 47 miles from the nearest U.K. territory (see Figure 8-10). Due to the configuration of the French coast and the arrangement of the islands, a full-effect equidistant boundary would connect the "shelf" of the Channel Islands with that of the U.K. To allocate the islands a twelve-mile zone would leave them as enclaves and would appear inequitable. The islands with full effect would influence an equidistant line approximately 24 miles to the north, 34 miles to the northwest, and 40 miles to west northwestward. The area between a line connecting these points and the twelve-mile limit measures approximately 1,100 square miles. The island area, in contrast, totals only 57 square miles (both areas are in square nautical miles). The entire French shelf area (beyond twelve miles) is estimated at 23,000 square miles.

The Channel Islands could thus affect about 5 percent of the total

Table 8-5. Natuna Island Groups Boundary Effect

Points	Distance		Island Effect
	Indonesian Islands	*Malaysia*	
22	50	58	.86
23	103	139	.74
24	125	185	.68
25	132	236	.56
		Average	.71

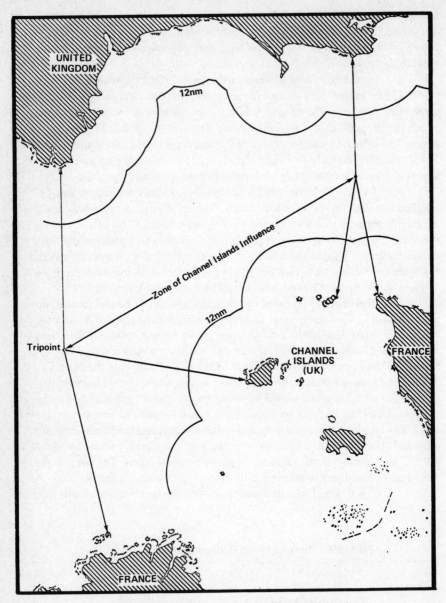

Figure 8-10.   Relationship of Channel Islands

French allocation. The percentage is sizable in comparison to the two land areas involved. Two solutions could prevail if partial value were to be required: (1) A delimitation could be made that would maintain a contiguity of the seabed with that of the U.K. A greater area could be allocated in the north to permit a worthwhile interconnection, while a lesser value would be assigned to the west as compensation. The result could approximate a half-effect value. (2) A zone of shelf jurisdiction could be allocated at a distance greater than twelve miles for the entire area. The region would remain an enclave within French shelf area jurisdiction if the value assigned did not exceed 24 miles. A value between 17 and 20 miles would appear to grant the half-effect. While the enclave would be a rare occurrence, it would not be unique; in fact, as limits of maritime jurisdictions are delimited throughout the world, enclaves will probably become increasingly more common.

In the St. Pierre example, no question exists of the isolation of the jurisdictional area from other than Canadian territory. Because of coastal configuration, the islands appear to exert an effect on equidistant limits for approximately 200 miles seaward of the islands. The zone forms a relatively narrow triangle, which would contain a significant area of shelf and seabed in relation to the limited population (6,000) and small area (90 sq. miles) of the territory. The need to restrict the base point value would seem to be apparent.

A fourth category of islands that could warrant a partial effect on equidistant limits are small islands (islets and isles) which constitute significant segments of national territory. Several conditions advanced earlier might lead to these small islands being discounted entirely in equidistant boundary delimitations. However, they should not be totally disregarded if both a significant number of these islands exist or have a relatively widespread distribution and if they constitute a significant part of the area of a state. One might conceive, for example, that isolated keys such as the Morant and Pedro Cays of Jamaica could be questioned as base points due to their small size. Jamaica, however, possesses a limited area, and the Cays constitute a relatively significant segment of it. They should not, as a consequence, be totally disregarded for the sake of equity. Since each situation of this type is unique, it is difficult to generalize further without additional examination of the individual situations.

Finally, under certain circumstances the islands of adjacent or opposite states may be assigned relative values of differing weights by agreement. In the shoreward sector of the Fenno-Soviet continental shelf boundary, the boundary relates to the Finnish and Soviet islands in a nearly constant 4:5 ratio. More seaward areas, however, are virtually equidistant. One may hypothesize reasons, e.g., security, for such actions, but it may be sufficient to note that an agreement has been made.

Islands: Special Conditions

The previous discussion has dealt with islands as individual base points. Islands, of course, may be integrated by systems of straight baselines in which the lines, rather than the islands, become the national baselines. In this event, two potential problems may occur:

1. A straight baseline system may incorporate within it rocks, islets, and/or isles which, by prior criteria, should be discounted as base points. If this situation prevails, an inequity will obviously develop and will be compounded by the characteristics of the system. The straight baselines system should then be restricted to the development of the territorial sea and eliminated for the purposes of constructing an equidistant shelf or seabed boundary. Again the degree of inequity may be found by developing boundaries with and without the use of the straight baselines. Many national systems contain excesses that should not be perpetuated in the shelf and seabed boundaries, thus creating (because of distance) even greater inequities.

2. One state may opt to draw straight baselines within the intent of the Convention while the adjacent or opposite state may not elect to establish a system. The construction of an equidistant boundary between straight (base) lines and random points (islands) results in a sinuous boundary. Along any line segment, an infinite number of points exists between turning points. To create equidistance between the line and one point (island) requires an infinite number of perpendicular bisectors to determine the equidistant points. An arc results (see Figure 8-11). This type of boundary would be difficult, if not impossible, to develop and intolerable to administer.

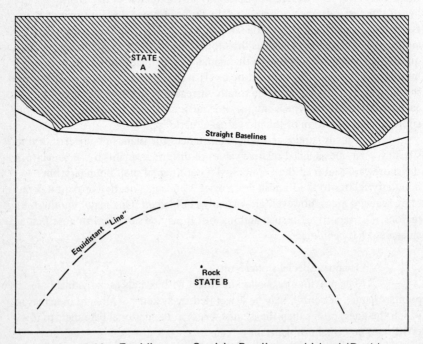

Figure 8-11. Equidistance: Straight Baselines and Island (Rock)

Two obvious solutions become available. The straight baselines of the one state should be ignored for the purposes of delimitation, or the second state should construct a straight baseline system for the purposes of determining the boundary. In the latter event, the system should be designed as nearly identical as possible to the existing system. The parameters will relate to: length of line, angle of the line to the coastline's general direction, and maximum distance of the lines from the intervening shoreline. Should a marked difference in insularity exist, the straight baseline system should be drawn, as feasible, to mainland basepoints to conform with length of line and coastal azimuth. Generally, an equidistance boundary will be easier to construct between straight lines, i.e., bisectors of the angle made by the intersections of the lines, than between random points, i.e., perpendicular bisectors of the lines joining the points. The former will also tend to be less complex and should produce fewer disagreements in the ultimate administration of the line.

The prior discussion has generally assumed that islands, isles, islets, and rocks have been situated upon the same area of continental shelf or seabed. Obviously, under the complexities of the physical environment, discontinuities and other aberrations will eixst on the floor of the ocean. (See Figure 8-6 for an illustration.) How these variations should be treated will depend directly on the ultimate definition of the national limits on the seabed approved by the United Nations Conference in 1974. Under present parameters, the delimitation experts have to choose a loose or a strict construction for the language of the existing Convention. Naturally, each nation tends to select the construction that presents the greatest advantage to it. Since the 200-meter limit has not yet been breached, one state might declare that the deep is the absolute factor and that it should serve to limit national jurisdiction.

Bottom topography, however, is normally uneven and is quite complex. In the Norway-United Kingdom agreement in the North Sea, Norway "jumped" a sizable trench of sub-200-meter area with U.K. approval. One may argue that this "trench" really constitutes an integral part of the shelf since it is not continental slope. On the other hand, the depth is a break in the "shelf" that adheres to the Norwegian coast, although to the south the shelf arcs about the "trench" end to envelop it. To whom does it belong? The question is relevant elsewhere in the world, e.g., in the East China Sea, where a nearly identical situation prevails. Does adjacency become the principal factor in this situation, or does depth continue to prevail? Does the question demand the same answer when the trench represents the identical geologic feature differentiated only by depth?

Under present rules, depth presents the complicating factor, particularly when modified by adjacency and exploitability. A state such as Norway might better refuse to negotiate should the trench become a factor of limitation pending the technical developments to increase exploitability that are bound to occur soon. Then the depth factor will be rendered superfluous.

Should a distance or a greater depth criterion be selected by the Seabeds Committee for the future limit of national jurisdiction, the complications will be reduced but not eliminated. Islands will still constitute major stumbling blocks in national delimitations. Nevertheless, until the new Convention is drafted, signed, and in force, the present reliance on the three factors must be considered to temper these proposed insular factors.

Even now, however, one may question the relevance of depth. The Anglo-Norwegian, Danish-Norwegian, Italo-Yugoslav and Italo-Tunisian agreements, among others, all traverse sub-200-meter seabed. Admittedly, all of these agreements occur in semienclosed seas, which offers an additional complication. Apparently, most coastal states perceive these semienclosed seas as the domain of the bordering states regardless of depth of intervening waters. Adjacency dominates depth under these conditions.

Islands: The Seabed Beyond the Shelf

The new convention presumably will have to face additional problems with the extension of national jurisdiction beyond the relatively limited shelf to the more expansive seabed. Insular inequities have been noted to increase with distance; as a consequence, islands will cause even greater concern to seabed delimitations unless specific language is provided. Unfortunately, the history of international conventions shows a use of the least specific language in an effort to obtain consensus. A 200-mile boundary about Clipperton or Ascension, for example, allocates to each approximately 125,000 square miles of seabed. Do they warrant such great areas with the corresponding reduction in the international zone? The uninhabitable rocks may or may not deserve one-eighth of a million square miles of seabed; however, to avoid future disputes, the negotiators must be aware of their significance and must face the issue. The effects of the scattered islands of the Trust Territory of the Pacific Islands and of French Polynesia will be astronomical.

Most of the islands that will significantly affect the seabed are situated in midocean. They will not normally complicate boundaries as currently being considered to a great degree, except among themselves. However, there are exceptions. The islands will serve to reduce the zone available for international development. The states of the world must, in concert, determine specifically how they should be treated.

ISLANDS—NATURAL BUT ARTIFICIAL

The Convention on the Continental Shelf, in discussing artificial islands, states in Article 5 (4):[31]

> 4. Such installations and devices, though under the jurisdiction of the coastal State, do not possess the status of islands. They have no territorial sea of their own, and their presence does not affect the delimitation of the territorial sea of the coastal State.

The perception in the Convention obviously involved artificial installations designed for shelf exploitation. Technology and the demands of population growth will soon lead to an expansion in the number and a change in the character of these "artificial" installations—atomic power plants, artificial harbors, floating airports, and perhaps inhabited places. Most of them will remain "artificial" in the sense man builds them of iron, steel, concrete, etc. These installations could cause grave political problems that might require special legal regimes. However, when the installations are sufficiently developed to be permanently inhabited by a specific people, will a special regime suffice? I doubt it. If people living on land demand a territorial sea, people living on "artificial" land also will. The seabed factor, however, is not as apparent.

Man's ingenuity will further complicate the issue of "artificial" islands. In the Arctic, permafrost islands exist as a result of natural processes:

> They are comprised of ordinary sand, gravel, clays, and silt. But the individual grains of these materials are rigidly cemented together by interstitial ice to depths of several hundred feet. This icy matrix gives the islands more than enough structural strength to resist any lateral forces that might be exerted by the thermal expansion and contraction of the recurring ice sheet.[32]

The Imperial Oil Company plans to duplicate these natural islands by artificial means for use as drilling platforms. If successful, once constructed, these permafrost islands will be difficult to distinguish from their natural counterparts. How shall these islands be legally viewed—artificial or natural? Are they similar to the spoil banks, which may conceivably become natural islands, or do they constitute "ice islands"? Several techniques are under consideration, and in time engineers will construct "natural artificial" islands in the Arctic.

In another part of the world, the so-called "Republic of Minerva" has proposed the construction of "islands" on otherwise submerged reefs in the South Pacific. While the government of Tonga has taken strong exception to the perceived threat of the "Minervan" operation, the concept raises questions again. The plan conceives of dredging unconsolidated materials from the lagoons and dumping them on the submerged reefs. These materials probably would have to be protected or stabilized to insure that future storms will not destroy them. The "Republic" campaigns actively to be recognized as a "state." To date, the efforts have been fruitless but the ramifications of the endeavor need to be considered. If successful, islands would exist which could, according to plan, have a permanent population. In addition, a government of sorts (the proposals are quite unique) would be present. The "government" has already issued maps of the Minervan "territorial sea." What may be a hoax, can also be a problem. If Minerva succeeds with the engineering problems, what will limit other states from attempting the same?

Several years ago a plan was formulated to construct an "island" on the Florida reefs beyond the U.S. territorial sea. The Federal Government opposed the project, and the Courts terminated the activities. Would the results have been the same if the Federal Government had supported rather than opposed the project? Would the artificial island have become, with time and nature, a true island? It is believed that it might have. Lawyers and negotiators should address the issue either by granting rights to these islands or by more specifically defining islands so as to exclude them and other types of manmade insular phenomena.

SUMMARY

National efforts have been directed toward a new seabeds convention that may provide the framework for a world order within the finite space and resources of the oceans. However, in the quest for the solution to the "big" problem, little effort has been directed toward the resolution of the numerous technical problems that nations must face in the delimitation of existing national limits. Many oil companies have withdrawn from concessions because of overlapping national claims that undermine the required security of tenure. These disputes are difficult to rationalize because technical advice is limited or contradictory; and few examples exist as evidence of state practice. Many of these problems flow from islands.

Both 1958 conventions on the territorial sea and on the continental shelf recognize islands as factors for the determination of national sovereignty and jurisdiction over and under the sea. Both, moreover, acknowledge the relative influence of islands on the delimitation of the territorial sea and continental shelf boundaries between adjacent and opposite states. Yet the two conventions stress the factor of "special circumstances" which, while undefined, obviously correlates to islands in the main.

Nearly all claims to "special circumstances" in boundary negotiations in the sea regard islands as particular causes or sources of inequity. There can be no question that islands, depending on their locations and relationships, cause gross deflections in equidistant boundaries. While equidistance is not the sole basis for the delimitation of territorial sea, continental shelf, or seabed boundaries, the principle has become enshrined as a veritable "conventional wisdom" for maritime limits. It is the only method specifically mentioned in both conventions and, as a consequence, states find the concept easy to accept due to its proper "sanctification."

The solution to the issues raised by the effects of islands on equidistant boundaries and seabed allocations may be rationally determined by varying the effects of islands on the limits under specific circumstances. Developing international practice and law point out several examples of categorization of islands in their relationships to maritime boundaries. From these examples, an effort has been made here to classify islands further by size, relative importance, and occupation (both human and political). These empirical generalizations have been applied to the territorial sea and its boundaries as well as to the continental shelf and seabed and their limits.

Islands, except in a few specific instances, do not greatly distort territorial sea boundaries due to the narrow limits involved. They may, however, produce tortuous boundaries, difficult to administer unless modified through a process of simplification or the choice of an alternative method of boundary delimitation. Inequities become prevalent with increasing distance from the national baselines. Shelf boundaries based on islands and and equidistance may prove to be unacceptable without considerable modification. Consequently, restrictions must be placed upon the use of certain small islands in order to remove or reduce their distortions and to preserve a semblance of equity.

An effort has been made here toward an objective analysis of islands as special circumstances within the limitations of the conventions on the territorial sea and the continental shelf. Certain seabed problems for which law has not yet developed have been pointed out. It is hoped that the proposals in this chapter may ultimately assist in alleviating certain vexing problems of maritime boundary delimitations.

Chapter Nine

Special Circumstances: Semienclosed Seas

Lewis M. Alexander
Department of Geography
University of Rhode Island

The physical variations existing along the margins of the world ocean are the source of many of the difficulties encountered in compiling a uniform code of rules for the law of the sea. The configuration and breadth of continental shelves, for example, vary considerably from place to place,[1] and there are wide differences in the nature of shorelines and in the presence of offshore islands and rocks throughout the world. Few similarities exist between one archipelago and another. Some of these differences in geography were provided for in the articles of the 1958 Geneva Conventions, but many were left unresolved.

In the years since Geneva the tendency has grown for states, both alone and in combination with one another, to gradually expand seaward their claims to competence in the oceans at the expense of the free seas. One result of this has been a trend toward smoothing over coastal irregularities, drawing straight baselines along indented or island-studded coasts, and closing off gulfs and bays to foreign users. But beyond this lies the potential threat of treating major bodies of coastal water as somehow different in status from the world ocean—a situation which could in time result in denying international community rights within some of the most important maritime areas of the world. The purpose of this chapter is to present a few of the major parameters of such a global "enclosure" movement.

Along the margins of the ocean are literally hundreds of partially enclosed seas, gulfs, straits, channels, and sounds, varying in size from a few square nautical miles to over a million. In order to reduce this group to manageable proportions, the term "semienclosed sea" has been introduced here, together with a number of suggested criteria. In order to qualify for consideration, such a sea must have an area of at least 50,000 square nautical miles and be a "primary" sea, rather than an arm of a larger semienclosed water body. At least 50 percent of its circumference should be occupied by land, and the width of the connector between the sea and the open ocean must not represent more than 20 percent of the sea's total circumference. By these definitions there are 26 semienclosed seas of the world today (See Figure 9-1 and Table 9-1).

These qualifications for "semienclosed" status are, of course, highly arbitrary and are intended in part to illustrate the complexities of any global classification system. One important part of such a system is the question, What was left out? The 50,000 square mile requirement eliminates the Molucca, Irish, White, and Ceram Seas, as well as the Gulf of Oman, leading into the Persian Gulf. Subsidiary seas, such as the Gulf of Siam, and Australia's Gulf of Carpentaria, do not receive special treatment, nor do "open" seas, such as the Norwegian, Coral, Philippine, Tasman, and Barents, where less than half the circumference is occupied by land. The Arabian Sea and the Bay of Bengal are really arms of the Indian Ocean with extremely wide entrances, and they too are therefore excluded. Finally, a point might be made that the Arctic Ocean itself is really a semienclosed sea, although measuring nearly 5 million square miles in extent. But because of the Arctic's unique characteristics it was not considered as one of the group.

It should be pointed out that the coastal states bordering on, or located within, any type of partially enclosed water body may come to think of that body as an entity separate from the world ocean, regardless of whether or not it conforms with the criteria described above. But the contention here is that among the 26 water bodies covered are probably the most likely candidates for the imposition of some form of special juridical status within the foreseeable future.

The 26 seas combined represent about 7 percent of the water area of the world ocean and 55 percent of the global continental shelf out to a depth of 200 meters. Of the 148 independent countries of the world, 76 (or just one-half) border on, or are located within, one or more of the seas—a fact that could prove significant should some effort be made in the U.N. to win approval of the principle of special regimes being established for semienclosed water bodies. All or most of the other half of the world's nations might tend to resist such a move.

About one-quarter of the global commercial fisheries catch comes from the 26 seas.[2] Among the most important for fisheries are the North, South China, and East China Seas, the Sea of Japan, and the Sea of Okhotsk. It is estimated that several of the seas, particularly those in the southwestern Pacific, have a high unutilized potential. The bulk of the world's offshore oil and gas comes from the semienclosed seas, about two-thirds of the total from the Persian Gulf and the Gulf of Mexico.[3]

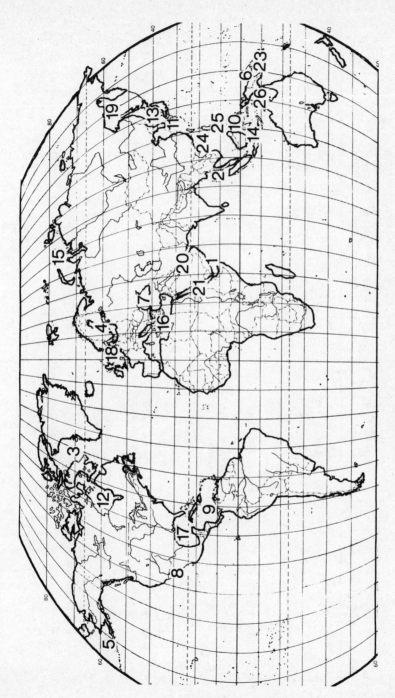

Figure 9-1.   Map of World (Key Is Table 9-1)

Table 9-1. Key to Figure 9-1

Key No. on Map	Semienclosed Sea	Littoral States and Territories	Area (000 sq. nautical miles)	Percent of Seabed Below 200 m.	Percent of Area Beyond 200 mi. limit	Estimated Average Annual Catch (000 Tons)	Major Ports
1	Aden, Gulf of	Somalia, Yemen (Aden) Afars & Issas (Fr.)	58	93	0	25	Aden
2	Andaman	Burma, India, Indonesia, Thailand, Malaysia	233	55	0	150	Penang, Rangoon, Port Sweetenham
3	Baffin Bay-Davis Strait	Canada, Greenland (Den.)	450	85	0	n.d.	
4	Baltic	Sweden, Denmark, West Germany, East Germany, Finland, Poland, U.S.S.R.	123	1	0	400	Stockholm, Leningrad, Copenhagen, Gdynia, Riga, Helsinki, Turku, Oslo
5	Bering	U.S., U.S.S.R.	661	60	8	750	
6	Bismark	Papua-New Guinea/ Bismark Archipelago (Aust.)	64	53	0	25	Madang*, Rabaul*
7	Black	Turkey, Bulgaria, Romania, U.S.S.R.	124	67	0	400	Odessa* Istanbul*, Batumi*, Verna*, Constana*
8	Gulf of California	Mexico	50	55	0	n.d.	
9	Caribbean	Mexico, Guatemala, Honduras, Nicaragua, Costa Rica, Panama, Colombia, Venezuela,	566	87	0	250	Kingston, San Juan, Port of Spain, Willemstad, Baranquilla,

No.	Sea	Bordering states					Major ports
		Trinidad & Tobago, Dominican Republic, Haiti, Jamaica, Cuba, (territories of France, Netherlands, U.K., U.S.)					La Guaira, Cienfuegos, Charlotte Amalie
10	Celebes	Philippines, Malaysia, Indonesia	125	75	0	250	Manado*
11	East China/Yello	Peoples Republic of China, Republic of China, Japan, South Korea, North Korea	362	26	0	1,800	Shanghai, Tsingtao*, Hangchow, Nagasaki, Inchon, Kitakyushu
12	Hudson Bay	Canada	359	2	0	neg.	Churchill*
13	Japan	Japan, South Korea, North Korea, U.S.S.R.	294	88	0	1,500	Pusan, Vladivostok
14	Java/Flores/Banda	Indonesia	328	52	0	500	Djakarta, Surabaja*, Makassar*
15	Kara	U.S.S.R.	400	25		n.d.	
16	Mediterranean	Spain, France, Monaco, Italy, Malta, Yugoslavia, Albania Greece, Turkey, Cyprus, Syria, Lebanon, Israel, Egypt, Libya, Tunisia, Algeria, Morocco	865	77	0	600	Barcellona, Marseilles, Venice, Genoa, Naples, Trieste, Rijeka, Palmero, Oran, Algiers, Piraeus

Table 9-1. (cont.)

Key No. on Map	Semienclosed Sea	Littoral States and Territories	Area (000 sq. nautical miles)	Percent of Seabed Below 200 m.	Percent of Area Beyond 200 mi. limit	Estimated Average Annual Catch (000 Tons)	Major Ports
17	Mexico, Gulf of	U.S., Cuba, Mexico	464	66	2		Mobile, New Orleans, Galveston, Houston, Tampico, Vera Cruz, Havana, Cristobal
18	North	U.K., France, Belgium, Netherlands, West Germany, Denmark, Norway	169	18	0	3,350	London, Dundee, Dunkirk, Antwerp, Ghent, Rotterdam, Bremerhaven, Amsterdam, Hamburg*
19	Okhotsk	U.S.S.R., Japan	445	72	3	1,000	Okhotsk
20	Persian Gulf	Iran, Iraq, Kuwait, Saudi Arabia, Qatar, Bahrain, United Arab Emirates, Oman	70	0	0	75	Abadan, Khorramshahr, Basra, Ras Tannurah
21	Red	Egypt, Israel, Jordan, Saudi Arabia, Yemen (San'a), Sudan, Ethiopia, Afars & Issas (Fr.)	128	55	0	30	Eilat*, Port Sudan*, Jidda*
22	St. Lawrence, Gulf of	Canada	76	30	0	250	Sept Isles*, Sydney*

23	Solomon	Papua-New Guinea/ Bismark Archipelago (Aust.), Solomon Is. (U.K.)	150	80	0	n.g.	
24	South China	Malaysia, Thailand, Cambodia, South Vietnam, People's Rep. of China, Rep. of China, Philippines, Indonesia, Singapore, Hong Kong (U.K.), Macao (Port.)	676	48	0	2,200	Bangkok, Singapore, Hong Kong, Manila, Saigon, Tainan
25	Sulu	Indonesia, Philippines	102	47	0	250	Sandakan*
26	Timor/Arafura	Indonesia, Australia, Papua-New Guinea (Aust.)	243	12	0	n.d.	Port Darwin*

= Large port.
* Small port.

Many of the major world ports are located on one of the semi-enclosed water bodies. Among the exceptions are (1) U.S. ports (except those on the Gulf of Mexico); (2) ports of South America (excluding Venezuela and northeastern Colombia); (3) East and West Africa; (4) the Indian subcontinent; (5) Australia (except for Port Darwin) and New Zealand; and (6) the east coast ports of Japan. If one studies the map of major world shipping routes it becomes apparent that most of them, at least at some point in their trajectory, pass through a part of one of the 26 seas.[4] Of some forty "strategic" international straits of the world all but five are connected with the semi-enclosed group (see Table 9-2).[5]

Several of the semienclosed bodies, at least in some part of their waters, face serious pollution problems, although little has yet been done in the way of regional pollution abatement and control measures. And it goes without saying that a number of these seas—e.g., the North, the Mediterranean, and the Caribbean—are of great strategic importance in terms of the movement of military vessels.

There are, of course, wide differences among the individual seas with respect to their significance to international community interests. On the one hand are such water bodies as the Soviets' Kara Sea, Canada's Hudson Bay, Mexico's Gulf of California, and the Baffin Bay/Davis Strait area between Canada and Greenland. These are little used by the world community. By contrast the list includes quite a number highly significant to international ocean use. One of the important elements of a semienclosed sea is the possibility that a special juridical regime might be imposed on such a water body by all or most of the littoral states, with resultant difficulties for international community interests. Such a regime might take any one of several forms.

National competence over maritime uses may be expanded seaward so as to enclose all or most of an entire sea. This may be done in the name of "historic waters," of poorly defined "closed sea" status, of designating extensive areas of inland or internal waters behind straight baseline systems, or of extension seaward of territorial limits. In December 1957, for example, Indonesia delimited straight baselines about the outer limits of the archipelago (including the Java-Flores-Banda Seas) and declared that all the enclosed waters were "inland or national." Six of the seas—Kara, Bismark, the Java-Flores-Banda group, Hudson Bay, and the Gulfs of California and St. Lawrence—are bordered by only one state.

Where two or more states border a semienclosed sea some sort of bilateral or multilateral jurisdiction could be established, at least for certain types of activities. The Bering Sea, the Sea of Okhotsk, the Sulu and Celebes Seas, the Solomon Sea, and the Timor-Arafura group involve only two countries, in contrast with the eighteen littoral states on the Mediterranean, and the seventeen involved in the Caribbean. The net effect of multilateral regimes may be to exclude participation by nonlittoral countries, or to permit only certain states to participate in marine activities there, and under certain prescribed conditions. There questions, then, are important: (1) What types of special regimes might be

Table 9-2. Major International Straits

1. On Semienclosed Seas

Western Hemisphere

Cabot	Canada
Florida	United States, Cuba
Yucatan Channel	Cuba, Mexico
Windward Passage	Cuba, Haiti
Mona Passage	United States (Puerto Rico), Dominican Republic
Anegada Passage	United Kingdom (Anegada, Sombrero)
Dominica Channel	France (Guadeloupe), United Kingdom (Dominica)
Martinique Channel	United Kingdom (Dominica), France (Martinique)
St. Lucia Channel	France (Martinique), United Kingdom (St. Lucia)
St. Vincent Passage	United Kingdom (St. Lucia, St. Vincent)
Bering Strait	United States, U.S.S.R.

Eastern Hemisphere

Dover Strait	United Kingdom, France
Skagerrak/Kattegat	Norway, Sweden, Denmark
Ore Sund	Denmark, Sweden
Gibraltar	Spain, Morocco
Dardenelles/Bosporus	Turkey
Bab el Mandeb	Yemen (Aden), France (Afars & Issas)
Hormuz	Iran, Oman
Malacca/Singapore	Indonesia, Malaysia, Singapore
Torres	Papua/New Guinea, (Aust), Australia
Sunda	Indonesia
Lombok	Indonesia
Ombai	Indonesia
Sapudi	Indonesia
Gaspar	Indonesia
Makassar	Indonesia
Wetar	Indonesia, Portugal (Timor)
Surigao	Philippines
San Bernardino	Philippines
Verde Island Passage	Philippines
Bashi Channel	Philippines, Republic of China
Formosa Strait	People's Republic of China, Republic of China
Osumi Kaikyo (Van Diemen)	Japan
Western Chosen	Japan, South Korea
Tsugaru Kaikyo	Japan

2. Not on Semienclosed Seas

Old Bahamas Channel	Bahamas, Cuba
Magellan	Argentina, Chile
Juan de Fuca	United States, Canada
Mozambique Channel	Malagasy Republic, Portugal (Mozambique)
Palk Strait	India, Sri Lanka

set up for such water bodies? (2) What chances seem to exist for the establishment of special regimes within specific seas? and (3) What legitimate rights might littoral states have for imposing restrictions on activities within a semienclosed sea?

One category of special regime relates to the seabed. As a first step in any form of regional arrangement, decisions should be made as to where are the limits of national jurisdiction on the seabed of a semienclosed sea. Two areas where offshore boundary agreements have been worked out among most of the littoral states are the North Sea and the Persian Gulf. By contrast, boundary delimitations in the East China and South China Seas are complicated by disputes over the ownership of islands such as the Senkakus and the Paracels. And even if territorial problems on land have been resolved, there may still be serious offshore delimitation questions, such as between Greece and Turkey, Venezuela and Colombia, Thailand, and Cambodia, and South Korea and the People's Republic of China.

In both the North Sea and the Persian Gulf, water depths do not exceed 200 meters (except for the Norwegian trough). But what happens if a substantial portion of the seabed is well beyond the 200-meter isobath, as in the Caribbean and Gulf of Mexico, the South China and Bering Seas, and the Sea of Japan? Do the littoral states divide up these deeps, following the median line or some other principle, and make no provisions for the allocation of funds derived from the exploitation of these deeper areas to an international authority? If present trends continue, a substantial portion of the world's offshore oil and gas activities beyond the 200-meter isobath may be taking place in semienclosed water bodies whose seabed and subsoil might turn out to be partitioned among coastal states.

In the superjacent waters a variety of special regimes could be imposed by littoral states. One of the more obvious would be with respect to fisheries—excluding nonlittoral fishing except under specific conditions. Such already is the case, for example, in the Sea of Okhotsk and the Gulf of the St. Lawrence. The Soviets in 1956 proclaimed a conservation zone embracing the entire sea of Okhotsk, and prohibited foreign fishing therein except during specified seasons. In the case of the Gulf of St. Lawrence the Canadian Government has banned all foreign fishing except by vessels of countries which have in the past fished there. The rights of six of these countries are gradually being phased out, so that within a few years only U.S. vessels will continue to enjoy historic fishing rights within the fisheries closing lines of the Gulf.

Littoral states about a semienclosed sea might claim that as a group they are better able to determine conservation needs, and to compile and enforce fisheries regulations, than would some worldwide organization. On the other hand, the transition from conservation to allocation arrangements may, in the perception of at least some coastal states, be a relatively simple one, so that nonlittoral countries find themselves not only faced by unilateral conservation measures, but also excluded, partially or in toto, from fisheries resources of the semienclosed sea. If a universal 200-mile economic zone eventually comes into being, littoral states about the multinational semienclosed water bodies may then come to work out regional agreements with one another for reciprocal fishing privileges, particularly within overlapping economic zones.

A second form of restriction may be on freedom of navigation, either through controlling straits or in the entire seas themselves. Three types of situations may be involved. First, the military vessels of nonlittoral countries, including surface ships and submersibles, may be excluded. The concept of declaring a sea to be a "peaceful zone" may have a wide appeal, at least to some littoral countries. On the other hand, one or more of these states may themselves be major naval powers, and be interested in excluding the vessels of other naval powers from the waters in question, as might well be the case in the Black and Baltic Seas.

Another type of unwelcomed vessel would be the potential polluter—particularly the oil tankers, the LNG ships, and the ammunition carriers. Declaring a national pollution control zone to cover at least the entrances to a semienclosed sea may be one way of dealing with this problem. Another is to establish sufficiently rigid international rules concerning pollution from ships so that the coastal states which border on semienclosed seas may feel confident their national needs and interests regarding pollution hazards are adequately protected.

A third situation is one in which foreign vessels of any type attempt hazardous routes of transit involving a semienclosed sea. Such is the case of the Soviet Arctic route (including the Kara Sea), where navigation conditions are such as to require special knowledge and skills—and at times, perhaps, assistance from the littoral state—in order to be successfully completed. The coastal state may in such cases feel justified in monitoring passages of this type, and perhaps ruling on the admissability of passage within the framework both of weather and ice conditions and of conditions of the transiting vessel itself and its crew.

Restrictions might also be placed by the littoral states on freedom of scientific research involving vessels of noncoastal countries on the grounds that the sea itself is perceived as being within the domain of the surrounding nations. Apparently such a move has not to date been attempted, at least in seas bordered by a group of countries. But the threat may come from a different source, namely the efforts of some coastal states to exclude or limit oceanographic research within their broad economic zones. If such zones turned out to be 200 miles in extent, the international community might be seriously handicapped in learning about physical conditions within all or most of the 26 seas.

Finally, the littoral states may seek collective action with respect to pollution control and abatement. On the one hand they must face the problems of pollution arising from their own activities. Since most of the countries bordering on these seas are in the developing rather than the developed category, financial investments in marine pollution activities may be difficult to come by. On the other hand, the littoral states must also reckon with marine pollution caused by agents of countries located outside the basin itself. In these cases, rigid requirements may in time be imposed on outsiders—requirements that could go well beyond accepted international norms.

Turning now from potential to existing regimes, it should be noted that Hudson Bay is claimed by Canada as historic waters; that Kara Sea is considered by the U.S.S.R. as a "closed sea," and efforts have been made to treat the Sea of Okhotsk in a similar category; and that Indonesia treats the Java-Flores-Banda Seas not necessarily as inland, but as territorial in nature. Mexico has closed off the northern part of the Gulf of California as internal, behind a series of straight baselines, and, as already noted, Canada has limited foreign fishing in the Gulf of St. Lawrence. But for the most part the semienclosed seas remain free to international use beyond territorial limits. The question then is, are they likely to continue to do so?

With regard to "closed seas" Butler writes[6]

> ... merchant vessels of nonlittoral states would have the same rights, including access to a closed sea, as those of littoral states. Except in time of war, the regime for merchant vessels in the closed sea would be identical to that of the high seas, apart from whatever straits regulation may be necessary. The warships of littoral states would enjoy a right of free and unrestricted navigation in closed seas beyond the territorial waters of other littoral states, but the warships of nonlittoral powers would have no right of access to closed seas.

Predicting international actions is always a risky business, and in the case of over two dozen separate situations, prediction borders on the impossible. There may be ideological or other differences among littoral states which makes joint action regarding maritime regimes extremely difficult. Israel's presence on both the Mediterranean and the Red Sea, along with that of the Arab states, the two Koreas and the two Vietnams, the U.S.S.R. and the People's Republic of China, Taiwan, the U.S., and Cuba—conditions such as these with respect to a single sea exacerbate an already tenuous situation in terms of establishing multinational control groups.

It might seem reasonable to assume that the greater the number of littoral states, the less chance there is for multilateral action with regard to marine control mechanisms. But two points should be noted. First is that all or most of the littoral states may be accustomed to working together on issues of common concern. Such is certainly the case in the North Sea, where most of the coastal countries are members of the EEC and other regional bodies; or of the Black Sea, where three of the four littoral states belong to COMECON and the Warsaw Pact. Even in the case of the Persian Gulf there is some commonality of interests among most of the coastal states (despite the problems between Iraq and its Persian Gulf neighbors). But in many cases, such as the South and East China, or the Andaman Seas, the tradition of joint international action on matters of common concern is not a strong one.

A second point is that regional maritime regimes might be established by some of the littoral states while omitting others. A Caribbean regime for resource exploitation which ignored the interests of the colonial powers having territories bordering that sea might nevertheless turn out to be a viable arrangement. The People's Republic of China could conceivably forge special international regimes for both the East China and South China Seas without reference to the interests of the Republic of China (Taiwan) beyond a narrow territorial belt. In the case of the Mediterranean there might in time be separate western and eastern regimes. The point here is that a variety of quasiregional arrangements could be worked out, once the principle of special semienclosed systems becomes accepted. But would such acceptance conform with general world community interests? And if so, would viable multilateral arrangements necessarily be the result?

My own bias is that any claims to encroachments of national or multinational controls on the regime of the free seas is a matter in which the burden of proof is on the claimant, not the international community. To automatically close off all or a part of the semienclosed seas of the world to international usage merely on the grounds of proximity, is to the disadvantage not only of the over 70 states that do not border on such water bodies, but also of a number of coastal countries with wide-ranging maritime interests whose vessels might be deprived of (or at least whose activities would be curtailed in) the use of such areas.

Many coastal countries have the potential for actions beyond their immediate coastline, even if at some point they are not utilizing this potential. In years past, who could have foretold that the vessels of East Germany, Romania, and Thailand would in time be operating close to foreign coasts, or that South Korea would become a major distant-water fishing country? To restrict freedom of access in semienclosed seas may be to foreclose future options for countries which have not yet begun to realize the potential of the world ocean.

It is possible, of course, that the prospects for truly restrictive multinational regimes in semienclosed seas may be too remote at this time to warrant concern, although single-state, or even some bi-state water bodies may be handled as "special circumstance" situations within the framework of coastal state competence. Since no specific international rules exist for such situations there seems to be little to counteract unilateral or multilateral claims to control in partially enclosed areas. It also would appear that such assertions of competence seem likely to continue in the future, not only for some of the major water bodies identified here, but also for "secondary" systems, as perhaps someday for the Adriatic, the Gulf of Tonkin, and the Gulf of Venezuela.

A distinction must be made here between those regional maritime arrangements which on the one hand represent agreement among littoral states over allocation of territory or resources, or for investment in conservation or environmental protection measures, and on the other hand are arrangements which seek to deny or limit access to use of waters or resources of a semi-enclosed sea by nonlittoral states. It may at times be easier for two or more countries to agree on measures in the latter category than in the former. Certainly, if the principle of broad resource zones is adopted by the international community, all or most of the areas of the 26 semienclosed seas will be closed off to foreign exploitation, except under special arrangements. Many of these zones will overlap one another. Will the littoral countries be able to agree with one another over procedures for joint development schemes? And will they continue to recognize certain rights of the international community—particularly rights of navigation and of scientific research—within these water bodies?

Earlier I noted that it may be some years before really viable regional maritime arrangements may be worked out among the littoral states of the world's multinational semienclosed seas. But the potential for such arrangements exists, and in the absence of any agreed-upon rules for regional regimes, flagrant abuses of world community rights may conceivably develop in one or more situations. I would therefore suggest that the United Nations might do well to address the problem of semienclosed seas in terms of all or some of the following criteria.

1. There should be established some concrete definitions of "semienclosed seas"; special provisions for these seas could in time apply.
2. The rights of the international community within semienclosed seas should be clearly spelled out. The question of single-state control of semienclosed seas should be addressed in terms of international community rights in these waters.
3. Littoral states should be encouraged to join into regional maritime resource development agencies for individual seas. These agencies should concentrate particularly on those sectors where the limits of national contiguous and/or resource zones overlap one another. The U.N., or some other international body concerned with ocean development, should be prepared to provide technical, scientific, and economic assistance to such agencies.
4. Regional arrangements should provide for safety of navigation within semienclosed seas. Under certain circumstances it may be appropriate for the littoral states to join with other major users of narrow waterways in some form of international regime with respect to certain forms of transit.
5. Littoral states should also be encouraged to take joint action with respect to pollution control and abatement, within the framework of internationally agreed-upon pollution measures. Again, technical, scientific, and economic assistance should be available from an international body in support of such efforts.

6. The international organization should also be prepared to assist littoral states in the resolution of marine related disputes, such as those involving the delimitation of offshore boundaries, or the operation of multilateral fisheries.

The issue of semienclosed seas is inexorably bound up with many other topics concerning the law of the sea, and it is only within such a context that the problem can be reasonably approached. It is of little value to delimit regional units of the world ocean, unless in some way the delimitation leads to a more rational approach to law of the sea problems. If the effect of regional consciousness is merely to hasten the maritime enclosure movement, then papers of this type may tend to be counterproductive. On the other hand, geographic assessments of marginal irregularities of the ocean may provide a basis for imaginative arrangements such as evolved in Articles 3 through 13 of the 1958 Territorial Sea Convention with respect to baseline delimitation involving a wide variety of coastal conditions.

Chapter Ten

Special Circumstances: Superports

Allan Hirsch
Director, Marine Ecosystems Analysis Program
Office of Coastal Environment
National Oceanic and Atmospheric Administration

Offshore superports, which are emerging as a new use of the sea, represent a special situation to be considered in discussions on law of the sea. In addition, they represent a broader class of special problems, those that are inherent in the coastal zone regime.

THE COASTAL ZONE

In considering problems relating to use of the sea, the coastal zone clearly represents a special situation. First, it is the area of greatest direct impingement of human activities on marine processes. Second, it is an area of complex, little understood, but certainly fragile ecosystems. Its estuaries and marshes are areas that very easily can be affected by man's activities.

Third, it is an area very rich in environmental resources. A very high percentage of all the fish and shellfish utilized in the United States spend some portion of their life history within the estuaries and within the coastal zone. It also has a very high recreational potential. So it represents a classic conflict ground for the struggle, all too prevalent today, between environmental protection and economic development. It is also extremely complex jurisdictionally, perhaps even more domestically than from an international standpoint. A host of interests, institutions, and authorities—state, local, federal—come to play within the coastal zone, and these are often in conflict.

In the United States the coastal zone is increasingly beset by a variety of problems: dredging for navigational purposes and filling of adjacent lands, heavy use of coastal areas for waste disposal, problems associated with improper land use, coastal erosion, and so on. These are all impacts of a rather unique kind that are not reflected in the same way on the high seas. There has been an accelerating tempo of governmental concern and governmental action directed towards management and protection of the coastal zone. At both state and federal level, there is a wide range of environmental legislation under which various environmental problems such as water and air pollution have been addressed. This legislation has been greatly strengthened in recent years as a consequence of the environmental movement and increased awareness of the need for environmental protection.

In addition, last year two important federal laws were enacted dealing specifically with environmental problems of the coastal zone. The first of these is the Coastal Zone Management Act of 1972, which would provide federal funds to support the states in development and implementation of orderly coastal zone management programs. These programs will provide a more effective way of managing land use in the coastal zone—and of elevating to state level a number of decisions previously fragmented at local level. The coastal zone, for purposes of this Act, includes coastal waters and the lands thereunder to the outer limit of the United States territorial sea, and inland from the shorelines to the extent necessary to control shorelands with a direct and significant impact on coastal waters.

The federal funds authorized by this legislation to support state coastal zone management programs have not yet been provided. Basically, this is tied to a broader issue relating to proposed federal comprehensive land use legislation currently being considered before the Congress. However, the Federal government has initiated this program in its planning phase—and is in the process of providing technical support and encouragement to the states. Significantly, a number of the states have already moved ahead with legislation and programs of their own providing for planning or control of their coastal areas. In summary, the Coastal Zone Management Act provides a national mechanism to encourage and support the use, management, and development of the coastal lands and resources. It provides a means of addressing the problem of fragmented decision making and jurisdiction within the coastal zone area, and it places the focus for this at the state level.

The second significant piece of federal legislation affecting the coastal zone was the Marine Protection, Research, and Sanctuaries Act of 1972. This act provides for the regulation of ocean dumping, which is the practice of barging wastes to sea. These wastes are municipal sewage, industrial wastes, and the spoils that result from dredging operations. Ocean dumping had been very loosely regulated up until passage of this Act, which now provides for stringent regulation, and also provides for a program of research and monitoring to support that regulatory effort. The Act also authorizes establishment of marine sanctuaries in areas of ocean waters as far seaward as the outer edge of the continental shelf. Where a sanctuary is designated which includes an area of ocean waters outside the territorial jurisdiction of the United States, the Secretary of State is authorized to negotiate with other nations to seek agreement concerning protection of the sanctuary area.

The program under the Marine Protection, Research, and Sanctuaries Act is now in the early stages of implementation. At the international level an International Convention on Ocean Dumping was signed in London last winter as a follow-up to the recommendations of the United Nations Stockholm Conference. The Convention has comparable provisions for regulating this type of ocean waste disposal. The United States legislation is largely compatible with the International Convention, and steps are being taken now to amend our own national legislation to make it entirely consistent.

Despite such progress in providing means of addressing man's impact on coastal areas, it seems clear that we in the United States still face major challenges in developing adequate national mechanisms for dealing with the coastal zone regime. The offshore superport issue, as an emerging use of the coastal zone in the United States, illustrates the need for new institutional mechanisms, technological capability, and environmental predictive capability for dealing with the coastal environment. Although my subsequent remarks will be confined to superports, other offshore structures now on the horizon will present quite similar problems. These include offshore nuclear power plants now under development; offshore waste disposal islands, where an ocean area can be enclosed and the wastes from an entire metropolitan area can be contained; offshore airports, and the like.

THE SUPERPORT QUESTION

In the United States the superport question arises from several basic circumstances. Oil imports will increase very sharply in the remainder of this decade, basically as one of the important components in meeting the so-called energy crisis. It is cheaper to ship oil in large vessels than it is in small vessels. For example, by increasing tanker size from what might be termed a conventional size tanker of 65,000 dead weight tons to what might be called a middle range supertanker of 325,000 tons, the unit cost of shipping oil from the Persian Gulf to the United States can be reduced by 25 percent.

The trend is towards large tankers. In the last five years, the number of supertankers has increased very sharply to account for 25 percent of the world's oil shipments, and this trend is expected to go up more sharply in the future. Ports in the United States are not adequate to handle these larger vessels. There are about 60 true deep draft ports or offshore buoy facilities in the world in operation, in construction or in advanced planning at this time. There are no such ports or facilities in the United States. Most United States ports are limited by depth to vessels in the 50,000 to 80,000 DWT range. A few on the West Coast can handle 100,000 tons. However, it appears that 200,000 to 300,000 DWT tankers will become the standard carriers of the future, and ships in the 500,000 to 700,000 DWT range are already being planned and ordered. So there is a problem.

United States oil imports could increase through transshipments from Canadian or Caribbean superports to the East Coast and to the Gulf, but this poses a number of economic, balance of payment, and national security issues. Transshipment from foreign superports on smaller tankers will increase the costs to United States refineries. So, it seems quite clear that the United States requires superports, and that development of these is somewhere on the near-scale time horizon. Several are under active consideration. The President, in his Energy Message of April 18, 1973, pointed to the need to make provision for construction of deep water ports.

At the same time, superport proposals have led and will continue to lead to major controversy, centering basically around the environmental issue. The question is, What impact will these superports have on the very important recreational and environmental values of the coastal zone? Proposals for deep water ports in Delaware, Maine, and off the coast of New Jersey have already met very determined public opposition. In an effort to come to grips with this energy-environment issue, the Council on Environmental Quality headed a government effort to study the superport question. The final report of this study should be available in the near future.

This study examined the environmental impact of sites at Machiasport, Maine, in the New York Bight, Delaware Bay, the Louisiana Gulf Coast, and the Texas Gulf Coast—all candidate areas for superports. The potential sites were grouped into three classes: inshore sites (those, for example, where the vessels would come up into Delaware Bay); offshore sites, where vessels would be moored offshore and transfer their oil to a pipeline, which would either go directly to the shore or to an artificial island with a series of storage tanks; and far offshore sites, basically the same concept but farther away from the shore.

The potential environmental damage associated with superport development is of three types: (1) oil spills, (2) construction impacts stemming from channel dredging and construction of breakwaters, and (3) shore-side effects associated with development of secondary industries. The study findings were that with respect to primary environmental impacts—namely, those associated with the superport and the transportation process itself—the environmental damage would be greatest for those superports located inshore, and it would be least for those located farthest from shore. The reasons for this seem obvious. The estuarine and coastal wetlands are the most biologically productive areas. They are also the areas most sensitive to damage from construction or from oil spills. If a spill does occur some distance from the shore, by the time the oil reaches a biologically sensitive area inshore it may be weathered, the toxic properties may have been diminished, and therefore it is less likely to do damage to the biota.

The close-in sites are more congested, thus also increasing the probability of navigation accidents and oil spills. As part of the Council on Environmental Quality study, a statistical analysis was made of the probabilities of accidental oil spills if one were to use conventional tankers versus supertankers to transport the same amount of oil. The study showed on the basis of accident probability that the total oil spilled would be less from supertankers of 250,000 DWT serving offshore deep water ports than it would be from conventional tankers of the 50,000 ton class serving conventional inshore ports. The total amount of oil that would be spilled on a probabilistic basis over a 20-year period would be very substantially less, using supertankers.

The construction effects associated with superports are also greater inshore, where it is necessary to do channel maintenance and dredging, while they are minimized offshore. The dredging necessary to maintain the depths of channels associated with inshore superports can cause major impact at inshore sites, because the dredged spoil must be disposed of. If it is disposed of by dumping it into the sea, this can create pollution problems and interfere with areas of biological productivity. Also, dredging these deep channels can create problems of seawater intrusion into areas that were previously less saline. This can have a devastating effect on those ecosystems dependent upon certain salinity characteristics. In addition, in some areas this salt water can penetrate into underlying fresh water aquifers, creating water supply problems.

The study also shows that superports will generate very substantial secondary environmental effects—those consequences that are felt on the land. Superports will be accompanied by development of refineries and petrochemical complexes that will require substantial quantities of land in the coastal zone. They will require substantial quantities of water and will generate very significant air and water pollution loads. They will frequently conflict with recreational or aesthetic uses of these areas. A very substantial population increase or population growth will be associated with these developments, and that in itself will exercise a demand for roads, sewage facilities, schools, and public services of all sorts, and change the complexion of land use in the vicinity. The full effect of these secondary impacts will depend on the region concerned. These kinds of impacts will tend to be easier to cope with in the Gulf region, where water supply and space are more abundant, but will be more difficult in the Middle Atlantic region, where congestion and environmental problems are already intense.

What about the jurisdictional aspects of this issue? The Congress currently has several legislative proposals before it, providing for regulation of superports. Among these, the Administration has sponsored proposed legislation entitled the "Deepwater Port Facilities Act of 1973," which would amend the Outer Continental Shelf Lands Act to regulate the construction and operation of deep water ports, constructed off the coast of the United States beyond the limits of the territorial sea. This is fairly complex legislation. Basically, it would provide for licensing by the Department of the Interior for the construction and operation of such superports.

The proposed legislation takes into account the interests of the states in the coastal zone. Facilities connected to a deep water port facility licensed under the legislation such as pipelines and cables, which extend above and into submerged lands or waters subject to state jurisdiction would be subject to all applicable laws of the state concerned, to the extent not inconsistent with federal law. Further, the legislation would require the Secretary of the Interior to consult with the Governor of any state off whose coast the facility is proposed to be located, to determine whether the operation of the facility and directly related land-based activities would be contrary to the state land use planning program. Thus there would be a close relationship between implementation of the Coastal Zone Management legislation previously described and the proposed deep water port legislation.

From an international standpoint, the proposed legislation would declare the construction and operation of deep water port facilities by United States citizens or corporations to be a reasonable use of the high seas, and in licensing a facility the determination would have to be made that it would not unreasonably interfere with international navigation or other reasonable uses of the high seas. The Constitution of the United States and, to the extent not inconsistent with the proposed Act, the laws and treaties of the United States, would apply in the same manner as if the facility was located within the navigable waters of the United States. In summary, superports reflect the full range of complexities and issues that must be addressed in attempting to manage the coastal zone, in the face of competing and conflicting demands for its resources.

Chapter Eleven

Artificial Islands in the North Sea

Albert W. Koers
Institute of International Law
University of Utrecht, The Netherlands

This chapter is concerned with some recent developments in the North Sea, particularly the proposed construction of an artificial sand island on the Netherlands continental shelf. The legal questions raised by that proposal reaffirm that in several respects the North Sea continues to act as a catalyst in the formulation of the rules and principles of the law of the sea. In fact, substantial parts of what now has become the "traditional" law of the sea emerged from the conflicts and disputes among the North Sea coastal states.

I do not intend to prove this remark through a detailed analysis of the available state practice, but I will give a few examples. The principle of the freedom of fishing on the high seas, for instance, can be traced back—at least in part—to such disputes among North Sea states as the sixteenth century conflict between the English and the Dutch with regard to the Dutch herring fisheries off the coast of England and Scotland. Similarly, the three-mile limit for the territorial sea was developed to a large extent by the practice of the North Sea coastal states.

FOCAL ROLE OF NORTH SEA

In the past this focal role of the North Sea was based primarily upon two factors: (1) the political influence of its coastal states; and (2) the fact that many legal problems associated with using the sea arose for the first time in that area.

Although the first factor is no longer of significance, the second factor still holds, largely because the North Sea is one of the most intensively used sea areas of the world.

A few figures will illustrate this point. The port of Rotterdam is one of the busiest of the world with more than 33,000 ships docking annually; at any given time more than 90 ships can be found in the confined waters of the Straits of Dover. Since 1964 about 500 exploration wells have been drilled in the North Sea; presently, about 25 drilling rigs are in active operation. More than 260 miles of pipelines can be found on the bottom of the North Sea, largely on the United Kingdom continental shelf; plans call for an additional 900 miles of pipelines, of which the pipelines between the Norwegian Ekofisk field and Teeside in England and Emden in the Federal Republic of Germany account for about 500 miles. Fishing operations in the North Sea involve a substantial number of vessels and produce a total catch of about 3 million kilos annually.

These few figures raise the question of what the reasons are for a proposal to build an artificial sand island in the middle of all these activities. Reclaiming land from the sea is not exactly a novel activity in the North Sea. Land reclamation projects in progress, or being planned, include: (1) Maplin Sands to the Northeast of London for a large international airport and a deep sea harbor; (2) Sea City on the Haisborough Tail; (3) the Plan Zeestad off the Belgian coast; (4) plans for an island on the Thornton and Akkaert Bank off the Belgian coast for a terminal for large tankers; and (5) the already completed Maasvlakte, the westernmost part of Rotterdam harbor. Such plans and projects have in common that they are prompted by a lack of available space on land for such activities as chemical industries, deep draft harbors, power plants, airports, or waste disposal facilities. Indeed, the intensive use of the North Sea merely reflects an even more intensive use of the land space surrounding it.

These considerations are also at the root of a study of the Bos Kalis Westminster Dredging Group concerning the feasibility of an artificial sand island on the Netherlands continental shelf.[1] Three types of islands were reviewed: (1) a small island with an area of about 50 hectares (one hectare is about 2.5 acres) to be used for such specialized activities as the treatment of waste; (2) an island with an area of about 300 hectares that could be used as oil terminal and for other industrial activities; (3) a large island with an area of about 1,000 hectares to be used for a variety of purposes. Such islands would be constructed in waters averaging a depth of 20 to 30 meters.

The Bos Kalis study reviews some of the criteria on which a decision concerning the precise location of an island should be based. These include

1. The effects on the environment
2. The distance to existing industrial centers on the mainland
3. The draft of ships using the island
4. The availability of sources of energy

5. The effects of the island on the existing coastline
6. The prevailing currents and waves
7. The water depth itself
8. The availability of building materials such as sand and gravel.

The islands would be constructed of a sand body protected by a sea defense wall. Such sea defenses could consist of sand beaches; a sea defense wall composed of gravel, quarry stone and concrete blocks; and a monolith construction consisting of caissons. The Bos Kalis study concludes that for the time being the second possibility appears to be the most attractive one, particularly for relatively small islands.

The costs of constructing an island consist of two elements: (1) the costs involved in building the inner sand body; and (2) the costs of building the sea defense wall. For small islands the costs of building the sea defense wall are high in relation to the costs of building the sand body; for larger islands the costs of the sea defenses become a less decisive factor. Assuming a water depth of 20 meters, the Bos Kalis study gives these figures for the total costs per square meter: for an island of about 40 hectares, in the order of $115 to $130; for an island of about 325 hectares, in the order of $47 to $52; and for an island of about 1200 hectares, in the order of $31 to $39. This also includes the costs of building the necessary harbor basins with unloading docks.

In conjunction with this study, Bos Kalis issued another one dealing with the feasibility of locating a waste processing facility on a small artificial island.[2] It is interesting that the Bos Kalis figures suggest that the balance sheet of such an operation will show only moderate losses—losses that could be quite acceptable in view of the social benefits derived from a better treatment of waste materials. Recently a North Sea Island Group has been formed by a cooperative agreement among about fifteen Dutch companies. Bos Kalis remains the leader of the Group, whose main objective is to further examine the feasibility of a large artificial sand island on the Netherlands continental shelf.

LEGAL QUESTIONS

Now to the legal questions raised by the construction of such an island on the continental shelf. The following observations are not directly concerned with the somewhat different problems of island structures that are built on sea mounts, rather than in the relatively shallow waters above the continental shelf. As far as artificial sand islands on the continental shelf are concerned, in essence three legal questions must be answered: (1) Is the construction of such islands lawful? (2) Which state has jurisdiction over these islands? (3) Do such islands have a territorial sea of their own?

With regard to the lawfulness of artificial sand islands, a first observation must be that, at least to my knowledge, there is no rule of international law that either explicitly prohibits or permits their construction. Consequently, an answer to this question must be found in the general rules and principles of the law of the sea.

There is no doubt whatsoever that coastal states have the right to construct artificial sand islands in their maritime internal waters and in their territorial sea.[3] However, if an artificial sand island is constructed in the territorial sea, a problem may arise in connection with the right of innocent passage of foreign vessels. It is conceivable—and maybe even likely—that such an island will hamper the exercise of this right, which would create a conflict with Article 15 of the 1958 Geneva Convention on the Territorial Sea and the Contiguous Zone.[4] The permanency of artificial sand islands and the fact that their purpose is probably unrelated to considerations of national security also prevents a coastal state from invoking its right to temporarily suspend innocent passage for the purpose of protecting its security.[5]

On the other hand, the right of innocent passage is not absolute: the fact remains that a coastal state does enjoy sovereignty over its territorial waters and their resources. I would therefore submit that coastal states have the right to construct artificial sand islands in their territorial waters, provided that they respect to every extent possible the right of innocent passage of foreign ships. This condition would, for example, prohibit a coastal state from building an island in a strait that is used for international navigation between one part of the high seas and another part of the high seas or the territorial sea of a foreign state.[6]

More complicated is the question of the lawfulness of an artificial sand island constructed in the waters of the high seas above the continental shelf. Two sets of rules appear to dominate this question. First of all, Article 2 of the 1958 Geneva Convention on the High Seas[7] provides that no state may validly purport to subject any part of the high seas to its sovereignty and that the freedom of the high seas comprises, inter alia, the freedom of navigation, the freedom of fishing, the freedom to lay submarine cables and pipelines, and the freedom to fly over the high seas. It also provides that "These freedoms, and others which are recognized by the general principles of international law, shall be exercised by all States with reasonable regard to the interests of other States in their exercise of the freedom of the high seas."

The fact that an artificial sand island can be constructed only in relatively shallow waters implies that Article 2 of the 1958 Geneva Convention on the Continental Shelf is equally relevant.[8] It provides, inter alia, that coastal states exercise over the continental shelf sovereign rights for the purpose of exploring and exploiting its natural resources. The Continental Shelf Convention also grants coastal states the right to construct on the continental shelf "installations and other devices" necessary for its exploitation and exploration.[9]

This last provision seems to leave little doubt that a coastal state has the right to construct an artificial sand island in the waters of the high seas above its continental shelf if it is required for the exploration and exploitation of the natural resources of the continental shelf. The term "installations and devices" used in Article 5 para. 2 of the 1958 Geneva Continental Shelf Convention is sufficiently broad to include artificial sand islands. The exclusive nature[10] of its sovereign rights also gives a coastal state the right to prohibit the construction of an artificial sand island by foreign states for the purpose of exploiting the natural resources of its continental shelf.

The situation becomes more complex if the island is not used for the exploration and exploitation of the natural resources of the continental shelf. (The proposed Bos Kalis island, for example, would be used for a variety of purposes, only a few of which would concern the exploration and exploitation of the continental shelf.) For such an island the following three questions arise: (1) Does its construction violate the rule that no state may subject any part of the high seas to its sovereignty? (2) Is its construction in accordance with the general principles of international law and with the requirement that states must use the sea with reasonable regard to the interests of other states?[11] (3) Can it be constructed without violating the sovereign rights of coastal states over the natural resources of the continental shelf?

To begin with the last question, the permanency of an artificial sand island and its potential size imply that it will interfere with the exploration and exploitation of the continental shelf more severely than, for example, navigation and fishing. As a result, such islands cannot be constructed without the consent of the coastal state. If this view is accepted, they may be built either by a coastal state (or its nationals) on its own continental shelf, or by other states (or their nationals) with the express consent of the state on whose continental shelf the island would be situated.

One could take the view that the construction of any artificial sand island in the waters of the high seas violates the rule that no state may subject any part of the high seas to its sovereignty. There would be much to support their view if states would exercise sovereignty over such islands and if they would have a territorial sea. However, artificial sand islands could be subject to the jurisdiction of a certain state, rather than to its sovereignty, while they could have a safety zone, rather than a territorial sea.[12] Moreover, even though the construction of an artificial sand island infers that a state reserves a certain area of the sea for its exclusive use, such a reservation of exclusive use should not be equated with an extension of sovereignty.

Installations for continental shelf exploitation, fishing operations with fixed gear, scientific data buoys, weather stations, offshore oil terminals, large oil storage tanks, etc., all require exclusive use of a certain area; but few will take the view that their construction in the waters of the high seas amounts to subjecting a part of the high seas to national sovereignty. However, artificial sand islands may present new problems in this respect in view of their permanency and potential size. Nevertheless, I am inclined to take the view that their construction does not a priori conflict with the rule that no state may subject any part of the high seas to its sovereignty.

This would leave one other problem: the requirement that an artificial sand island must be constructed and used with reasonable regard to the interests of other states.[13] This implies, for example, that the precise location of the island must be selected with a view towards minimizing the adverse effects on navigation and fishing; it also implies that the island and the activities thereon do not abuse the marine environment.[14] A waste processing facility on an artificial sand island should not simply solve land-based pollution by transferring it to the marine environment!

In view of the importance of this requirement, it seems desirable to set up special procedures for making sure that it will be met. In this respect it is of importance that artificial sand islands cannot be constructed without the consent of coastal states, which suggests that these states could be made responsible for ensuring that an artificial sand island would not unreasonably interfere with any other use of the high seas. To this end coastal states should consult with all states concerned and attempt to solve any problems through negotiations. Such a procedure would also reflect the fact that the coastal state is in all probability the primary beneficiary of an artificial sand island on its continental shelf.

The second legal issue raised by the construction of artificial sand islands concerns the question of which state has jurisdiction over a certain island and over the people living and working on it. In a number of cases this question is not difficult to answer. If the island is located in the territorial waters of a state, whatever their limits, the coastal state will not only have jurisdiction, but sovereignty over the island.[15] And if an island is located beyond the territorial sea, but within the contiguous zone, a coastal state would have jurisdiction for certain purposes.[a] If the island would be constructed beyond the territorial sea and the contiguous zone in the waters of the high seas, a distinction must be made between islands used for the exploration and the exploitation of the continental shelf and islands used for other purposes. The first category of islands could be considered "installations and other devices" in the sense of Article 5, para. 2 of the 1958 Geneva Convention on the Continental Shelf. Therefore, they would also be subject to the jurisdiction of the coastal state.

The real jurisdictional problems occur in connection with the second category of islands: those not used for the exploration and exploitation of the continental shelf. If the island were used as a deep water port, the coastal state concerned could designate the area as a roadstead in the sense of Article 9 of the 1958 Geneva Convention on the Territorial Sea and the Contiguous Zone.[16]

---

[a]Article 24 of the 1958 Geneva Territorial Sea Convention provides that in a contiguous zone beyond the territorial sea a coastal State may exercise jurisdiction for the purpose of preventing infringements upon its customs, fiscal, immigration, or sanitary regulations within its territory or territorial sea; the contiguous zone may not extend beyond twelve miles from the baseline of the territorial sea.

Such action would include the area in the territorial waters of that state. However, I am not quite sure that Article 9 can be used for the purpose of giving a coastal state jurisdiction over an artificial sand island that is located at a considerable distance from its coast. Article 9 refers to loading and unloading areas that are " . . . otherwise . . . situated wholly or partly outside the outer limit of the territorial sea. . . . " It seems to me that these words restrict the area that can be designated as a roadstead to the immediate vicinity of the territorial sea.

In addition, even if the roadstead solution could be applied, it would still fail to solve the jurisdictional problems of islands not used for continental shelf exploration and exploitation or for port facilities. For such islands jurisdiction could be assigned to states on the basis of nationality.[17] Persons on the island would be subject to the jurisdiction of their state of nationality, ships would fall under the jurisdiction of the flag state, etc. However, in my view this would result in a very complex situation and it could be very difficult to determine which state would have jurisdiction with respect to a certain incident on the island. It also seems to me that this nationality-based approach could be unacceptable to coastal states. For example, if an accident occurs on the island and if its effects are felt within the territory of the coastal state, I am convinced that the coastal state in question would like to investigate the matter and to take measures against a repetition.

More generally, I also have some reservations with regard to the idea of assigning jurisdiction over artificial sand islands in the waters of the high seas on the basis of the purpose served by the island. Most of these islands will have a variety of purposes, which raises the question of whether or not a coastal state may invoke its continental shelf rights or the rules applicable to roadsteads for the purpose of exercising jurisdiction over an artificial sand island that is used only in part for the exploration and exploitation of the resources of the continental shelf or for the operation of a deep water harbor facility.

A more simple solution to the jurisdictional problems of artificial sand islands in the waters of the high seas would be a unilateral extension of the jurisdiction of the state on whose continental shelf the island would be located. Several considerations support such a solution: (1) existing rules of law give coastal states jurisdiction over certain categories of islands; (2) coastal states are most directly affected by such islands and their activities; (3) they cannot be constructed without the consent of the coastal state; and (4) coastal state jurisdiction over artificial sand islands constructed on their continental shelf avoids the complexities of a nationality-based approach.

A unilateral extension of the jurisdiction of coastal states could be accomplished by enacting appropriate domestic legislation.[18] In this respect it is of interest that in 1964 the Netherlands adopted an act that makes it possible to apply specifically designated laws to all installations on the Netherlands continental shelf.[19] The act was used to stop the operations of a television broadcasting station on an artificial structure erected just beyond the Netherlands territorial sea. It could, however, also be used by the Netherlands for the purpose of extending its jurisdiction over the artificial sand island proposed in the Bos Kalis study.

The third question involving artificial sand islands is whether or not they have a territorial sea. In this respect the most relevant provisions are Article 10, para. 1 of the 1958 Geneva Territorial Sea Convention and Article 5, para. 3 of the 1958 Geneva Continental Shelf Convention. The first provision defines an island as a " . . . naturally-formed area of land, surrounded by water, which is above water at high tide." It will be clear that the phrase "naturally-formed" prevents artificial sand islands from falling within the definition of islands adopted by the Territorial Sea Convention. Consequently, para. 2 of Article 10, which states in effect that islands have a territorial sea, is not applicable to artificial sand islands. Article 5, para. 3 of the Continental Shelf Convention stipulates that installations and devices required for the exploration and exploitation of the continental shelf have a safety zone of 500 meters. They do not have a territorial sea.

These two articles lead to the conclusion that under existing international law artificial sand islands cannot have a territorial sea—a conclusion which also avoids a conflict between the construction of artificial sand islands and the rule that no state may subject any part of the high seas to its sovereignty. It is also clear that artificial sand islands used for the exploration and exploitation of the continental shelf have a safety zone of 500 meters. I would suggest that islands used for other purposes have such a safety zone as well. The conclusion that artificial sand islands cannot have a territorial sea also implies that the construction of such an island does not alter the delimitation of the territorial sea of the coastal state in question. However, an exception could be made for an island that primarily provides port facilities and that is located relatively close to the outer limit of the territorial sea. In this case there would be sufficient justification for applying Article 9 of the 1958 Geneva Territorial Sea Convention and to consider the island a roadstead included in the territorial sea of the coastal state. Article 8 of the same Convention could also be used for that purpose since it does not specifically require the outermost permanent harbor works from which the territorial sea may be measured to be actually connected with the land; they merely have to form an " . . . integral part of the harbor system . . . , " which can very well be the case with an offshore terminal located on an artificial sand island.

The topic of "artificial islands and installations" is included in the list of subjects and issues to be considered at the conference on the law of the sea.[20] This provides an opportunity for solving the legal questions raised by artificial sand islands through international agreement and I hope that this opportunity will be used. I also hope that the North Sea coastal states will enter as soon as possible into consultations with each other with regard to the island proposal of the Bos Kalis Westminster Dredging Group. Only international cooperation can prevent this new use of the sea from becoming the object of disputes, rather than an instrument for the benefit of mankind.

* * * * * *

Commentary
H. Gary Knight[b]

I would like to address myself briefly to some of the international legal problems involved in nonextractive uses of ocean space. Before I do so, though, I feel duty bound to reply on behalf of the lawyers who were disparaged (albeit facetiously) at the hands of Dr. Alexander this morning, by giving you a quotation I came across a couple of years ago. It went something like this: "If all the geographers in the world were laid end to end, they could not reach a conclusion." I think the truth of this is borne out by Lew's comment that relations among coastal states bordering on semienclosed seas may get better, may get worse, or may stay the same.

The problem of nonextractive uses of ocean space is not a new one. Three years ago, Arvid Pardo included two articles on the subject in his draft ocean space treaty. Two years ago I wrote a short article on the subject, and as Albert Koers mentioned, the topic was inscribed last year by the United Nations Seabed Committee on the list of subjects and issues relating to the law of the sea. The types of uses contemplated include offshore ports, floating airports, floating cities, offshore nuclear power plants, and man-made general purpose islands. Indeed, the range of nonextractive uses of the sea is limited only by one's imagination.

My favorite such enterprise, however, is the one that some California entrepreneurs developed about six years ago. They were going to sink a vessel on the Cortez Bank 100 miles or so off the coast of Southern California for the purpose of establishing a resort and gambling center. The location, of course, was chosen to avoid the jurisdiction of the United States. This artificial island was to be established as a kingdom—the Kingdom of Abalonia—and as king they had selected a professional golf player from the San Fernando Valley. The enterprise was greatly worrying the Interior Department which was naturally concerned about the jurisdictional problems involved. Fortunately (or unfortunately, depending on your point of view) the positioning maneuver went awry and the vessel sank in a great depth of water, thus bringing the Kingdom of Abalonia to a precipitous end.

I have the feeling that some of our current offshore entrepreneurs are going to be better financed and their plans a little more sound. I believe we will see more new economic investment in offshore uses of the type that you

---

[b]Louisiana State University Law Center

have heard about today than we are going to see in terms of new uses in any other development in the ocean. I therefore think it is very critical that we begin to develop the appropriate institutions and rules to govern this type of activity.

I have written a lengthy paper on this subject which will be published in the third of the series of "Workshop" publications by the Law of the Sea Institute. Here I shall give just a very cursory overview of the types of issues I have addressed in that paper and which I think the international community must address in the relatively near future. My comments are directed primarily to installations situated beyond the limit of the territorial sea, i.e., beyond total national competence. Installations within the territorial sea—with few limitations, such as with respect to protection of the marine environment—are within the competence of the coastal state to construct and regulate, but serious questions arise concerning the respective interests and roles of the coastal state and the international community at large when these fixtures occupy areas of high seas and continental shelf.

Customary versus Conventional
International Law

The first issue is whether we should try to codify the laws to govern these nonextractive uses of the sea or should we rely on the customary international law process whereby the actions of states over a long period of time result in the development of rules. I think it is vital that we seek the route of codification. For one thing, it will give us certain rules by which all nations will be bound, and second, it will avoid potential abuses of traditional inclusive uses of the ocean, such as fishing and navigation, which might occur if nations were left on their own to decide where such structures would be constructed, how they would be constructed, and what rules would govern them. In other words, we should try to avoid that "patchwork quilt" development of law which Richard Young mentioned in his introductory remarks.

National versus International
Jurisdiction

A second issue is whether these types of installations should be regulated exclusively by international or national law. It is unquestionable that coastal states have vital economic and security interests in anything that is built near their coastlines. It is also true that other coastal states and, indeed, the international community as a whole have some broader interests in such issues as navigational safety, protection of the marine environment, and protection of traditional inclusive uses of the sea such as fishing.

The recommendation I made in my study—which does, incidentally, conclude with some draft articles and commentaries on the subject—was that we rely on some international institutions, such as IMCO or the new ocean space institution that will emerge from the law of the sea conference, to establish *standards* concerning such matters as size, location, construction methods, and so forth, and then allow the respective coastal states to administer the facilities so long as they comply with the international standards.

Problems of Existing International Law

A third issue concerns what we do while waiting for the new rules to emerge. What is the existing law? Dr. Koers has given a good summary of it, and I will not belabor you with it further except to note that in the absence of any express permission or prohibition in the Convention on the High Seas, the Convention on the Continental Shelf, or customary international law, it would seem that we must rely on the theory of "reasonable use" of the high seas. That approach requires a unilateral act by a state followed by a period of waiting to determine the amount of protest or acquiescence received from other members of the international community. I am not sure we can afford to go through that time-consuming process, as I mentioned earlier.

Unfortunately, this is the approach that has been taken in the United States draft legislation submitted to Congress by the Nixon Administration which Dr. Hirsh outlined for you. Because he did raise that issue, I would like to digress for just a moment to comment on two aspects of that proposed legislation. First, the approach of positing that the construction of a superport (or any other facility for that matter) is a reasonable use of the high seas is a unilateral act. In other words, the United States is not basing its right to build these facilities on any existing permissive law. It is saying simply that we are going to build them, and that this is in our view a reasonable use of the high seas. Second, the draft legislation contains an implied consent jurisdiction provision. I have found no basis in international law to support the concept of implied consent jurisdiction—i.e., subjecting a foreign national to the jurisdiction of another state merely by virtue of that state's own law—in the absence of some *other* jurisdictional basis such as territoriality or nationality. I think it probably is invalid and will need some reworking.

Navigational Safety

Another problem that is going to arise in connection with such offshore structures is navigational safety. Large supertankers, which are going to be using superports, require a tremendous amount of maneuvering room. If you place one of these in the Gulf of Mexico (which, as many of you know, is already studded with offshore oil installations), you are going to imperil both the operation of the vessels and the conduct of the exploitation of seabed resources. Some form of withdrawal of areas, single-use regimes, or mandatory sea lanes for ingress and egress approach will be required.

The Baseline

Another issue concerns whether these facilities should constitute part of the baseline and thereby generate a territorial sea of their own. Probably what is needed are *functional* zones, not territorial seas. Functional zones could be geared to the particular needs of the installations, such as ensuring navigational safety, and would not necessarily need to involve aspects of sovereignty. There are some other issues I have addressed in the paper, such as the impact of the superport proposals on United States' foreign policy, and the potential use of such facilities by landlocked states. In the interest of conserving time, I am not going to elaborate on those now.

In conclusion, I would like to express my personal view that this issue of nonextractive uses is not a peripheral issue, in spite of the fact that it stands number 18 on the Seabed Committee's list of issues. I think it is a vitally important matter both from an economic standpoint and from the standpoint of international cooperation. I believe we have to come to grips with the issues involved, that we have to reach international agreement on these issues, and that we have to do so soon, before the international law of the sea is overtaken by technological developments.

* * * * * *

Commentary
John S. Bailey [c]

I have been asked to make a few brief remarks about the special situations confronting states with broad continental shelves. The shortness of time for these remarks necessitates leaving aside such practical problems as policing and surveillance and logistic support for operations so far offshore and the problem of mapping large shelves; also I shall leave aside for the most part the problem of common and adjoining shelves and the related question of boundary agreements.

I should like to turn my attention to the fundamental question of the determination and delineation of the borders of the continental shelf. The lawyer will tell you that the International Court of Justice in the *North Sea Continental Shelf Cases* reaffirmed that the most fundamental of all rules of law relating to the continental shelf, which was enshrined in Article 2 of the 1958 Geneva Convention though it was quite independent of it, was that a coastal state, by virtue of its sovereignty over its land, had certain rights over the area of the continental shelf that constitutes a natural prolongation of its territory.

The question to be decided, of course, is where does the natural prolongation end. Other than referring to this point (wherever it may be) as the margin, the lawyers stop short at indicating how to determine its position. The court in the *North Sea Continental Shelf Cases* referred to physical indicia but were not entirely clear as to what these were.

Various physical tests have been proposed. First, geological charac-

[c]Law of the Sea Section, Department of Foreign Affairs, Canberra, Australia

teristics. It is said that essentially there is no geological characteristic to distinguish between the continental shelf proper and the slope as such, and that both differ geologically from the rise and the deep sea floor. The shelf and slope, it is said, are of a light rock structure, and the latter of heavy structure. Using this test to its logical conclusion, volcanic islands such as Fiji, which are upthrusts of the deep sea floor, either have no continental shelf or have shelves that extend indefinitely into the abyssal plain. Furthermore, many areas are geologically complex, lending themselves to no simple division, at least by present tests such as the gravity method.

The second test is that of morphology. It is said to be the foundation of the continental shelf doctrine that a continental land mass of a coastal state is prolonged and slopes down to the point where it merges in the deep ocean floor or abyssal plain. Any of you who have looked up this question in an encyclopedia will have found a standard map set out that indicates the continental shelf proper, the slope, the rise and the abyssal plain.

Mr. Hollis Hedberg, in an occasional paper produced by the Law of the Sea Institute, suggests that a natural boundary does exist in the prominent, worldwide, geomorphic feature known as the continental slope to which I have referred, and that the base of this slope should be recognized as the logical and equitable guide to the precise boundary between national and international jurisdiction; but he goes on later to stress that this should only be a guide to the boundary and not a precise boundary itself. Indeed, towards the end of his paper he even questions whether this line can be designated with sufficient accuracy and with sufficient accord among expert opinion even to allow its use only as a general guide to a boundary line.

Mr. Hedberg advocates the establishment of a wide boundary zone by means of points fixed by coordinates of latitude and longitude and connected by straight lines and arcs set up by a boundary commission within which a state may establish its own definite boundaries. The wide zone he advocates noticeably includes the continental rise or part of that. The experts, however, will tell you that the exception is more frequent than the rule when you talk about morphology. For instance, between the South Island of New Zealand and Lord Howe Island off the East Coast of Australia there is very little change at all in morphology. It should be emphasized, I think, that whereas the 200-mile limit can be readily plotted on the basis of agreed cartographic procedures, the limits of the continental margin apparently depend on scientific interpretation.

Recent work by the Australian Bureau of Mineral Resources and by Joides in waters around Australia has provided some information on the apparent limit of the continental margin, particularly off some parts of Eastern and Western Australia. Data available off the coast of New South Wales and off some parts of Western Australia suggest that the 4,000 meter isobath approximates the position of the edge of the continental margin, but in some localities it approximates the 3,000 meter, and in others the 5,000 meter isobath.

For practical reasons, and at this point, we in Australia are using the 4,000 meter isobath as an indication of the edge of the margin. Off Western Australia both the Exmouth plateau and the Naturalist plateau, as delineated by the 4,000 meter isobath, extend far into the Indian Ocean, and there is another plateau called (probably characteristically so) the Wallaby plateau, which may or may not represent another continuous prolongation westward of the margin. This plateau, a very large one, is joined to the main continental shelf structure of Australia by a small sill or peninsula which, it could be argued for purposes of delimitation, should be cut off at that point from the main continental shelf of Australia.

Again, south of Tasmania, the 4,000 meter isobath does not close around the island but diverges southwards from a comparatively narrow sill to embrace a large sea of the southern ocean. This problem, of course, again might be solved by an agreement to connect the 4,000 meter isobath across the sill south of Tasmania.

In the area around Queensland the 4,000 meter isobath trends eastward from the coast and there the extent is not currently known. If we proceed eastward we face the problems of how and on what basis should a continental margin be defined in regard to the islands and island arcs of the deep ocean floor.

I suggest that the problem will to a very large extent be solved by the establishment of a 200-mile economic resources zone, and I do not feel as pessimistic as Dr. Gamble is on this point. The number of difficult areas of continental margin would then be considerably reduced. There exists a current estimation that there are seventeen state members and observers in the Seabed Committee with a continental slope beyond 200 miles, and 39 such countries with continental rises beyond 200 miles.

Perhaps a combination of factors, such as morphology, geology, and depth could be used to determine a precise and arbitrary point of delimitation beyond 200 miles. It could be argued that the easiest solution is to have the above-mentioned countries give up their rights to the continental margin where it extends beyond 200 miles. This would lend itself to a certainty, and furthermore it would give the international community some share in oil rights and oil deposits. However, some states, like Australia, would regard this as equivalent to asking the United States to give up its rights to Texas.

* * * * * *

Commentary
Richard Young[d]

I have great sympathy with Bob Hodgson's desire to see a convention that will lay down some really useful, clear, and workable rules on how you deal with

[d]Attorney and Counsellor at Law

islands and related problems (Chapter 8). He certainly has made a heroic effort to develop a basis for working out such rules. But I cannot be very optimistic about the Law of the Sea Conference's actually being able to agree on clear, concise, workable, satisfactory rules sufficiently detailed to solve all the problems that can be thought of in this field.

The difficulty is that, in situations of this kind, by the time you finish the multilateral drafting process, the result may be a good deal fuzzier than many of us would like to see. This leads me to an observation which is certainly not novel but which I think needs to be underlined again: that there is in the foreseeable future no real substitute for negotiation as a means of settling these offshore boundary problems, whether or not complicated by islands. Individual situations *do* differ. National interests, as the participants perceive them, vary from region to region, from place to place, from island to island, and the good old-fashioned horse trade may still be the best answer in arriving at a boundary agreeable to all the parties concerned.

We have authority from the *North Sea Continental Shelf Cases* that there is an obligation to negotiate boundaries in good faith and to settle them on equitable principles. I would hope very much that that would be written into the convention, much as the doctrines of the *Corfu Channel Case* and the *Anglo-Norwegian Fisheries Case* were written into the 1958 Territorial Sea Convention. Some negotiations, of course, will prove to be unfruitful and another method of settlement must be sought. For such cases I certainly would like to see (and this also has been said often) an adequate obligation to resort to third-party settlement in the event of disagreement. It seems to me that this also should be an essential feature of a convention.

One other observation derives from Lew Alexander's paper (Chapter 9). I share his concern that steps may be taken, in some of the semienclosed seas which he has described, to establish regional arrangements of one kind or another in the relatively near future, and that these steps may not take sufficient account of global community interests. Yet I can understand very well what the pressures are for such measures in some of these areas. For example, in the gulf which some of my friends call the Persian Gulf and others call the Arabian Gulf (I shall call it the Persian Gulf today for the sake of convenience) I think these problems are very acute. As Bob Hodgson has pointed out elsewhere, the Strait of Hormuz is the third or fourth busiest international strait today in terms of tonnage. With the recent extension by Oman of its territorial sea to twelve miles, this has now become a territorial sea strait between Iran and Oman. And this obviously presents potential problems.

There are rich fisheries, particularly shrimp, in the Gulf, and the water is shallow. The hazards to navigation can be severe. There is every reason for strict controls on traffic of all kinds in those restricted waters. So I think we shall probably have to look forward to regional arrangements to govern closed bodies of water of this kind. I do not think that anyone could object to reasonable regional arrangements, in view of the interests to be served, but regional arrangements can also be abused as against outside parties. Unlimited discretion is always a dangerous thing.

This suggests to me, again, the importance of a point which has been made by others, that the sooner we can agree on certain basic international standards—particularly with respect to such matters as pollution and environmental protection—with respect to management of sea traffic and similar questions, the better it will be, because then we will have a uniform standard of reference against which to measure the fairness and appropriateness of the measures that regional groups of states may see fit to take.

Discussion

Alexander: I would just mention, in relation to what Mr. Bailey said, that out beyond the 200-mile zone various criteria may be used for finding where the outer edge of the continental margin is. He said that there might be a combination of criteria. Was it also implied that governments might look for a combination of criteria in order to get the most advantageous outer boundary?

Bailey: Yes, naturally each state, in negotiating a means by which a boundary could be assessed, thinks of the most advantageous system by which it could arrange the boundary. So, we would ourselves try to assess which type of boundary would give us most.

I have a couple of comments I would like to make with regard to Dr. Alexander's paper. There are only two of the 26 of Dr. Alexander's enclosed sea areas which, I believe, have a breadth at any point greater than 200 miles. Would there, then, be any reason why these seas should have any special status if they were accepted at an international convention as being part of a 200-mile economic zone? It could be argued that the establishment of such a zone would lessen the possibility that a special juridical regime might be imposed on such a water body by most of the littoral states, with the resultant difficulties, as Dr. Alexander says, for the international community interests. So, I would imagine that if there were established a 200-mile resources zone, you would have less trouble with special regimes having to be established. Would this not be so?

Alexander: For one thing, you would have a great many cases of overlap of these 200-mile zones within semienclosed seas, so that littoral states would presumably have to work out some sort of an arrangement for such situations. On the other hand, both within the 200-mile zones and in the areas beyond them, the littoral states should think not only in terms of restricting foreign access, but also of joint development programs, such as for pollution control and abatement activities for resource management, or for navigation facilities—which are things that the United Nations could help them out with considerably. But you are right that if there were a 200-mile resource zone established, this would effectively close off almost all the seas. I think the only two principal exceptions are the Bering Sea and the Sea of Okhotsk, each of which has only a very small percentage of its area more than 200 miles from the shore.

Bailey: I have just two more questions I would like to ask. Dr. Alexander says that if present trends continue, a substantial portion of the world offshore oil and gas activities beyond the 200-meter isobath may be taking place in semi-enclosed water bodies whose seabed and subsoil might turn out to be partitioned among coastal states. In our agreement with the Indonesians, it was assumed that both our countries had rights extending beyond 200 meters. One of the agreements which we made with the Indonesians includes part of the Timor Sea area; this area, I think, goes down to a depth of over 2,000 meters. In our negotiations the argument was never raised that a country that had rights over its continental shelf did not have rights beyond 200 meters. What was in dispute between Australia and Indonesia was the question of whether there was one shelf or two shelves, Australia arguing that its continental shelf and slope went very gently down and ended up very close to the Timor coast, whereas the Indonesians were saying that there was one shelf, an integrated shelf, and there should be a median line.

Another point made by Dr. Alexander: he said that in such zones which in the closed seas turned out to be 200 miles in extent, the international community might be seriously handicapped, as far as scientific research went, in learning about physical conditions within all or most of the 26 seas. Could we not use a similar provision to that used in the continental shelf convention, which states that a state shall not normally withhold permission to scientific bodies to carry out scientific research within these areas? We could have a provision that it shall not reasonably withhold permission.

Nweihed: I just noted prima facie that Dr. Hodgson classifies, under Number 6, uninhabited and disputed islands together. I should like to raise some doubts over the question because I cannot find, really, any valid reason for combining both issues. For example, the big island of Irian, West New Guinea, was disputed in the decade of the 1960s between Holland and Indonesia, but it was never uninhabited; and when the British had to abandon their colonial possession in the South Atlantic Ocean, Tristan da Cunha, for a few months in 1962 after the island was overflooded, nobody rushed in with his flag to take possession of the island. They are entirely two separate concepts. I should like to see a more explicit definition of this new concept of habitability of islands in order to qualify as such. Actually, I should say the concept of habitability might be properly discussed only when taken as an indirect consequence of an extreme case of smallness of an island, but it would set a precedent to accept it as a cause of jurisdiction generation per se, for it has never been so considered in international law.

Dr. Hodgson also lists a group of islands that are detached from their mother country, among them explicitly the Monges Archipelago, off the coast of a neighboring country but which pertain to Venezuela, with the remark that they are an exception, inasmuch as all the other groups he mentions are inhabited, but Los Monges are not. Two observations about that: first, around 1952 and up until that date, it is true that this archipelago was not inhabited, but the islands are under no dispute whatsoever with our neighbors. There exists in the Venezuelan Ministry of Foreign Affairs a diplomatic note dated November 22, 1952, whereby the neighboring government explicitly recognizes Venezuelan sovereignty over this archipelago and says that they have no valid titles for any claims on it. The second remark is that since then, the islands have been gradually submitted to settlement, both by navy officers and by construction teams which are working on them.

Now, my question raised by Dr. Hirsch's paper on superports is, I think, on the minds of many of us when we talk of a superport to be installed at a distance of more than three miles from the coast of the United States; though he did say that it was not his intention, probably, to raise the legal issue. But could we then ask what are the legal measures to be taken for such a superport to be built after or beyond the three-mile limit without a substantial change in the United States policy toward its territorial limits in the ocean? Will it be maintained at three miles, or are you suggesting an advancement of probably three or nine more miles?

Hirsch: I can only respond to that with respect to the question of distance. They are generally considered to be beyond three miles. Maybe Dr. Knight can speak to the other part.

Knight: This raises one of the points covered in my paper but which I did not address in my comments here, namely, the U.S. foreign policy interests in nonextractive ocean space uses. The objective of the United States on this topic is to ensure consistency between its desire that all states refrain from extensions of jurisdiction and unilateral acts in the ocean and the perceived national interest in constructing and operating superports. The United States does not wish to be in the position of making territorial claims beyond the existing three-mile territorial sea, or for that matter of engaging in unilateral acts. The attempt that was made in the bill was to find a way around that problem—in other words, to create a jurisdictional base not dependent upon a territorial claim—and as I mentioned the route taken was to assert that the use did not constitute a use of the seabed at all. It was only a use of the water column (the high seas) and this constituted a "reasonable use" of the high seas on the basis that nations are free to make any reasonable use of the high seas that they see fit.

Now, as I said before, this is clearly a unilateral act, because it requires national action followed by a period of time in which there can be acquiescence or protest to that action. I cannot envision any protest to this sort of thing, but that is the framework of decision making. There is no intent in this proposed legislation to make a territorial claim beyond the three mile limit, at least as I interpret it.

Hodgson: The comment on uninhabited and disputed islands is a good point. What I should have stated, perhaps, is uninhabited disputed islands, not uninhabited *and* disputed. The main thrust of this particular section is that disputed islands—islands which are under no sovereignty or no jurisdiction—should not be used as base points. On Los Monges I did not mean to imply that they are in dispute. I know there is no dispute between Colombia and Venezuela over the sovereignty of these islands. They are Venezuelan. They have been Venezuelan. They are settled in the sense that has been stated, i.e., naval personnel and construction personnel are there. I was categorizing them in the paper as being different from the others in the sense that they did not enjoy a local autonomy which was characteristic of the rest of the islands—the Channel Islands, for example, which have an anachronistic situation of being a crown fiefdom; the Saint Pierre and Miquelon, which are an overseas territory; and Aruba, Bonaire, Curaçao, the Netherlands Antilles, as being a locally autonomous portion of the Netherlands realm.

It was not in my intent—the concept may have been conveyed as a result of poor writing—to imply that these were either in dispute or anachronistic other than the situation that they were not a locally autonomous entity.

McKnight: I would like to say a little bit about superports. I wonder whether we have a feasible alternative, such as delaying going forward with establishing superports even though it would require a unilateral act. At the present time we are importing 30 percent of our crude oil and refined products. It has been estimated—and I think these estimates are conservative—that by 1985 we will be importing some 50 percent of our requirements. That means importing each day about 10 to 11 million barrels of oil. This would require, if you assume the oil originated in the Persian Gulf, some 400 tankers of 250,000 deadweight tons. If you do not go forward with the superport program, the alternative—if you equate the 400 very large crude carriers with the 70,000 DWT tankers that are now in use to import oil—would require about 1,500 of the smaller tankers. Another alternative, of course, is to cut down on our use of energy products—oil and gas in particular. If our increasing demand requirements continue and oil is imported in small tankers because of the lack of port facilities to berth larger tankers, transportation costs will be greater, further complicating our balance of payment problems. So, I just wonder whether there is any feasible choice other than to go ahead with establishing superports in the very near future.

Obviously, if the superport issue were to be negotiated separately from other issues in the law of the sea this might be a practicable alternative. I would agree with the alternative that Gary [Knight] proposes. But if this issue is tied in with all the other complex issues in the Law of the Sea Conference, I would not agree. I do not think anybody here would have an optimistic estimate of less than two years to negotiate a Law of the Sea treaty. And then there is the ratification process. Judging by the experience of the Geneva Conventions of 1958, some five years transpired before the conventions came into force. We are looking, therefore, at a minimum of seven years. Can we afford to hold off superport construction for five to seven years because of the niceties of international law? In any event, it seems to me that superports can well be justified as coming within the reasonable use doctrine of the 1958 High Seas Convention.

Knight: Max, I will not argue here with you about the energy crisis or its validity. On your other point, I believe there is an alternative which we can take. If we are going to take unilateral action, let us seek international solutions at the same time. There is a very interesting parallel here between what Canada did with respect to its 100-mile pollution zone and what the United States is doing on the superport issue.

Canada perceived a threat to its national security, and because the international community was not able or willing to act, Canada acted on its own. The United States now perceives a threat to its national security in terms of a shortage of fuel supplies. The international community is not prepared to act, so the United States has decided to act on its own. I do not really see any significant difference in the two approaches, but I think we ought to approach the problem as the Canadians did by seeking international solution at the same time. We could probably have treaty articles by the time superports are ready for operation, if things go well.

Ellis: I speak here in the capacity of a special assistant to the attorney general of the State of Louisiana on offshore matters. Let me first observe that it is a real delight to, for a change, speak in support of an official United States policy on the law of the sea. I refer to the policy concerning reasonable use of the high seas, and I must beg to differ with my colleague, Gary Knight, with respect to the analyses made, for I do not think it is a unilateral action to take an action under law which has been multilaterally created. The High Seas Convention was multilaterally created. No more than any decision to grant a lease on the outer continental shelf or to drill an oil well on the outer continental shelf, no more than that is unilateral, because it was multilaterally authorized. So I think there is a multilateral authorization for the construction of the very much needed superports.

Turning from that to points of disagreement with another distinguished speaker on the matter of islands, of which we have some in Louisiana, and of the very brilliant geographical analyses which have been made on this subject, I emphasize here the slight humorous friction that was raised on the platform between the professions of law and the professions of geography. I note that in the brilliantly reasoned paper of Dr. Hodgson, the reasoning was brilliant geographically but totally devoid of any mention of the legal history with respect to islands and the legal criteria of the existing jurisprudence and of the existing writings and of the assertions heretofore made: such as by the Ambassador of the United States before the British High Admiralty Court in the case of Guiana in 1805; such as the recognition of the claims of the British Government in the Bahamas; such as the ten-mile standard that was the official position of the United States in 1950 in the confection of the Chapman line, where islands within ten miles of each other and within ten miles of the mainland were recognized as a basis for the delineation of base lines, according to Shalowitz's writings. This present attitude of the United States was only a latter-day change from its position relating to islands, and there is a great wealth of history in the legal literature, which perhaps explains the absence of a historical treatment of the law on islands at this Conference.

These are, of course, points in litigation between the United States and the State of Louisiana in which, perhaps, we may have some further enlightenment from the Supreme Court, but I notice also on the question of inhabitability, for example, there is a void of mention of the fact that the Supreme Court of the United States has already rejected any notion of the significance of inhabitability in the Louisiana boundary decision; and as to size, this too has been rejected. The tiniest of low water elevations off the Louisiana coast have been recognized by the Supreme Court of the United States.

So, I do not know, as was very diplomatically asserted by the gentleman from Venezuela, that the flood of new ideas is not really innovative suggestion for changes in the law rather than recognition of what has long existed in the law. I could not resist pointing this out in this New England state in connection with the comment that had been made by one of the speakers, the distinguished geographer from Rhode Island, in respect to developing nations discovering historic waters, when their international titles perhaps stem from countries which are noted as conservative in the delineation of boundaries in the sea. For example, it is rather amazing how some of the ancient history of these countries has been forgotten and gets rediscovered, as for example, the 100-mile boundaries of the Massachusetts Bay Colony in the Atlantic Ocean which were rediscovered. . . . The specific questions to which these observations relate are that I think it would behoove the United States' positions in these matters to relate these positions to existing law in an attempt to codify what is, as well as to recommend innovations.

Lapointe: I guess the reaction of the audience is related to the fact that the name of my country seems to be brought into the picture fairly often in these discussions. I would like to start by expressing some disagreement, unfortunately, with the previous speaker, who comes from a great coastal state. He has not got the same interpretation as I have of the legitimacy of certain actions that are now being taken or are about to be taken by the United States. I feel that there is an inherent contradiction among some of the proposals advanced by a number of speakers. There seems to be some confusion between the interests of the international community and the interests of the United States on the one hand, and then the so-called "reasonable measures" that can be taken on the other hand.

Apparently, in 1945, when the United States decided unilaterally to claim the seabed of the continental shelf, I suppose that was a reasonable measure. A few years later, when Canada decided to have a 100-mile pollution zone, apparently that was no longer reasonable. I would like some clarification, perhaps from some of the distinguished panelists, as to exactly where the boundary is between the interests of the international community on the one hand (which most of the time seems to boil down to navigation) and on the other the "reasonable measures" that are being taken which I suspect might greatly interfere with freedom of navigation if one could imagine 1,000 offshore casinos, as Mr. Gary Knight has mentioned. I suppose that would involve criminal jurisdiction, as well as all kinds of other jurisdictions being extended to such places.

Superports or airports or whatnot—how is it intended by the American authors of these projects to reconcile the interests of the international community with the very real national interests that the United States would obviously have over an airport, for instance? I do not want to deny the national interests of the United States—far from that; but I have trouble reconciling this defense of their own national interests with the protection that they seem to want to give to the international community as a whole—insofar at least as the international community interests do not go too far towards interfering with the coastal state interests of the United States. This bothers me, and the main reason it bothers me is not so much that it may affect or not affect the position of my country; but given the importance of the United States within the law of the sea context, and the major say that the United States will have during the forthcoming negotiations, I am a bit concerned that the package that they are now trying to sell to other countries will be a very difficult one to put together.

Breuer: I will confine myself to one point in Professor Alexander's paper. He is, as I see the European and especially the German conditions, completely right that we are mostly interested in regional solutions concerning the North Sea and other waters near the European coast. Any general regulation giving to each coastal state a patrimonial sea in addition to the national territorial seas would break up the national unity in Europe. Only one short example: Germany, with its very special coastline, would on the one side have no profit by a 200-mile patrimonial sea regulation, and on the other side, the high sea waters in which Germany and its neighbors are mostly interested (for instance, the fishing grounds around Iceland) would be locked. Germany and Great Britain and others would have no more opportunity to fish in the sea area around Iceland containing the best and most fish, because these waters would be given definitely to Iceland. The 200,000 inhabitants of Iceland would definitely get the present European fishery zones, and 130 million inhabitants of other European coastal states would be deprived of these waters, which they urgently need.

Alexander: You have made a very interesting point that half of the nations of the world would gain little or nothing geographically from a 200-mile extension, and some of the other half would probably lose more than they would gain. However, you will notice that in the international deliberations, the half or more of the world's states that would gain nothing have never gotten together to stop the movement toward a 200-mile patrimonial sea.

Schram: I would like to point out that Iceland is not claiming a 200-mile patrimonial sea. It is still doubtful that Iceland would, even if permitted by a Law of the Sea Conference, do that, simply for the reason that the Icelandic coastal fisheries and spawning grounds are situated on the continental shelf, which reaches only out to 50 and in some areas 70 miles. Proximity to other countries is also a limiting factor here. This is simply a matter of information.

 I think the last speaker was highly controversial and on quite difficult grounds when he started speaking about a nation of 200,000 depriving the rest of Europe of the fisheries in that part of the world. There are quite a few very good fishing grounds apart from the grounds off Iceland in the Northeast Atlantic, and of course, as you know, in the Northwest Atlantic. I do not think we really can regulate these fisheries on a per capita basis or on the question of the value of each ton of oil or each ton of iron ore mined from the bottom of the sea. The question is really not that simple.

 The trend, of course, has been towards extended fisheries jurisdiction. There is little doubt that the next Law of the Sea Conference will accept a patrimonial sea. We realize the difficulties of nations like West Germany, but undoubtedly in such a patrimonial sea there will be stipulations regarding states' fishing in the patrimonial sea of another state, if that coastal state cannot fully utilize its own patrimonial sea. But I must say that the fact that West Germany can possibly not, in coming years, take the 100,000 tons of fish out of Icelandic waters which it has been used to, is certainly not a very serious blow for the West German economy. It is only a tiny fraction of West Germany's economy and is much more than equalled by the enormous riches, oil and mineral, that West Germany is mining out of the seabed in the North Sea. I would like to point out that Iceland does not have any such riches in its own continental shelf and, in spite of that, is not going to claim any part of Germany!

Part Four

Chapter Twelve

Where Trends the Flow of Merchant Ships?

Charles C. Bates and
Captain Paul Yost, USCG *

From time immemorial, ship operators and owners have been able to proceed under the premise that the operation of ships was the dominant and preeminent use of the sea. In fact, it is estimated that commercial shipping generates some $40 billion of revenue from the sea, in comparison to less than $10 billion each for the fishing and offshore oil industries. Nevertheless a vast body of international maritime law and tradition, with its associated economic, engineering, and military practices and considerations, is now coming into question as nonseafarers demand that more attention be paid to their maritime interests as well. For example, if the one time sacred three-mile limit for territorial waters is moved out to twelve miles on a global basis, 116 of the world's straits may no longer be considered to be waters of the "high seas." Similarly, at this conference of the Law of the Sea Institute, there is much discussion about artificial islands, superports, marine research, marine pollution, and technology transfer.

       In order to evaluate these discussions against the background of the modern world of shipping, we have attempted to provide an overview of what this special "world" actually consists. We therefore have here briefly reviewed the composition of the merchant fleet, touched upon the major routes taken and the larger ports used, summarized the statistics of the accidents these ships are

      *The authors wish to stress that conclusions interpreting the presented data and statements as to the relative threat of ship source pollution represent the views of the authors. These conclusions and statements should not be taken as representing the position of the U.S. Coast Guard or the U.S. Delegations to IMCO or to the UN Committee on Peaceful Uses of Seabed and Ocean Floor Beyond the Limits of National Jurisdiction.

involved in, and pointed out some of the national and international actions being taken or contemplated with respect to protecting the marine environment from pollution generated by maritime shipping.

The classic authority for the composition of the world's commercial fleet of vessels is *Lloyd's Register of Shipping Statistical Tables.*[1] The 1972 statistics from this *Register* provide the following highlights for vessels of 100 tons gross (200 tons deadweight approximately) and up.[2]

1. During the past eleven years, the world's merchant fleet has nearly doubled in tonnage to 268 million tons; even in the past year, the world has grown over 21 million tons or about 8 percent.

2. Thirty nations now have fleets of over one million tons each. The ranking by nations for both tonnage and number of ships is shown in Table 12-1. It is interesting to note that Liberia remains in first place, followed by Japan, Great Britain, and Norway. Russia has moved up into fifth place, while the United States has dropped back to seventh place, behind Greece.

3. Despite the scrapping of over four million tons of merchant ships during 1971, there are still some 57,000 ships in the world, of which 5,000 are tankers. Tonnage-wise, these ships break down as shown in Table 12-2. Oil tankers make up about 42 percent of the total, followed by 29 percent for general cargo, and 30 percent for ore and bulk carriers. Newer types of ships are beginning to enter the picture, however. Thus bulk/oil carriers make up about 6 percent of the total tonnage, container ships 2 percent, and liquified gas carriers 0.25 percent.

4. While 62 percent of the world fleet is under ten years in age, 54 percent of the United States' fleet is over 25 years old in contrast to 7 percent for the world fleet as a whole. The most modern fleet is that of Japan, with 83 percent being under ten years in age. Norway, Sweden, and West Germany also have fleets in which over 75 percent of the vessels have been built since 1961, followed closely by Denmark with 74 percent.

5. Giant ships, i.e., those of 100,000 gross tons (approximately 200,000 deadweight tons) and above, already number 228 oil tankers and 11 bulk ore/oil carriers. Ships of this size were not built at all until six years ago. Already the draft of such vessels, of the order of 70 feet (21 meters) or more, has become a limiting factor in operating them in many coastal zones of the world such as the North Sea, the coasts of the United States, and Malaysian waters. These limitations have led to the creation of offshore unloading terminals in over a score of countries. In addition, Sanko Steamship Company of Japan has recently announced the construction during the next two years of 56

Table 12-1. Nationality of Major World Merchant Vessel Fleet

Country	Ship Tonnage (millions of gross tons)	Number of Ships (all kinds)	Tanker Tonnage (millions of gross tons)	Number of Tankers
Liberia	44	2,234	25.5	790
Japan	35	9,943	12.7	1,465
United Kingdom	29	3,700	13.7	600
Norway	23	2,826	10.7	367
USSR	17	6,851	3.7	470
Greece	15	2,241	5.2	304
USA	15	3,687	4.6	327
West Germany	9	2,546	1.9	142
Italy	8	1,684	3.1	308
Panama	8	1,337	4.0	208
France	7	1,390	4.2	124
Sweden	6	875	2.0	123
Netherlands	5	1,452	1.9	106
Spain	4	2,313	1.9	108
Denmark	4	1,331	1.9	84
India	3	412	0.3	18
Canada	2	1,235	0.25	64
Cyprus	2	394	0.02	21
Poland	2	617	0.05	9
Brazil	2	444	0.5	48
Finland	2	402	0.8	55
Yugoslavia	2	364	0.25	28
Taiwan	1	399	0.3	13
Argentina	1	343	0.5	63
East Germany	1	436	0.2	14
Belgium	1	224	0.3	18
Australia	1	370	0.25	15
China	1	286	0.2	33
South Korean	1	446	0.4	38
Portugal	1	407	0.25	25
Total:	253	50,679	101.75	5,988
World Total:	268 (414 million tons deadweight)	57,391	105.1 (188.4 million tons deadweight)	6,462

Source: Lloyd's Register of Shipping Statistical Tables 1972, London, 1973.

new ocean tankers in the 75,000 to 90,000 ton range that will likely find increasing use in shuttling refined oil products from superports in Nova Scotia, the Caribbean, and Ireland to European and U.S. ports that are capable of handling this class of vessel, which draws about 45 feet (13 meters) of water when loaded.

Three other new classes of ships are worth mentioning for they, too are introducing their own special problems into the law of the sea. The new speedsters of the ocean are the 33-knot container ships operated by Sea-Land, Inc. In May 1973, one of these vessels crossed the North Atlantic in 3 days, 20

Table 12-2. Types of Ships in World Fleet Trading Commercially

Type of Ship	Total Gross Tonnage (in millions of tons)
Oil tankers	105.1
General cargo	70.6
Ore and bulk carriers	48.4
Bulk/oil carriers	15.1
Container ships	4.3
Liquified gas carriers	1.9
Chemical carriers	0.6
Other vessels	1.7
Total	247.7
(Non-trading type vessels: 20.7)	

hours, for an average speed of 33 knots; in the same month, a sister ship made the crossing from Seattle to Kobe, Japan with an average speed of nearly 31 knots.[3] Ships of this type are able to turn around inside a port within less than 24 hours; hence, delays caused by congested coastal waters and poor visibility sharply affect the economic reasons for operating such vessels.

The world's major developed nations are much interested in using the vast amounts of natural gas now being flared to the atmosphere as waste during the production of crude petroleum in poorly industrialized nations. Thus, there is a rapid and evolutionary growth in the building of liquid natural gas tankers to provide the seaborne link between producer and consumer. During the next twenty years, Peebles[4] estimates that the demand for these unique tankers carrying their cargo at a temperature of $-259°F$ $(-162°C)$ can range from 75 to 170 ships assuming that such a ship has an average capacity of 120,000 cubic meters (2.65 billion cubic feet of gas). As of the moment, there are 27 or these ships with a volume of over 50,000 cubic meters (300 barrels) capacity, the oldest being 10 years of age. Table 12-3 shows one possible pattern of liquified natural gas traffic by the mid or late 1980s.

A third class of unusual merchant ship is presently in limbo—this is the icebreaking tanker capable of routinely operating in heavily ice-infested waters. Based on experimental operations of the 115,000 deadweight ton *Manhattan* during 1969-1970, including a round trip through the Northwest Passage, the Humble Oil and Refining Company has concluded that the use of ice-breaking tankers to transport crude oil from Alaska's North Slope to U.S. markets is technically and commercially feasible, although pipeline transportation has the economic edge for the time being. If built, such arctic tankers might well have an 80 foot (24 meter) draft, a length of 1,250 feet (375 meters), and a tonnage of about 300,000 DWT.

Wiederkehr[5] of the SACLANT ASW Research Centre has also published an informative forecast of the composition of world shipping in the 1970-1985 period. He predicts that there will be large increases in the order to 200 to 400 percent in the fleet capacity, annual trade, and average tonnage of bulk carriers and tankers during this period but that there will be very little change in the average speed (14 to 16 knots) or total number of these ships. Container ships would also increase to four to five times their present number with an associated major increase in fleet capacity and annual trade. Other types of cargo ships, however, would undergo little change. Some of Wiederkehr's predictions are plotted in Figures 12-1 through 12-4. His conclusions are also listed in Table 12-4.

To summarize, the world fleet of merchant ships is expanding rapidly in tonnage and design in order to handle the ever-increasing amount of world trade, particularly that related to the needs of developed countries for increasing amounts of energy and minerals. At the moment, the doubling rate in ship tonnage is about eight years, with much of this need being met by building supertankers and ore carriers exceeding in size the largest warships afloat today. According to British Petroleum[6] 60 percent of the tonnage of new tankers building and under order at the end of 1972 were in the 200,000 to 285,000 DWT category, and another 17 percent was in even bigger tankers. In contrast, tankers under construction of less than 25,000 DWT made up less than 1 percent of the total tonnage being built, even though the T-2 tanker of World War II that dominated the immediate post war period were of the 17,000 DWT class.

ROUTES AND PORTS PREFERRED BY THE WORLD MERCHANT FLEET

Forty percent of the world tonnage of merchant ships is made up of tankers; hence the global shipping pattern is dominated by the flow of crude petroleum and refined products from their points of origin in the Middle East, the South China Sea area, the north coast of South America, and the Gulf Coast of the United States. Figures 12-5 and 12-6 show how this pattern has shifted between 1967 and 1973; the biggest change, of course, came with the closing of the Suez Canal, creating the extremely heavy traffic flow past the Cape of Good Hope. The burgeoning growth of Japan has also created a major traffic pattern through the Straits of Malacca.

Today some 50,000 vessels transit these straits yearly, even though the straits have a least depth of 61 feet (19 meters) thereby requiring supertankers of about 210,000 DWT and above to swing to the east of Sumatra, adding nearly a thousand miles to the voyage. During 1972, 75% of the tanker voyages originated in the Middle East, in contrast to 4% in the U.S., 5.5% in the Caribbean, 5% in North Africa, and 10.5% elsewhere. The major destinations of these voyages were: Western Europe and North Africa, 54.5%, Japan, 16%, USA, 11.5%, Canada, 2.5%, and other Western Hemisphere countries, 7.5%. A tabulated matrix of these voyages is given in Table 12-5.

Table 12-3. Possible Import Patterns of Liquified Natural Gas by the Mid or Late 1980's

Supply Source	Delivery	MMcf/day	
		Lower Level	Upper Level
	INTO U.S.		
Algeria	East Coast	1,000	3,000
Alaska	West Coast	500	800
Ecuador	West Coast	....	400
Nigeria	East Coast	1,200	3,000
Trinidad	East Coast	400	400
U.S.S.R.	East Coast	1,000	3,000
Venezuela	East Coast	400	800
Total U.S.		4,500	11,400
	INTO JAPAN		
Arafura Sea area		500	1,000
Alaska (existing)		150	150
Australia		700	1,400
Bangladesh		....	500
Brunei (existing from 1972)		700	700
China Sea basin (excl. Brunei but inc. Sarawak)		700	1,400
Middle East (various countries)		400	1,000
Total Japan		3,150	6,150

INTO WEST EUROPE

Existing or firmly planned			
Algeria	UK and France	150	150
Algeria	France	450	450
Algeria	Spain	150	150
Libya	Italy and Spain	400	400
	Subtotal	1,150	1,150
Possible			
Algeria	Southern Europe	500	1,000
Algeria	Northern/Central Europe	1,000	1,500
Nigeria	N.W. Europe	600	1,200
Eastern Mediterranean	Southern Europe	....	500
	Subtotal	2,100	4,200
	Total Europe	3,250	5,350

Source: Presentation to Third International Conference and Exhibition on Liquified Natural Gas, Washington, D.C., 1972, by M.W.H. Peebles, Shell International Gas Ltd.

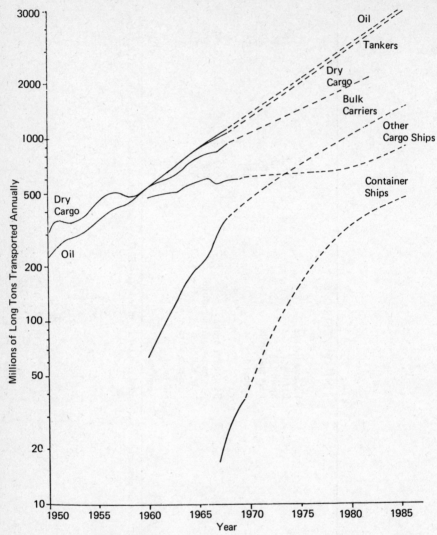

Figure 12-1. Increase of Annual Seaborne Trade, Actual and Projected, 1950-1985

Under presently recognized jurisdictional limits, ships utilizing these major ocean routes pass through jurisdictional waters for only a small fraction of the normal trip. For comparative purposes, were the world community to agree to a 200-mile pollution control zone, the ratio of transit through jurisdictional waters would become dramatically different. For example, the route between

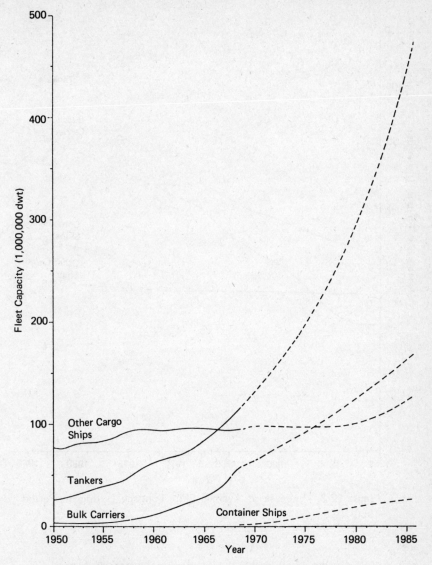

Figure 12-2. Increase of Merchant Fleet Capacity, Actual and Projected, 1950-1985

U.S. and Japan is 4,600 miles of which 1,350 miles would fall within jurisdictional waters; the route between Libya and the United Kingdom is 2,700 miles of which 2,650 miles would fall within jurisdictional waters of seven different coastal states; the route between South Africa and France is 6,400 miles of

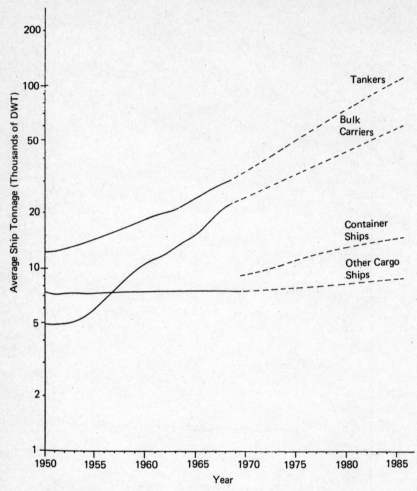

Figure 12-3. Increase of Average Ship Tonnage During the Period 1950-1985

which 4,000 miles would fall within the jurisdictional waters of thirteen different coastal states; the route between Venezuela and New York is 2,200 miles of which 1,540 miles would be within jurisdictional waters of five different states; and the route between Panama and France is 4,450 miles of which 1,150 miles would be within the jurisdictional waters of eight different states. All of these figures are approximate but close enough to demonstrate the change that would occur if a 200-mile pollution control zone was introduced.

Merchant ships make thousands of ports of call. Table 12-6 shows

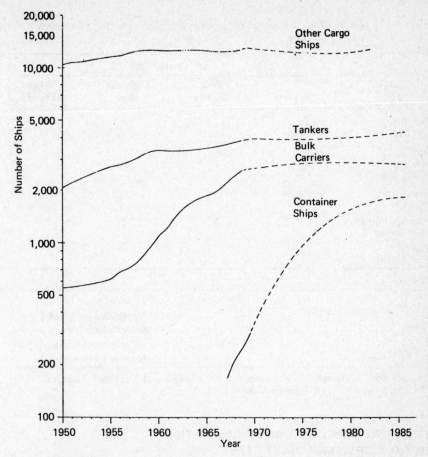

Figure 12-4. Increase in Number of Ships, Actual and Projected, 1950-1985

the total tonnage of cargo handled during 1970 at 30 selected world ports as compiled by the U.S. Maritime Administration. Although the tabulation omits Persian Gulf ports, the listing does provide insight into "where the action is." "Europort" at Rotterdam, with about 250 ship passages per day, is very much the world leader with 241 million tons of cargo handled annually, an amount approaching that handled by the next four European ports reported on— Antwerp, Marseilles, London, and Genoa. Second and third rank in the world listing are held by New York and New Orleans, respectively, followed by Kawasaki in Japan. It is interesting to note that Chicago, located in the center of North America, handles more tonnage than Singapore or Milford Haven, England. Similarly, the Lakehead ports of Duluth/Superior in Minnesota handle more tonnage than Le Havre, France, and Tokyo, Japan.

Table 12-4.   Expected Changes in Merchant Shipping Between 1970 and 1985

Change in		Class of Ship		
	Tankers	Bulk Carriers	Container Ships	Other Cargo Ships
Number			* * *	
Average Speed			*	
Average Tonnage	* *	* *	*	
Fleet Capacity	* *	* *	* * *	*
Annual Tonnage Transported	* *	* *	* * * *	*
Fleet Productivity		*	*	
Key				
			Little increase	
*			Increase by factors of 1.2 to 2	
* *			Increase by factors of 2 to 4	
* * *			Increase by factors of 4 to 8	
* * * *			Increase by factors of >8	

Source: R.R.V. Wiederkehr, "A Forecast of 1970-1985 World Shipping," Technical Report No. 199, SACLANT ASW Research Center, 1971.

FREQUENCY AND NATURE OF CASUALTIES IN THE WORLD MERCHANT FLEET

The operation of over 57,000 vessels round-the-clock and through all kinds of weather leads, of course, to a continuing number of accidents. During the past five years (1967-71), 1,768 ships have been totally lost at sea, as shown in Table 12-7. This works out to an average of 812,000 gross tons lost annually, or a loss rate of nearly 0.4 percent per annum. The number of accidents annually appears to be relatively constant, even though the number of merchant ships has increased in this period. The nationality of the ten nations losing the most merchant vessels during 1970 and 1971 is given by Table 12-8, both by total gross tonnage and by percent of total tonnage. Tonnage-wise, the greatest losses are suffered by Liberia, Greece, Norway, Panama, and Spain in decreasing order. In terms of percentage lost of available tonnage among the major ship-owning nations Cyprus, Panama, Spain, and Greece each lost over one percent of their fleet through accident or "acts of God" during 1971. Record losses were by Lebanon, with a loss of over 10 percent, Hong Kong with a loss rate over 3 percent, and the Philippines with a loss rate of 2.6 percent.

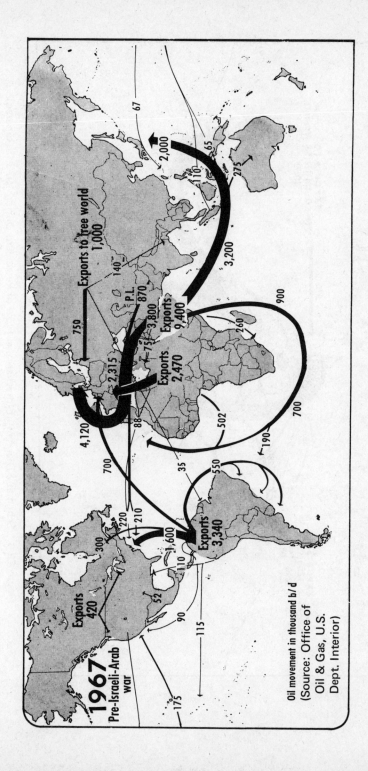

Figure 12-5. Schematic Diagram of International Flow of Petroleum Just Prior to the Israeli-Arab War in 1967

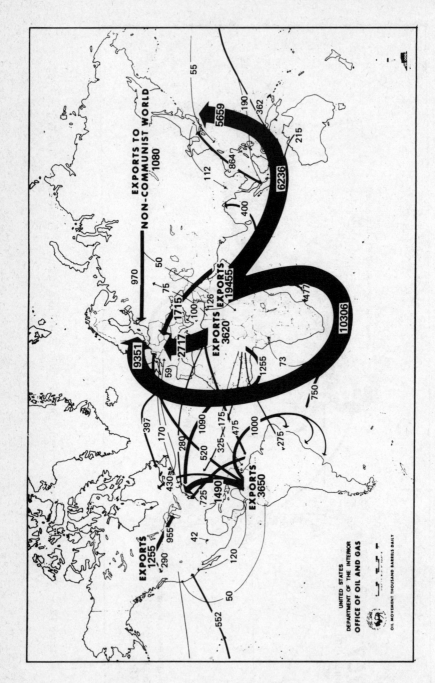

Figure 12-6. Schematic Diagram of International Flow of Petroleum During 1973 (Estimated)

Table 12-5.   Employment of Tankers 1972 (Estimated Proportions of World's Active Ocean-going Fleet on Main Voyages)

	Voyages From					
Voyages To	*U.S.A.*	*Caribbean*	*Middle East*	*N. Africa*	*Others*	*Total*
U.S.A.	4.0%	3.0%	2.5%	0.5%	1.5%	11.5%
Canada	–	1.0%	1.0%	–	0.5%	2.5%
Other Western Hemisphere	–	–	5.5%	0.5%	1.5%	7.5%
Western Europe, N. & W. Africa	–	1.5%	44.5%	4.0%	4.5%	54.5%
E. & S. Africa, S. Asia	–	–	2.0%	–	–	2.0%
Japan	–	–	14.0%	–	2.5%	16.5%
Other Eastern Hemisphere	–	–	4.5%	–	–	4.5%
U.S.S.R., E. Europe & China	–	–	1.0%	–	–	1.0%
TOTAL	4.0%	5.5%	75.0%	5.0%	10.5%	100.0%

Source: BP Statistical Review of the World Oil Industry, 1972, British Petroleum Company, London, 1973.

What is the nature of maritime accidents? A good understanding of what can and does go wrong can be obtained by studying the extremely comprehensive set of annual statistics prepared by the United States Coast Guard relative to all accidents in domestic waters and to those of U.S. flag vessels on the high seas and in foreign waters. Coast Guard Regulations call for such casualties to be reported whenever

1. physical damage to property exceeds $1,500
2. material damage affects the seaworthiness or efficiency of vessel
3. loss of life occurs
4. stranding or grounding occurs
5. injury causes associated persons to be incapacitated for over 72 hours

Fiscal Year 1972 (July 1, 1971 through June 30, 1972) casualty statistics of this type have already been published in the Proceedings of the Marine Safety Council for January, 1973[7] (see Table 12-9). During this period, 2,424 casualties were reported involving 4,117 vessels and a loss of 177 lives. These values are generally comparable to the six year (1967-72) average values (see Table 12-10) of 2,531 casualties, 3,983 vessels and a loss of 189 lives on a per annum basis. The data in Table 12-10 indicate that of the 4,117 vessels involved in casualties in 1972, 618 were in collisions during ship passages, 168 collisions were in fog, and 1,641 were in collisions due to other causes. There were also 177 explosions of various types, 442 groundings with damage, 123 founderings and floodings, and four heavy weather damage situations. Overall damage costs from these casualties in 1972 was about $106 million, of which $82 million was to vessels, $13 million to cargo, and $11 million to other property.

Table 12-6. World Port Tonnage as of 1970 (Based on Total Volume of All Types of Cargo Handled in Waterborne Commerce at 30 Selected World Ports)

Order[1]	Ports	Total All Cargo (Short tons[2])	Order[1]	Ports	Total All Cargo (short tons[2])
1	Rotterdam, Neth.	241,560,000	16	Chicago, Ill.	48,254,387
2	New York, N.Y.	174,008,108	17	Singapore	46,420,000
3	New Orleans, La	123,674,208	18	Baton Rouge, La.	45,535,281
4	Kawasaki, Jap.	91,426,074	19	Milford Haven, Eng.	44,000,000
5	Antwerp, Bel.	80,322,330	20	Willemstad, Neth. Ant.	43,800,000
6	Marseilles, Fr.	68,200,000	21	Duluth/Sup. Minn./Wis.	42,758,965
7	Nagoya, Jap.	67,236,060	22	Le Havre, Fr.	41,250,000
8	London, Eng.	67,100,000	23	Tokyo, Jap.	35,000,000
9	Yokohama, Jap.	66,635,800	24	Southampton, Eng.	33,012,753
10	Houston, Tex.	64,654,263	25	Toledo, Ohio	31,932,493
11	Genoa, It.	58,828,420	26	Tampa, Fla	31,356,522
12	Norfolk, Va.	53,544,337	27	Detroit, Mich.	31,241,263
13	Hamburg, W. Germ.	52,690,000	28	Amuay Bay, Venez.	30,800,000
14	Philadelphia, Pa.	52,224,396	29	Beaumont, Tex.	30,480,706
15	Baltimore, Md.	51,084,394	30	Portland, Me.	30,016,945

[1] Based on total of all cargo, both foreign and domestic.
[2] Tons of 2,000 lb.

Source: Various world port directories, but primarily "Ports of the World," Benn Brothers, Ltd., England.

Marine casualties are of great interest to the ship operators, crew, owners, and marine underwriters involved. Moreover, when the casualties result in coastal explosions or in spills of petroleum-derived hydrocarbons and other hazardous polluting substances, there is often marked local and even national and global interest, as has happened in the cases of beach contamination result-

Table 12-7. Ships Totally Lost at Sea

Year	Ships Lost	Tons Lost (gross tons in thousands)	% Lost of Total Tons Available
1967	337	832	0.46
1968	326	760	0.39
1969	327	825	0.39
1970	352	613	0.27
1971	377	1,031	0.42
	1,718	4,061	1.93
Average	344	812	0.39

Source: Lloyd's Register of Shipping Statistical Tables, 1972, London.

Table 12-8. Nationality of Ships Totally Lost at Sea During 1970-1971

Highest Losses in Total Tonnage Per Nationality

Nationality	Ships	1970 Gross Tonnage Lost (thousands)	Ships Lost	1971 Gross Tonnage Lost (thousands)
Liberia	12	96	21	195
Greece	16	70	30	147
Norway	16	36	19	117
Panama	20	81	29	93
Spain	15	7	14	57
USA	13	14	14	49
Cyprus	5	14	9	32
France	7	2	9	39
United Kingdom	94	49	9	27
Philippines	4	4	8	25
Soviet Union	1	4	No Data	No Data
World Total	352	613	377	1,031

Ten Highest Losses by Percent of Tonnage Per Nationality

	% in 1970	% in 1971
Lebanon	1.9	10.4
Hong Kong	No Data	3.4
Philippines	0.4	2.6
Cyprus	1.2	2.2
Panama	1.4	1.5
Spain	0.2	1.5
Greece	0.6	1.1
Denmark	0.06	0.6
Brazil	0.2	0.6
Liberia	0.3	0.5
(Soviet Union)	0.03	No Data
(USA)	0.08	0.3
World Total	0.27	0.42

Source: Lloyd's Register of Shipping Statistical Tables, 1972, London.

ing from such groundings as the *Torrey Canyon* of England (1967), the *Ocean Eagle* off Puerto Rico (1968), and the *Oregon Standard* and the *Arizona Standard* off San Francisco (1971).

In an international workshop during May 1973[8] a preliminary tabulation has been worked up indicating that petroleum hydrocarbons actually entering the ocean ca. 1971 totaled approximately 6 million metric tons. Of this amount, approximately 44 percent was from industrial and metropolitan activities, including sewer and river runoff, 33 percent was from marine transportation, 10 percent each from atmospheric fallout and natural oil seeps, and 2 percent from offshore oil production. Brummage's[9] initial analysis indicates that of

Table 12-9.   Statistical Summary of Casualties to Commercial Vessels

REPORTS TO U.S. COAST GUARD 1 July 1971 to 30 June 1972 Fiscal Year 1972	Nature of Casualty							
	Collisions; crossing, meeting and overtaking	Collisions, while anchored, docking, or undocking	Collision, fog	Collisions with piers and bridges	Collisions, all others	Explosion and/or fires—cargo	Explosion and/or fires—vessel's fuel	Explosion and/or fire—boilers, pressure vessel
Number of casualties	188	159	58	426	254	12	25	2
Number of vessels involved	618	459	168	787	395	12	27	2
Number of inspected vessels involved	164	131	60	285	159	10	3	2
Number of uninspected vessels involved	454	328	108	502	236	2	24	
PRIMARY CAUSE								
Personnel fault:								
Pilots—State	5	7	12	12	1			
Pilots—Federal	25	27	9	73	18			
Licensed officer—documented seaman	37	20	17	78	15	3		
Unlicensed—undocumented persons	145	39	32	141	40	1	3	
All others	36	44	11	32	19	4		
Error in judgment calculated risk						1		
Restricted maneuvering room				1				
Storms—adverse weather	1	13	5	35	39	1		
Unusual currents	1	1		11	1			
Shear, suction, bank cushion	2			1				
Depth of water less than expected					2			
Failure of equipment	10	21	3	31	20	2	15	2
Unseaworthy—lack of maintenance	1			1				
Floating debris—submerged object		1		4	110			
Inadequate tug assistance	1	1		1				
Fault on part of other vessel or person	350	285	79	359	125		2	
Unknown—Insufficient information	3			7	4	1	7	
TYPE OF VESSEL								
Inspected vessels:								
Passenger and ferry—large	4	3		6	3		1	
Passenger and ferry—small	3	8	3	4	12			
Freight	19	30	11	101	49	4		2
Cargo barge	7	15	10	24	12		1	
Tank ships	11	23	6	13	32	2		
Tank barge	112	46	25	128	45	4	1	
Public	2	2	1		2			
Miscellaneous	6	4	4	9	4			
Uninspected vessels:								
Fishing	68	40	9	12	43		15	
Tugs	208	91	42	280	117		5	
Foreign	35	71	24	29	18	2		
Cargo	103	83	18	160	32			
Miscellaneous	40	43	15	21	26		4	

Explosion and/or fire—structure, equipment, all others	Grounding with damage	Grounding without damage	Founderings, capsizings and floodings	Heavy weather damage	Cargo damage	Material failure—structure and equipment	Material failure—machinery and engineering equipment	Casualty not otherwise classified	Totals
131	304	236	85	3	31	341	145	24	2,424
136	442	304	123	4	42	409	148	41	4,117
39	155	162	13	1	28	181	103	11	1,507
97	287	142	110	3	14	228	45	30	2,610
	5	19						1	62
	28	40	1			2		1	224
7	48	37	5		5	11		1	284
9	106	36	24		3	14		4	597
18	14	14	4		2	10		6	139
	3								4
	1					1			3
	33	19	11	4	19	74	2		256
	2	2							14
	13	37							7
									52
55	33	19	10		2	118	140	3	483
1	5		14			36			58
	5					2		1	123
		3							6
5	143	74	36		11	134	6	10	1,619
41	3	4	18			7		14	109
1	5	2	2			5	3		34
8	17	7				13	5		81
13	27	65	1		19	103	55	8	507
1	14	4	3		8	14		1	114
6	13	50		1		18	30	1	206
8	71	32	6			16	2	1	497
	2		1			6	3		19
2	6	2			1	6	5		49
45	101	22	32			79	27	6	499
27	119	65	42	1	9	63	5	6	1,080
6	15	40	2		1	5	1		249
4	37	11	24		3	50		14	539
15	15	4	10	2	1	31	12	4	243

Table 12-9 (cont.)

REPORTS TO U.S. COAST GUARD 1 July 1971 to 30 June 1972 Fiscal year 1972	Nature of casualty							
	Collisions; crossing, meeting and overtaking	Collisions, while anchored, docking, or undocking	Collision, fog	Collisions with piers and bridges	Collisions, all others	Explosion and/or fires—cargo	Explosion and/or fires—vessel's fuel	Explosion and/or fire—boilers, pressure vessel
GROSS TONNAGE								
300 tons or less	283	171	67	260	197		23	
Over 300 to 1,000 tons	163	126	44	255	57	2	3	
Over 1,000 to 10,000 tons	140	79	37	214	95	6	1	1
Over 10,000 tons	32	83	20	58	46	4		1
LENGTH								
Less than 100 feet	252	140	50	207	164		24	
100 to less than 300 feet	303	193	81	424	139	5	3	
300 to less than 500 feet	25	32	16	62	27	2		1
500 feet and over	38	94	21	94	65	2		1
AGE								
Less than 10 years	312	182	92	322	146	7	9	1
10 to less than 20 years	176	152	49	223	98	2	5	
20 to less than 30 years	73	80	17	141	77	2	7	1
30 years and over	57	45	10	101	74	1	6	
LOCATION OF CASUALTY								
Inland–Atlantic	21	36	8	69	42	2	5	
Inland–Gulf	83	51	25	137	54	4	3	1
Inland–Pacific	11	26	5	23	47	3	7	1
Ocean–Atlantic	6	2	6	1	7		1	
Ocean–Gulf	14	3	1	7	24	1	1	
Ocean–Pacific	9	3	2	2	9	1	4	
Great Lakes	9	4	1	71	29			
Western Rivers	28	17	6	93	23		3	
Ocean–other		3		1	2		1	
Foreign waters	7	14	4	22	17	1		
TIME OF DAY								
Daylight	77	93	32	207	151	10	14	1
Nighttime	104	56	24	192	87	1	11	1
Twilight	7	10	2	27	16	1		
ESTIMATED LOSSES								
Vessel	5,280	3,363	1,744	4,088	3,757	469	3,854	47
Cargo	4,282	28	26	323	270	481	3	
Property	18	1,388		8,202	625	50	7	
VESSELS TOTALLY LOST								
Inspected	1		1	2		3	1	
Uninspected	19	8	4	10	31		14	

Explosion and/or fire— structure, equipment, all others	Grounding with damage	Grounding without damage	Founderings, capsizings and floodings	Heavy weather damage	Cargo damage	Material failure— structure and equipment	Material failure— machinery and engineering equipment	Casualty not otherwise classified	Totals
87	232	98	83	1	12	188	44	16	1,762
12	88	27	29		2	63	8	16	895
27	97	87	8	2	17	77	44	5	937
10	25	92	3	1	11	81	52	4	523
80	206	84	70	1	6	156	41	16	1,497
31	179	66	48	1	14	118	17	16	1,638
14	21	40	2	1	8	36	26	5	318
11	36	114	3	1	14	99	64	4	664
38	157	105	41	2	14	136	53	15	1,632
41	120	80	43		10	101	21	9	1,130
35	94	66	23	2	15	103	53	11	800
22	71	53	16		3	69	21	6	555
16	70	87	18		2	38	18	6	438
31	66	63	22	1	1	38	7	3	500
24	64	22	14	1	3	49	22	2	324
11	8	4	5	1	6	45	21	1	125
8	14	10	4			35	7	2	131
22	16	1	12		17	72	44	1	215
4	17	25	1			24	11		196
11	31	6	8		1	21		3	251
1	9	2	1				8	1	29
3	9	16			1	19	7	5	125
88	132	107	54	2	17	238	94	13	1,330
38	148	113	29	1	12	89	40	10	956
5	24	16	2		2	14	11	1	138
21,316	19,587	76	6,330	122	71	8,527	3,109	735	82,475
792	3,096		557		1,085	1,806	10	107	12,866
84	157	2	170	178	2	54	8	160	11,105
2	9		1			2			22
46	56		24	1		64	5	5	287

Table 12-10. Vessel Casualties Reported to the U.S. Coast Guard, 1967-1972

Year	Number of Casualties	Number of Ships Involved	Loss of Life
1967	2,353	3,373	178
1968	2,570	4,011	140
1969	2,684	4,183	217
1970	2,582	4,063	178
1971	2,577	4,152	243
1972	2,424	4,117	177
Average	2,531	3,983	189

the 2,400 million metric tons of oil produced in 1971, about 1,355 million tons moved in the marine mode of transportation. Table 12-11 gives a breakout of how two million tons of petroleum hydrocarbons were lost during this phase of transportation. The single biggest loss was from the ballasting of tankers without using the load-on-top technique. Nevertheless, losses of crude petroleum and its by-products during accidents are much more dramatic and concentrated than the losses through everyday ship operation; hence a great amount of political and public attention is paid to the oil spill problem.

Probably the best oil spill from all causes data yet developed, of which marine transportation contributes only a part, is that tabulated by the

Table 12-11. Petroleum Hydrocarbons Lost in 1971 During Marine Transportation Phase (According to Brummage)

Type of Loss	Likely Amount of Loss (Millions of Metric Tons)
Tanker ballasting not using load-on-top technique (20% of tanker fleet)	0.75
Tanker ballasting using load-on-top technique	0.25
Cleaning for dry-docking purposes	0.25
Terminal operations	0.03
bunkering and cleaning bilges	0.5
Tanker accidents	0.2
nontanker accidents	0.05
Total	2.03

Table 12-12. Numerical Distribution of Water-Polluting Spills of Petroleum Hydrocarbons in the United States During 1970, by Size

Weight of Spill (metric tons)	Number of Spills	Total Weight of Petroleum Spilled (metric tons)	% of Total Weight Spilled
Greater than 3,250	4	32,200	65
325 to 3,250	12	10,400	21
32 to 325	45	4,400	9
Less than 32	3,648	2,500	5
Total:	3,711	49,500	100

NOTE: 1 metric ton equals 308 gallons of crude oil, approximately.

Source: "Polluting Spills in U.S. Waters—1970," Internal Report by U.S. Coast Guard dated September 1971 (data covers only six months of 1970).

U.S. Coast Guard in response to authority contained in the Federal Water Pollution Act as amended by the Water Quality Improvement Act of 1970. Based on data for the last half of 1970, Table 12-12 indicates that the very occasional catastrophic spill, i.e., one of over approximately one million U.S. gallons (3,250 metric tons), occurs ten times per year but contributes about two-thirds of the total spilled fluid. In contrast, the small spill of less than 1,000 gallons occurs thousands of times each year but only contributes about 5 percent of the total. The Coast Guard has also tabulated the geographic location of spills into U.S. waters during 1971 (see Table 12-13). Out of 8,736 spills logged in that year, 7 percent of the incidents and 16 percent of the total tonnage spilled occurred in inland waters, while 86 percent of the incidents and 76 percent of the total tonnage spilled occurred in coastal waters.

MEASURES BEING TAKEN TO AMELIORATE MARINE POLLUTION BY SHIPPING

The discussion so far has indicated that merchant vessels of the world operate under many different flags, are undergoing dramatic changes in type and size, are subject to a relatively high rate of annual casualties, and provide a sizeable contribution of spilled and waste petroleum hydrocarbons to the world ocean each year. Leadership in reducing such losses has been taken on the international scene by the Intergovernmental Maritime Consultative Organization (IMCO) comprised of 78 nations. In London, for example, there will be a major conference to determine how these nations can jointly establish regulations and introduce technical practices for reducing drastically the petroleum now entering the world ocean.

In the United States there are, of course, many initiatives underway

Table 12-13. Geographic Distribution of Polluting Spills into U.S. Waters During 1971

Geographic Locale	Number of Incidents	% of Total	Weight of Spills (metric tons)	% of Total
Inland waters				
1. Roadsteads	99	1.1	47	0.2
2. Ports	63	0.7	581	2.0
3. Terminals and docks	141	1.6	255	0.9
4. Beaches	7	0.1	129	0.5
5. River areas	252	2.9	2,281	8.0
6. Nonnavigable areas	69	0.8	1,270	4.4
Total	631	7.2	4,555	16.0
Coastal waters (including Great Lakes)				
1. Bay, estuaries, and sounds	2,933	33.6	6,835	23.9
2. Ports	1,452	16.6	2,621	9.1
3. Terminals and docks	869	10.0	1,530	5.3
4. Beaches	93	1.1	56	0.2
5. Channels, canals, and inlets	869	10.0	1,589	5.6
6. River areas	938	10.7	2,075	7.3
7. Nonnavigable area	47	0.5	7,060	24.6
8. Open waters (Great Lakes or territorial sea)	315	3.6	122	0.4
Total	7,516	86.1	21,688	76.4
Contiguous zone	396	4.5	2,104	7.4
High Seas	193	2.2	66	0.2
Total	8,736	100.0	28,413	100.0

Source: "Polluting Spills in U.S. Waters—1971," Internal report of U.S. Coast Guard, Washington, D.C. (date unknown).

Note: About 1 percent by weight of these spills are unknown as to type of material or sewage, refuse, dredge spoil, or other material.

to achieve this goal of making major strides forward in reducing marine pollution during the marine transportation phase. Among the leaders in this area are the Congress, Council on Environmental Quality, Coast Guard, Environmental Protection Agency, Maritime Administration, Navy, Army Corps of Engineers, American Petroleum Institute, and the shipping industry. For example, President Nixon signed into law the "Port and Waterways Safety Act of 1972," which allows the U.S. Department of Transportation to operate vessel traffic systems for waters subject to congested vessel traffic and to require vessels that operate in the area of such a system to utilize or comply with that system.

In addition, the Secretary of Transportation is directed to establish regulations not earlier than January 1, 1974 that set forth minimum standards of design, construction, alteration, and repair of bulk liquid cargo vessels for the purpose of protecting the marine environment. These regulations shall include but not be limited to standards to improve vessel maneuvering and stopping ability to reduce the possibility of collision, grounding or other accidents, to reduce the cargo loss following such casualties, and the damage to the marine environment from normal vessels operations such as ballasting and deballasting, cargo handling, and other activities. If comparable rules are not developed by international treaty for foreign vessels by January 1, 1976, then the U.S. Secretary of Transportation shall make the rules equally applicable to foreign bulk liquid cargo vessels operating in United States waters.

Needless to say, the tanker industry has been paying great attention to how liquid bulk carriers can better protect the marine environment. For example, Madsen, Nicastro, and Schumacher[10] of the Standard Oil Company (New Jersey) presented a paper last year to the Seventeenth Annual Tanker Conference of the American Petroleum Institute comparing the safety practices employed in the aviation and shipping industries. They found that safety practices are much more advanced in the aviation industry with respect to the training, licensing, and proficiency demonstration of the operating officers, the attention paid to traffic separation and control and the use of elaborate all-weather control systems for the approach and departure phases at ports of call. Some of their recommendations for the shipping industry to consider included

1. Establishment of mandatory traffic separation lanes in heavily trafficked international waterways of the world along with an enforcement mechanism to ensure compliance.
2. Encouragement of governments to establish mandatory sea lanes in their coastal waters (*Note:* The United States has voluntary traffic separation schemes for approaches to New York, San Francisco, Seattle, Boston, Cape Cod Canal, Portland, Maine; Providence, Rhode Island; Los Angeles, The Chesapeake Bay, Delaware Bay, and Santa Barbara Channel.)
3. Establishment of radar monitoring and enforceable traffic control systems in critical pilotage waters, including such straits as the English Channel.
4. Requiring vessels to establish and maintain radio contact with existing harbor radar networks.
5. Establishment of English as the universal maritime language for communication between pilot and master, pilot and local harbor advisory service, and pilots and tugs.
6. Provision of preplanned route information for frequently traveled trade routes.
7. Provision of coded radar transponders in fixed key positions as all-weather navigation aids in pilotage waters.
8. Establishment of international rules requiring that all marine navigation equipment must meet certain minimum performance and reliability standards. If the vessel in question would be operating in an IMCO traffic separation scheme, then this navigation equipment should include radar, Loran/Decca, or a similar electronic navigation device.

9. Encouraging development of more accurate navigational equipment for use in coastal waters, as well as advanced collision avoidance systems.
10. Preparing better instructions to ship masters defining minimum safety navigation conditions considering limitations of his navigational equipment and the local geography.
11. Stiffening international maritime licensing requirements for ships' officers so there is included performance testing under both normal and stress conditions, periodic proficiency checks to hold the license, and some restriction as to size and class of ship the individual is licensed to operate. (*Note:* Licensing examinations today are written tests, and in some countries licenses are issued for life.)
12. Updating curriculum of maritime training academies to include modern problems in shiphandling, navigation, and collision avoidance, and cargo handling, including the handling of liquid cargo, with some stress placed on the operations of very large vessels that are now becoming commonplace.
13. Introduction of additional formal training before an officer can advance in grade; such training might take the form of working with special simulators for enhancing navigation and collision avoidance skills.

Both the United States Congress and industry are placing greater emphasis on the desirability of using various types of vessel traffic systems (VTS). The first VTS of any consequence was installed using radar in the port of Liverpool in 1948. By 1964, the ports of Hamburg and Rotterdam had fully developed systems in operation, each comprised of a series of shore-based radars and a VHF communications network. Their success in reducing accidents is demonstrated by the experience of Rotterdam where the number of collisions in the approaches to the world's busiest port has been reduced four-fold even while there were significant increases in port tonnage.[11]

The U.S. Coast Guard initiated an experimental harbor advisory traffic system in San Francisco Bay during 1970; this system is now the most heavily computerized in the world employing some thirteen modest-sized computers to provide digital displays at varied scales, automatic target acquisition, suppression of sea state and rain clutter, and alarm signals indicating incipient collisions, buoys off station, and ships taking courses outside of recommended channels. In addition, to an operating VTS in the U.S. portion of Puget Sound, VTS systems are being designed for other major congested ports, including Houston, New Orleans, New York, and the Delaware River/Bay area. Such systems could have five varying degrees of increasing complexity and management as shown in Table 12-14.

Although not as dramatic, there are also major actions being taken within the United States relative to discharge of shipboard sewage, bilge, ballast, and other waste waters. Under the provisions of the Federal Water Pollution Control Act Amendments of 1972, the U.S. government is working towards no

Table 12-14. Degree of Complexity Possible in Vessel Traffic Systems

Type of System	Degree of Traffic Management	Example
Conventional traffic separation scheme based on posted information	Passive	Approaches to Port of New York
Vessel movement reporting systems	Advisory	U.S. waters of Puget Sound
Basic surveillance system using conventional radars	Advisory or Active	Initial Model of San Francisco Bay VTS
Advanced remote sensor surveillance system using direct displays (Note: Sensors could be radar, infrared, acoustic, television, etc.)	Advisory or Active	Present San Francisco Bay VTS using conventional displays linked to special high resolution radars
Automated advanced remote sensor surveillance systems using digitally processed displays	Advisory or Active	Present San Francisco VTS operating in automated mode

harmful discharge from vessels into U.S. waters by the late 1970s. In addition, greatly improved equipment and procedures for improved law enforcement and regulatory activity are being developed, with special emphasis being paid to making these enforcement systems capable of operating day and night, in adverse weather, and identifying vessels that cause the numerous "mystery" spills.

The Coast Guard also has research underway to develop a formal spill risk assessment methodology that would yield two basic output measures: (1) the probability that a spill occurs given the single occurrence of one type of standard conflict situation, and (2) the expected total number of spills per year per specific conflict type. This methodology will draw on three basic models— that of specific ship interactions leading up to collisions or groundings, that of the degree of ship rupture relative to position and speed, and that of ship traffic patterns in different types of ports and approaches. It is hoped that this formal methodology will provide the basis for the reduction, in a *cost-conscious manner*, of the risk associated with future spills that cause death or injury, property damage or loss, and environmental damage, both ecological and esthetic. The methodology will place some emphasis on avoidance of major accidents not yet experienced by the shipping industry, e.g., massive releases of ammonia, chlorine, or liquified natural gas in close proximity to a heavily inhabited area.

On the international scene, the United States is also playing a leading role in combating marine pollution around the world. The Hon. R.E. Train, Chairman of the President's Council on Environmental Quality, has personally proposed to IMCO in London that that international organization should set up a new standing committee—perhaps called the Marine Environmental Protection Committee—to identify sources of the various forms of ocean pollution, e.g., petroleum, chemicals, sewage, garbage, etc., and to recommend international rules for controlling such pollution. If formed, this new Committee would then take over the antipollution functions of IMCO's Maritime Safety Committee, which primarily specializes in developing regulations for the safety of life and property at sea. The Committee could take account of new types of cargoes to be transported, the changing technology in ship design, and any ecosystems in specific ocean areas that may be endangered by marine pollution.

OBSERVATIONS AND CONCLUSIONS

Data offered here suggest that the tonnage of commercial shipping in the world is doubling in the order of eight to eleven years. However, the growth is primarily taking place in the rapidly increasing size of liquid bulk carriers, particularly those associated with the petroleum industry. As a result, the total number of ships afloat is staying about the same. The accident rate is also staying about the same, whether expressed in number of casualties or in percent of tonnage involved. Because ship casualties have a predominant tendency to take place in the coastal zone and because of the growth in size of liquid bulk carriers in particular, the general public in many nations is demanding the introduction of safer designs and operational practices for the world's merchant fleet. This demand is also spreading to the partial international prohibition of the release of waste materials from seagoing vessels and barges as well. In addition, more and more of the world's coastal zone is acquiring specific values in terms of fishing, mineral development, siting of offshore power plants and shipping terminals, recreation, and esthetics.

Thus, the mariner's age-old belief that navigation under his own terms is the paramount use of the sea is now held in serious question by many deliberative bodies throughout the world. As a consequence, the ground rules will be changing rapidly over the next decade for operating merchant vessels on both the high seas and in coastal waters coming under national jurisdiction. For individuals who enjoy "challenge and change," it will be an exciting period; for individuals who enjoy the status quo, it will undoubtedly be a trying time.

It will particularly be a time when the seafaring man, the petroleum operator, and the environmentalist must sit down and reason together. This is a necessity if there is to be a proper balance between regulation and freedom of navigation, between protecting the marine environment and supplying energy to our industrial society, and between providing for multiple uses of the ocean and for political control of valuable resources in the broad oceanic areas that lie outside the territorial sea. This balance must be struck if the IMCO 1973 Marine Pollution Conference and the United Nations 1974 Law of the Sea Conference are to produce lasting international law. Our only alternative to this type of balance is increasing anarchy in the oceans.

Discussion

Krause: Your projection of tankers and their size, of course, requires an ever-increasing amount of petroleum coming in, and if we project the potential requirements for petroleum this is very true. But certainly some economic factors are going to come in to reduce a perpetually increasing petroleum input to a good many nations, simply because of foreign exchange problems. Has that gone into your predictions for the tonnages?

Bates: Those graphs of tonnage were by Wiederkehr of the SACLANT/ASW Research Center. Somewhere after 1985, you should reach the peak of the world oil production curve, and from there on it is downhill. We had already reached it in United States oil production about six months ago. Wiederkehr's curves are still based on the premise that drilling a hole in the earth, putting in a valve system, and opening up the valve is the cheapest way to obtain energy. On the other hand, there are lots of tricks to the trade in this energy supply business, particularly the use of nuclear power or going back to mining coal, if we can find the coal miners. There was a very excellent business hauling coal from Norfolk, Virginia, to Europe in the 1950s and hauling it to Japan in the 1960s.

   The other thing that always puzzles me regarding these petroleum projections is that no one bothers to comment on what the Middle East can be given in return for all this raw energy. You can give them air conditioners. You can give them Mercedes and Cadillac automobiles. You can give them radios. In other words, you can give them a good life, but there are just not that many people over there to balance out the exchange.

Labastida: Would you please clarify for us whether cargo ships that use the method of "load-on-top" do not cause pollution at all, or cause only minimal pollution as compared with vessels not using such technique. Assuming that this method is useful to minimize or prevent pollution from cargo ships, who takes the decision whether to use it or not? Is it the ship owner, the cargo owner, or the authorities of the flag state?

Bates: First, some people may not know what "load-on-top" means. In the case of a tanker, after you have discharged the cargo of oil, you have to put some sea water back in to ballast the ship so that it does not capsize on the way back to pick up the next cargo. About four-tenths of one percent of the crude oil cargo clings to the sides of these tanks after unloading. Thus, if you put sea water in for ballast and then you pump the water out as you go into the next loading port, you obviously take out an identifiable fraction of the cargo that had been carried by that ship. I noted this practice discharges 80 percent of the oil into the ocean generated by the global tanker operation, even though the tankers doing this make up 20 percent of the total tonnage. The newer ships are designed to actually have an "oil slop tank" where instead of pumping the mixture of ballast water, wash water, and oil clingage directly overboard, this mixture is pumped into the slop tank, left to settle out, and then decanted off as clear sea water from the bottom of the slop tank.

   Coming to your question as to who decides which way you build your ship, it is up to the ship owner. As I have said, at least the United States has proposed a committee to look at the problem of how to reduce the amount of pollution going into the ocean on international high seas. In the United States, the Congress has said that by 1974 the Department of Transportation has to specify what is a safe tanker in terms of the environment, as well as in traditional terms of crew and ship safety. Right now, as I understand it (and Captain Yost may want to correct me), the decision on how to build really is up to the ship owner.

Gantus: Part of your data was that the very occasional catastrophic spills that, it says here, occur ten times per year, cause two-thirds of the amount of oil spilled during that year. Now, with this figure in mind, can we infer from that that you do not recommend the increased construction of very large crude carriers?

Bates: You heard yesterday that there has been an operational analysis done the other way—this indicates that if you are careful and eliminate the major accidents like the *Oregon Standard-Arizona Standard* case, you have a good start to solving two-thirds of your problem. In other words, all I am trying to say is that the more we can reduce the catastrophes, the more we reduce this major contribution of oil into the sea.

Gantus: But you indicated that at the same time the rate of accidents is remaining static?

Bates: Because, again, there has been no pressure on the ship owners by the governments at large to require a standard set of navigation gear on the bridge, as for instance in an aircraft. In fact this was quite thoroughly gone into in the Esso paper I referred to as to what would make a good suite of bridge navigation equipment. It has always amazed me that when you look at a $15 million ship, the amount of navigational gear up on the bridge to get that investment safely from Point A to Point B is a very miniscule amount of the ship's total cost. It certainly is not comparable to the ratio of costs true for aircraft.

Bello: An area which I expected you to deal with was the one concerning the ships operating under flags of convenience. It is an area very heavily exploited by the developing nations, but one which is also thoroughly detested by many of the maritime nations. I would like to ask two questions in this regard. First, what is the effect of the ships operating under the flags of convenience on the maritime world? Secondly, what are your observations on the disadvantages of such ships?

Yost: Of course, flags of convenience are those flags which have a large number of merchant ships owned primarily (or at least a significant number of them) by other countries, and as all of you know much of the merchant fleet that is actually owned by U.S. corporations does fly flags of other countries. I think that many of the coastal states of the world are concerned that flags of convenience, as we call them, maintain the same standards for pollution equipment and antipollution control measures as do flags of other countries. Most of the ships owned by the United States that do fly flags of other countries are, by the way, among the leaders in pollution control. There are flags of convenience where the standards are not as high as for U.S. flag ships, and of course the U.S. would like to see those standards raised. I would like to see exclusively international standards that all ships, regardless of their flag, regardless of their owner, regardless of their builder, would have to comply with; I feel that that is the best way of reducing pollution in the oceans. I also feel that this is the fairest way to allow flags of all ships to compete equally.

Schatz: Notwithstanding the exploitation of the Prudhoe Bay pool, we have a good deal of oil and gas flowing out of the general region of the Gulf of Alaska, which is highly seismic. Could you address the problem of protection of port and loading facilities from seismic danger and tsunamis?

Bates: In a place like Alaska, you had better be careful where you put your tank farm. I think the most famous case that I dug into was Alaska's Lituya Bay, where a tidal wave reached up apparently 400 feet above normal sea level. It is hard to believe; but men were not around to observe such a wave. As I remember it, the Coast Guard personnel at Scotch Cap Lighthouse were all lost, even though this light was about 100 feet above sea level. I have also been at Seward, Alaska, where a tank farm was pretty well destroyed. Even here in Narragansett Bay, tank farms must face major changes in sea level. Thus, sea level changes are definitely an engineering hazard that must be taken into account.

There are ways to beat this type of hazard, but they cost money. So this puts a real responsibility on our friends in the Department of Interior to make sure that tank farms can stand up under that once-in-a-hundred years phenomenon. My trouble as an industrial meteorologist was, however, that the once-in-a-hundred-years storm always seemed to occur about every tenth year. For example, Hurricane Agnes was supposedly the once-in-200-years storm, which means going back to 1773, or a very long time. Thus, it is a real problem when you are designing economic trade-offs out on the absolute tail of a gaussian distribution.

Wells: Since you are designing a presumably comprehensive maritime safety regime, I would like to ask if the IMCO regulations cover or have considered the special problems posed by high-speed surface craft, such as hydrofoils, cross-channel hovercraft systems, possibly the oceanic surface effect ships that the U.S. Navy is working on and their eventual commercial successors.

Yost: I will turn it over to Dr. Bates in just a moment, but I think that we are often accused of planning for today instead of planning for tomorrow, and maybe this is an area where we can be so accused. At the Law of the Sea Institute workshop in Nassau, we had an interesting paper presented by a Dr. Frankel from M.I.T. where he indicated the type of vessels that we need to plan for in the future and the type of ports that we need to plan for them, and the speeds that we are going to be faced with, and the rapidity of which things happen at these speeds are far beyond anything that today's mariner is used to. Even two ships approaching each other at 30 knots, with a 60 knot closing rate, is certainly something that most of us who have been going to sea all of our lives do not see very often. I am not sure we are really ready to deal with closing rates significantly higher than this.

When you are talking about IMCO, you are really talking about a group of nations, and so perhaps I would talk instead about the 1973 Marine Pollution Conference in London. There is a fifth draft of articles for that convention. These articles consider many of the things that Dr. Bates addressed here today as far as protection of the marine environment is concerned. That conference will consider vessel traffic schemes in the congested areas of the world, including the English Channel, for instance, where I understand there is some cross traffic of ground effect type vessels which are moving very fast and in areas of normal shipping lanes.

Bates: It is in the paper, though I did not mention it, that Europort has, by introducing a strict vessel traffic control system scheme, reduced the number of accidents by a factor of four while the tonnage actually went up. I have visited Europort, and the harbor approaches are run just as tightly as at any aircraft control tower at an international airport. I mean you do not move anything through that port without permission of the Dutch Government pilot, in order to avoid random ship intersections.

The high resolution radars now used in San Francisco Bay are amazing, too. We can track a small boat out to nine or ten miles and not lose it in the sea clutter. In fact, the other day one of our own Coast Guard utility boats had all of its navigation gear go out while in a dense fog. This craft was tracked completely through the harbor and brought into the pier simply by using this high resolution radar. I might also point out that radar transponders can be put on your high speed vehicles. There are other sorts of things one can do as well to keep two pieces of moving metal from intersecting, and much can still be done while introducing more electronics into the ship operations business.

McKnight: Dr. Bates, you have not addressed yourself to the problems that may arise in connection with superports. I was wondering what your views and Captain Yost's might be in connection with the advantages of superports as opposed to having an increased traffic inshore in the harbor areas. Also, what would be the Coast Guard's regulatory jurisdiction and functions in regard to superports 10 or 20 miles offshore?

Bates: You can get a personal opinion or you can get an official opinion. I had better let Captain Yost give you the official opinion.

Yost: The first thing I intended to say, Doctor, was that this is certainly not an official opinion. Actually, we are well aware, as is the entire Executive Department, of the need for superports to accommodate these large tankers, and as you know, there has been an administration bill that Gary Knight talked about yesterday, an administration bill submitted to Congress, and there are also two companion bills that have been submitted by members of Congress at the same time. So, there are at least three bills that I know of that are currently under consideration by the Congress.

In my own personal opinion—and this is not official in any way—I think that any country who has a superport needs some type of minimum safety zone around that superport so that within that safety zone they can control the traffic using the superport, and I would hope that those safety zones would be internationally agreed upon. I would think IMCO, for instance, might be an excellent organization to take a look at the plans a country might have for a superport—the location, the proximity to traffic lanes, and a number of other things—and advise that that superport needs X number of yards or X number of miles as a safety zone around it, and then that would be an internationally designated zone. Within that zone the coastal state which has the responsibility for the port would control traffic. They might also enforce laws regarding pollution. They might need to do some things in customs and other things within that zone, but I would hope that zone would be internationally agreed upon, internationally designated, and the things that the country can do within the zone be agreed international law.

Bates: Our Coast Guard philosophy in doing research and development for pollution control is to be essentially anywhere in a country within a matter of a few hours with the right gear to contain and pick up the spill. There are hazardous chemical spills, but it is oil that gets on television. Hence, our goal is to have the oil never get over a mile from the point of rupture; then we will place the necessary pickup equipment inside the contained pool of oil.

Our third generation oil containment boom can actually be air transported to the area. By the time the barrier arrives, our local buoy tenders will have necessary anchors out. We also have in final prototype two different kinds of high-speed oil pickup devices. By high speed, I mean on the order of picking up 50 barrels of oil a minute, a rate nearly 50 times greater than what anybody else has at present. All our oil catastrophe equipment fits into Coast Guard C-130 aircraft. The Coast Guard also has twin turbo helicopters for some air delivery, which might be supplemented by towing "sea sleds." There was a picture in the *New York Times* of a typical sea sled operation with a marine helicopter towing a minesweeping device off Vietnam.

The third point is that we really cannot contain spilled oil if the current is stronger than about 1.25 knots. Hence, if anybody is going to design a superport, current speeds should be kept down below about a knot, for after that the barriers do not "barrier" any more.

Gold: I have enjoyed your presentation, particularly regarding the imminent dangers. I think you made the point very well that we are still sailing in the dark ages on the seas, and the analogy to the aviation industry is a point extremely well taken. You seem to have a lot of faith in the regulatory ability of IMCO. It seems to me that IMCO is not really a regulating body; rather it is a self-regulating body which is, of course, run by the major shipping nations of the world. I think we can make the analogy to other industries with self regulations. It is never very effective.

You feel that IMCO is going to make increasing safety regulations. They may do so, but these will be regulations which will be set out much more in an advisory capacity than anything else. Will they be followed? The Council of IMCO, of course, is composed of the major shipping nations; and as you have said yourself, the major shipping nations have been very, very slow in implementing increasing safety on their ships.

So, I feel that even if the United States regulations in 1974 and 1976 will perhaps unilaterally bypass the lack of IMCO regulations, you will just drive more ship owners into, as Dr. Bello has already indicated, flags of convenience—or flags of necessity, as they are called by the oil industry. I would like to know whether this faith that you have in IMCO in 1973 and so forth is really well fixed?

Bates: I would hate to speak for anybody's delegation to the IMCO conference on marine pollution. Rather, I would re-raise the question that in the final analysis the law of the sea has to be postulated and worked over by the United Nations as a group, for this is the world body to which most of the countries of the world subscribe. In fact, the United Nations already has four organizations— IMCO, WMO, FAO, and UNESCO—all interested in the oceans. Unfortunately they are located in different cities. The fishery people, Food and Agriculture Organization, is in Rome. The Intergovernmental Oceanographic Commission is in Paris with UNESCO. The Intergovernmental Maritime Consultative Organization is in London, the World Meteorological Organization is in Geneva, and of course the United Nations headquarters are in New York. Thus, there are a lot of "cracks" for items to fall through, but that is also why the United Nations exists—to somehow or other work on global problems of the type you cite. In the final analysis, it is no better than the leadership exerted.

Reuben: First of all, I would like to commend Captain Gold for his incisive question. My question deals also with IMCO. There is a doctrine of shared jurisdiction now being pushed by coastal states whereby if there is a pollution incident from a ship even though it is beyond the territorial sea, the nearest coastal state would have a right to prosecute in its own ports, as well as the ports of, let us say, Panama or Liberia. What especially, Captain Yost, would be your opinion of this doctrine of shared jurisdiction?

Yost: First, one comment on Captain Gold's question. I am always concerned to see that in many countries of the world who have delegations both to IMCO and to Law of the Sea that as of yet many of these delegations do not seem to really be talking to each other; and I would say, Captain Gold, that your IMCO delegation is, I believe, much more enthusiastic about IMCO than you have indicated yourself.

       I think IMCO is capable of putting together a rational regime for the oceans so far as pollution goes. It is a very young organization, and its achievements to date have been remarkable, considering its age. However, there are some 75 nations now belonging to IMCO. The 1973 Marine Pollution Conference is a plenipotentiary conference at which we hope to see, as does Canada, many many more than 75 nations there. We would like to see the coastal nations who are concerned about pollution come to that conference and make their feelings felt and make the regulations that are negotiated be very, very meaningful; and of course the enforcement aspect of it comes from port state, flag state enforcement.

Rueben: The question was on shared jurisdiction where there was a pollution incident off the coastal state; the coastal state would have the right not to rely on the feelings of the Panamanian court but be able to prosecute in its own court.

Yost: I think that shared jurisdiction is a relatively new term in that context to me. I am familiar with the proposals for pollution zones well beyond the territorial sea, and any violation within that zone would be enforced by the coastal state. The proposal that you have is that anywhere on the high seas, without regard even to a zone, an offense that is committed would be an offense against the nearest coastal state, and that is certainly an interesting concept. I would be more inclined to discuss the concept of that enforcement before I would be willing to discuss the standard setting which I think is more important. If the state which was closest to a vessel had the right to set standards for discharge and construction, then I think we would have utter chaos on the oceans. If, on the other hand, we have exclusively international standards that are set by IMCO or a plenipotentiary conference, and then you are asking who is going to enforce, I think that your suggestion merits some discussion. I am sure it will be discussed at the law of the sea conference.

Reuben: I think the point that Captain Gold and I are trying to make is that since 1948 IMCO has been making regulations and setting standards. I am thinking in particular since 1954 of the oil pollution rates, and you know every three or four years we see another treaty or another set of regulations being passed. The problem is that the major shipping states, the ones whose vested interests are in maximization of the freedom of navigation, have refused to sign these or have had many great exceptions to different articles in the treaties, and I am wondering or questioning your optimism with respect to the October-November IMCO conference.

Yost: Yes. I understand that there are many nations concerned that we are not going to get effective standards out of this conference, and even if we do get effective standards we are going to be unable to enforce them throughout the seas.

I think this is a very real fear, and I am optimistic, but maybe I should say cautiously optimistic, even hopeful that we will be able to work out a system of standards within IMCO and jurisdiction within law of the sea for enforcement that will be effective. The only way I see of doing that is if all the nations in the world who are interested will not sit back and criticize what we have now, and I do not mean that Canada is doing that in any way; but there are many nations who have not become as yet active within either IMCO or the Law of the Sea that I hope will come out in a forthcoming way and sit down and work out a system that we can all live with. So, I am cautiously optimistic.

Chapter Thirteen

The Role of the Marine Insurance Industry in the Emerging Regime of the Oceans

George W. Handley
Senior Vice President and Director
Marsh & McLennan, Incorporated

It is my privilege to have this opportunity to discuss the role of the marine insurance industry in "The Emerging Regime of the Oceans" and to review with you the industry's major problems and its view of the future.

A BRIEF LOOK AT THE INDUSTRY

With your many different backgrounds and activities, your exposure to marine insurance will vary considerably so we should begin with a brief look at the marine insurance industry. I hope I will cover the areas that interest you most and that you will not find my approach to be too general.

Marine insurance is truly international in scope; it must adapt quickly and efficiently to changing international relationships and it must be particularly sensitive to worldwide economic conditions and exposures. It is essential to world trade, and the dependence of each upon the other goes back many centuries, first to the Phoenicians and later to the then very sophisticated fellows who met at Edward Lloyd's coffee house in London to underwrite, as they called it, each others' ships and the cargoes they carried.

Marine insurance available to vessel owners generally fits three main areas of exposure: (1) loss of or damage to the vessel itself, (2) liabilities arising out of the operation of the vessel, and (3) loss of income to the owner if the vessel is unable to operate because of a damage. In addition, insurance to cover loss of or damage to the cargo carried aboard the vessel is available to shippers, and to those who buy or sell the manufactured products, merchandise, or the commodities being transported.

Vessel insurance—that is, hull and machinery coverage for the vessel and liability coverage—accounts for approximately 75 percent of the world's marine insurance business. According to the best available estimates, marine insurance produced a worldwide premium of about $2,500,000,000 in 1972. Of this total, approximately 60 percent was written by the British Market, including Lloyd's Underwriters. Approximately 25 percent of the total was underwritten in the United States, with the remaining 15 percent divided among all the other markets, which are located in most of the maritime nations of the world. The company I am with, Marsh & McLennan, Incorporated, is an international brokerage firm, and represents clients of all nationalities with exposures all around the world; thus we are in constant communication with all the major insurance markets.

The figure of $2,500,000,000 is, on its own, a rather substantial sum, but is it when related to the exposures the marine industry will be faced with and expected to protect? In a year or two, liquid natural gas carriers, valued at more than $125,000,000 each, will be in service, and even before then two or three of these unique vessels will be lying side by side under construction at several shipyards around the world. Referring again to the $2,500,000,000, American insurers' share is about 25 percent or $625,000,000—the worth of only five liquid natural gas carriers or perhaps ten very large crude carriers. I should point out that the $625,000,000 does not all come from large vessels, and includes premium for all marine policies, outboard motor boats, yachts, tugs and barges, drilling rigs, and cargo, for instance. The largest underwriting group in the United States had a premium volume of about $75,000,000 in 1972 spread over about 3,800 vessels, and its participation in several exceeded $25,000,000 each—that does not leave much to pay claims on the other vessels.

THREE PROBLEMS

As those of us in the industry see it, the major problems we will have to contend with during the next few years fall into three broad categories: financial, legal, and physical; and while each does present its own particular areas of concern, each has a very significant effect on the other. If the insurance industry cannot produce the necessary capacity because it does not have sufficient security to support the underwriting demands put upon it, it makes little difference how good a risk the highly valued specialized vessels may be. On the other hand, even if sufficient capacity is available, underwriters will not commit it to a risk that is poorly engineered (to put it simply) or is influenced by legislation, as we are seeing today, that imposes unlimited liabilities while permitting virtually no defenses. The mission of marine insurance is to absorb the risks undertaken by those who follow the sea and to spread those risks among the members of the insurance market. This spreading of risk, coupled with the assurance of prompt indemnity to those who suffer loss, is the business of marine insurance.

Financial

Let us examine the financial problem first. As vessels have grown in size and complexity their values have risen substantially. Modern vessels, together with their cargoes, represent a tremendous concentration of capital. In fact, except for aircraft, there is probably no other exposure where so much money is at risk and where a few moments' lack of concentration by those in charge can have such catastrophic results. As recently as five or six years ago we did not think in terms of a $25,000,000 value; yet today such values are commonplace.

One new large vessel will often replace four to six conventional vessels, and considering building costs today, the value of that one vessel will exceed the combined values of those it will replace. With the substantially increased values and reduced spread producing greater concentrations of risk, underwriters are exposed to the effects of what we call shock loss—the situation where only a few such losses can produce unsatisfactory loss results. This is the financial problem. In such circumstances, underwriters will reduce the participation they are prepared to take in each risk and it becomes necessary for us to find more underwriters to complete the risk to be insured. Furthermore, as underwriting is supposed to be profit-making business, the more unsatisfactory the results, the less enthusiasm there is to join the club. Would you invest your money in a losing business? It is only in the last two years that we have seen a return to profitability, albeit modest, after a long period of extremely poor results.

Right now, because of capacity limitations, it is not possible to insure a $125,000,000 vessel completely in one insurance market, be it London, Lloyd's, the United States, or Japan. This question of capacity is something which I feel is sometimes not fully understood, and I would like to review it with you. Very simply put, if underwriting results for a given class of business or a particular type of exposure are poor, insurers will restrict the resources they make available for writing such risks. The fewer the risks there are to be insured, the smaller the participation insurers are willing to take in each risk. If he has $100,000 to commit, an underwriter would obviously prefer a $25,000 share in four risks than a $100,000 share in one; and if, for instance, the underwriter's maximum permissible line is $100,000 we will need more underwriters to insure a $1,000,000 risk than we would for a $500,000 risk. Underwriting resources are not unlimited and we are approaching the maximum of the worldwide insurance resources presently available.

For instance, just about everyone has heard of Lloyd's of London—and just about everyone thinks Lloyd's is a very large and wealthy insurance company, but it is not. It is a market made up of about 7,000 individuals who in various combinations form syndicates that underwrite insurance for the personal account of the members. When you insure your property or your exposure with Lloyd's it is insured not with the Corporation of Lloyd's, but with one or more of the syndicates, and every member of each syndicate is directly liable to the policyholder for his share of any loss that may fall on the policy in which his syndicate participates. Lloyd's capacity—that is, the amount of insurance that an underwriting member or a syndicate can write—is determined according to a rigid formula and is dependent upon the personal funds the member has pledged to the Corporation of Lloyd's to support his book of business.

I hasten to assure you that the problem is not insoluble; however, we are going to have to attract substantial additional capacity to the market place. The endeavor has been underway for a couple of years, led mainly by the international brokerage firms, who must be sure of continuity of coverage if they are to properly protect their clients—who are, in turn, committing themselves to 15- and 20-year finance agreements. I am happy to report that our endeavor, aided immeasurably by the improved underwriting results since 1970, has already produced some additional capacity. But there is still a long way to go, given the very large numbers we are looking at. This additional capacity must come from insurers new to the marine field, such as the large life insurance companies, as well as from the companies now in the business who must be willing to increase their participations. Also, we may need an increased involvement on the part of ship owners in the form of pooling arrangements with each other as the TOVALOP Scheme. There, the participants share among themselves the first $1,500,000 of each claim and purchase commercial insurance in excess of this figure.

Legal

Now, what about the legal problem? At a time when the underwriter is concerned about his diminishing spread of risk, he is being asked to provide even more coverage for each of the fewer risks he insures. The unprecedented proliferation of marine pollution liability legislation over the last few years illustrates the point I want to make here. The general feeling these days seems to be that all that is necessary to develop insurance capacity for pollution liabilities is to enact legislation imposing such liabilities upon the ship owner. In virtually all cases, the ship owner and his underwriter must provide the appropriate authorities with a financial guarantee that they will pay for the cleanup of a spill.

Heretofore, an underwriter's liability under his policy may have been, say, $14,000,000 for all claims arising out of one accident; but if he gives a financial guarantee for cleanup he must, in effect, separately reserve an additional $14,000,000. This means he will write $14,000,000 less coverage during the year whether on hull and machinery, cargo, or for loss of life and personal injury claims or for the other liabilities for which the ship owner must be protected. From the point of view of the marine insurance industry, it is important that we have pollution legislation providing for uniform liability limits, uniform defenses, and uniform financial responsibility requirements if the insurance market is to provide the coverage for all the liabilities that may be imposed upon ship owners. The problem here is obvious. Never mind the two limits we mentioned earlier. Suppose Canada and the United States and, say, the State of New York, each required evidence of financial responsibility to comply with their pollution laws: Ship owners and their underwriters would be tripling their pollution liability in case of one spill in the Thousand Islands area, for example; and add that to the value of the vessel and the cargo if they are lost in the accident.

I am not attempting to minimize the pollution problem, to be sure; and who can object to reasonable legislation that will protect our water resources and environment from pollution? What I am saying, however, is that the answer is not the enactment of more and more onerous legislation that establishes financial requirements that are guaranteed not by the polluter but from a not unlimited reservoir of funds that must also be available to absorb the other risks undertaken by those who follow the sea. Rather, we should be as much concerned about preventing the spill so it won't happen. Are we giving as much thought to the location of terminals, traffic handling, personnel training, and enforcing regulations established by bodies such as IMCO as we are to politics and unlimited liability? Reasonable legislation, then, is the key to the solution of the legal problem. Reasonable limits of liability and uniform responsibilities and defenses that clearly define and establish the exposures to be faced are necessary if the marine insurance industry is to be able to intelligently measure its exposures and thus provide the security expected of it by its policyholders.

Physical

And now we come to the physical problem. After World War II, and during the early 1950s, the T-2 tanker, as it was known, was the standard petroleum carrier, and its 16,600 deadweight tons carried the oil cargoes of the world. The war-built T-2, which was later strengthened, was a sound, seaworthy vessel and caused underwriters very little trouble. Everyone thought it was impossible to sink the tanker—and these models had a top value of only about $2,500,000. There was some difficulty in the early 1960s due to several explosions, but the cause was quickly traced and the problem resolved by 1964. Despite this, underwriters generally regarded the tanker to be one of their better classes of business.

However, it was all changing. During 1957, more than 400 vessels of over 24,000 DWT were delivered. Four were 85,000 DWT, then the largest tankers ever built. It was in 1958 that the average size of the world's tanker fleet exceeded, for the first time, the 16,600 DWT of the T-2. By the end of 1961, the average deadweight tonnage of tankers in service was 21,200 tons and the average size of tankers under construction was only 44,700 tons. Only eight years ago construction of the first of the Bantry class tankers was begun. These vessels measure 326,000 DWT and are over 1,100 feet in length and 175 feet wide. They can carry 2,500,000 barrels of oil. The first Bantry was delivered on September 9, 1968. Two years ago a 378,000 tonner was delivered, and February of 1973 produced a 486,000 tonner—the largest moving object ever built by man! An $80,000,000 egg in one big basket. I was personally involved in the insurance negotiations leading to the placing of the coverage for each of these VLCCs and I can attest to the difficulties we faced in completing the insurance required around the world.

The new age of the VLCC had dawned, and in 1967 two catastrophes, one of which was the infamous *Torrey Canyon*, occurred within weeks of each other and shocked underwriters into realizing the impact of the large loss of a single unit with its great concentration of value. The great awakening came in December 1969 when, within two weeks, three VLCCs, *Mactra, Marpessa*, and *Kong Haakon VII*, suffered explosions while cleaning tanks. *Mactra* was lost, the largest vessel ever to sink, and the other two were severely damaged. Despite extensive investigations into the circumstances of these catastrophes, the exact cause of the explosions has not been conclusively established. Now the tanker is suspect; it has grown much larger and it is no longer considered to be the good risk it once was, despite the fact it is adding considerable premium into underwriter's accounts.

The significant point here is that it all happened so quickly. The smart marine underwriter is supposed to know everything that happened in the past; he has all kinds of statistics on past losses and performance—but there were no statistics and past performance records for VLCCs, and there aren't any for liquid natural gas carriers either. So the underwriter is deprived of the most important tools he needs to work with and he must underwrite the future, rather than the past, when he is dealing with 500,000 tonners and $125,000,000 LNGCs. He has never had to underwrite so much with so little experience, and the stakes are very high. He tends to be very cautious. But marine underwriters are going to have to learn to work without these tools because we are in a period of rapid and farreaching change in technological development, and for this reason past experience will become a less important factor in the art of underwriting.

As we moved into the 1960s, technological development was overcoming previous limitations on speed, power, size, and cargo handling capabilities. Innovative design changes were being made, but as is so often the case, such development is usually accompanied by periods of experimentation and uneven growth. Structural adequacy had been demonstrated only on the drawing boards. Safety programs were inclined to lag behind design changes. The increase in draft of vessels ran well ahead of channel marking and dredging activities. Ports were opened before their approaches were adequately charted, and vessels found themselves disabled oceans away from tugs of sufficient power to tow them to the few drydocks that could hold them. Officers and crewmen were faced with maneuvering characteristics unlike anything experienced before, and very few had knowledge of the operation of an automated engine room. All of us have in fact embarked upon a new voyage into the unknown—the naval architects, builders, owners, classification societies, seamen, and the marine underwriters.

This is the physical problem, and with talk of deep-sea ports, offshore nuclear power stations, advanced offshore oil exploration, 1,000,000 tonners, undersea mining, and underwater pipelines, underwriters say they have good reason to wonder if they can ever catch up with the new technology. Traditionally marine underwriters have been reluctant to attempt to force change on the ship owner, insisting they are simply part of the owners' financial support and thus they are in no better position than the designers, the professionals, or the classification societies or other technicians to know how effective a piece of equipment will be. In fact, underwriters' attempt to involve themselves in this area of the owners' domain has often been strongly resisted.

But as underwriters must now work without their old tools they will need new ones, and the marine underwriter is going to have to involve himself to a much greater extent than he has been inclined to in all the physical areas of the highly valued, complex exposures of the future. Any meaningful contribution the underwriter can offer should certainly be welcomed. The importance, or rather the necessity, of a dialogue among the partners in the venture—the owners, the underwriters, the brokers, and the many technicians—is now at least fully appreciated, and I am satisfied we are all going to be much better informed about our risks than we were in the past. We will have to be if we are going to overcome the fears of the unknown that are prevalent in underwriting circles today.

If we were to ask underwriters today what their principal physical concerns are, I am certain these would include

1. The necessity to install inerting systems or other effective means to reduce the gas vapors in tankers
2. The relationship of tank size to explosion potential
3. Whether or not it is necessary to fix vessels with inner bottoms to protect the cargo tanks
4. Whether dual propulsion units and bow and stern thrusters are necessary
5. The development of advanced collision avoidance systems
6. The establishment of sea lanes in congested waterways and their mandatory use
7. The updating of crew training and licensing programs
8. Effective methods of pollution prevention and control

For the most part, I have confined my comments to tankers and VLCCs, but they do not, of course, pose all the problems. What about LNGCs? There is precious little we know about the hazards of liquified natural gas spills on water. The Coast Guard acknowledges that LNG is a hazardous cargo but is satisfied that it can be safely transported by vessels if the proper precautions are taken. The enormity of the LNG problem has fortunately generated considerable research, and we are certainly much farther along than we were at a similar period in the development of the VLCC. The Coast Guard has already formulated plans to take absolute control over the LNGCs entering New York Harbor, isolating them from other traffic to ensure that a collision does not happen.

But suppose there is a leak or spill and vapor clouds are formed as the super cold liquid warms into a gas? Tests indicate that the gas cloud disperses poorly and remains flammable for long distances downwind. Vapor trails, if ignited, can provide a flashback to the vaporizing LNG spill. How much damage would be caused? How much insurance would you want to buy if you owned an LNGC? It could very well be that the $125,000,000 the vessel is worth would represent the smallest part of the loss.

As you will appreciate, there are a number of areas I have not covered; but whatever the function, whatever the exposure, the insurance problems are the same—financial, legal, and physical. I hope that I have been able to give you some idea of the insurance industry's problems. We have come a long way with you from clipper ships to steam and nuclear powered vessels, from T-2s to 500,000 tonners and pollution coverage, and now liquid natural gas carriers valued at $125,000,000. And while it does not look as if the next twenty years will be the easiest, I am confident we can cope with the financial problem if you will help us in the legal and physical areas. If the marine insurance industry is not willing or able to absorb the risks undertaken by those who follow the sea, we have nothing to offer.

Chapter Fourteen

Offshore Petroleum: Its Geography and Technology

John P. Albers
U.S. Geological Survey

I will discuss first where known oil and gas reserves exist offshore, and second the nature of petroleum operations and their relation to other uses of the sea-bed. I shall not attempt to discuss specifically where additional oil and gas resources will be found, for our level of knowledge is not yet sufficient to do so. Suffice it to say, that so far as the offshore is concerned, oil and gas resources are largely confined to the continental shelves, slopes, rises, and small ocean basins. Because these areas commonly contain a substantial thickness of Tertiary and Mesozoic sedimentary rocks from which most of the world's petroleum production comes, they are generally favorable from a geologic viewpoint for petroleum. However, there are many other factors that determine whether or not oil and gas are present in a given area, and only a small part of the broadly favorable areas actually contain producible oil and gas accumulations.

EXPLORATION

During the past few years the search for petroleum on the submerged continental margins of the world has continued at a rate of acceleration surpassing earlier forecasts. The floor of the world's oceans and seas adjacent to the continents is the major exploration focus of the petroleum industry and the offshore search underway has been referred to as the beginning of one of the most massive oil-hunting eras in history.

Offshore exploration during 1972 was in progress on the continental shelves and slopes of 80 countries and involved 134 companies. Some 400 drilling units are now operating on the continental shelves of 70 countries and, at the end of 1972, commercial offshore production was reported from 26 countries. Discoveries of commercial potential have been made off 13 additional countries, but development has not as yet progressed to production.

The current status of knowledge about worldwide offshore petroleum resources and their distribution is best revealed by examination of the production and reserves figures for those areas where exploration and development drilling have progressed to the point where production has become substantial and where recoverable reserves can be estimated with reasonable definity. The distribution and magnitude of offshore oil production and reserves by continent and country to January 1, 1973, are shown in Table 14-1; natural gas production and reserves to January 1, 1972 are shown in Table 14-2.

The tabulations are classified as provisional because only in the past two years have offshore statistics begun to be reported separately from total production in many countries. Consequently, some inconsistencies exist in both production and reserves statistics for some of the fields that straddle the shoreline and produce from both onshore and offshore. Furthermore, some of the estimates are based on a minimum of discovery wells and, in general, recoverable reserves estimates are not available for many of the smaller fields, as indicated in the tables.

Nevertheless, in all cases, the reserve estimates tabulated are based on discovery drilling and not on broad favorability factors. The offshore recoverable oil reserves, as reported in Table 14-1, represent 25 percent of the total world estimated recoverable reserve at this time and of the offshore recoverable total, 57 percent is in the Persian Gulf. Worldwide production from the offshore increased from 2.6 billion barrels in 1970 to 3.3 billion barrels in 1972 and now accounts for about 18 percent of total world production if Lake Maracaibo is included as offshore production.

Figure 14-1 illustrates graphically three main points relevant to world petroleum. First is the relation between oil produced through 1972 and known proved reserves. It will be seen that reserves are a little more than twice as much as the oil produced so far. On the graph, production is above the horizontal line and reserves are below. Second, the graph illustrates, more or less by continent, where production has come from so far and where the presently known reserves are. Obviously the Middle East—specifically the Persian Gulf area—stands out as the big area of reserves. Finally, the graph illustrates the proportion of production and reserves that are offshore.

Data are still not sufficient for making either a complete estimate of potential world subsea petroleum resources or for making a meaningful revision of Lewis Week's 1969 estimate of 700 billion barrels, a figure that is based on

Table 14-1
Worldwide Ultimate Recoverable Offshore Oil Reserves and Cumulative Production (millions of barrels)

WORLDWIDE ULTIMATE RECOVERABLE OFFSHORE OIL RESERVES AND CUMULATIVE PRODUCTION (MILLIONS OF BARRELS)

	ESTIMATED ULTIMATE RECOVERABLE	CUMULATIVE PRODUCTION	NUMBER OF OFFSHORE FIELDS	
			GIANT	OTHER
AFRICA	9,401	1,317	7	49
ASIA				
• PERSIAN GULF	95,933	6,039	21	16
• FAR EAST	3,654	296	1	30
TOTAL	99,587	6,335	22	46
EUROPE	12,011	679	7	33
SOUTH AMERICA	23,949	15,817	9	11
NORTH AMERICA	17,764	7,280	9	290
OCEANIA	2,876	312	4	6
WORLD TOTALS*	165,588	31,740	58	435

*OF THE WORLD TOTAL, 81 PERCENT IS IN THE 58 GIANT FIELDS.

Source: *Offshore Petroleum: Its Geography and Technology*, by John P. Albers

Table 14-2
Worldwide Ultimate Recoverable Offshore Gas Reserves and Cumulative Production (billions of cubic feet)

WORLDWIDE ULTIMATE RECOVERABLE OFFSHORE GAS RESERVES AND CUMULATIVE PRODUCTION
(BILLIONS OF CUBIC FEET)

	ESTIMATED ULTIMATE RECOVERABLE	CUMULATIVE PRODUCTION 1-1-72 (EXCEPT AS NOTED)	NUMBER OF OFFSHORE FIELDS	
			GIANT	OTHER
AFRICA				
• EGYPT	1,000	NA		1
• GABON	NA	NA		1
TOTAL	1,000	NA		2
ASIA				
MIDDLE EAST				
• SAUDI ARABIA	3,600		1	
• KUWAIT-NEUTRAL ZONE	875	37		1
• UNION OF ARAB-EMIRATES	2,165	NA		NA
TOTAL	6,640	37	1	NA
EUROPE				
• UNITED KINGDOM	29,500	1,131	4	19
• NORWAY	10,000	0	1	1
• DENMARK	500	0		2
• NETHERLANDS	NA	NA		11
• ITALY	NA	300		12
TOTAL	40,000	1,431	5	45

Table 14-2 (cont.)

WORLDWIDE ULTIMATE RECOVERABLE OFFSHORE GAS RESERVES AND CUMULATIVE PRODUCTION
(BILLIONS OF CUBIC FEET)

	ESTIMATED ULTIMATE RECOVERABLE	CUMULATIVE PRODUCTION 1-1-72 (EXCEPT AS NOTED)	NUMBER OF OFFSHORE FIELDS GIANT	OTHER
NORTH AMERICA				
UNITED STATES	39,463	20,606	NA	
TOTAL	39,463	20,606	NA	
CARIBBEAN				
TRINIDAD-TOBAGO	3,500	39		6
TOTAL	3,500	39		6
OCEANIA				
AUSTRALIA	10,300	48	3	8
NEW ZEALAND	6,000	0	1	
TOTAL	16,300	48	4	8
WORLD TOTALS	106,903	22,161	10	INCOMPLETE

Source: *Offshore Petroleum: Its Geography and Technology*, by John P. Albers

broad geologic favorability factors. The world subsea petroleum potential is unquestionably large, but the magnitude cannot yet be accurately defined. Offshore exploration for petroleum, now worldwide in scope, is becoming increasingly intense in many areas of the world. Results, though initially disappointing to date in some areas, have been spectacular in others. Over the next few years, the worldwide recoverable reserves of petroleum will be substantially increased,

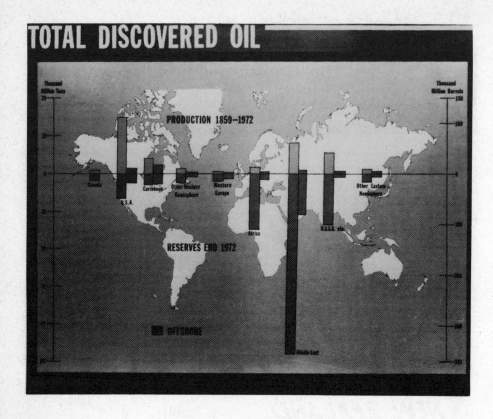

Figure 14-1.   Total Discovered Oil

and by the end of the next decade offshore data should be sufficient to permit meaningful estimates of world subsea potential.

Cumulative natural gas production, to January 1, 1972, and offshore reserves are shown in Table 14-2. As is evident, the bulk of the presently known reserves are in the North Sea and on the shelves of the United States.

Some indications of where the new reserves will be found and what the ultimate geographic distribution of the reserves might be can be obtained from a review of the exploration activities underway around the world and of the results that have been obtained over the past several years. Let us focus on the most active areas and the general prospects for the future.

Foreign Areas of High Offshore Activity

1. The *North Sea* in 1972 was one of the world's most active and successful discovery areas. Some twenty new fields were discovered, thirteen oil and seven gas. Of these, three are classed as giant oil fields, two in the U.K. sector and one in the Norwegian sector, bringing the number of North Sea giants to five. Interpretation of seismic work suggests that other large oil finds can be expected in the northern part of the North Sea. Estimates of ultimate potential range from 31 to 42 billion barrels.

2. Exploration in the waters off *Indonesia* became extensive in 1971, and some fifteen companies were active at the beginning of 1973. Six offshore fields have been discovered since 1971, four oil and two gas. No ultimate potential reserve estimate is available, but geologic conditions across the extensive Sunda Shelf and in locally developed sedimentary basins along the margins of land areas indicate a large potential.

3. Nine companies were active off *Trinidad-Tobago* at the beginning of 1973, and newly licensed areas are in water depths up to 2,000 feet. In addition to earlier discoveries of both oil and gas, two other big probable commercial finds have been recently reported. No ultimate potential reserve estimate is available, but the area is considered to have a large gas reserve and has the potential of becoming a major petroleum producer.

4. The number of large sedimentary basins that lie along the continental margin of *West Africa* makes its shelf one of the world's most promising hunting grounds. Exploration activity has been high all along the West Africa shelf for several years, but to date the greatest success has been obtained off Nigeria, where drilling has been intense. Three new field discoveries have been announced in recent months. No estimate of ultimate potential oil reserves is available for Nigeria, but prospects for additional discoveries are considered good. Potential gas reserves, as yet unconfirmed, are estimated to be 10,000 billion cubic feet. For other areas off West Africa some promising discoveries have been made, but the giants have been elusive. The tempo of exploration off West Africa is expected to increase in the months ahead.

5. Exploration in the past three to four years has proved the shelf off *Northwest Australia* to be a major new supply of natural gas. Five fields have been discovered in the past one and a half years, and one of these is in the super giant class. Prospects are considered good for additional discoveries as the search broadens.

Prospects in Other Foreign Areas

1. The *Mediterranean Sea* is believed to have good potential for major sources of gas. Search along the offshore margin of Africa has been de-

layed because of major success in onland discoveries in the countries of northern Africa, particularly in Algeria and Libya. Activity in the offshore of northern Africa has increased in the past several years and the first discoveries off Tunisia and Libya have come in the past two years. The Tunisian-Sicilian platform, the Adriatic Sea, and the submerged part of the Nile Delta are considered highly prospective areas in the Mediterranean for new finds.

2. The *South China Sea* area has been the scene of major exploration activity within the past two years and new discoveries have been made off Sarawak. More than 70 wells have now been drilled in the waters of Malaysia.

3. Attention in *Canada* has been focused for the past half dozen years on the Scotia shelf where a significant discovery has been made on Sable Island. Prospects for large supplies of natural gas in that area are judged excellent. More recently, activity has become heavy in the MacKenzie Delta, where major land discoveries have been made, and on the Arctic islands of Canada. Drilling is planned this year in the Beaufort Sea off the MacKenzie Delta. The northern coastal area of Canada, including parts of the shelf where ice problems can be handled by drilling from constructed offshore islands, has the prospects for significant petroleum production.

4. In the *Soviet Union* the rate of land discoveries has been so rapid over the past ten years that the offshore has not received much attention. Offshore petroleum exploration in the U.S.S.R. is still in its infancy. However, fifteen new fields have been discovered in the Caspian Sea within the past five years, and Soviet sources state that total reserves there are "enormous." First discoveries by the U.S.S.R. in the Sea of Azov, Black Sea, and Sea of Okhotsk have been announced within the past two years. Exploration activity is now under way in the southern part of the Barents Sea and prospects for major discoveries are considered excellent. It is worthy of note that of 82 super giant oil fields in the world (ultimate recoverable reserves of more than one billion barrels) nineteen are in the U.S.S.R., seven more than Iran, which has twelve.

5. The overall discovery rate in the *Persian Gulf* has been comparable to the phenomenally high success ratios that have characterized the land areas peripheral to the Gulf. Furthermore, the size of the field discoveries in the offshore has been so consistently large that much of the drilling activity has been absorbed in field development rather than in continued exploratory drilling. Production rates for the Gulf remain well below potential capacity both because of deliberate control and because one or the largest fields in the offshore straddles a territorial boundary and has yet to be put into production. Considering the discovery history in the Persian Gulf to date, one cannot conceive of an indefinite continuation of large discoveries. Yet, experts feel that additional large reserves will be found.

6. In *South America* the fields of Lake Maracaibo have been a world leader in production for a number of years. A recent discovery in the Gulf of Venezuela opens a new offshore area for that country and the continental shelf area of Northeastern Venezuela offers good prospects. Other offshore areas of Latin America have received somewhat less attention than other areas of the world, but exploration activity is increasing. Field discoveries have been made off Brazil, Argentina, Peru, and Ecuador, though none to date have been large. Nevertheless, the continental shelf off the mouth of the Amazon River and off southern Brazil, the very broad shelf off Argentina, the shelf off Southern Chile, and parts of the Peru and Ecuador shelves offer promises for future discoveries.

7. In the U.S. the northern shelf of the *Gulf of Mexico* off Louisiana and east Texas has been the most intensely explored and developed offshore area in the world and it is one of the world leaders in offshore production. The entire outer shelf off Florida and much of the southern shelf of Texas remain untested by drilling. Prospects for additional discoveries in those areas, though less promising for large production than the northern shelf, are nevertheless considered good. The most promising area for future large production is the continental slope of the northern Gulf in water depths of 600 to 2,500 meters. Though as yet untested by drilling, this area of the sea floor could rival the northern Gulf of Mexico continental shelf, as a source of petroleum.

8. The offshore of southern *California*, and particularly the Santa Barbara Channel area, must be classed as a major U.S. petroleum source. The State of California estimates its offshore potential (i.e., to 3 miles offshore) to be 30 billion barrels.

9. The *Gulf of Alaska*, the *Bering Sea*, the *Chukchi Sea*, and the *Beaufort Sea* shelf have potential for large amounts of petroleum if appraised on the basis of broad geologic favorability. Geologic structures and sizable sedimentary basins are known. Various estimates of potential have been made, but with exception of the north Alaska coastal area, reservoir conditions in the areas otherwise favorable are unknown and must stand the test of the drill before meaningful estimates of potential can be made.

10. Along the *Atlantic Continental Margin* off the U.S. from Florida to Canada are three known sedimentary basins of the size and thickness favorable for the occurrence of petroleum. These are the Georges Bank basin, the Baltimore Canyon basin, and the Blake Plateau basin. These structures lie beneath the outer continental shelf and extend seaward beneath the continental slope and possibly beneath at least part of the continental rise as well. Although geophysical exploration has been underway along the U.S. Atlantic margin for some eight years, its reservoir characteristics offshore remain as yet untested by drilling. Nevertheless the extent of the area and the size of its sedimentary basins

are such that it must be considered at this time as a prospectively favorable area. But until it is tested by drilling, estimates of ultimate potential must be classed as speculative. To summarize the status of knowledge about the petroleum prospects of the submerged continental margin of the U.S., it can be safely stated that less than five percent has been studied in the detail necessary to make meaningful estimates of the ultimate offshore petroleum potential of the U.S.

11. For completeness, mention must be made of two of the world's most extensive shelf areas, the shallow sea floor beneath the *Laptev* and *East Siberia Seas* north of Siberia, and the shelf basin area off China, extending for 2,000 miles southward from the Yellow Sea, through the East China Sea to Hainan off southeast China. The geology of the vast Arctic Siberian shelf is not well known but the area cannot be overlooked as a potential oil-producing province for the somewhat distant future. A recent offshore discovery was made in an inland arm of the Yellow Sea off China. Otherwise, exploration has been very limited along the China Shelf. Geologic conditions, insofar as known, indicate a good potential for discoveries.

TECHNOLOGY

Let me turn now to offshore petroleum technology, which may be subdivided into four component operations. These operations include exploration, production, transportation, and storage. I will try to describe the relation of these operations in relation to other uses of the seabed.

The exploration phase of operations normally commences with seismic surveys, in which the geophones or recording devices are trailed behind the exploration vessel and record reflections of artificial earthquake waves created in the vicinity of the vessel. These seismic operations have virtually no effect on other uses of the sea, except as they add another vessel to fishing areas or sea lanes.

Following such geophysical exploration the next step is the drilling of an exploratory well. Such wells are drilled from four types of vessels. In the first case the vessel consists of a barge which is sunk to the sea floor, the superstructure remaining above the surface of the water. Such vessels are no longer constructed and their use is confined to the Gulf of Mexico. A second type of vessel is the semisubmersible, which is towed or self-propelled to its drill location and is then partially submerged in the water, thereby increasing stability under adverse water and weather conditions. A third type of exploratory vessel is the jack-up rig, the emplacement of which requires the lowering of the legs to the sea floor which are then jacked up to maintain the drilling platform at the appropriate elevation above the water surface. The fourth exploratory drilling vessel is the drill ship, which operates like other vessels but contains on its deck a drilling rig as well as the other pertinences required for the drilling of wells.

Until the present time, virtually all exploratory activities have been in water depths not greater than 600 feet. Drilling vessels are under construction, however, to extend this water depth capability to as much as 2,000 feet. Exploratory drilling in this type of vessel leads to very little interference with other uses of the sea or the seabed. If the vessel is stationed in or near a regular shipping lane, appropriate precautions must be taken to avoid accidents. There is, of course, some possibility of an oil spill but such spills are rare during exploratory drilling operations. The most common problem raised by the exploratory phase of offshore operations is that of interference with fishing operations. Normally, however, no more than one exploratory drilling vessel is located in a large area of water.

The second phase of offshore petroleum operations takes place after the discovery of a petroleum deposit. In this case a means is required for both the drilling of wells in the field discovered and their production. At the present time the practice is to install permanent platforms the legs of which are emplaced in the sea floor. From this platform as many as 62 different wells may be drilled directionally to produce the oil or gas reservoir. Platforms of this type are restricted to waters of 600 or 700 feet in depth. In greater water depths it will be necessary to drill the wells from either a floating vehicle of the type used for exploratory drilling or from some sort of self-contained unit on the sea floor.

At the present time several production units are being developed which can produce wells with all equipment located on the sea floor, the drilling platform being removed. The production platforms are more likely sources of interference with other uses of the sea and the seabed than the removable drilling vessels used in exploratory operations. Because the platforms are more numerous and the number of wells is large, there is more chance of an oil spill. Experience in the United States does not suggest that this is a serious problem, for of the 16,000 wells drilled in U.S. waters only 25 have resulted in blowouts and of these only three were serious enough to cause severe pollution and consequent interference with commercial and pleasure uses of the sea.

The large number of platforms located in the Gulf of Mexico and the many that will be installed in the future in the North Sea and in certain other heavily travelled seas will require particular precautions to prevent accidents involving the collision of tankers, freighters, and fishing boats with the platforms. The platforms will also result in interference with surface fishing and with the operations of draggers. And obviously such platforms may also interfere with eventual sea-floor mining in places where mineral deposits may be found coextensive with the outlines of oil and gas fields. In addition, the large numbers of production platforms may result in some diminution of esthetics because such platforms are visible up to distances of about twenty miles on clear days. At the same time, the drilling platforms in the Gulf of Mexico are reported to serve as artificial reefs, and result in a notable increase in sport fishing in their vicinities.

A third aspect of offshore petroleum operations is related to the transportation of the petroleum from the fields to shore. In some places the production is simply stored on one or more of the platforms of the field and transferred to barges, which carry it ashore. In other cases, and necessarily in the case of gas fields, gathering lines are laid on the seabed between the various platforms in the fields and these gathering lines are then hooked into trunk lines for transportation of the crude oil or natural gas to a point onshore. In many places these pipelines are buried in the sediment of the sea floor, but in other cases they lie on its surface and therefore may cause severe interference with dragger operations and with the fouling of large fishing nets. There is also the possibility of such pipelines breaking and therefore resulting in pollution. However, such breaks are quickly obvious from either the platforms or the shore terminal either visually or by pressure drops and may be quickly shut off until the break can be repaired. Such breaks are rare.

The fourth aspect of offshore petroleum operations is the storage of the petroleum. In most cases the storage is in facilities onshore. In some cases, however, the oil is stored on platforms and transferred to barges. At any transfer point the possibility of spills exists. In addition, the barges result in a greater amount of vessel movement in a given area, therefore leading to the possibility of greater interference with other sea traffic and with fishing operations. In some places the petroleum is stored in very large tanks which rest on the sea floor. Obviously such a tank would prevent the development of seabed mineral deposits that might be located in the same area. However, such sea floor tanks are necessarily restricted to special conditions of stable seabed and calm waters, such as are found in the Persian Gulf. These tanks are not used elsewhere in the world.

In addition to the above there is always the possibility of some additional interference with seabed operations as a result of junk material lost during the development of a field, or as a result of abandoned wells, the casing of which has not been cut off at a sufficient distance below the sea floor. Only in the United States is the offshore producing industry sufficiently mature that some fields have been produced to exhaustion and abandoned. Such abandonment and the ensuing cleanup operations are closely monitored by both the state and federal governments. Such monitoring will be required in other parts of the world as new fields being discovered eventually reach their economic limits and are abandoned.

In conclusion, it is my view that, overall, offshore petroleum operations, properly conducted, will result in relatively little interference with other peaceful uses of the seabeds.

Discussion

Bello: My first question is directed to the gentleman from the insurance company. I would like to know what your policies are *vis-à-vis* the development of the merchant marines of the young nations. I understand from what I have been told a number of times that there is an assertion by these nations that there is a kind of complicity between the top insurance companies and the conference lines. This has subsequently dampened the enthusiasm of these young nations to develop their merchant marines, which are not in any position at all to compete with the old ones, the traditional lines. Complicity is a very strong word to use, but I would like to know if you consider it to be a fair comment?

My second question is to Dr. Albers. I think your exposé is a very brilliant one, and I like it very much, but I just want to ask you a very simple question. That is, how do you effect the transfer of technology in the offshore petroleum areas to the young nations in whose coastal states you carry out these inspections?

Handley: As to the question of insurance insofar as the merchant fleets of the emerging countries are concerned, as I said earlier, I am with a brokerage firm, and it is our job to buy insurance for our clients. I am not with an insurance company. The brokers' role is quite different, and as international brokers we are becoming involved now in insurance for exposures around the world. Our domicile is in the United States, but we are developing a network around the world so that we can be involved in the local markets. There is certainly no complicity between the large insurance companies. As a matter of fact, we are on the threshold of seeing a greater competition among insurance companies for the better classes of business. We have been involved in recent situations in Spain, for instance, Japan, other countries, where marine insurance has heretofore been required to be placed in those countries because of the local regulations. The owners in those countries had to buy their insurance from insurers in the local market. The insurers in the local market could fix the rate, as there was no question of competition with other insurance companies around the world; but of course, they reinsured in other areas.

In many cases the reinsurance purchased by the direct company or the original company was bought at much cheaper rates than the local company was charging the local ship owner. We (I keep saying "we" only because my company is involved around the world) negotiate in all the leading marine markets, and we have seen the insurance rates come down over the last few years, despite the loss experience, because of an increased capacity. I should not say an increased capacity, but rather the desire to spread the business more.

Japanese insurers kept the business in Japan. Now, this is being mixed with American business in the American market, and European business, for instance, is coming into the American market where it used to go into the London market. So, as the world becomes much smaller, and marine insurance is mixed more than it used to be, we are not going to have situations where rates are arbitrarily kept up in a particular area of the world. If that continues, in my judgment (and I am satisfied this is correct) it will be simply because of local regulations; but if the marine insurers in your country will seek reinsurance elsewhere in the world from where they are buying it now, they may see that there is a competition, and there can be a better rate level. I would say that there is absolutely no complicity among the leading insurance companies of the world.

There is one other illustration of that. I mentioned earlier the major market in the United States which is called the American Hull Insurance Syndicate. It is composed of 50-plus companies. It operates under the Merchant Marine Act of 1920 as its authority, but heretofore it wrote exclusively United States business or vessels owned by United States corporations. In the last three or four years about 40 percent of its premium volume is foreign business—non-U.S. business—which gives some indication of the radical change in the spread or the mix of insurance business around the world. As it is mixed the rate level will reduce. There is no question about that.

Albers: In reply to your other question, I am not aware that there is any overall policy for transfer of technology. I would point out that all offshore petroleum exploration and production overseas is done by individual companies who have agreements with the coastal state governments. It may be, and I am not aware of this, but it may be there are provisions written into those agreements individually which address this problem. In any case, I believe it is the policy of most companies to train local employees in various technical aspects of the operations and to move them into responsible positions as time progresses. Maybe Max McKnight might be able to answer that a little better.

McKnight: I am not aware of the actual details in the contractual arrangements that are made by various multinational companies that are operating offshore in the different developing countries. I know that several countries do require, as their people are trained and gain experience, that their nationals replace foreign employees. I think this is particularly true of Indonesia. It is the practice of foreign companies as people of the host country are trained to promote them to higher managerial positions. It is very expensive to have American employees overseas. It is much less expensive to train the host country nationals and to promote them in the managerial structure to the extent of their abilities.

Now I have a question for Mr. Handley. I found his talk very illuminating. That is no reflection on Dr. Albers, because I am a little bit familiar with his subject matter. I agree with Mr. Bello that it was a brilliant statement. My question to Mr. Handley is, in terms of the various schemes you mentioned such as Tavelop, what the underwriters think of a scheme such as I believe Maine has proposed to provide a cleanup fund for marine pollution by taxing the import of petroleum products into the state. This is, of course, a cost of doing business and is probably passed on to the consumer. It seems to me that that particular device to build up a fund by a coastal state to be used in the event of a pollution catastrophe ties up a lot of money. I was wondering what the underwriters' thoughts might be on such a scheme?

Pontecorvo: We are a little bit out of phase. Dr. Bates would like to make a comment about Dr. Bello's question. Then we will answer your question, Max.

Bates: On the problem of a developing nation's acquiring enough technology so it can run its own oil business, there are five steps involved: exploration, production, transportation, refining, and marketing. The transportation, refining, and marketing are very easy to get into because most of your agreements with the producing oil companies are on a royalty basis. Most people prefer to take it in cash or gold bars, but there is nothing against a nation saying that it would take it in kind, in actual oil and gas. Then you have a nice volume to work with.

If you want to get into exploration and production, this is a very sophisticated business. It takes a lot of skills that in the United States exist only due to competitive enterprise. For example, it is interesting that at least two of the major U.S. companies knew of the Prudhoe Bay structure and passed it up as being uneconomic. The British Petroleum Company then got about a third of the Prudhoe Bay oil field; in this case the British know-how was better than the local know-how.

In the case of Japan, with which I familiar through the U.S.-Japan Program of Natural Resources headed by Interior, we have found that Japan, as sophisticated as she is, is moving into the exploration field very gingerly. Japan owns less than, I think, two percent of all the oil she consumes; but tends to do what she does well, such as make transistor radios and television sets, and leave the oil exploration to others who do that very well.

Handley: I think the fund is a pretty good solution to the problem. In saying that, I do not want to give the impression that I do not think the insurance companies should respond. Mind you, I am an insurance broker, and if there were another policy I could sell I would be the first one to attempt it, but the insurance companies must recognize their responsibilities. They were very late in doing this four or five years ago. We criticized them. We criticized them all around the world. To their credit they seem to be devoting more funds to pollution exposure. I am not saying that this is a liability or a responsibility for which you should not expect to be able to buy insurance in the commercial market. You should. What I was saying before is that we are having all sorts of conflicts with overlapping treaties and international agreements and laws, and this is what makes it difficult, because marine insurance is an international business.

If you could underwrite only those vessels in the United States or in the United Kingdom for instance, and you knew exactly what the laws were, that would be one thing; but if you insure a vessel that goes around the world to many jurisdictions, then you are faced with all these different pollution laws and other laws.

The insurance market must insure pollution as it insures other marine liabilities, and it seems to be moving in this direction. Insurance companies are being prodded by many people, but there is certainly nothing against a fund or the supplementary convention, for instance. There is nothing wrong with that, I would not think, and there are those who will say that the burden should not be completely on the ship owner, that it should also be on the owners of the cargo, for instance. I am not going to get into that controversy, but this is a proper subject matter for insurance within the framework of the capacity and the resources of the companies around the world.

Logue: I have some rather elementary questions to put to the same gentleman. First, how many voyages does the supertanker make per year? And how much profit does it make per voyage? In other words, how much time does it take to pay off the original investment?

My second set of questions has to do with pipelines. Can you put pipelines under the oceans? What is the longest underwater pipeline? And why can't we build an underland pipeline from the Middle East to Europe? I do not want to put tanker companies out of business, but I am curious why pipelines can't replace some tankers. It certainly should cut down on pollution.

Handley: First of all, Marsh & McLennan are general insurance brokers, and if the business does not come on the marine side, perhaps it will come on the property side. So, it does not make any difference. I do not know the length of the longest pipeline. I am just not competent to pursue that. There are some underwater pipelines. There is nothing wrong with underwater pipelines. Again, this is not an area I should even speak to, but on the question of the voyages, the VLCCs that run from the Persian Gulf to European distribution ports—Bantry, Rotterdam and so on—make the round voyage in about 42 days or 40 days. So, they are making about seven or eight voyages a year. The time in port is very limited. They load and unload very quickly.

The average value for these vessels, the 250,000 tonners, VLCCs, is about $45 million for the hull insurance. In addition, they have liability insurance as well as pollution coverage. The total premium for one of these vessels varies among ownerships. Some have good experience records. Others have somewhat different records. Some carry large deductibles. Some insure subject to a deductible of $5 million, some $10 million, some $250 thousand, some $20 thousand. The average premium would be in the neighborhood of about $800 thousand to $1 million per annum.

Albers: It certainly is technologically feasible to construct a long pipeline over land. We have had pipelines of that sort in the United States for several decades. Now, of course, in some parts of the world, say in the Middle East, these pipelines would have to go across several different countries to get to their destination, and there you have a political factor entering in. But from a technological standpoint, I would think that there should not be any problem with this mode of transportation.

Russell: I have a question for Dr. Albers. The United States Department of Interior recently called for nominations for leasing areas beyond the 200-meter isobath offshore Louisiana. The call for nominations included the statement that leases issued beyond 200 meters would be subject to the terms of whatever international accord the U.S. later became a party to. Other nations you have noted have either initiated or licensed exploration for and development of petroleum resources also beyond 200 meters. Have there been any similar provisions or calls in the agreements between the explorers or developers in these other offshore areas for subjection to the terms of an international agreement when it is agreed upon?

Albers: Not to my knowledge. I might say that there are about 40 nations which now have leased offshore beyond 200 meters, and as far as I know most of them at least are following the 1958 Geneva Conference in their leasing.

Wolf: I would like to follow up on Mr. McKnight's question to Mr. Handley by inquiring whether or not the industry has given any consideration to—or if not, what Mr. Handley thinks of the possibility of creation of—an international or perhaps intergovernmental organization, corporation or what have you, modeled on something like the American Security Investors Protective Corporation, which could then provide either reinsurance or excess coverage for these pollution exposures?

Handley: There were those who advocated something like this a few years ago because it was felt that the insurance industry was not moving fast enough to do this. The large brokers in the United States and in the United Kingdom met and in an unofficial effort, if you will, it was left to them to scour the world to see how much capacity they could put together and whether the free enterprise method, so to speak, was the proper way to do it. This joint unofficial effort was undertaken, and as a result of it, the capacity that is available today for pollution was put together. Prior to that there was absolutely nothing. I am not suggesting that the companies themselves would not have offered capacity for pollution coverage, but it was through the effort of an international endeavor, made up of the leading brokers of the world and some of the leading insurance companies, that put this capacity together. But at this point, it seems to be resting on that, and there is no additional effort underway at the moment.

I would offer one other comment. We were talking before about competition and complicity and so on, and I said earlier that companies were concerned about their concentration of risks, and this is what happens in the insurance market. Even though they are concerned about their concentration of risk and the fact that they want to limit their participations in the high-value risks, today happens to be a very good time. It is a buyer's market for insurance because as the companies see themselves left with just a couple of high-value risks, they are seeking to involve themselves in all sorts of other business, be it pollution or risks of another country and so on. So they are reaching out; insurance companies are reaching out to be involved in more and more risks in other areas of the world. The competition is becoming rather severe at the moment, and as this happens, and as they need additional sources of revenue, we will see them going into additional lines, but the participation will be on a reduced basis although into more classes of insurance.

Lockwood: Mr. Handley, I wanted to follow up just with that last part and with Mr. Bello's first question, respecting insurance for the younger nations. I got confused in the statistics. I thought you had said in the beginning that 75 percent of the insurance was done by Lloyd's of London, and then you indicated later that there had been radical changes, and you sort of continued that with your last statement. Did Lloyd's have significantly more of the insurance prior to the last five years, or is there some trend where it is more competitive? The 75 percent suggests that.

Handley: Yes, that is exactly right. It was not 75 percent. I said that 75 percent of the world's marine insurance premium volume or 75 percent of the world's marine insurance business is hull business, and I said that about 60 percent of that was in Lloyd's, but 75 percent of the insurance volume by premium applies to hull—to vessel insurance, let us say. The remaining 25 percent is for oil rigs, outboard motor boats, cargo, and all sorts of things; and of the vessel insurance about 60 percent of that was written in the British market. The British market, and Lloyd's in particular, has really been the insurance market of the world for many years. They were way ahead of everyone else. It started there. They were more sophisticated than most other people until the last five or ten years. In the United States the American Hull Insurance Syndicate, which is the largest hull insurance underwriting group in the United States, is now a factor in the world market. It has increased its premium volume by 50 percent in the last five years, and most of the business that it has taken—I should not say most of it, but a good portion of it—is business it has taken from other markets by competition.

The American market is writing British business. It is writing Japanese business. It is writing Italian business, Norwegian business, that in the past went exclusively to the London market, that is the share that was not handled in the local country. So the London market does not have the influence or the position in the world insurance market that it had not many years ago.

Part Five

Chapter Fifteen

Ocean Pollution: Status and Prognostication

John A. Knauss
Provost for Marine Affairs
University of Rhode Island

INTRODUCTION

About three years ago I attempted an analysis of the developing issues of the forthcoming Law of the Sea Conference such as fisheries, oil, deep sea mining, transportation, military uses, and scientific research.[1] I felt least comfortable with my analysis of ocean pollution as it relates to the Law of the Sea Conference, and nothing in the intervening three years has changed my mind.

One thing I do perceive, or at least believe I see, is an increasing interest in the subject. Part of this concern is certainly related to other issues, such as navigation through straits, but part I believe relates to a fundamental concern with pollution, quite independent of other subjects. More than most issues I believe the pollution issue is time dependent. By that I mean the following: if the Seabeds Committee had begun working in 1965 and had brought forth a successful treaty in 1970, I suspect that ocean pollution would have played a smaller role than it does presently. If, on the other hand, we were aiming for a 1980 Law of the Sea Conference, I suspect the ocean pollution issue would loom larger than it does at present. The time-dependent nature of this issue is a major theme of this chapter.

Much has been written recently about ocean pollution and the immediate dangers we face. A good part of this material strikes me as nonsense, and I am concerned that too many strident voices prophesying immediate doom

313

will eventually lull into complacency the public and their political leaders. This would be unfortunate because I do not believe we dare be complacent about the future.

Although I have attempted to review the factors affecting ocean pollution, I have made no attempt at a survey of all the relevant literature, nor is this a comprehensive review of what is known. I believe I have at least touched on the major points, but the examples are chosen because they highlight certain processes and outline certain trends. The message can be simply stated. It is that ocean pollution is a very complex problem and our present level of knowledge is inadequate to the task. Insofar as we can judge, although open ocean pollution is measurable, it does not pose an immediate threat to the future of man on this planet. Given present and projected trends, however, I am less optimistic about the future.

Note that throughout I am referring to the threat of ocean pollution beyond internal waters. Most of my emphasis is on open ocean pollution. Critical pollution problems are known to exist within internal waters of a number of states, including the United States.

THE GEOCHEMICAL CYCLE

Each year the rivers of the world bring from three to four billion tons of material from the land to oceans where it mixes with the water.[2] Additional material is blown into the ocean from the land. For example, desert sands from the Sahara have been found in air samples collected in the Caribbean.[3] The very saltiness of the ocean is a measure of this constant movement of material from land to sea.[4]

This movement of material from land to ocean has been continuing since early geological times. The material brought from the rivers and the air to the ocean mix with the waters. Most of this material eventually finds its way by one means or another to the seabed, where it becomes part of the thick layer of sediments that cover the ocean bottom. Using the time scale of geologists, the elements that comprise the ocean salt spend but a moment in the ocean on their way from their original source on land to their ultimate resting place on the ocean bottom. For different elements, the time is different. The small amount of iron that washes down the rivers, so that the average residence time in the ocean is about 100 years. On the other hand the sodium that enters the ocean spends an average time of at least 100 million years in the ocean before it finds its way to the ocean floor.[5]

The system is more complex than I have outlined. Some material that reaches the bottom redissolves into the water. Additional material can be added to the ocean from underwater volcanoes, and a limited amount of salt finds its way from the ocean back to land by salt spray from bursting bubbles in the ocean. However, the point I wish to emphasize is that the ocean is the ultimate repository for all the material from land whether blown by the winds or brought by the rivers, and the composition of seawater reflects the balance between the rate at which material enters the ocean and is ultimately deposited on the ocean seabed. This process has been continuing since earliest geological times and the ocean has achieved something of a steady state. We are reasonably certain there has been no significant change in the composition of seawater for tens of thousands of years, and probably not for tens of millions of years.[6]

More precisely, I mean there has been no average change. It takes time for the waters of the oceans to mix. The huge outfall of the Amazon can be seen several tens of kilometers into the ocean by the casual observer in an airplane and a careful chemist can trace the water of the Amazon several hundred kilometers from its mouth.[7] Nor is the amount of material brought by a river always the same. We have just suffered the worst flood of the Mississippi River in recent history and it seems certain that the amount of material brought to the ocean by the Mississippi this year will be much more than its average sediment load of 500 million tons a year.

WHAT IS POLLUTION?

Let us now consider what we mean by pollution and let me start by defining what I think we can all agree pollution is not. Pollution does not result from the natural processes that occur which bring the atmospheric dust from the Sahara and the erosion products of the rivers to the ocean. The fact that one can trace the outfall of the Amazon many miles into the Atlantic does not mean the ocean in that region is polluted, even though the biological communities that can survive near the Amazon outfall are different from those some miles distant from the mouth of the Amazon. Nor does the fact that the oyster and shrimp fishery off Louisiana may be measurably affected by the spectacular flooding of the Mississippi River mean necessarily that the Mississippi is polluted this year.

Most of us assume that a natural phenomenon, no matter how irregular or how devastating, is not pollution, even though the physical processes and the biological consequences may be strikingly similar. By pollution we mean those processes to which man contributes (and presumably, therefore, processes that man can control) that cause measurable and undesirable effects on the natural world. This, at least, is the definition of pollution I am using.

Sometimes it is difficult to tell what is man's contribution, (and therefore pollution) and what is nature's contribution (and therefore not pollution). As an example, consider the controversy surrounding the well documented data on mercury in swordfish and tuna. The story is not yet complete but the situation, as near as I can reconstruct it, is as follows: In 1970 a Canadian graduate student found that some samples of freshwater fish contained mercury levels of over one part per million.[8] He publicized his finding. Other chemists found similar values in other areas; particularly high levels were found in swordfish.

The Federal Food and Drug Administration put a ban on the sale of swordfish in this country which is in effect to this day. The effects of mercury poisoning are well known and documented and few people at the time seriously questioned the FDA prohibition, at least until more evidence could be gathered.

Several points should be noted. First, the amount of mercury is very small and measuring that level of mercury is not routine. In fact, it is a measurement that probably could not have been made with any degree of confidence some twenty-five years ago.[9] At present there are any number of laboratories that can make 50 observations a day. The second point to note is that apparently the mercury observation in swordfish took the scientific world by surprise. No one was sufficiently confident that he knew enough about the sources of possible mercury pollution and its pathways into the ocean that he was prepared to attempt an explanation of the swordfish observation. This inability of scientists to provide a reasonable explanation of the mercury level in swordfish was perhaps at least a secondary reason for the FDA to move as quickly as it did.

Since then, of course, there have been a number of investigations. Although the evidence may not be all in, the present consensus of my colleagues is that although the level of mercury in swordfish may be too high for safe consumption, that level is due to natural causes and not to man. Let me attempt to explain why.

The source of the mercury for the swordfish is the seawater. Swordfish are predators. They live on small fish, which in turn live on smaller fish, zooplankton and phytoplankton, which in turn take up the mercury from the seawater. Somehow in this process, the swordfish concentrate the mercury so that the levels found are 10 to 100 thousand times that found in seawater.[10] How, where, and under what circumstances this concentrating mechanism occurs is not known. The levels of mercury in seawater is known, and although it is a measurement that has not been made routinely until recently, the data suggest that there has been no increase by a factor of five or ten in the amount of mercury in seawater in recent years. Somewhat more reassuring evidence has come from measuring the mercury content in old swordfish and tuna. Soon after the original observations, museums and laboratories were canvassed; a few measurements have been made on preserved specimens of tuna and swordfish that were caught from 25-93 years ago. There is no appreciable difference in the mercury concentration in these samples than in modern specimens.[11]

However, the evidence that many of my colleagues find most persuasive is indirect evidence. It is an argument which requires rather sophisticated scientific reasoning, and not all decision makers are convinced. The scientists' argument is as follows: Mercury is fairly volatile; that is, it evaporates into the air. Scientists are reasonably convinced that nearly all mercury, both from natural sources as well as man-produced sources, reaches the ocean from the atmosphere rather than flowing into the ocean from rivers. One way of determining whether the amount raining into the ocean has increased significantly in recent years is to measure the mercury content of glaciers. The topmost layer of a glacier is rain and snow that has fallen in the past few years. As you core deeper into the glacier you reach layers that were laid down in successively earlier years. We have cored deep into the Greenland glaciers and have samples that date back 2,700 years. Although the data are not unequivocal, it would appear that there has been little significant increase in the mercury fallout over this period.[12]

These data would appear to confirm the most critical part of the scientists' arguments, which is that man's use of mercury is less by a factor of ten than the amount of mercury that escapes each year into the environment from natural causes. One of the largest sources of man's mercury contribution is the burning of coal. Although the mercury content of coal is small it is estimated that more than 1,000 tons of mercury a year are released to the atmosphere by the burning coal. However, large as that number is, it is still small compared with how much mercury escapes to the atmosphere by natural causes. Ten times as much mercury is released to the atmosphere from volcanoes, hot springs and similar phenomena as is produced by man.[13] Thus, the consensus in the scientific community today is that if swordfish are unsafe to eat, because of its mercury content, this is not a new phenomenon. Man's contribution of mercury to the ocean is small compared with nature's contribution. If swordfish are unsafe to eat now, they were unsafe to eat three hundred years ago.

I have gone into this example in some detail because I want to emphasize several points in the remainder of this paper and the mercury-swordfish case is a good example of a few of these. The first is that we can measure levels of potential pollution with much more accuracy and ease than we could before. The second point is that it is sometimes difficult to distinguish what is a natural phenomenon and what is man's contribution. The third point is that our scientific base for understanding pollution is very inadequate. For example, no one predicted that swordfish concentrated mercury, and we still do not know how and under what circumstances this occurs. The fourth point is that pollution sources are not always obvious. If mercury is indeed an ocean pollutant, a major source for man's contribution (at least on a worldwide basis) may be the thousands of homes, businesses, and factories around the world that burn coal as a fuel.

HOW DO POLLUTANTS ENTER THE OCEAN?

Pollutants can enter the ocean in four general ways. The first, and perhaps the easiest to monitor, are man-built outfalls that lead directly into the ocean. Examples are the sewer outfalls of Long Beach and San Diego, California. The effluent from these sewage treatment plants leads directly to the ocean. Although the number of such outfalls is large and will increase in numbers, they are at fixed locations and the amount and kinds of material discharged from these outfalls can be monitored with any degree of completeness for which society is willing to pay.

The second way pollutants reach the ocean is by man's activities in the ocean. Included in this category are ocean dumping and vessel pollution. It includes the carrying of New York's sewage offshore in barges and dumping, or the pumping of ballast from an underway tanker. It also includes accidents, such as pollution resulting from a ship running aground and sinking or the blowout of an offshore oil well. Deliberate dumping can be monitored as easily as are outfalls. Accidents, of course, are more difficult. Sometimes it is not possible to get more than a rough estimate of the amount of pollutants entering the environment from an accident.

The third route is rivers and estuaries. Material can be dumped into a river many miles upstream and carried to the ocean. Just as the natural material from the Mississippi and Amazon can be traced many miles from shore, so can pollutants added to the rivers and estuaries from sewers, land drainage, and dumping. In principle, the sources of material and the amounts entering the ocean can be monitored. In practice, this can be difficult and expensive. However, present technology would appear to be sufficient to the task, if society decides it is sufficiently important.

The fourth and last route is via the atmosphere. A surprisingly large amount of material, including mercury, lead, and DDT reaches the ocean from the land via the atmosphere. All the material returns to earth eventually, most of it by rainfall. Of all the routes, this is the most difficult to trace to its source and the most difficult to monitor with any degree of precision. Science has made considerable progress in the past few years in measuring airborne pollutants, but it is perhaps fair to say that our present level of understanding is best characterized by saying that we believe we have some estimate of the magnitude of the problem.

I have not made any attempt to develop a complete inventory of how much material is entering the oceans. The few selective figures given are not as important as the trend they signify. For example, ocean dumping off the U.S. for a twenty year period for 1949-68 increased at a rate of nine percent a year, a doubling time of less than eight years.[14] In 1946 about 200 million tons of oil were moved by tankers; today the figure is about 1.5 billion tons a year. The present growth rate is equivalent to an increase of 9 percent a year.[15] the number of offshore oil platforms has gone from essentially zero in 1948 to more than 9,000 off the U.S. alone.[16] All projections for future oil reserves point to an increasing percentage of our oil coming from the offshore regions.[17] Around the world we are considering offshore ports, and in the U.S., at least, we are making plans for offshore nuclear power stations. One of the main points I wish to make today is that when we consider ocean pollution, it is not enough to consider the extent to which ocean pollution is a problem today, we must consider the prospects of significant ocean pollution tomorrow.

FUTURE PROJECTIONS

Whether or not you believe that ocean pollution will become a problem in the future depends in part upon your view of man's future. There is a school of thought that claims that we cannot continue to expend our natural resources at the present rate or we will run out of these resources. It is not simply a question of expending oil and gas reserves, but of running out of important metals like copper, tin, zinc, and even iron and aluminum.[18,19] They suggest that man will have to change his way of living if he is to survive; at least there will have to be changes in the highly developed nations such as the U.S., which presently consumes about one-third of the nonrenewable resources each year with only 5 percent of the population.[20] The statistics which can be marshalled in making their case are good and their arguments are persuasive. If they are correct, then I think we can reasonably hope that as man returns to a less resource-consuming mode of life the chances of major ocean pollution will diminish.

There is another view of the future, however, which argues that by present standards of consumption, man has an almost unlimited supply of energy. Before we run out of coal, oil, and natural gas, we will develop the breeder nuclear reactor, controlled nuclear fusion, or find an efficient way of converting and transporting the potential thermal energy, either directly from the sun or that stored in the oceans. With an unlimited energy supply we can solve the problems of recycling limited natural materials and we can develop synthetic materials. We can continue to strive for a comfortable standard of living for all the world's population. If this is your view of the future, then I think it is also necessary to begin to worry about ocean pollution. My view of the future is more in tune with this latter school, and thus I worry about the future of the oceans.

Without going into any great detail, let me sketch a few future projections. The present population of the world is about 3.6 billion and is growing at 2 percent a year. One projection has the world population stabilizing at 15 billion in about a century.[21] There are many ways to estimate the effects of a nation's standard of living on pollution. None is ideal, but all conclude that pollution potential increases as the standard of living increases. Thus, the developed world with a higher standard of living contributes proportionately more to worldwide pollution. One can compare uses of fertilizers, consumption of raw materials, or solid waste disposal, and arrive at different versions of the same conclusion.

A simple projection can be made by comparing energy consumption. The U.S. with about 5 percent of the world's population uses more than 34 percent of the total energy.[22] In a very simple-minded way I think we can relate standard of living and pollution potential to energy consumption. *If* you allow the U.S. a continuing modest growth rate of 3 percent a year per capita in energy consumption, *and* if you should project the rest of the world catching up to the U.S. annual energy consumption rate by the year 2000, you have a total annual energy consumption which is 15 times the projected 1980 value.

I don't suppose that the political and social problems of the world are such that the rest of the world will catch up to the U.S. by the year 2000, but it is obvious that this is the goal of most of the world; and, if you believe as I do that energy is unlimited, then I think one might assume that it is only a matter of time. If it isn't the year 2000, it will be 2073.[23] It is this view of the future that causes me concern about ocean pollution.

When the world's population is using energy at that rate, we will be perturbing the natural environment in so many ways that it will require constant vigilance to see that we do not do something that inadvertently upsets the system. Let me give an example of what I mean. One of the few reasonably well documented cases of ocean pollution is that of dissolved lead found in the ocean. The amount of lead in the surface water of the ocean is 5-10 times higher than was apparently present 40 years ago.[24] The comparison of lead distribution in the ocean with chemicals of similar characteristics, the distribution of lead as a function of depth in the Greenland glacier, along with other indirect evidence, have clearly identified the source as man. The probable cause is the gasoline used by modern automobiles. Some 50 years ago we began adding tetraethyl lead to gasoline to reduce engine knocking. Much of the lead from this additive is split off in the combustion process and passes out the exhaust system of the automobile and into the atmosphere. Although most of the lead presumably comes to rest close to the highways, some travels great distances. All of it eventually comes to earth, most of it scavenged by the rainfall. Although the amount of lead in the ocean is appreciably more than was the case 40 years ago, there is yet no clear evidence that this increase has had a harmful effect on ocean life. Some of my ecology friends would argue that the lack of such evidence is more a measure of our lack of knowledge of ocean ecology than proof that there has been no effect.

The reason for the example, however, is not so much to argue the case for or against the effect of lead pollution in the ocean, but rather to suggest the kind of almost inadvertent pollution that can occur with a high standard of living. If you will allow your imagination to project a future where the entire population of the world is consuming energy at a rate equal to or greater than that in the U.S. today, then perhaps you can begin to imagine the ways in which pollution may occur. Fertilizers and pesticides are two obvious examples, but consider for a moment, some not so obvious examples; it has been estimated that 350,000 tons of dry cleaning fluid and a million tons of gasoline evaporate each year.[25] What is the ultimate fate of all the growth hormones fed to beef cattle? Or the antibiotics made by the pharmaceutical companies? I give these examples, not because of any evidence to suggest they are harmful, but only to help you think about all the unexpected events that might occur in the world of the future where we all live well. New chemical substances are being produced commercially at the rate of 400-500 a year.[26] A population of 15 billion a hundred years from now, with a standard of living equal to or better than what we now enjoy in the U.S., will of necessity depend increasingly on synthetic material, intensive agricultural techniques, and complex social structures. The danger of inadvertent pollution will be much greater than it is today.

OCEAN AS A SINK

The next point I wish to make is that if the oceans become polluted it is not easy to unpollute them. If a pond, a small lake, or a river becomes polluted, it can be made clean again in a relatively short time. How long depends upon a number of factors, but one can make a first estimate by comparing the volume of water in the lake with the average amount of water running into and out of the lake. A small lake with a volume of 40 cubic kilometers that has a river inflow and outflow of 80 cubic kilometers a year has its water renewed every six months. If the pollution was caused by the incoming river and if that pollution source was stopped, one would expect to see a marked change in the pollution level of the lake in a very few months. Probably the pollution would not be completely eliminated in six months, or even a year, because in all likelihood much of the past polluted material has sunk to the bottom where it now serves as a secondary source, as some of this material is redissolved in the lake water.

The volume of water in a lake or estuary, divided by the rate of flow into or out of that body of water is defined as the *residence time*. In the above example the residence time of a water particle in the lake is six months. The residence time can be used as a lower limit on the time necessary for a small body of water to cleanse itself. Leaching of polluted material from the bottom can lengthen that time and occasionally degradation of the polluted material within the water column can shorten the time. The residence time of most small lakes and estuaries are the order of days or months. If such a body of water becomes badly polluted and society wishes to pay the price necessary to reverse the situation, it is usually possible to do so. One simply cuts off the source of the pollutants and waits for nature to take its course. In a matter of months or a few years the pollution can be stopped. As a result of federal legislation and new pollution control standards we are presently witnessing such a reversal in a number of bodies of water in the United States.

Generally speaking, the larger the body of water, the longer the residence time and the longer it takes to see an effect once the source of pollution is eliminated. For example, the residence time of water in Lake Erie, the most polluted of our Great Lakes, is two and a half years, the shortest of any of the Great Lakes.[27] Thus, even if it were possible to stop all sources of pollution flowing into Lake Erie tomorrow, the time required for Lake Erie to cleanse itself would be long compared to most lakes and estuaries within the U.S.

When one moves into the ocean, the time scale increases. The residence time of the Mediterranean is 50-100 years.[28] Thus a major pollution problem in the Mediterranean will take a very long time to clean up. For time scales of 50-100 years other processes cannot be ignored. However, at least the concept of residence time has some meaning, since there is a flow into the Mediterranean from rivers, and a flow out through Gibraltar.

The residence time concept has little meaning for a particle of water in the ocean. Although such a calculation can be made by comparing the volume of the ocean with the total river inflow it has little significance. There is no flow-through in the ocean in the usual sense. The river waters that enter into the oceans are returned to the land via evaporation from the ocean surface and subsequent rainfall on land. Generally speaking, the pollutants do not evaporate. They remain in the ocean until such time as they are degraded or sink to the bottom.

The ocean is the ultimate sink. The oceans have served as a natural receptacle of the debris of this planet long before man became a factor and the oceans will continue to do so long after we pass on. Presently the oceans serve as the final receptacle for nearly all of the by-products of man's activities. They are carried by land drainage and erosion down the rivers, or into the atmosphere and blown from the land. The oceans' ability to assimilate wastes is tremendous whether they be man-produced or natural. However, once the material reaches the ocean it has no place to go. One does not talk about cleaning up the oceans as one talks about cleaning up Narragansett Bay or Lake Baikal. If the oceans become polluted they will probably remain polluted on any time scale meaningful to man.

To people like myself the greatest worry about ocean pollution at this time is the unknown. Few believe that there is a serious immediate danger of oceanwide pollution. Our worry is based on combining the following concepts: (1) once the ocean is polluted, cleaning it up as you do a lake or estuary is probably not feasible; (2) the exponential growth in energy use, natural resource consumption, and man's activities in general suggest that the possibility of oceanwide pollution within the next century is not as radical an idea as one might have thought as little as 25 years ago; (3) our low level of knowledge of what is getting into the ocean and what effect it is having in the ocean does not insure that we will be in a position to sound the alarm in time before the situation becomes acute.

PRESENT STATUS OF OCEAN POLLUTION

A useful way of considering ocean pollution is to consider: (1) the possible sources and the routes the pollutants follow to the ocean; (2) what happens to the pollutant once it reaches the ocean, i.e., does it mix with the water, sink to the bottom, change its chemical characteristics, and if so at what rate? (3) What effect does the pollutant have on the environment? Do some forms of plants or animals die because of it? Do others prosper? I think one can safely generalize by saying that although our knowledge of sources and routes is incomplete, understanding in that area is further advanced than our knowledge of what happens to the pollutant once it reaches the ocean. The least satisfactory of the three subjects is our present understanding of the effects of pollutants on ocean ecology.

Sources of Pollution

One of the most effective ways of monitoring ocean pollution is to measure or estimate the material produced and what percentage of it reaches the ocean. For example, I suspect it would be possible to estimate within a factor of two how much oil reaches the ocean from tankers by knowing the number and size of the worldwide tanker fleet, how often each pumps ballast, and some details of the technique, such as whether or not it is "load-on-top."

It is more difficult to estimate seepage and leaks from offshore oil platforms and coastal oil refineries although reasonable order of magnitude calculations can probably be made. However, the largest single source of oil to the ocean may come from such sources as old crank case oil from automobiles.[29] Although much of the oil is removed by sewage treatment, that which is not passes through sewage treatment plants virtually unmodified. For example, we are reasonably certain that the largest single source of oil pollution in Narragansett Bay is not spills from tankers, oil storage facilities, or similar obvious sources, but our sewage treatment plants.[30] To further complicate the picture of oil reaching the ocean, it has been suggested that a significant source on a worldwide basis is the exhaust fumes of gasoline and diesel engines. Some of this vaporized material reaches the ocean via the atmosphere.

For a second example, consider DDT and its fate, about which there has arisen one of the most vocal and emotional controversies of recent years. Its importance to agriculture productivity and in reducing malaria and similar insect-carrying diseases is well known. Coupled with these very obvious benefits has been a growing concern about the side effects. It has been suggested that DDT drains off the agricultural land and into the streams where it kills fish. DDT has been implicated in the depletion of the Brown Pelican population on Anacapa Island.[31] There has been concern about DDT in man.[32] DDT is somewhat volatile; much of it evaporates and is carried to the ocean where it falls out with the rain. Equally important, DDT and its derivatives are long lived. How long DDT and its toxic derivatives remain before they are further broken down to harmless chemicals by microbes is not known presently.

A few years ago it was reported that perhaps as much as 25 percent of all DDT produced to date could be found in the ocean.[33] The calculation was made on the best available evidence at the time. In part because the result was so startling, a major effort has been made to verify this conclusion. Happily, it would appear that the estimate was high, perhaps by a factor of 100, certainly by a factor of 20. However, the data are not all in, and not everyone is satisfied with the present revised estimate.[34]

In the process of studying DDT, scientists came upon another potentially dangerous pollutant, the PCBs (polychlorinated biphenyls). They are sufficiently similar to DDT in their chemical structure that the two were often confused in some of the early analysis. PCBs are useful substances that have been produced for the last 40 years. Like DDT much of it reaches the ocean via the atmosphere, and they are apparently even more resistant to natural breakdown processes than DDT. As a consequence, there is some evidence to suggest that there are more PCBs in the ocean than DDT and that they are potentially more troublesome.[35]

Man's contribution of synthetic chemicals such as DDT and PCB is easily determined, because there is no natural background with which to compare it. Man's contribution to heavy metal pollution is not as easy to determine. We have already noted the problem of attempting to determine whether the present mercury level in swordfish is a relatively new phenomenon or whether this is a natural level. However, this does not mean that mercury poisoning does not occur in local regions. Mercury poisoning did result from eating shellfish taken from Minamata Bay in Japan, which was subject to the continuous discharge of mercury from a nearby chemical plant.[36] To date, however, the only unequivocal example of heavy metal pollution in the *open* ocean is from lead.[37] There have been some suggestions that cadmium, arsenic, selenium, zinc, cobalt, and antimony may be present in the ocean in higher than normal levels, especially in coastal areas.[38]

What Happens to the Pollutant?

Let us next consider what happens to the material once it reaches the ocean. If it is solid material, and has a specific gravity larger than seawater, it of course sinks to the bottom. If it is dissolved material in river water or if it enters the ocean via the atmosphere it usually mixes with the seawater. Occasionally a chemical reaction takes place as one moves from fresh water to seawater that results in the material precipitating to the bottom, but most of the potential pollutants we hear about stay in the seawater rather than precipitating to the bottom. Most of us learned in school that "water is the universal solvent." The oceans are not saturated with respect to very many elements. The heavy metals such as lead and mercury are dissolved in the ocean as are the chlorinated hydrocarbons such as DDT and PCB. The nutrients such as phosphate and nitrate which result from the breakdown of organic sewage products are dissolved in seawater and so are the primary radioactive material from nuclear power plants or nuclear bombs.

Either in seawater or on the bottom, some chemical changes occur, particularly in the complex organic materials which are broken down into simpler products. The breakdown of food and human wastes by bacterial action is well known. Given sufficient time, bacteria will even reduce oil to carbon dioxide and water and will break down DDT and PCB into less toxic products.[39]

As with most biological reactions, biodegradation is generally faster at higher temperatures than at lower ones, which is one reason for the special concern about oil spills in polar regions. In this light one might consider some recent experiments conducted at the Woods Hole Oceanographic Institution and at the University of Rhode Island where human food has been left on the bottom of the ocean for some months. The ordinary bacterial breakdown is very slow. In fact, the first Woods Hole experiments suggested it was almost nonexistent.[40] The reasons for this slow biodegradation are not completely understood at this time. There is apparently more involved than the fact that the deep water is close to freezing.[41]

Whatever the reasons, the deep ocean does not appear to be an efficient place to dispose of garbage. The inorganic materials do not break down, at least in the sense of biodegradation where bacteria can so completely alter the chemical structure that the original material is destroyed. Lead, mercury, phosphate, etc., may form different complexes in seawater, and by so doing make it less likely that they will be incorporated in the food chain of plants and animals; but these changes are reversible. Once added to the ocean this material remains in that form until it is removed.

One of the more difficult concepts to discuss is how these pollutants are transported throughout the ocean once they reach there. Perhaps the primary reason for this difficulty is not so much conceptual but the lack of agreement among oceanographers as to what occurs. However, I think the following examples are sufficiently vague as to marshall general agreement from my colleagues.

The first is that vertical mixing in the ocean is slow. For example, the high lead values in the ocean are found in the near surface water, not the deep water.[42] The lead enters the surface water from the atmosphere and mixes in the top few meters. In time it mixes deeper and deeper. Consider the question: suppose we stopped adding lead to gasoline, and no more lead entered the surface water of the ocean; how long would it take for the present lead to be distributed more or less equally throughout the water column? The answer is more than ten years and perhaps more than fifty years. In some parts of the ocean, such as the mid-Pacific, it might be a couple of hundred years. Similarly, if canisters filled with radioactive waste material were dumped on the ocean bottom and broke open, releasing the material into the deep ocean water, it would take a comparable time for the material to reach the surface waters.

Horizontal mixing is comparatively rapid. For example, a mid-depth source of radioactivity was traced over an area of 40,000 km^2 in 40 days. During this period it mixed vertically only 60 m.[43] However, although horizontal mixing is greater than vertical mixing, it still takes many years for the water of one ocean to mix with that of another. For example, imagine that somehow the

North Atlantic ocean between the U.S. and Europe became badly polluted from top to bottom. How long would it take for the pollution to be spread more or less equally throughout the North and South Atlantic? Again, the answer is well over ten years. The mixing of the deep water of the North and South Atlantic is probably closer to a few hundred years,[44] although the surface waters may be mixed much more rapidly. For the pollutant to find itself spread throughout all the oceans would require the order of a thousand years. Thus, although we speak of ocean pollution we must always bear in mind that it takes time for the pollutant to mix throughout the ocean from its source. As the pollutant mixes it becomes more diluted.

The spreading of pollution from ocean dumps, outfalls, or river mouths can be traced. It is obviously possible to build up high levels of pollution in semienclosed seas such as the Mediterranean or the Baltic long before their effects are seen in the Atlantic. Generally when one speaks of ocean pollution he is referring to a specific area of the ocean, which is related to a specific source that can be traced. However, given sufficient time, the pollution spreads. Oceanographers are reporting tar balls in their plankton nets from throughout the North Atlantic and Mediterranean.[45]

There may be one major exception to the concept that ocean pollution can generally be related specifically to a given source and that is airborne pollution. Airborne material in the Northern Hemisphere can be distributed around the world in a matter of weeks. Mixing in the lower atmosphere between the Northern and Southern Hemisphere is longer, but is probably accomplished in one to two years.[46] Thus, material like lead, mercury, DDT, and PCB, which mostly enters the ocean from atmospheric fallout, can be expected to be distributed more evenly throughout the surface layers of the oceans. For these types of material, one can truly speak of potential oceanwide pollution even today.

Effect of Ocean Pollution

Let me finally say a few words about the most difficult, but also the most important aspect of the problem. What effect does this pollution have on man? For example, we know that man can get very sick and die from the buildup of lead in his body tissues and this buildup can occur from eating food that has lead in it. We know there is added lead in the surface waters of the ocean. However, if this increase in the ocean is not reflected in any of the food that we eat, why worry? Is it even reasonable to call it pollution if there is no direct effect on man? This is a philosophical, and ultimately a political, question which I prefer to stay clear of, at least as far as this paper is concerned. However, one's view of pollution depends in large part upon its potential effect on man.

Broadly speaking, there are the direct and indirect effects. The residents of Minamata Village who suffered nerve damage from eating mercury laden shellfish are an acute example of the direct effect of marine pollution. The decimation of the Brown Pelican population near Los Angeles is a rather far removed indirect effect.

There are those who claim that the total of the indirect effects may be the most important. For example, although we may not eat any seafood with an increased lead content, the high level of lead in the surface waters may effect the growth patterns of certain planktonic plants and animals and lead to a change in the ecological balance of the ocean which may have a very profound effect upon man. From time to time there have been suggestions of a change in the ecological balance in the ocean which would cut off the oxygen supply of the earth. This idea has been rather soundly refuted;[47] but other possibilities may exist. The one attracting the greatest interest at the present is only indirectly ocean related. Because of the increase burning of coal and oil in the last hundred years, the amount of carbon dioxide in the atmosphere has steadily risen and it is presently increasing at a rate of 0.2 percent a year.[48] The increase in the CO_2 content of atmosphere affects the balance of the radiation from the sun and the heat escaping from the earth. Present meteorological theory is barely equipped to·consider the consequences in all its detail, but an incomplete analysis of the problem predicts a slight increase in the mean temperature of the surface atmosphere.[49] It should also be noted that others have predicted that dramatic changes, such as the triggering of a new ice age, could result from a small change in the mean condition of the atmosphere.[50]

At present I am not aware of any plausible hypothesis of ocean pollution that could trigger catastrophic events of this kind. However, when you consider that the ocean is the source of all life on this earth, that it is the climatic control that makes life bearable, and that we really know so little about it and the life within it, it is not surprising that otherwise rational scientists can become very emotional when they talk about the possible effects of ocean pollution.

There is a potpourri of evidence that suggests that ocean pollution has some effect by whatever criteria one wishes to use. Fish have been observed with measurable amounts of DDT and PCB in their flesh.[51] There have been fish kills in coastal waters in which pollution has been implicated.[52] There have been marked changes in the dissolved oxygen and nutrient level in the Baltic which can be expected to have a measurable effect on the distribution of plants and animals.[53] The stomach contents of ocean fish have been found to contain many of man's discarded artifacts.[54] Measurable changes in the ecology of benthic communities have been observed two years after an oil spill.[55]

Probably none of these separately or in total constitutes a serious pollution problem at present. If tomorrow we should all go back to a way of life and a standard of living comparable to that in Europe or the U.S. in the eighteenth century I do not expect there would be any cause for concern. But we are not going to turn the clock back. In my view today's energy "crisis" is simply that, a crisis, and not a signal for a change in our standard of living. Because of lack of foresight we may face a temporary problem between supply and demand.

Some in the U.S. agree with Wordsworth that "the world is too much with us," but I do not believe that attitude is shared in the developing world, nor do I believe it is really shared by most in the U.S. If you see the future as I do, then perhaps you can also understand why some are worried about ocean pollution in the future.

* * * * * *

COMMENTARY   COMMENTARY

Earle E. Seaton[a]

I remember very well when I used to represent Tanzania in discussions at the United Nations that it was not so easy to use against some of the U.S. representatives, particularly Mr. Hargrove, the invectives which his country's policies deserved, and one of the reasons that I allowed myself to be persuaded to come to this Institute was because I saw the familiar names of Hargrove and Oxman, and Mr. Oxman has agreed that if I say anything that is two years out of date he will correct it.

We have had a very illuminating paper by Dr. Knauss and of course one recognizes the expert in his field on the scientific aspects of marine pollution. One could not hope for a better presentation. I shall try, perhaps in a judicial manner, to make some comments on different aspects of marine pollution, saying things which I am sure you already know, but perhaps inviting you to look at them in a different manner so that at the end you may reach clearer perceptions of these problems.

As I approach the topic of marine pollution I cannot help going back to the fact that we evolved from the oceans, and having achieved our security on land, we proceeded to use the oceans as the place for disposing of our wastes. We thought that because most of them would sink, thereby they would go away. Of course we continued to exercise our prerogative of using a minute fraction of the creatures of the oceans for our food. We continued to disport ourselves on the areas where the oceans met the lands, and we used the oceans to communicate with our friends on other continents when we wished, or to get closer to them for hostile purposes at other times.

We did not think too much of the life in the oceanic depths from those minuscule plants whose life is measured in hours to those mammals who dwarf even man in bulk, and unwittingly or deliberately, on an increasing scale in recent years, we deposited foreign matter. Of course, not all this matter is harmful. Some of it is innocuous; some of it, because of a combination of the chemistry of seawater, the atmosphere, or the creatures that still live in the ocean, is assimilable. Some of it disperses. Some is baneful to certain forms of life while stimulating other forms.

---

[a]Puisne Judge, Supreme Court, Bermuda

Then, of course, there are the residues of this matter, which are driven back upon the land, reducing its beauty, destroying its amenities. The common term, rather loosely used for all of this foreign matter introduced into the sea—pollution—is rejected by scientists, and we heard from Dr. Knauss his definition which probably is currently accepted as the proper term, the "unusual deterioration of a biological community as a result of something done by man."

One reaches the conclusion that in this field of pollution the scientists candidly and humbly admit they cannot advise us too precisely. All they can do is begin to point to certain areas of concern. We heard Dr. Knauss mention oil pollution as one of these causes of concern. This may be caused either in the process of extraction, in the process of transportation or in the aftermath of delivery.

In certain parts or the oceans it is more a problem than in other parts. In the Baltic where, we understand, there is great pollution, oil represents a mere 3 percent. In the North Atlantic, partly as a result of the closing of the Suez Canal and the diversion of ships from the Mediterranean, we now have oil pollution on a scale which is fast approaching catastrophe. Some of those places in the North Atlantic that depend on tourism find it necessary regularly to clean the beaches, or I should say try to keep down the tar lumps on the beaches.

Of course, a little island like Bermuda does not have oil production, does not have refineries, yet still finds itself compelled to combat oil pollution. We are told this is the unfortunate result of being in the Gulf Stream. It enables tourists from North America to enjoy the milder weather when the temperatures are severe in their own country, but it also causes, because of the effect of the trade wind drift and the north equatorial current, formation of the Sargasso Sea.

The peculiar characteristic of the Sargasso Sea is that—something like imperialist countries—what it has, it holds; so that floating tar lumps are attracted into the Sargasso Sea, and once within, 20 to 50 percent remain. So, if one has for the whole of the North Atlantic in a given year about 87,000 tons of tar lumps, some 66,000 tons would be found in the Sargasso Sea, and of course this increases yearly. It has been increasing since 1970, with the result that countries near the Sargasso Sea, like Bermuda, find great danger to their amenities.

Rather interestingly, the attitude of the international community towards pollution has undergone changes. There was, at first, the unawareness of the problem. The 1958 Conferences on the Law of the Sea gave the impression that even though scientists were aware of the potential dangers of pollution, they could not anticipate its growth sufficiently to provide for detailed antipollution measures.

The present position seems to be a rather feverish attitude of prohibition—no deliberate spillage of oil. This attitude, of course, can be explained by the nature of oil pollution, the persistence of certain kinds of oil, the difficulty of dispersing or eliminating all of the oil lost in the oceans; but it seems to ignore the trend of modern life. It seems to ask the impossible, somewhat like those laws which Puritans passed which could even before being passed be anticipated would be broken.

Perhaps the next stage will be a more realistic approach, not total prohibition, but rather utilizing the spillages, the leakages which will inevitably occur for constructive purposes. In this connection we have all heard with great interest of the discoveries of two Israeli scientists, who hold out the hope not only for a significant reduction of spillage or deliberate leaking, if you like, not only to reduce this, but to utilize the bacteria who will be responsible for the reduction as protein animal food.

I pass from oil pollution to consider some aspects of ocean dumping which can occur, of course, by actual dumping from vessels of containerized wastes or by dispersal from vessels or even from coastal towns. The effusion into the ocean is often insidious. It is not the kind of spectacular pollution which, like the disasters of the Torrey Canyon or the disaster in the Santa Barbara Channel, causes everyone's attention to be directed. It is rather the type that Dr. Knauss mentioned in his paper that occurred in Minamata where the coastal inhabitants continued eating fish and shellfish for years, and the inhabitants began to get eye diseases, and pregnant women began to give birth to deformed children, and eventually, after some seventeen years, the causes were traced to methyl mercury having been discharged by the company manufacturing fertilizer, just as an incident to its production.

Interestingly enough, the defense that the manufacturers raised of not having known of this kind of pollution did not avail them in the courts. Here again we see this trend, which to me appears to be transitory and one which will probably change. We see this trend to make the offense absolute and to hold the offender responsible whether or not he had knowledge of its causes.

One could perhaps say a few words also about thermal pollution, which refers to the discharge of heat into the water as a result of human activity. It is perhaps difficult for creatures who have the capacity to regulate their body temperature, such as man, to appreciate the harm that might be done to cold blooded creatures, such as fish, who can adjust to seasonal variations in temperature but who must find great difficulty in reacting to abnormally abrupt changes of temperature. This danger is being increased by the construction of large generating plants fueled by nuclear energy. The combination of thermal pollution with discharge of human wastes can give rise to very interesting phenomena, odorous sometimes, sometimes causing growth of undesirable blooms. So far, prohibitions have been attempted, but thought is also being given to more constructive use, suggestions as to fish farming, for example.

We find in this type of activity a possibility that one could not hope for complete prohibition. Nuclear energy development is almost inevitable, and so the thought must change from one of prohibiting it to using it for its constructive purposes. We have become aware, of course, of the prohibitions of the Geneva Convention on the High Seas that could permit states to prevent pollution of such substances as radioactive wastes. We are aware of conventions, such as the International Convention for the Prevention of Pollution of the Sea by Oil, which could deal with the specific problem there. But however many specific international conventions may be negotiated, we come upon the rather fundamental principle of the freedom of the seas that might even invite freedom to pollute, unless one has recourse to the customary international law principle that everyone must so exercise his rights that he does not harm the enjoyment by others of their rights.

Therefore, we are beginning to see suggestions for the dealing with marine pollution problems on an international or global basis. In this respect one is aware of the numerous United Nations agencies with activities in the sphere of marine pollution. We know that UNESCO and its IOC are dealing with the problem, also FAO, IMCO, WHO, WMO, and IAEA. They have set up the joint group of experts on scientific aspects of marine pollution, GESAMP, supported by all of these organizations. They have their program—global investigation of pollution in the marine environment; and then of course, there has recently been set up the United Nations Environment Program. All these agencies have their legitimate interests, their legitimate jurisdictions. Of course the difficulty, the danger is of overlapping, of competition. What one requires urgently in the field of marine pollution seems to be an interconnected, scientific, institutional, and legal approach. It should be based on four prongs.

First, there should be a registration and monitoring system to record and check upon all discharge of pollutants into the oceanic space. Second, there should be reform and standardization of national regulations for the control of pollution. Third, there should be preservation of the marine environment, which should be the responsibility of an overall international authority which should have jurisdiction to hold offenders liable for damage caused by them. Fourth, provision should be made for financial and/or technical assistance to be given when needed to countries confronted with major pollution crises. All these steps are being considered. All of them eventually will be taken.

The Law of the Sea Conference is preparing to achieve these results. Countries which at the moment seem indifferent, perhaps (and I refer here to the developing countries), may not be so indifferent because of lack of realization of the problems or of the remedies but possibly because the financial and manpower requirements do not permit all the attention to be given. One only has to remember the difficulties that beset Great Britain when it was trying to deal with the disaster that faced it from the breakup of the *Torrey Canyon* tanker near its shores to consider how would a country such as Tanzania deal with a similar problem off the coast of Dar es Salam.

To retain in the country itself machinery to deal with such a problem would be very expensive, and probably, because of the rapid development of technology, by the time the need for the machinery occurred the machinery would have become outdated. To call for assistance from its neighbors, Kenya and Uganda, would probably be futile, finding them in the same position.

So, there seems to be a need for international provision, either on a global basis or on a regional basis, for financial and technical assistance to be ready to be made available if needed. I want to close by stressing the necessity for international authority over this problem. The existing agencies no doubt all wish to retain and expand their jurisdictions, but with the approach of the Law of the Sea Conference, thought must be given to where these existing agencies will fit in the proposed international seabed resources authority which itself may wish to assume jurisdiction over pollution that is caused in the area within its jurisdiction. One must beware lest the competing and overlapping jurisdictions clog the system. It is coordination which will be most urgently needed in dealing with these problems in the future.

Chapter Sixteen

Preservation of Marine Environment with Special Reference to the Mediterranean and Adriatic Seas

Branko Sambrailo
Scientific Adviser, Yugoslav Academy
of Sciences and Arts

Specialized agencies and other organizations of the United Nations family, as well as many states and scientific institutions and organizations, are taking steps to find scientific, legal, technical, and financial means to prevent all kinds of pollution of the marine environment. Let us mention the activities of the IMCO on the question of sea pollution from oil by ships, and those of FAO on marine pollution and its effects on living resources and fishing.

WMO and UNESCO have established a joint group of experts on scientific study of marine pollution. The Intergovernmental Oceanographic Commission's comprehensive outline of the scope of long-term and expanded program of oceanic exploration and research provide for scientific studies of ocean pollution. The Economic Commission for Europe held in 1971, in Prague, Czechoslovakia, a symposium on problems relating to environment.[1]

The UN Conference on the Problems of Human Environment, held in Stockholm in 1972,[2] produced three documents: recommendation for an action plan to tackle the planet's environmental ills; a resolution outlining a scheme for new United Nations machinery including an environmental fund to focus international efforts on these problems; and a Declaration on the Human Environment containing the 26 principles which the nations assembled at Stockholm believe should guide them in the years ahead.

Also, the Ottawa session of the intergovernmental group of experts on maritime pollution of the U.N. elaborated 23 principles on marine pollution, which were endorsed by the Stockholm Conference and which provide the guidelines and general framework for a comprehensive and interdisciplinary approach to all aspects of marine pollution problems.

The Conference, convened by IMCO in the fall of 1973 (as this book goes to press), will take into consideration the draft convention prepared under IMCO auspices, which is intended to achieve the complete elimination of pollution of the sea by oil and other noxious substances and the minimization of accidental spills. In other words, it is intended to provide for the prevention of all forms of ship-generated pollution, whether accidental or deliberate.

Finally, the United Nations is scheduled to hold the third law of the sea conference at the end of 1973, which is expected to lay down the foundations for a comprehensive approach to the preservation of the marine environment. Within this system will be elaborated a "head" treaty in the form of several fundamental legal principles: (1) the fundamental obligations of all states to preserve the marine environment and protect it from pollution; (2) application of management concepts to the preservation of the marine environment; (3) development of an effective system for monitoring changes in the marine environment and the effects of various activities within that environment; (4) adoption and improvement of internationally agreed-upon criteria, technical rules, and standards to ensure the prevention of pollution; (5) resolution of jurisdictional issues arising in connection with the preservation of the marine environment in coastal areas and on the high seas, including in particular the elaboration of effective provisions for the enforcement of international conventions; (6) further elaboration of a regime for compensation for victims of marine pollution damage, including clarification of state responsibility in this regard; (7) development of internationally agreed-upon measures for the prevention and control of pollution arising from exploration and exploitation of seabed mineral resources both within and beyond the limits of national jurisdiction; (8) provision of assistance to developing countries to strengthen their ability to discharge their obligation for the preservation of the marine environment.

All these efforts are concentrated on one practical problem—i.e., to find ways and means of reducing marine pollution of all harmful agents and toxic materials to a prescribed minimum, coming from any source, whether land based or marine based, e.g., from coastal industries located on seashores, from vessels, and from exploitation of submarine areas, seabed, and subsoil—because the concept of "marine environment" includes the submarine areas and waters above from coast to coast.

I feel I should repeatedly underline that Yugoslavia has taken a very positive view of the above-mentioned proposals and agreed to participate very actively in the solution of the problem of sea pollution. This is particularly important considering that the Yugoslav seashore lies on the east side of the Adriatic Sea, which is a semienclosed sea, and that it is very narrow, about 120 miles. That is the reason why both sea and shores will be seriously endangered in case of pollution occurring owing to an accident on a tanker, or to eruption of oil from the seabed deposits caused by the exploration and exploitation of the mineral resources of submarine areas of this sea.

Consequently, the only solution we can find is a bilateral agreement with Italy, which lies on the other side of the Adriatic Sea, and thus obtain intergovernmental cooperation and establish mutual internationally agreed-upon measures and standards against all kinds of pollution, whether from land-based or marine-based sources, in the whole Adriatic Sea. This should be made in the interest of the living resources and also of domestic and foreign tourism, human health, and protection of marine environments in general. This problem is very urgent just now after the establishment of the pipeline "TAL" from Triest to Ingolstadt, Germany, with capacity of 35 million tons a year and from Urinj, Rijeka, to Pancevo, Yugoslavia, which is soon to be built. For the purposes of both these pipelines, an ever greater number of tankers will come in the northeast part of the Adriatic, so that the problem of the pollution would become very acute and very dangerous. The two governments, Italy and Yugoslavia, are now exchanging views on these matters following an initiative from the Italian side on the parliamentary level.

On the other hand, Yugoslavia is interested in regional arrangements against pollution in the whole Mediterranean involving all the countries along the Mediterranean coasts. Preparatory work for these regional arrangements was undertaken during the session of the intergovernmental group of experts of the U.N. on sea pollution held in London in 1971. On this occasion a paper was drafted entitled "Note on Advisability of a Regional Agreement on the Control of Marine Pollution in the Mediterranean."[3] This document notes the need of a regional agreement, not only because the Mediterranean Sea is one of the more threatened seas, but also because its pollution sources are "exportable," like the pollution from the River Rhine, the Baltic, and the North Sea. Consequently, for all these "exportable" areas of the seas international standards and antipollution measures are required.[4]

During the above-mentioned session of IWGMP in London in 1971, the majority of the Mediterranean countries and also some others too, drafted a paper entitled "Proposed Resolution on Monitoring, Surveillance, and Control of Marine Pollution in Relation to Assistance to Developing Countries."[5] This was done because most of the Mediterranean countries are at the developing level.[6] In spite of all these efforts, it will be rather difficult to reach a regional agreement on control and prevention of pollution in the Mediterranean sea as a whole, because of very complicated political and economic reasons. In connection with this political situation, Professor Dupuy of the University of Nice has said, "The Mediterranean was always a world of conflict. It still remains so: industrial countries and developing countries, Israel and Arab countries and oil conflicts." Then Prof. Dupuy asked himself, "Will the Mediterranean governments be capable of overcoming these political and economic tensions to safeguard their common heritage?"[7]

According to our opinion, these difficulties in respect to the elimination of pollution of the Mediterranean as a whole can be surpassed by international arrangements between France, Italy, Spain, and Malta on one side, and by arrangements among developing countries of the Mediterranean coast on the other side. Yugoslavia, meanwhile, is interested in taking an active part in both arrangements and will support all peaceful programs.

Consequently, we should agree with the Italian government's proposal that the inclusion of a provision should be made in the draft convention of IMCO prepared for the 1973 conference on marine pollution for dealing with certain "special areas" which, because of their geographic characteristics and particular problems relating to the transportation of oil, may call for the complete prohibition of discharge of oil and other toxic mixtures and substances. These might include such areas as the Baltic, the Black Sea, and the Mediterranean, including the Adriatic Sea. Besides, it is welcome news from IMCO that a new complex of measures will be submitted for acceptance to the forthcoming conference in London that will greatly facilitate the preservation of areas such as the Adriatic Sea to the benefit of all bordering countries and people of other nations who enjoy its amenities.[8]

THE REVISION OF EXISTING INTERNATIONAL CONVENTIONS AGAINST POLLUTION OF THE MARINE ENVIRONMENT—THE HIGH SEAS

It is a well known fact that exploration and exploitation activities in submarine areas of the sea, the breaking of the pipelines, as well as dumping in the seas of the radioactive waste, pose a much greater threat toward pollution of the marine environment than the ships which pollute the sea and the shores accidentally or deliberately. This threat was discussed in detail in the report I delivered at the International Congress on Petroleum and the Sea in Monte Carlo in 1965, and in my proposal submitted to the IMCO in 1967.

At that time no actual cases of pollution had been recorded, but since then there have been cases that must cause concern in every coastal country. The danger of this new form of pollution has been well illustrated by the flow of oil from submarine spills near Santa Barbara in California and in the Gulf of Mexico. The damage caused to the shores of the United States was very serious and the cost of cleaning the shores from the oil brought by ocean streams and the wind was huge. It amounted to dozens of millions of dollars, to which should be added the loss to the tourist industry, fishing, shipping, and so on. We must also mention the accident of the *Torrey Canyon* in the Northeast Atlantic between the English and French coasts. Since oil and its derivates float on the surface of the sea, they can spread over hundreds of miles within a very short period of time and reach the shores and harbors of many countries. It is precisely for this reason that the international significance of the problem of pollution has been recognized.

In spite of these facts, the 1958 Geneva Convention on the High Seas leaves it to the states engaging in such activities (mentioned in Articles 24 and 25) to adopt their own national protective legislation and measures for the prevention of pollution of the seas and air space above.[9] Also, the 1958 Geneva Convention on the Continental Shelf (Art. 5, par. 7) obliged the coastal states to undertake in the safety zones within 500 meters around the installations and other devices which have been erected, all appropriate measures for the protection of the living resources of the sea from harmful agents.[10]

These approaches are clearly inadequate, precisely because of the already discussed tendency of oil and other harmful agents to spread over large areas notwithstanding state boundaries, which automatically gives an international dimension to this problem. Besides, leaving it to individual countries to take their own measures and draw up regulations to prevent pollution of the seas, puts the entire effort on a subjective basis, and it is not inconceivable that a country should follow its selfish interests in this respect and take measures and regulations which might damage the interests of other, including neighboring, states. That is why it is increasingly felt that this question should be tackled only *internationally*, through an international convention.

Meanwhile, in addition to these general provisions in respect to pollution of the high seas, there exist also many special conventions about various kinds of pollution caused by vessels (ordinary or a special class, i.e., tankers), compensation for damage, remedial measures, etc., which have been concluded under the auspices of United Nations and its specialized agencies. One is the *International Convention for the Prevention of Pollution of the Sea by Oil*, concluded by IMCO in London, 1954, amended in 1962 and 1969.[11] This convention deals with only one marine-based source of pollution, namely ships polluting the "prohibited zones" of the high seas. Its gaps will be explained in further detail below.

Another convention that has been concluded is the International Convention Relating to the Limitation of the Liability of Owners of Seagoing Ships (1957).[12] This convention limits the liability of shipowners for damage caused by their vessels, in the absence of actual fault or privity on other part, to a maximum of approximately 7 million dollars. It does not deal with the question of state responsibility, nor is it designed to deal specifically with pollution damage.

The Convention on the Liability of Operators of Nuclear Ships (1962),[13] which is not yet in force, makes provision for a regime of strict liability of the operators of nuclear ships and sets the limitation of that liability at 100 million dollars. It makes no provisions for preventive measures. It implicitly recognizes the right of a coastal state to exclude nuclear ships from its waters and ports. The Treaty Banning Nuclear Weapons Tests in the Atmosphere, in Outer Space, and Under Water (1963),[14] while more often viewed as a disarmament measure, also represents by its express terms a very important environmental protection agreement. It prohibits states, who are parties to the treaty, to carry out nuclear explosions in any environment if such explosions cause radio-active debris to be present outside the territorial limits of the state under whose jurisdiction or control such explosion is conducted.

The International Convention Relating to Intervention on the High Seas in Cases of Oil Pollution Casualties (1969),[15] not yet in force, provides for the right of the coastal state to take such measures on the high seas, without any limitation as to distance, as may be necessary to protect its coastline or related interests from pollution of the sea by oil, following upon a maritime casualty that may be reasonably expected to result in major harmful consequences. The convention makes no provision for a similar right of intervention in pollution casualties not involving oil-carrying vessels. It is essentially oriented to remedial rather than preventive measures; that is, to action that may be taken after an accident has occurred rather than to action that should be taken to prevent such accidents.

The International Convention on Civil Liability for Oil Pollution Damage (1969),[16] not yet in force, imposes strict liability (exception being made for acts of war or natural catastrophes, international acts of a third party, or negligence on the part of those responsible for the maintenance of navigation aids) on the owner of any oil tanker from which oil has escaped after an incident at sea which has caused damage in the territory or territorial waters of a con-tracting state. No provision is made for compensation for damage to coastal re-sources or other coastal interests in any "economic zone" beyond the territorial sea. It sets the limit to such liability at approximately 14 million dollars per inci-dent. In addition, being restricted to one form of marine pollution damage, it does not deal with the question of state responsibility, nor does it remove pro-cedural difficulties standing in the way of satisfying pollution claims.

The International Convention on the Establishment of an Interna-tional Fund for Compensation for Oil Pollution Damage (1971),[17] not yet in force, relieves ship owners from the "additional financial burden" imposed by the 1969 Convention on Civil Liability and provides additional compensation for oil pollution victims to a limit of 30 million dollars. It represents a special com-pensation regime for damage from a special class of vessels—i.e., tankers—but even in this sense it is incomplete in that it does not provide for compensation for damage caused by intentional discharges of oil not connected with a mari-time incident, and excludes compensation for damage resulting from an act of war or from oil escaping from a warship or other government-operated vessels in noncommercial service. Finally, it does not provide for compensation for dam-age caused by the pollution of coastal resources and other coastal interests in any "economic zone" beyond the territorial sea; nor does it help to resolve pro-cedural difficulties in satisfying claims over and above the 30 million dollars limit.

The Convention for the Preservation of Marine Pollution by Dump-ing from Ships and Aircraft (Oslo, 1972)[18] establishes an absolute prohibition against the dumping of certain highly toxic substances and regulates the dumping of all other substances in the region of the North Sea and the North Atlantic.

It is evident from the above survey that all existing conventions deal with only some particular forms of marine pollution, and even in respect of these forms do not fully settle such important issues as enforcement jurisdiction, state responsibility, and compensation for damage. Guidelines for a comprehensive approach that would fill these gaps are provided by the Declaration on the Human Environment passed by the Stockholm Conference of the United Nations (1972) and the 23 Principles on Marine Pollution elaborated at Ottawa (1971) and endorsed by the Stockholm Conference.[19]

CONTROL AND JURISDICTION OF STATES

The practical implementation of any such international agreement will depend on the possibility of control, surveillance, and jurisdiction in the process of detecting violators and forcing them to pay compensation to the coastal state for the damage caused to their shores and economic interests. Many of the proposals made so far provide for the control by the states which have exploration and exploitation equipment already installed in a given area: offshore drilling platforms, drilling vessels, dredging vessels, and so forth.

According to the United States draft convention on the submarine areas regime, for instance, both the authority to maintain order and the power of jurisdiction remain with the state whose ships or installations are engaged in such submarine activities.[20] In cases of pollution by passing ships through discharge of oil or other pollutants, without the knowledge of the inspection service of the country under whose flags the ships sail (according to the already mentioned 1954 London Convention), any contracting government may only furnish to the government of the relevant territory "in writing of evidence" that any provision of the Convention has been contravened in respect of that ship, wheresoever the alleged contravention may have taken place (Art. X). But it has no right to visit or search the suspected ship to determine whether it is in fact responsible or not. Unfortunately, the new draft convention of IMCO against pollution by ships was based on the same principle of flag-state in respect to control and jurisdiction.

The difficulty of determining which ship or installation on the sea, seabed or subsoil is responsible for the pollution of the high seas is well known. There exists the cromatography method of spectral analysis in the laboratory of samples of pollutants found in the sea, which would have to be compared with the samples of oil from the ship or installation. The difficulty is particularly pronounced since a sample of oil from the ship can be taken, and its Oil Record Book inspected, only "while within a port of that territory"—i.e., when the ship enters in one of the contracting state ports (Art. IX, par. 5 of the London Convention).

Since the convention does not allow the visit and search of the suspected ship for contraventions made on the high seas, the only other way in which the inspection vessel of a foreign country may proceed is by informing the government of the transgressor, in writing, that the violation has been directly observed. It is clear from everything said here that the machinery of surveillance or inspection on the high seas should be changed to allow foreign authorities, in cases of reasonable suspicion of the violation of internationally agreed-upon measures and standards, to visit and search the ship and its cargo both in the territorial sea and in the so-called "prohibited zones," as well as to inspect its Oil Record Book in order to determine the contravention and escort the ship to a port of that country under whose flag it sails for an inquiry before competent authority.

FINANCIAL QUESTIONS WITH RESPECT TO ORGANIZING POLLUTION CONTROL SCHEMES

It is clear that it is not possible to work efficiently on the solution of the problem of sea pollution, which in its essence is very complex in nature, only by legal means. This is why the correct conclusion should be reached in accordance with the results of legal studies and investigative work into the technical aspects of sea pollution, without neglecting the search for adequate means for its prevention as well as the carrying out of economic analyses of the most efficient and least costly methods and means to fight sea pollution. All these parallel investigations, which are of a very complex nature, can serve as a basis for future national and international regulations.

At the same time it is absolutely necessary that competent scientific institutions and practical organizations should determine the actual state of pollution data along the coast and of the marine environment of all countries, and that they should determine the already available means, or those they would recommend to be introduced, in order that pollution of the marine environment might be suppressed as much as possible.

Accordingly, developing countries should take into consideration the financial question with respect to the organized struggle against pollution of the marine environment. Namely, that it is necessary to find sources to cover the considerable costs of expensive technical means and equipment—port facilities for the reception of residues and oily mixtures, inspection vessels and helicopters, organization of administration in the port, training program for experts, laboratories for research, and so on.

The answer can be found only by providing immediate help to the developing countries or indirectly by establishing an international fund for the protection and improvement of the marine environment, as well as for the compensation of damage in cases where a violator is unknown. This help is quite justified because industrialization as a whole is responsible *in grosso modo* for the causes and consequences of pollution of the marine environment, either directly or indirectly. Consequently, the industrial countries are obliged to help the developing countries to be protected against the consequences of pollution for which they are not guilty.

Chapter Seventeen

Ocean Pollution: What Can the Law of the Sea Conference Do?

Bernard H. Oxman
Assistant Legal Adviser for Ocean Affairs
Department of State*

The 1958 Law of the Sea Conventions contain certain general provisions regarding marine pollution. Article 24 of the High Seas Convention obliges states to draw up regulations to prevent pollution of the seas by discharge of oil from ships, pipelines, or seabed exploration and exploitation activities. Article 25 obliges states to take measures to prevent pollution of the seas from the dumping of radioactive waste, and to cooperate with competent international organizations in taking measures for preventing pollution of the seas or airspace above from any activities with radioactive materials or other harmful agents. Article 5 of the Continental Shelf Convention obliges the coastal state to undertake, in safety zones around seabed exploration and exploitation installations and devices, appropriate measures for the protection of the living resources of the sea from harmful agents.

  To these one might add the basic legal obligation in the High Seas Convention of "reasonable regard" for the interests of other states in their exercise of the freedom of the high seas, and a similar obligation in the Continental Shelf Convention prohibiting "any unjustifiable interference with navigation, fishing, or the conservation of the living resources of the sea."

  The significant number of specific treaties regarding marine pollution that have been negotiated in the Inter-Governmental Maritime Consulta-

---

  *The views expressed in this paper are those of the author, and do not necessarily represent the views of the Department of State or the United States Government.

tive Organization and elsewhere since the 1958 Law of the Sea Conference reveal that the general provisions of the Law of the Sea Conventions were not considered adequate or sufficiently precise, particularly as the seriousness of the ocean pollution problem has become increasingly apparent in recent years. Indeed, the text of the Law of the Sea Conventions clearly reveals that their drafters contemplated such developments.

This experience probably indicates at least two general conclusions regarding the next Law of the Sea Conference. First, the Law of the Sea Conference can establish a stronger legal foundation for further efforts to prevent pollution of the marine environment. Second, the Law of the Sea Conference need not and probably cannot itself deal with the details of precise water quality, construction, or other standards needed to achieve these purposes.

The public proposals of the United States indicate that it has reached a third conclusion of considerable significance. Stated broadly, it is that in important respects regarding ocean pollution problems, traditional treaty negotiating processes should be replaced by international regulatory processes in order to ensure needed flexibility and responsiveness.

Thus the August 1971 draft seabeds treaty introduced by the United States would give the new seabeds authority important regulatory authority to establish rules and recommended practices to prevent pollution from exploration and exploitation of seabed resources in the deep seabeds as well as continental margin areas. In the continental margin, the coastal state could of course establish higher standards, but it would have to observe the international standards as a minimum.

In June of 1973, Russell Train, the Chairman of the President's Council on Environmental Quality, made an analogous proposal in the Inter-Governmental Maritime Consultation Organization regarding pollution from ships. Looking toward the October IMCO Conference on Marine Pollution, Mr. Train proposed that IMCO establish a Marine Environment Protection Committee, open to all IMCO members, with regulatory authority as follows:

1. With regard to marine pollution from vessels, the Marine Environment Protection Committee would be empowered to consider, develop, adopt, and communicate to governments new regulations under the conventions for which it was responsible or modifications to existing regulations.

2. Such new or modified regulations would enter into force on a date specified by the committee unless objections were received from a substantial number of states party to the relevant convention, including a designated number or category of states to ensure a balance of maritime and coastal interests.

3. The committee would be empowered to adopt and bring into immediate force appendixes to regulations, without further consideration by

contracting states, when the action received the unanimous consent of those participating in the committee.

This proposal, as well as a companion proposal to establish an ad hoc committee to elaborate the idea, were well received in the IMCO Council. Favorable comments were made by such countries as Belgium, Brazil, Canada, the Federal Republic of Germany, India, Poland, the USSR, and the United Kingdom. The drafts prepared by Subcommittee III pollution working group of the U.N. Seabed Committee provide that measures taken by states "shall, . . . in respect of marine-based sources of pollution of the marine environment, conform to generally accepted international standards." If this is to have dynamic meaning, action must be taken by IMCO and its October conference, as well as the law of the sea conference, to ensure that there are international institutions equal to the task of promulgating such standards.

The importance of a viable system of international standards cannot be emphasized too strongly. Marine pollution is a global problem. For environmental as well as economic reasons, it is necessary to take international action to deal with the problem. Flag states are clearly not the only states that might be affected by pollution from vessels under their jurisdiction; coastal states are clearly not the only states that might be affected by pollution from activities under their jurisdiction or control. Strong international standards, with compulsory dispute settlement, are the best means to ensure that legal obligations are formed by all those concerned, will be met by those responsible for the activities, and will in fact protect all those affected.

Everyone is a potential victim of pollution. Decisions regarding jurisdiction over navigation, resources, or other activities should be made on the basis of the substantive requirements involved, not on the basis of potential harm from pollution. The responsibility to ensure that an activity does not result in pollution should, as a rule, be placed on the state that exercises jurisdiction over an activity. As a minimum, that state would have to ensure compliance with applicable international standards. International machinery should be strengthened to ensure that international standards are developed in a timely and responsive manner. Compulsory dispute settlement should exist to ensure compliance by the state exercising jurisdiction, and the remedies available should be equal to that task.

This of course does not mean there are no situations where two states exercise jurisdiction or control. For example, a port state is of course free to establish conditions of port entry for vessels of all flags. The "Intervention Convention" provides for action by a state with respect to foreign vessels in carefully defined and urgent circumstances. But let us not confuse the extraordinary with the ordinary, and bear in mind that jurisdiction and protection of the marine environment are not the same thing.

Virtually every major proposal for an overall law of the sea settlement is predicated on the assumption that freedom of navigation and coastal state jurisdiction over resources can be exercised in the same area. Attempts to solve pollution problems in a manner inconsistent with that approach could send us all back to the drawing boards for a long time to come.

A strengthened international system to deal with marine pollution can resolve the problem. It would be tragic indeed if the energies of those who believe the current system needs improvement were diverted by jurisdictional formulas from the real objective, which can be achieved: protecting the marine environment.

* * * * * *

COMMENTARY

Raul Bazan [a]

We are discussing the scientific effects of ocean pollution, and I propose to consider it in the light of the juridical science, having in mind a case that just happened in Chile. I am going to express my personal views.

The Geneva Conventions on the High Seas and on the Continental Shelf mention some devices for the states to prevent contamination. The first of these conventions established that every state is obliged to dictate its positions, to take certain measures, and to collaborate with competent organizations in order to avoid contamination. The second of these conventions prescribes that the coastal state is obliged to adopt in the security zone adequate measures in order to protect all the living resources of the sea against noxious agents, but these norms are subjects to limitations and deficiencies that make them insufficient.

The Convention for the Prevention of Pollution of the Sea by Oil, written in 1954 and amended in 1969, imposed some prohibitions to the owners of oil tankers. It also is insufficient because it leaves enforcement exclusively in the hands of the flag state. The Nuclear Test Ban Treaty, signed in 1969, prohibited states from making any nuclear explosion that could discharge radioactive matter beyond their own territorial limits. This treaty has not been able to avoid nuclear experiments in the Pacific and further fails in that it implicitly admits that the states can contaminate their own territory.

Some other recent conventions are attempts at preventing ocean contamination, but they have not yet come into force. It is interesting to remind one of the international convention relating to intervention on the high seas in cases of oil pollution casualties, signed in 1969. This convention recognized the right of the coastal state to adopt in the high seas the necessary measures to protect their interests against contamination by hydrocarbons as a result of a mari-

_____
[a]Permanent Mission of Chile to the United Nations

time accident. From these dispositions we conclude a contrary essential that the states which are not part of the convention have no right to adopt these measures of protection. This would be unacceptable.

Looking at all these conventions, it is obvious that they offer only partial solution to the prevention of ocean pollution. They just include some particular causes of contamination and forget others. They do not explicitly forbid the states to pollute their own national territory. They do not recognize that the coastal states have, per se, the right to adopt in the high seas the necessary measures to protect them against contamination from maritime accidents. They do not resolve the very important question of competent jurisdiction, and they do not express any concern about the indemnification of the damages caused.

The voids that exist in the conventional system justify the progressive Latin American position in the matter of ocean pollution which has been developed under the umbrella of the 200-mile doctrine. The first declaration of sovereignty over the sea adjoining the coast to a distance of 200 miles was formulated by Chile on June 23, 1944. It contains no reference to contamination. The Santiago Declaration signed by Chile, Ecuador, and Peru on August 18, 1952, also about the 200 miles, does not mention contamination either, but all subsequent Latin American declarations on the 200 miles express a growing concern for marine contamination. The Montevideo Declaration of May 8, 1970, endorsed by nine Latin American countries, mentions the danger of alteration of the ecological conditions.

Three months later the Lima Declaration, signed by sixteen countries, especially proclaimed the right of coastal states to prevent the contamination of their waters and other dangerous effects that could result from the use of the oceanic milieu adjacent to its coast.

The Santo Domingo Declaration signed on July 20, 1970, by eleven Caribbean countries showed considerable progress in the enunciation of the Latin American principles about oceanic contamination. This Declaration expressed that the adoption of the necessary measures to avoid contamination of the oceans is not only a right of the coastal states, it is also a duty. It adds that every state has to abstain from any act that may pollute the oceanic waters or the seabed within or without their own jurisdiction, and it asserts finally that every physical or juridical entity who pollutes the ocean water has an international responsibility.

The principles of the Santo Domingo Declaration have the greatest importance in doctrine and in practice. They affirm that no state has the right to pollute its own environment. This idea contradicts the implicit acknowledgment of such a right which is contained in the Nuclear Test Ban Treaty. It was necessary to proclaim this idea, and it is a pity that it has not been included in the declaration of June 19, 1972.

It is obvious that a state should not damage the environment because it would be jeopardizing the lives of its own people. Since the ultimate responsibility of the state is to defend and to preserve its own life, it cannot permit anybody else to harm it in such a way. The state, first of all, has the right to prevent those threats, and this implies that it has the power to adopt all necessary measures. The state has, furthermore, the duty to act in this way. Then, nothing could justify its failure to act. The state cannot ignore any situation which causes or may cause pollution of its own environment. No consideration would excuse its leniency because, when facing this menace, the defensive reaction of a state has to be immediate and will be always as legitimate as the right of personal self-defense; and if the damage has already occurred, the state has the right to be compensated for that damage.

The Santo Domingo Declaration defines the responsibility of those who produce the damage as an objective and absolute responsibility. The responsibility to compensate exists even if there was no fault on the part of the polluter. That responsibility is generated by the sole fact that somebody has damaged the marine environment of another country.

Some time ago a Liberian tanker collided with some rocks off the southern coast of Chile. As a result of the collision oil began to be released, threatening to destroy certain of the fish and oyster nurseries and other fishery resources necessary for feeding the Chilean population. The critical position in which the tanker stayed and the bad weather made it evident to the Chilean and foreign experts that the ship was going to break apart, thus releasing its whole cargo of oil. The threat was imminent, and the damage would have been irreparable. Since the Chilean Navy had saved all the crew, it was decided to eliminate all possibility of damage by bombing the ship and burning all the cargo.

I am not trying to defend this decision because it is unnecessary. The Chilean Government action was based on its sovereign rights in its national territory, and was fulfilling its fundamental duty to preserve the marine environment and the fishery resources of its population. What I want, rather, is to show you this case as an example of the threat posed by oil tankers all over the world and of the urgent necessity for the coastal states to adopt adequate measures for their protection.

We cannot eliminate the tankers, but we can—and we have to—improve the legal system to prevent the damages that the tanker used to cause. I think that the adoption of the principles of the Santo Domingo Declaration in a convention which has to be approved this year in London or next year in Santiago would be a constructive solution. Those principles empower the coastal states to act immediately and effectively even in the open seas to prevent any danger of pollution of the oceanic environment. So, the damage in cases of accident would be minimized. Those principles, furthermore, oblige the people who are responsible for any pollution to compensate for the damages. It is evident that this would alert the ship owners and the insurance companies to take extreme caution in order to avoid casualties, and it is quite possible that less tankers would then be involved in oil-polluting accidents.

DISCUSSION

Butler: I suppose that somebody should earn the odium by saying what I feel must now be said. First, I would like to note that we have been listening to five distinguished lawyers commenting on a scientific subject. Although I use the word "commenting," in fact in my notes I have substituted the phrase "reading their own prepared speeches." They had, in fact, little relevance to the topic in question. (I might add that five marine scientists discussing a legal problem probably would be quite as unconvincing.)

My next remark is addressed to Judge Seaton. He referred to a recent newspaper report concerning the work of two Israeli scientists on oil-consuming bacteria. He saw fit to emphasize the supposed potential of such bacteria as a protein resource for a hungry world. I consider that sort of unqualified statement to be irresponsible, similar in vein to the dangerous mythology generated by the Green Revolution propagandists.

I will now address myself to some of the statements made by Dr. Knauss. I found his paper very interesting. I would like, however, to question the excessively optimistic tone of some of his comments. Dr. Knauss states that deliberate dumping can be monitored as easily as outfalls. Most of us would agree with him but can the regulations to control such dumping be enforced? I recently attended the third International Conference of the International Association for Pollution Control held in Montreal. The problem of enforcement was highlighted by one of the speakers in referring to litigation in Canada in which a tanker had been taken to court for spilling oil. The defense lawyer pointed out that the government analyst was in fact an inorganic chemist and, as we all know, petroleum hydrocarbons are organic in origin. The case was accordingly thrown out! One could justifiably feel cynical.

Dr. Knauss goes on to say, if I may quote: "There is another view of the future, however, which argues that by present standards of consumption man has an almost unlimited supply of energy." The following paragraph then refers to the population explosion. Within this context, surely the world's lack of *food energy* and not *industrial energy* must be our primary concern—one cannot eat a controlled fusion reactor!

My next comment refers to a sentence that reads (and I am encouraged to note this): "To people like myself the greatest worry about ocean pollution at this time is the unknown."

May I now recall for you the paper presented this morning by Dr. Albers, in which he confidently referred to *only* three serious blowouts to date. I would like to know what "serious" represents quantitatively, and in this respect perhaps Dr. Knauss would enlighten us concerning some of the problems associated with even "nonserious" oil spills, including synergistic and sublethal effects.

Knauss: The question you asked about sublethal effects of oil pollution is a very difficult one to answer. As I said before, one can observe measurable changes in the biological community some three years after a major oil spill. I am not prepared to estimate at this time what effect this will have on the local ecology over the long term.

The sublethal effect of oil spills on man is a different matter. It is my impression that the most potentially dangerous effect is still somewhat speculative. Shellfish may get a little sick and may not taste very good if they are taken from an area of an oil spill, but that is a lot less critical than the suggestion that cancer-producing effects do occur. This issue has been raised by several people and has been bitterly denounced by others. It is my understanding (and I certainly am not an expert in this particular area) that it is very much an open question as to whether or not this is a real danger.

Seaton: I suppose that the comment that was made regarding the Israeli scientists' proposal comes from a scientist. I suppose so. I am not in a position to judge how valuable that proposal is. I suppose that the term "irresponsible" was applied to the first man who proposed that the earth revolved around the sun. What I had attempted to suggest was that we cannot, merely by prohibiting forms of pollution, solve the problem. If we have, for example, a huge quantity of nerve gas which the army in country X finds is excess to its needs, that nerve gas has to be disposed of. Country X is going to dispose of it somewhere, and if there is a prohibition against dumping it in the ocean, then the country must turn somewhere else. So I suggested that the emphasis must, in time, change from mere prohibition of dumping, prohibition of deliberate spillage of oil, to one of seeking ways and means of finding how to use wastes.

There have been proposals that wastes should be used in various manners. One of these proposals has come from Israeli scientists, and it may be that it will be found that it cannot work. But the suggestion alone that oil wastes might be used for protein animal food is not coming for the first time from the Israeli scientists; it has been made before, and is seriously being considered.

As far as the Green Revolution is concerned, I think it is now fashionable to deride it. There was a time when great hope was given to the peoples of the third world that they need not continue to live in poverty, that by the application of modern methods of farming, utilization of fertilizers, the problem of poverty could be solved. This was important to countries which had very low standards of living.

It has now been found that those promises were somewhat illusory because it was not just a question of improving the methods of agriculture. One had also to improve the capacity to repair the modern equipment that was sent out. One had also to consider the effect of fertilizers, and one then had to consider whether there might not be developed so much of a particular food that it disrupted the economy. I do not think that the Green Revolution was irresponsible. I think that lessons can be learned from it, and that we must still continue the task of trying all measures which may be helpful in the long run.

Logue: I have a question for Mr. Oxman. In the last paragraph of your paper you have a sentence which rather surprises me. You say that virtually every major proposal for an overall law of the sea settlement is predicated on the assumption that both freedom of navigation and coastal state jurisdiction over resources can be exercised in the same ocean area. Now I assume that the U.S. draft treaty is one of the major proposals for a law of the sea settlement. But the U.S. draft treaty does not provide for coastal state jurisdiction over resources. There is some coastal state administration of these resources, but the jurisdiction in the U.S. trusteeship zone proposal is a kind of mixed jurisdiction.

       Incidentally, I think the term "trusteeship zone" is a very unfortunate term. I raise this point because I think this benefit feature is the most valuable and the most striking part of the U.S. draft treaty proposal. As you know, it provides that the International Seabed Resources Authority gets 50 to 66 percent of the revenue from the area reaching from the 200-meter depth line out to the end of the continental margin.

       Maybe I have misunderstood, but this sentence suggests that, in fact, the U.S. position is in favor of coastal state jurisdiction over resources, period— i.e., complete coastal state jurisdiction over resources.

Oxman: I certainly did not intend to suggest that the U.S. position is in favor of "coastal state jurisdiction over resources, period." This was made absolutely clear in Mr. Stevenson's speech of August 10, 1972, which remains the fundamental policy of the United States on that issue.

       I do not want to get into problems of terminology, but if the coastal state has the right to determine the conditions of exploitation, as it would even in the earlier trusteeship zone, then I think it is fair to use the term "jurisdiction." If your question was, did the use of the term jurisdiction imply that the coastal state would not have any international treaty obligations in connection with the exercise of that jurisdiction, including appropriate revenue sharing obligations, then the answer is no, I did not intend to imply that.

Nweihed: Actually, my question is addressed to Judge Russell Train, but since he is not here, I expect Mr. Oxman to give me the answer for him. According to his proposition, the Intergovernmental Maritime Consultative Organization, known as IMCO, will be asked to establish a Marine Environment Protection Committee open to all IMCO members with regulatory authority to follow. We all know that developing countries have been a little bit recalcitrant as to approving or ratifying the IMCO Convention—not because we have anything fundamental against its aims, but just because, I understand, its voting power from the first moment it was created was based on a principle which we have not admitted: the relative size of the fleets of the countries that compose the organization. This we regard as an unjust principle. That is why, at the first opportunity when it was possible to shift the cargo reserve clause and related shipping activities to UNCTAD—where such a principle does not exist—that this was done by the developing nations, and UNCTAD took over those functions that had been allotted at the beginning to IMCO. As we all know, by the way, IMCO's treaty was not easily ratified. It entered into force ten years after it was initially signed. If this injustice, as we call it, would exist, how do you expect the developing countries to be receptive to such a committee when the same mechanisms, I should say, may accompany the new committee?

Oxman: First let me state that all members of the United Nations and other states can become members of IMCO. The IMCO membership, if I am not mistaken, is somewhere in the eighties. It certainly exceeds the number of developed states in the world. Its new Secretary General is a national of India.

Second, the proposal for a Marine Environment Protection Committee is that it be a committee which is open to all members of IMCO, as well as other state parties to conventions with respect to which the committee exercises responsibilities. There would not be elections to it. Any member of IMCO or party to the appropriate convention who wanted to participate in that committee could do so. That committee, not the Council of IMCO, would exercise the regulatory authority that Judge Train spoke of. Satisfaction or dissatisfaction with the way in which IMCO handles its shipping responsibilities would not be relevant; the environmental responsibilities would be in the hands of the Marine Environment Protection Committee.

The third point is that the rapid entry into force procedure—the objection procedure—should obviously have some kind of clause in it to make sure that there is something of a balance of interests involved. The precise formula, of course, has to be negotiated.

The record of United States participation in recent pollution conferences indicates that we do, indeed, share the concerns in this field of many other coastal states. I think it would be inconceivable for the United States, however strong its maritime interests are, to advocate a system which we felt was incapable of producing strong and adequate environmental measures because it was placing undue emphasis on the economic burdens on shipping. On the other hand, I must say that we have to realize that we also cannot set up a procedure that does the reverse.

I am not an expert in international organizations, but I must say that from the little I do know, I think it would not be regarded by most experts as realistic to assume that those states whose activities we are trying to regulate would agree to vest in UNCTAD, for a variety of reasons, the authority to impose binding legal obligations.

We can establish satisfactory procedures in IMCO to overcome the problems that you adverted to insofar as the pollution question is concerned. Accordingly, these problems should not be an impediment to using the very substantial expertise which has been built up in IMCO on this matter.

Bailey: I just had a comment to make on Mr. Oxman's statement. He refers to one of the drafts prepared by the Subcommittee III pollution working group of the U.N. Seabed Committee, and this draft article stated, among other things, that states shall in respect to the marine-based sources of pollution of the marine environment conform to generally accepted international standards. What Mr. Oxman did not say was that there was a footnote to this draft article that mentioned that many or a number of members of the drafting committee considered that a coastal state should have the right to take stricter measures if those international standards were not sufficient to protect its marine environment.

The problem at the conference will be to balance a coastal state's claim to take stricter measures if the international measures are not sufficient to protect its environment, and the abuse by that state of that right whereby it may unnecessarily hinder international navigation. It will be very difficult, in my opinion, to persuade many coastal states that unknown international standards not made as yet by IMCO will be sufficient to protect their interests.

Agosta: My question is directed to Dr. Knauss. I know your topic was mainly on pollution in the open ocean, but you did allude to the inland coastal areas, and this is, I think, where probably our major problem is today. One of the things I wanted to object to quite strongly was your flow-through time. Not the concept of it, but the fact that you tended, I think, to minimize the effect of pollution by using this very small flow-through time. True, the water does change, as you indicated, let us say, within two and a half years in Lake Erie; but I think you will have to admit that the biological effects are not remedied that rapidly. And while we are speaking of estuary areas and areas of the continental shelf where our major fisheries are located, I think you have to be much more careful in discussing pollution in this area and much more conservative than I believe your talk led us to expect.

Knauss: All I mean by the residence time is that this is the minimum time one should consider as required to clean up pollution. I am sure that in the case of Lake Erie it would take much longer than two and a half years. I think, however, residence time is still a useful concept in considering the question of how long it takes to clean up small bodies of water in comparison to larger bodies of water like the oceans, or the Mediterranean.

What I was trying to emphasize was that we should not extrapolate from the relatively short period of time it takes to clean up something like Narragansett Bay or Chesapeake Bay which we can do within a few years. In a place like the Mediterranean we are talking about a flow-through time of 50 to 100 years. In the ocean it is a meaningless question. You can make the calculation, and it comes out to a few thousand years. What I really meant to emphasize was that we make a dangerous extrapolation if we assume that we can clean up the oceans or large semienclosed seas in the same way we can clean up small estuaries and lakes.

Schatz: Dr. Fletcher, of the National Science Foundation, and the National Center for Atmospheric Research and scientists working with the Global Atmospheric Research Program, have so far modeled an effective demonstration of the influence of the polar oceans on world climate. I wonder if Dr. Knauss could enlighten us as to what is known and what needs to be known about the effect of oil on the ocean surface on the rate of ice formation?

Knauss: Although oil has been implicated in many aspects of pollution, I do not think that oil on the surface of the ocean would change the climate. Presumably its effect would be to change the albedo (the reflection of sun light) or the evaporation rate. It is my impression that the effect of oil on the surface of the ocean should be negligible, at least in part, because the oil that is spilled does not spread very easily. I think the burning of oil, and therefore changing the carbon dioxide content of the atmosphere, is a much more likely way to change the climate.

Stockman: I would like to acknowledge Dr. Knauss's very elaborate and very complete statement about the importance of scientific research in defining the dimensions of the marine pollution problem and perhaps also the uncertainties there.
　　　　　I have a question that would probably be most appropriate for Mr. Oxman. With respect to the very recent United States proposal to upgrade the capacity of IMCO to deal with marine pollution, it seems clearly accepted that their scientific capability is at best quite modest, while they do have a strong technological capability to deal with maritime matters and shipping. The marine scientific component of the IMCO staff and subordinate bodies is minimal with the possible exception of the interagency GESAMP. I would ask Mr. Oxman to respond on whether or not the United States is prepared to recommend any sort of measures to upgrade the scientific stature of IMCO and perhaps more particularly whether or not it is prepared to pay the extra cost of this?

Oxman: First, on the questions that go into the scientific basis for regulatory proposals or regulatory action, you really have to find out what the problem is and how best to deal with it. Traditionally (although not exclusively) in international negotiations, that expertise basically has been supplied by the individual states themselves. In other words, before making a proposal, a state normally engages in extensive internal consultation as to what the problem is and what a possible way is to resolve it. Thus the mere fact that in negotiating regulatory measures of this sort there is no visible scientific input does not mean that it does not exist. Obviously looking down the road there is an alternative, which is for an organization to hire scientists and experts itself to perform such services for all members. It has been argued that this avoids some unnecessary duplication and asymetry in certain cases. The U.N. Secretariat has provided good examples in its reports in certain technical fields, perhaps not precisely the scientific one, of that kind of procedure.

Another aspect of the problem which Judge Train did address was the entire issue of the dissemination of information and trying to encourage the improvement of pollution control techniques around the world. This inevitably gets into the kinds of assistance questions regarding developing country problems that have been raised on the panel here. Insofar as vessel pollution is concerned, he indicated that he certainly felt the new committee should concern itself with those problems. He stated explicitly that this would create new commitments on funds, and in this regard he said two things.

First, member states ought to be prepared to go ahead and support that kind of increase in expenditure. Second, he hoped that the Law of the Sea Conference would take into account this possible use of any international revenues generated from the seabeds. That, of course, remains to be seen. If international revenues are to be generated basically by manganese nodules only, I personally have serious doubts whether there will be enough revenue generated, at least in the near term. If they are to be generated from petroleum in continental margins also under coastal state jurisdiction, then it would seem that the international community—including the developing countries, who are intended to be the principal beneficiaries—could well decide on priorities of international technical assistance programs to developing countries, such as this one, as part of a general system for using the revenue.

Bates: Judge Seaton raised the question of technology transfer on oil cleanup. I would point out that we are now getting a lot of experience in the United States on cleaning up oil spills. For example, the Coast Guard manages the national fund for oil cleanup; already in the last twelve months there have been three spills that cost over $1 million each to clean up. In fact, one cost $5 million. So there is pressure to make cleanup more efficient. Hence, we have set up three strike forces, plus a two-week training school in port and waterway safety. Manuals from this school could be supplied if anybody is interested. However, we ourselves are still very much in the learning curve. In addition, the Coast Guard has run cleanup exercises to which observers from other countries could be invited. For example, this winter [1973-74] up in Alaska we will be doing actual oil spills and testing existing cleanup equipment.

Perhaps IMCO or the United Nations might want to consider having an international oil cleanup strike force, in view of the Chilean Ambassador's comments regarding the tanker recently grounded on his coastline. About three months ago there was a similar situation with a stranded tanker in the Aleutians; we flew specially developed pumps there designed to work on a stranded tanker without creating an explosive hazard. Remember the *Torrey Canyon* and what happened when the Dutch salvage crew tried to offload it? There was an explosion that promptly killed the salvage master. So yes, there is need for technology transfer, and it could be encouraged.

As far as the impact of oil on the oceans is concerned, when one listens to Dr. Blumer of Woods Hole, he is describing the worst kind of oil spill you can get. This is a spill of hundreds of thousands of gallons of Number 2 fuel oil very close to the beach. All three of these things—the type of oil, the amount of oil, and the beach location—are very bad.

On the other hand, the offshore oil fields in Louisiana produce about a million barrels a day of oil along with about 300,000 barrels a day of "bleed water" containing 40 to 50 parts per million of oil that is released into the ocean. Yet the fishing has actually improved in that region. Today, there is a very elaborate study by twenty universities going on there to find out what impact, if any, that development of offshore oil has had. So far it is slow going in finding anything finite in a major sense. If there is an adverse effect, it may be a problem much like smoking cigarettes, for I noticed a certain number of people up here on the stage still doing that. Smoking is obviously not good for you, but it is also not so bad as to cause the insurance companies to change the insurance rates.

Chapter Eighteen

A Final Word: Address to
the Law of the Sea Institute

The Honorable Edmund S. Muskie

I come from a state that lives by the sea, so it is a particular pleasure for me to be home in New England and to have the opportunity to talk to many of you who are dealing with the future of the world's seas.

To our ancestors on this continent, the sea was infinite—an infinite, if often dangerous, source of food and work; an infinite protection from foreign interference . . . a barrier and shield for a new country and its people; an infinite disposal for the refuse of man in his headlong pursuit of industrial development. In this century the safe havens of our ocean frontiers have disappeared one by one before the onward rush of technology.

Hence, the oceans no longer isolate us from the politics of other nations. Contamination and depradation of the sea and its inhabitants have risen to terrifying proportions. The technology that brings closer to hand the economic wealth of the seas also presents the prospect of the same short-sighted pursuit of wealth that has left our land scarred, our water poisoned, and our air polluted.

George Santayana once said that those who cannot learn from history are doomed to repeat it. To me this is the essence of the problems that confront us here in the United States and will confront all nations at the upcoming Law of the Sea Conference. The primary question is not whether the U.S. can reconcile its conflicting domestic pressures to pursue an equitable adjustment of international ocean problems. Nor is the question whether developing states can temper their understandably urgent quest for a share of the world's goods by claiming jurisdiction over the seas that others have so long controlled. The question is really whether the nations of the world have learned the lessons necessary to prevent the abuse of the seas from reaching the point some scientists predict will be our ultimate doom.

A hundred years ago, the British scientist Thomas Huxley wrote of this nation, "I cannot say that I am in the slightest degree impressed by your bigness or your material resources as such . . . the great issue is what are you going to do with all these."

Huxley's statement has a great deal of relevance today vis-à-vis man's use of the ocean. At present, more than a hundred nations are involved in probably the most significant international negotiations ever conducted concerning the seas. An orderly and equitable ocean regime has become both more vital to nations and more difficult for them to agree upon. They are more dependent than ever before on access to critical areas of the ocean, on its ecological health, and on its mineral and food resources.

As ocean users multiply—and as competition among them intensifies—the classical political question of "who gets what" is thrust to the center of the debate over the future of the oceans. With wise answers to this question, international cooperation and justice can prevail in the ocean. With short-sighted answers, 70 percent of the earth's surface could become an arena for serious international tension and conflict.

As everyone in this audience knows so well, highly nationalistic and parochial trends have become evident during preparations for next year's conference. Pressures against international solutions are powerful and growing—in developed as well as developing nations. The present cod war between Iceland and Britain, and the proliferation of all kinds of jurisdictional claims, painfully underscore this reality and the inadequacy of present law. A "beggar thy neighbor" world of ocean politics can no longer be considered a mere alarmist fantasy.

Despite these trends, I remain convinced that we can forestall that new colonial race in the oceans President Johnson warned about some years ago, and Dean Rusk spoke of before a Congressional committee more recently.

I remain convinced that international accommodation is possible in the ocean. I remain convinced that a broadly agreed-upon and comprehensive international ocean regime can serve both the world's interest and the national interest. I remain convinced that the international community can bring stability and justice to the seas without compromising the security or the welfare of any nation with high stakes in the ocean.

Indeed, I believe that only with concerted action can our collective interests in the ocean be satisfied. Concerted action will call for vision and statesmanship of the highest order. What outcomes are needed?

- New international law to regulate the multiple and often conflicting uses of the sea.

- New principles of national behavior and self-restraint to insure that sheer military might and technological prowess do not become the sole arbiters of ocean affairs.
- New institutions and processes to enable all concerned nations to participate in decisions about the oceans.
- New arrangements to facilitate scientific study and interpretation of the marine environment.
- New policies toward ocean resources to insure rational and fair distribution of ocean wealth.
- New initiatives to help the world's poor countries to benefit more fully from the potential of the ocean.

In sum, we must nurture a new sense of international community toward the ocean. With it must come an overarching conception of the common good, a capacity for handling our inevitable disputes peacefully, and a set of new political habits and reciprocity, good faith and mutual accountability for our activities in the ocean. These goals are no longer utopian hopes. They now are the imperatives of prudent diplomacy.

This helps explain why the upcoming law of the sea conference is so important. For the conference represents the opening of a new political process for working together on shared ocean problems. So awesomely complex an enterprise as the conference cannot realistically expect to succeed in all major respects. Most governments, including the U.S., will likely have to settle for less than their maximum demands. Some tasks needing international attention will remain incomplete. Some outstanding issues will be settled ambiguously, if at all.

I am not urging that we slacken our efforts to achieve productive and timely results. Or that we move any less vigorously towards agreements which can halt the extension of competitive nationalism into the seas. What I am urging, however, is that we anticipate what inevitably must be the equivalent of a continuing and permanent law of the sea conference. History will not judge next year's session by some scoreboard tally of completed actions on a long agenda. What will count in the end will be whether today's statements leave the ocean as a lasting international resource and whether future conferences will have a durable and flexible political framework for collective action.

Several Resolutions currently before the U.S. Congress endorse the objectives that were envisioned in President Nixon's statement on ocean policy in May 1970. These Resolutions—as well as the President's statement—are the culmination of several years of study within the American government, debate among government officials and private interest groups, and negotiations with other countries. The Resolutions envision:

1. Protection of the freedom of the high seas, beyond a twelve-mile territorial sea, for navigation, communication, and scientific research.

2. Recognition that the protection of the ocean environment requires certain internationally agreed-upon duties of the international community as a whole.
3. Establishment of an international regime to regulate the development of deep seabed mineral resources.
4. Protection of our fisheries resources through coastal zone management of coastal and anadramous species, and international management of migratory species.

These are notable and worthwhile goals for the United States to pursue. They reflect a genuine concern on the part of our government to establish the beginnings of effective international regulation in an area covering 70 percent of the globe. In Congress I have supported and intend to continue to support legislative efforts designed to achieve these objectives.

We should all realize, though, that these are long-run goals that may take many years to achieve. The Law of the Sea Conference is not scheduled to convene in Chile until next May and it may be several years after the conclusion of the conference before we have any international agreements governing the use of the seas.

In the short run, we must be aware of and deal with very real problems that cannot be filed away while treaties are negotiated. Specifically, in this country, it is important for our government to formulate and pursue an interim oceans policy responsive to the needs of both the American people and the international community. Let me emphasize that this does not mean that the United States, in the short run, should adopt short-sighted policies, such as the American Mining Congress bill currently before the Senate Interior Committee. That proposal calls for the mining of hard mineral resources of the deep seabed under government protection. The unilateral adoption of such a policy course by our government would likely trigger an international race to colonize the seas, jeopardize American credibility at the Law of the Sea Conference, and be prejudicial to the future conclusion of international accords on the oceans.

No, what I am talking about is the need for this country to adopt enlightened interim policies that on the one hand are responsive to the needs of the American people, and on the other hand will not prejudice the future conclusion of international agreements. Such an enlightened policy course will not be easy to formulate. Nor will it be easy to pursue.

Let me take the example of fishing, a subject which is of prime concern to the people of the State of Maine. In Maine, fishermen are currently losing the livelihood of generations because as a nation we have not responded adequately to global developments, allowing our fishing industry to sink to low estate in our national priorities. Within the last ten years, the fishing effort of foreign fleets off our coasts has increased several fold. At any given time today, hundreds of large foreign vessels can be sighted within 100 miles of our shores.

In fact, the world's fishing effort is now so much greater than even a decade ago that stocks can be decimated in a season or two, a rate much faster than our traditionally cumbersome international negotiations can impose effective regulation upon them.

The experience in the Northwest Atlantic is illustrative of the gravity and immediacy of the situation. From 1952 through 1960, the U.S. fish catch from New England waters averaged about 700 million pounds a year, or 99 percent of the total catch from that area. In the early 1960s, the Russians, the Poles, the Germans, and other foreign fleets moved into these waters in large numbers. By 1969 the Soviet fleet was taking 836 million pounds, or 50 percent of the total catch from New England waters, while the U.S. catch had declined to about 418 million pounds, or about 25 percent of the area's total harvest.

The efforts of the International Commission for the Northwest Atlantic Fisheries to manage fisheries resources off the New England Coast unfortunately have failed miserably. Enforcement of current ICNAF regulations is virtually nonexistent because the Coast Guard does not have the capability to adequately police the Northwest Atlantic. In addition, the Coast Guard is not permitted to search when boarding foreign ships; it has to rely on the information provided by foreigners as to their landings off the New England Coast, and it has to contend with a multitude of local, state, regional, federal, and international jurisdictions, often having conflicting objectives.

Clearly, if regulation is to have any meaning, we must strengthen our ability to deal with fishing problems. As one means of doing this, we need to improve our knowledge of our fish resources and the nature of the difficulties faced by our domestic fishing industry. Second, we have to have not only more effective but better coordinated regulation between various entities so that our fishermen can compete with foreigners fishing off our waters. And finally, we need better enforcement of existing regulations.

What do we have? We have a situation in which the agency that can provide us with additional knowledge of our fisheries resources is losing both money and status. We have a situation in which our domestic enforcement arm—the Coast Guard—cannot begin to police the area with available resources. And we do not have the kind of workable regulation that might overcome these handicaps.

When the National Ocean and Atmospheric Administration was established in November 1970 as a direct result of the findings of the Stratton Commission, it was hoped—and intended—that this organization would become a strong focal point for ocean research programs. That need has not begun to be met. Yet three NOAA Marine laboratories, including one in Maine, will be closed down at the end of this month and other urgent programs will be curtailed for lack of funds. The Nixon Administration on the one hand is urging for this country a leading role in the international effort to preserve the ocean environment, and on the other hand has severely slashed the funding of the agency concerned with the research that might tell us how best to do it.

At stake is not corporate profits, but much-needed research and people's jobs—not panaceas for a dying industry but means to restore it to health. Unfortunately, the Administration is providing neither the health measures nor the kind of constructive proposals needed to meet the difficulties faced by our domestic fishing industry.

I do not suggest there is nothing the industry and the states can do. Certainly the differing regulations in neighboring states and regions concerning the same stock are both unnecessary and remediable. Unfair advantage offered to one renders all measures ineffective and unenforceable. And certainly the government can provide means to help our domestic fishermen to adopt the vessels and the gear that will enable them to compete. Much as I suspect that some of our fishermen would prefer that the competition simply fade away, becoming competitive is a more realistic view of the future.

Finally—and I am sure that this will be one of the conclusions of the Law of the Sea Conference regarding fisheries—all coastal states must have a recognized interest, not only in a fair share of the catch, but in seeing that our fish resources are not destroyed by visiting fleets that have only a passing interest, easily transferrable to new and more promising grounds. In recent years the depletion of haddock stocks on Georges Bank in the Northwest Atlantic has been so great as to cause a recommendation by the National Marine Fisheries Service that haddock fishing be suspended. And now, many experts are predicting similar fates for cod, sea scallops, lobster, and yellow-tail flounder.

To the extent that fishing stocks continue to vanish, the pressures for unilateral action to extend our fishing limits to 200 miles or to the edge of the continental shelf will increase, and such action may well be the most effective way to produce the international approach to management of the oceans that we need. If, in upcoming months, international agreement on global fisheries problems appears increasingly unlikely in the short term, then unilateral steps may have to be implemented to ensure the existence of a strong U.S. fishing industry.

Let me add that I am aware of the apparent illogic of advocating measures to benefit American fishermen, while condemning national measures that would benefit our mineral industry or indeed any number of other countries that have made unilateral claims in defense of this or that vital interest or special circumstance.

As far as I know, there is no shortage of critical minerals that compels us to scoop up manganese nodules in the next six months or even in the next six years. There is, however, something to be said for the view of fishermen that international treaties will be of little value if by the time they are negotiated, certain species will have been severely, or, in some cases, totally depleted because of overexploitation.

Additionally, there seems to be a distinction with a difference in situations in which interim measures might follow the path of predictable outcome. I believe there would be little argument that in some form, the preferential rights of coastal states over both the control and distribution of catch off their coasts will be substantially increased, whether that increase is measured in distance or by species or by some combination of both. If in fact that is a fair prognostication, I think it should be possible to take immediate measures without prejudice either to negotiating positions or to the form in which such rights may ultimately be couched.

For these reasons and as one measure that would bring some light to bear on this situation, I have supported a Senate Resolution calling for a national fisheries policy in this country. This Resolution, which was recently passed by the Senate, expresses Congressional support for a U.S. oceans policy that will permit us to deal more effectively with excessive foreign fishing off our coasts, and that will facilitate better coordination among our states. This bill recommends the utilization of existing entities—the Atlantic States, Gulf States, and Pacific Marine Fisheries Commissions—to gather facts, ideas, and suggestions needed to formulate policy and insure a strong commercial fishing industry in this country.

Another measure I have recently supported in Congress is legislation to have the lobster designated a creature of the continental shelf. This legislation would limit foreign lobster fishing off our coasts and help conserve existing lobster stocks, which are being depleted at an unusually rapid rate. In the bill, it is explicitly stated that this legislation, if enacted, would remain in force only until future international agreement is reached.

These initiatives, interim though they are, should help our fishing industry. But their effectiveness—no matter how well planned or prepared the steps—will depend ultimately on our ability to enforce the measures. With more than fifteen foreign countries fishing off our shores for a wide variety of stocks, enforcement will be impossible unless the regulations are simple, straightforward, and subject to easy surveillance. Even then, it will be essential that the Coast Guard be fully funded so that it will have the vessels and aircraft needed to ensure that the regulations are obeyed and that the heritage—as well as the livelihood—of our fishermen are protected.

I have chosen to speak at some length about our fisheries problems only in part because I know that coastal fishing jurisdiction will be an important—and perhaps critical—element in the successful resolution of law of the sea problems. I also speak to this question because I recognize the kind of political pressure that can build from jobs and revenue lost and resources depleted while diplomats negotiate.

As someone who has spent a large part of his career concerned with the preservation of our land and water, I believe in the imperative of a regime for the oceans that will treat them as the one world they are—the legacy of all mankind. I do not think that this great objective is either inconsistent with, or would be ill-served by, sensible interim measures to alleviate immediate fisheries problems.

George Kennan once wrote, "A political society does not live to conduct foreign policy . . . it conducts foreign policy in order to live." This aphorism should be kept in mind by our government today, if we are to ensure that the oceans will live and that their riches will be justly shared and nurtured for future generations.

Appendices

Appendix A:
Conference Program

Law of the Sea Institute Eighth Annual Conference
"The Emerging Regime of the Oceans"
June 18-21, 1973

PROGRAM

Monday, June 18

9:00   Opening Remarks, *Lewis M. Alexander*, Director, Law of the Sea Insti-
            tute
       Welcome, *Werner A. Baum*, President, University of Rhode Island
       Introduction, *Giulio Pontecorvo*, Columbia University—Program Chair-
            man

9:30   "Bloc Thinking About the Oceans: Accelerating Pluralism?"
       Paper: *John King Gamble, Jr.*, Assoc. Director, Law of the Sea Institute
       Panel: *Leigh Ratiner*, U.S. Department of the Interior (chairman)
                  Arvid Pardo, Woodrow Wilson International Center for Scholars
                  Kaldone G. Nweihed, Universidad Simon Bolivar, Caracas
                  Paul Lapointe, Department of External Affairs, Canada
       Discussion

2:00   "How Will the Deep Seabed Regime Be Organized?"
       Chairman: *John A. Knauss*
       Paper: *Andres Aguilar*, Ambassador of Venezuela to the United States
       Discussion Groups, Independence Hall—Leaders:

Francis Cameron, University of Rhode Island
Henry Esterly, CUNY-NYC Community College
Margaret Galey, Purdue University
Albert Koers, University of Utrecht
John Logue, Villanova University (Monday)
Roger Mesznik, Columbia University (Tuesday)
Joseph Nye, Harvard University
Giulio Pontecorvo, Columbia University
Atwood C. Wolf, Attorney, New York, N.Y.

6:00   Buffet-Reception, The Dunes Club, Narragansett, Rhode Island

Tuesday, June 19

9:00   "Technology Transfer"—Chairman: *Giulio Pontecorvo*
        Papers: *Surendra Patel*, Transfer of Technology Branch, United Nations
        C. Weiss, Jr., International Bank for Reconstruction and Development
        Panel: *Warren Wooster*, Rosensteil School of Manne & Atmospheric Science
        Herman T. Franssen, Woods Hole Oceanographic Institution
        Nelson Marshall, Intl. Ctr. for Marine Resource Dev., URI
        Emannuel G. Bello, IOC, UNESCO, Paris
        Discussion

2:00   "International Organizations and Technology Transfer"
        Chairman: *Giulio Pontecorvo*
        Paper: *Ivan Silva*, Indian Ocean Programme, FAO, Rome
        Discussion Groups as listed for Monday afternoon

6:00   Barbeque, Thirty Acre Pond, URI Campus

Wednesday, June 20

9:00   "Regimes for Special Situations"
        Chairman: *Richard Young*
        Papers: Islands, *Robert Hodgson*, The Geographer, U.S. Department of State
        Semi-Enclosed Seas, *Lewis Alexander*, University of Rhode Island
        Superports, *Allan Hirsch*, University of Utrecht, Netherlands
        Panel: *Albert W. Koers*, University of Utrecht, Netherlands
        H. Gary Knight, Louisiana State University Law Center
        John M. Bailey, Dept. of Foreign Affairs, Canberra, Australia

Richard Young, Counsellor at Law, Van Hornsville, New York
Discussion

2:00   Choice of afternoon activities:
Canadian Film, "Who Owns the Seas?" Edwards Hall
Bus trip to Wickford and Point Judith Fishermen's Cooperative Association
Bus trips to beach

8:00   Open House, Dr. Alexander's, 28 Beech Hill Road, Peace Dale, R.I.

Thursday, June 21

9:00   "Consequences of Intensive Ocean Utilization"
Chairman: *Thomas A. Clingan, Jr.* University of Miami School of Law
Papers: Flow of Ships, *Charles Bates*, U.S. Coast Guard
       Insurance, *George W. Handley*, Marsh & McLennan, Inc.
       Offshore Petroleum, *John P. Albers*, U.S. Geological Survey
Discussion

12:00 Foreign Participants' Luncheon, Memorial Union, URI

2:00   "The Scientific Aspects of Ocean Pollution"
Chairman: *William T. Burke*, University of Washington School of Law
Paper: *John A. Knauss*, Provost for Marine Affairs, URI
Panel: *John Lawrence Hargrove*, American Society of Int. Law (chairman)
       Earle E. Seaton, Puisne Judge, Supreme Court, Bermuda
       Branko Sambrailo, Yugoslav Academy of Sciences and Arts, Zagreb
       Raul Bazan, Mission of Chile to the United Nations
       Bernard H. Oxman, U.S. Department of State
Discussion

7:00   Banquet Address, *Hon. Edmund S. Muskie*, United States Senate

Appendix B:
List of Participants

Participants List
8th Annual Conference

Kathleen Agosta
Department of Oceanography
Dalhousie University
Halifax, Nova Scotia

Andres Aguilar
Ambassador of Venezuela to the
United States

Paul Ake, Cdr.
Joint Chiefs of Staff
Washington, D.C.

John Albers
Associate Chief Geologist
U.S. Geological Survey

Abraham Alemayehu
Master of Marine Affairs Program
University of Rhode Island

Lewis M. Alexander
Department of Geography
University of Rhode Island

Richard B. Allen
Atlantic Offshore Fish & Lobster
Association
Narragansett, Rhode Island

Harry H. Almond, Jr.
Sr. Attorney-Advisor
U.S. Department of Defense

Amer Araim
First Secretary
Mission of Iraq to the United States

John Bailey
Department of Foreign Affairs
Law of the Sea Section
Canberra, Australia

Daniel Bardonnet
Paris, France

Jessie H. Bartlett
Barrister of the Middle Temple
New York State Bar

Charles Bates
Science Advisor to the Commandant
and Chief Scientist
Office of Research and Development
United States Coast Guard
Washington, D.C.

Raul Bazan
Ambassador
Mission of Chile to the United Nations

Emmanuel G. Bello
Consultant with IOC
UNESCO
Paris, France

M.S. Berryman
Professor of Marine Sciences
Washington Technical Institute

Jean-Pierre Beurier
University of Nantes
France

Richard B. Bilder
University of Wisconsin Law School

F. Gilman Blake
Science and Technology Policy Office
National Science Foundation

Robert Bogttcher
House Foreign Affairs Committee
Washington, D.C.

Kells M. Boland
Defense Mapping Agency
Hydrographic Center
Washington, D.C.

John Botzum
Ocean Science News
Washington, D.C.

Edward Bradley, Jr.
Marine Resources Section
Department of Justice

Raul Branco
Ocean Economics and Technology
Branch
U.N. Secretariat

Gerhard Breuer
Federal Ministry of Transport
Merchant Marine Department
Hamburg, West Germany

Burdick H. Brittin
Ocean Affairs
U.S. Department of State

James E. Brown, Jr.
U.S. Coast Guard

James P. Brown
New York Times

Ralph T. Brown, Jr.
Community and Resource
Development
Clemson University Extension Service

William Burke
School of Law
University of Washington

Bess Burton
United States Government

Morris Busby, LCDR
United States Navy

Michael J.A. Butler
Marine Sciences Centre
McGill University

Francis X. Cameron
Master of Marine Affairs Program
University of Rhode Island

Flora C.C. Carmichael
Solicitor's Office
St. Andrews House
Edinburgh, Scotland

Jack Corbett
Department of Church
Government Relations
United Methodist Church

Ronald P. Cundick, Major
Defense Advisory Group
on the Law of the Sea
Office of the Judge Advocate General
of the Army

Jonathan I. Charney
Vanderbilt University School of Law

Daniel S. Cheever
Graduate School of Public and
International Affairs
University of Pittsburgh

Chen Tsien
Permanent Mission of the
People's Republic of China
to the United Nations

Patrick N. Chipunqu
Central Fisheries Research Institute
Zambia

Francis T. Christy, Jr.
Resources for the Future, Inc.
Washington, D.C.

M.O. Clement
Department of Economics
Dartmouth College

Thomas A. Clingan, Jr.
School of Law
University of Miami

Burton T. Coffey
National Fisherman
Camden, Maine

Couglas Comitta
Office of the Legal Advisor
U.S. Department of State

E.J. Cooper
Marine Sciences Branch
Department of the Environment
Canada

W. Harvey Dalton
Ocean Law Program
University of Miami

Jose Carlos de Magalhaes
University of Sáo Paulo
Brazil

Frederic G. Derocher, LCDR
Law of the Sea Task Force
U.S. Department of Defense

John R. Dewenter, Captain
United States Navy
U.S. Department of State

Jean-Andre Diaz
Institute of the Law of Peace and
Development
Nice, France

Stuart Dill
Christian Science Monitor

Herbert Drechsler
School of Mines
Columbia University

Nora Kathryn Ducan
Tidelands Section
Office of the Attorney General
of Louisiana

W.R. Edeson
University of Wales Institute of
Science and Technology
United Kingdom

Clark Eichlberger
United Nations Committee to
Study the Organization of Peace

Frederick W. Ellis
Tidelands Section
Office of the Attorney General
of Louisiana

Octavio Errazuriz
Second Secretary
Embassy of Chile

Henry Esterly
CUNY-NYC Community College

Robert Farmer
Master of Marine Affairs Program
University of Rhode Island

Nelvin Farstad
Institute of Fisheries Economics
School of Economics & Business
Administration
Bergen, Norway

James R. Finnegan
The International Nickel Company
of Canada, Limited

Harold Fisher
Marine Board of the N.A.E.
National Academy of Engineering

Herman T. Franssen
Woods Hole Oceanographic Institute

Maureen Franssen
Woods Hole Oceanographic Institute

William E. Fuller
Fuller, Lawton and Moyle
New York

Margaret E. Galey
Department of Political Science
Purdue University

John K. Gamble, Jr.
Law of the Sea Institute

John Gantus
San Diego Law Review

Thomas R. Gill
San Diego Law Review

R. Del Giorno
U.S. Coast Guard

Martin Glassner
Department of Geography
Southern Connecticut State College

Edgar Gold
Faculty of Law
Dalhousie University
Halifax, Nova Scotia

Jim Griffin
ICMRD
University of Rhode Island

G.W. Haight
Forsyth, Decker & Murray
New York

George Handley
Marsh & McLennan
New York

John L. Hargrove
Director of Research
American Society of International Law

Charles M. Hassett
University of Louisville School of Law

Moritaka Hayashi
Office of Legal Affairs
United Nations Secretariat

William C. Herrington, Jr.
Staffordville, Ct.

Allan Hirsch
Marine Ecosystems Analysis
Program, NOAA
U.S. Department of Commerce

Robert Hodgson
The Geographer
U.S. Department of State

Ho Li-Liang
Permanent Mission of the
People's Republic of China
to the United Nations

Ann L. Hollick
Ocean Policy Project
Johns Hopkins University

Brian J. Hoyle
Law Department
Gulf Oil Co.

Donald L. Humphreys
Counsel
Utah International, Inc.

Michael J. Jacobs
Staff Attorney
U.S. Coast Guard

Jon L. Jacobson
School of Law
University of Oregon

Milton G. Johnson
Office of the NOAA Corps
U.S. Department of Commerce

Robert Johnson
Mardela Corporation
Burlingame, Ca.

Peter A. Joseph
Naval War College

Karl Wm. Kieninger
National Oceanic and Atmospheric
Administration
U.S. Department of Commerce

Judith Kildow
Massachusetts Institute of Technology

Campbell Killefer
Office of Coastal Environment
National Oceanic & Atmospheric
Administration

Charles P. Kindregan
Suffolk University

Lauriston King
National Science Foundation
Washington, D.C.

John A. Knauss
Provost for Marine Affairs
University of Rhode Island

H. Gary Knight
Louisiana State University Law Center

Albert W. Koers
Institute of International Law
University of Utrecht, The
Netherlands

Robert J. Korengold
U.S. Information Agency

Dale C. Krause
Division of Oceanography
UNESCO, Paris

Fernando Labastida
General Legal Division
United Nations

P.A. Lapointe
Law of the Sea Section
Department of External Affairs
Canada

Vincent D. Lasse
Mission of Trinidad and Tobago to the
United Nations

Peter Richard Latham, Lt. Cdr.
U.S. Navy
Naval War College

Horace Leavit
Master of Marine Affairs Program
University of Rhode Island

E.G. Lee
Department of External Affairs
Canada

Bert B. Lockwood, Jr.
Center for International Studies
New York University

John J. Logue
World Order Research Institute
Villanova University

D.C. Maclellan
Marine Sciences Center
McGill University

Dennis F. McCoy, Lt. Cdr.
Office the Judge Advocate General
Department of the Navy

John E. McCracken
Attorney
Shaheen Natural Resources Co., Inc.

Michael MacGwire
Dalhousie University
Halifax, Nova Scotia

Kay McKeough
Congressional Fellow
Senate Commerce Committee

Maxwell S. McKnight
National Petroleum Council

Scott Marston
Master of Marine Affairs Program
University of Rhode Island

Mary Anne Mason
Center of Concern
Washington, D.C.

Oscar Maurtua
Second Secretary
Embassy of Peru
Washington, D.C.

Yilma Makonnen
Imperial Ethiopian Navy and
The Fletcher School of Law and
Diplomacy

William R. Mansfield
New Zealand Mission to the
United Nations

Nelson Marshall
ICMRD
University of Rhode Island

Alexander Melamid
New York University

Roger Mesznik
Graduate School of Business
Columbia University

Hal Mills
Department of the Environment
Canada

Frederick Monroe
Center for Advanced International
Studies
University of Miami

David L. Moore
Institute for Marine Studies
University of Washington

Michael M. Moore
Counsel
Defense Mapping Agency

Chandler Morse
Cornell University

Gordon Napier
Master of Marine Affairs Program
University of Rhode Island

John Neery
World Magazine

Stewart B. Nelson
Special Assistant
Office of the Oceanographer of the
Navy

Frank Njenga
Mission of Kenya to the
United Nations

Robert D. Nordstrom
Fishery Products Division
National Canners Association

Kaldone G. Nweihed
INTECMAR
Simon Bolivar University
Caracas, Venezuela

Joseph Nye
Center of International Affairs
Harvard University

Hyman Orlin
Asst. for Science Activities
National Ocean Survey
NOAA

Francisco Orrego-Vicuna
Senior Legal Officer
Organization of American States

Bernard H. Oxman
Asst. Legal Adviser for Ocean Affairs
U.S. Department of State

Arvid Pardo
Ocean Studies Program
Woodrow Wilson International Center
for Scholars

Choon-ho Park
Woodrow Wilson International Center
for Scholars

Jeffrey C. Peck
U.S. Merchant Marine Academy

Alan F. Penn
Geography Department
McGill University
Montreal, Canada

David Peterson
U.S. Department of Commerce
Washington, D.C.

Donat Pharand
Faculty of Law, Civil Law Section
University of Ottawa

Giulio Pontecorvo
Graduate School of Business
Columbia University

Jean-François Pulvenis
Institute of the Law of Peace and
Development

Pemmaraju Screenivasa Rao
Fellow, Marine Policy Program
Woods Hole Oceanographic Institution

Leigh S. Ratiner
Office of Ocean Resources
U.S. Department of the Interior

Orlando Rebagliate
Mission of Argentina to the
United Nations

Jack H. Regentin
U.S. Government

Felix Reuben
Department of the Environment
Canada

G.A. Rogers
Toronto, Canada

Niels Rorholm
Department of Resource Economics
University of Rhode Island

Frank P. Rossomando, Jr.
U.S. Government

William F. Royce
National Marine Fisheries Service
Department of Commerce

Judy G. Russell
American Petroleum Institute
Washington, D.C.

Alan Ryan
Center for Advanced International
Studies
University of Miami

Jawad Sakka
Legal Department
Ministry of Petroleum & Mineral
Resources
Saudi Arabia

Branko Sambrailo
Yugoslav Academy of Sciences
and Arts
Zagreb, Yugoslavia

Steinar Sandvik
The Norwegian Fisherman's
Association
Trondheim, Norway

Frederick Schaefer
Englewood Cliffs, New Jersey

Gerald S. Schatz
National Academy of Sciences
Washington, D.C.

Gunnar G. Schram
Mission of Iceland to the
United Nations

Justice E.E. Seaton
Puisne Judge
Supreme Court
Bermuda

John W. Sellers
Master of Marine Affairs
University of Rhode Island

Caesar D. Sereseres
School of Social Sciences
University of California

John Seymour
Department of Management/Sea Grant
Texas A&M University

L.I.J. Silva
Department of Fisheries, FAO-UN
Rome

Marvin L. Skelton
Houston, Texas

Lucy Sloan
Press/GSO Associates
Cambridge, Massachusetts

Emory C. Smith
Legal Adviser
Office of the Oceanographer of the
Navy

Robert H. Stockman
Institute for Marine Studies
University of Washington

Terese Sulikowski
Brookings Institution
Washington, D.C.

Eisuke Suzuki
Yale University Law School

Joseph C. Sweeney
Fordham University Law School

Phiphat Tangsubkul
University Chiengmai, Thailand

Milan Thamsborg
Copenhagen, Denmark

G.K. Tikhonov
United Nations Secretariat
New York, New York

D.L. Tough
Department of Energy, Mines
and Resources
Canada

Pius Uchegbu
Institute of International Relations
University of West Indies
Trinidad

Roland Wachs
University of Hamburg
West Germany

Mary Hildegrade Walsh
Department of External Affairs
Canada

Lowell Wakefield
Sea Grant Program
University of Alaska

C. Weiss, Jr.
Science Adviser
International Bank for Reconstruction
and Development

Millie Weiss
Overseas Development Council
Washington, D.C.

Linton Wells, II
Graduate Student
The Johns Hopkins University

Jack Werner
Naval Oceanographic Office

James A. Wexler
National Oceanic and Atmospheric
Administration
U.S. Department of Commerce

C.I.J. Whebell
Department of Geography
University of Western Ontario

Wendy Witherspoon
Washington, D.C.

Atwood C. Wolf, Jr.
Counsellor at Law
New York, New York

Warren Wooster
Rosensteil School of Marine and
Atmospheric Science
University of Miami

Rebecca Wright
Office of Ocean Resources
Department of Interior

Captain Paul Yost
Special Assistant for Law of the Sea
Office of the Chief Counsel
U.S. Coast Guard

Richard Young
Attorney at Law
Van Hornesville, New York

James V. Zimmerman
Ocean Policy Project
Johns Hopkins University

James W. Zirkle
University of Mississippi School of Law

Notes to Chapters

Notes to Chapters

Notes to Chapter 1

1. William H. Riker, *The Theory of Political Coalitions* (New Haven: Yale University Press, 1962); Sven Groennings, E.W. Kelley, and Michael Leiserson (eds.), *The Study of Coalition Behavior* (New York: Holt, Rinehart and Winston, 1970).

2. Thomas Hovet, Jr., *Bloc Politics in the United Nations* (Cambridge, Mass.: Harvard University Press, 1960), p. 13.

3. William T. Burke, "Some Thoughts on Fisheries and a New Conference on the Law of the Sea." Law of the Sea Institute Occasional Paper #9, March 1971, p. 8.

Notes to Chapter 4

1. This paper draws heavily upon the author's earlier studies, "La Transferencia de Tecnologia a los paises en desarrollo" (Foro Internacional, vol. XIII, No. 1, El Colegio de Mexico, 1972); and "The Cost of Technological Dependence" (CERES, FAO, Rome, March-April 1973). The opinions expressed here are personal and should not be attributed to UNCTAD, of which the author is a staff member.

2. Lord C.P. Snow, *The Two Cultures and a Second Look* (New York, 1963) p. 73.

3. For details, see P.M.S. Blackett, "Technology and World Advancement" in *Advancement of Science*, Vol. XV (1957); Simon S. Kuznets, *Modern Economic Growth: Rate, Structure and Spread* (Yale University Press, 2nd printing March 1967) p. 463; and also David S. Landes, *The Unbound Pro-*

motheus: The Technological Change and Industrial Development in Western Europe from 1750 to the Present (Cambridge University Press, 1969), pp. 27-28.

4. For Details, see the author's "Economic Distance Between Nations: Its Origin, Measurement and Outlook," *Economic Journal*, March 1964.

5. Professor H. Dingle, in an extensive review of J.D. Bernal's pioneering work, "The Social Function of Science," pointed out ten different ways in which Bernal had used the concept "science." In reply to this criticism, Prof. Bernal stated that for a concept "so wide-ranging in time, connection and category," multiplicity of aspect and reference must be the rule. See J.D. Bernal, *Science and History* (Pelican Books, 1969), pp. 30-31.

6. For a discussion of some of these features, see Kuznets, *op. cit.* (Note 3), pp. 286, 287, and 501.

7. See the author's "World Economy in Transition (1850-2060)," In C.H. Feinstein (ed.) *Socialism, Capitalism and Economic Growth*, Essays presented to Maurice Dobb (Cambridge University Press, 1967), p. 257. During the last two decades, the growth rate has been as high as 5 percent, or even higher, for a number of countries in both the East and West.

8. See the author's study, "World Economy in Transition," in Feinstein (ed.), *op. cit.*, pp. 256-257.

9. Over a century ago, this idea was expressed, in words which have quite a contemporary ring, by Karl Marx in his Preface to the first edition of *Capital*. Talking of Germany in the context of developments in England, he stated: "The country that is more developed industrially only shows, to the less developed, the image of its own future." See *Capital* (Modern History Edition, New York), Vol. 1, p. 13.

10. For details, see Landes, *op. cit.*, particularly Chapter 3, "Continental Emulation" and Chapter 4, "Closing the Gap." As Landes put it: "The 1850's and 1860's then were the years when Western Europe caught up with Britain. Their very lateness now turned to their advantage." *Ibid.*, pp. 229-230.

11. See UNCTAD Study, Chapter III, "Transfer of Technology, Including Know-How and Patents; Elements of a Programme of Work for UNCTAD" (TD/B/310).

12. The elements of such technical knowledge may be grouped in stages: (a) *pre-investment and construction stage*: feasibility of studies and market surveys, choosing among a range of technological alternatives, engineering design and selection of machinery, plant construction and installation of equipment and process technology proper; and (b) operation stage: management and operation of production facilities, marketing and improving efficiency of established processes by minor innovations. For a detailed discussion of the direct and indirect ways of acquiring these elements, see "The Channels and Mechanisms for the Transfer of Technology from Developed to Developing Countries," a study by Charles Cooper with the cooperation of Francisco Sercovitch (UNCTAD doc. number TD/B/AC.11/5).

13. See Gunnar Myrdal, *Economic Theory and Undeveloped Regions* (Bombay: Asia Publishing House, 1958).

14. Based on UNCTAD study, "Transfer of Technology," prepared for the Third Conference, Santiago, in April-May 1972 (TC/106), paragraphs 9-14; also see for details, UNCTAD document TD/B/310, Chapter 11.

15. See Appendix 4-1, for a list of UNCTAD studies on the subject. Most of the factual information in this paper is based on these studies.

16. For details on the number of scientists and expenditure on science, see J.D. Bernal, *Science in History* (Pelican Books), Vol. II, p. 659 and Vol. III, p. 714. 17. "Policies relating to the transfer of technology of the countries of the Andean Pact: their foundations," a study of the Junta del Acuerdo de Cartagena (TD/107).

Notes to Chapter 8

1. See *International Boundary Study, Series A, No. 24*, "Continental Shelf Boundary: Iran-Saudi Arabia," July 6, 1970, Office of the Geographer.

2. Ian Brownlie (ed.), *Basic Documents in International Law*, Oxford: Oxford University Press, 1969, p. 72.

3. *Ibid.*, p. 73.

4. See *International Boundary Study No. 13*, "China-Hong Kong Boundary," April 5, 1962, U.S. Department of State, Office of the Geographer.

5. Brownlie, *op. cit.*, pp. 7-71.

6. See *International Boundary Study, Series A, No. 48*, "Straight Baselines: Finland," U.S. Department of State, Office of the Geographer.

7. International Court of Justice, *Judgment: Fisheries Case (United Kingdom v. Norway)*, 1951.

8. D. McLoughlin, "Statement delivered . . . [before the] Committee on the Peaceful Uses of the Seabed. . . . "

9. M. Kusumaatmadja, "The Legal Regimes of Archipelagoes: Problems and Issues," *The Law of the Sea, Needs and Interests of Developing Countries* . . . 7th Conference Proceedings, Law of the Sea Institute, (February 1973) University of Rhode Island, p. 166.

10. R.D. Hodgson and L.M. Alexander, *Towards an Objective Analysis of Special Circumstances* . . . , Occasional Paper No. 13 (April 1972), Law of the Sea Institute, Kingston, R.I.

11. *Ibid.*, p. 49.

12. *Ibid.*, p. 49.

13. Brownlie, *op. cit.*, p. 73.

14. Robert D. Hodgson, "Critique," in *The Law of the Sea: International Rules and Organizations for the Sea*, Proceedings of the Third Annual Conference of the Law of the Sea Institute, Kingston, R.I., 1969, pp. 194-196.

15. See *International Boundary Study, Series A., No. 45*, "Maritime Boundary: Mexico-U.S." (Aug. 11, 1972), U.S. Department of State, Office of the Geographer.

16. Brownlie, *op. cit.*, p. 98.

17. *Ibid.*, p. 100.

18. S.W. Boggs, "Delimitation of Seaward Areas under National Jurisdiction," *The American Journal of International Law* 45 (2) (April 1951): 257.

19. Hodgson and Alexander, *op. cit.*, pp. 17 ff.

20. *Ibid.*, pp. 17-20.

21. See *International Boundary Study, Series A, No. 2,* "Continental Shelf Boundary: Norway/Sweden" (Jan. 22, 1970), U.S. Department of State, Office of the Geographer.

22. See *International Boundary Study, Series A, No. 10,* "Continental Shelf Boundary: The North Sea" (Mar. 2, 1970), U.S. Department of State, Office of the Geographer.

23. Northcutt Ely, "Seabed Boundaries Between Coastal States: The Effect to Be Given Islets as 'Special Circumstances,' " ECAFE Committee on Industry and Natural Resources, *Seminar on Petroleum Legislation with Particular Reference to Offshore Operations,* Bangkok (Oct. 18-25, 1971), p. 23. Reprinted in *The International Lawyer* 219, 1972.

24. See *International Boundary Study, Series A, No. 9,* "Continental Shelf Boundary: Italy-Yugoslavia" (Feb. 20, 1970), U.S. Department of State, Office of the Geographer.

25. See *International Boundary Study, Series A, No. 24,* "Continental Shelf Boundary: Iran-Saudi Arabia" (July 6, 1970), U.S. Department of State, Office of the Geographer.

26. See *International Boundary Study, Series A, No. 18,* "Continental Shelf Boundary: Abu Dhabi-Qatar" (May 29, 1970), U.S. Department of State, Office of the Geographer.

27. Ely, *op. cit.*, p. 26.

28. See *International Boundary Study, Series A, No. 24,* "Continental Shelf Boundary: Iran-Saudi Arabia" (July 6, 1970), U.S. Department of State, Office of the Geographer.

29. Pantelleria: 32 sq. mi., c. 10,000 pop., isle; Linosa: 2 sq. mi., c. 44 pop., isle; Lampedusa: 8 sq. mi., c. 3,500 pop., isle; Lampione: less than 1 sq. mi., islet.

30. See *International Boundary Study, Series A, No. 1,* "Continental Shelf Boundary, Indonesia-Malaysia" (January 21, 1970), U.S. Department of State, Office of the Geographer.

31. Brownlie, *op. cit.*, p. 99.

32. D.M. Taylor, "Man-made permafrost islands for offshore drill sites?" *Ocean Industry* 7 (11) (November 1972), Gulf Publishing Company, Houston, p. 42.

Notes to Chapter 9

1. For data on the extent of coastal state's continental shelves, see *International Boundary Study, Series A, No. 46 Limits in the Seas,* "Theoretical Areal Allocations of Seabed to Coastal States . . . ." (August 12, 1972), Washington, D.C.: Department of States, Bureau of Intelligence and Research, Office of the Geographer.

2. Fisheries data in Table I from J.A. Gulland (ed.), *The Fish Resources of the Ocean,* FAO Fisheries Technical Paper No. 97, Rome: Food and Agricultural Organization of the United Nations, 1970.

3. For offshore oil and gas data, see John P. Albers, et. al., *Summary Petroleum and Selected Mineral Statistics for 120 Countries, Including Offshore Areas*, Geological Survey Paper 817, Washington, D.C.: United States Government Printing Office, 1973.

4. See "Relationship of Major Currents, Major Shipping Routes and a 200 Nautical Mile Pollution Zone," Map prepared by the Office of The Geographer, Bureau of Intelligence and Research, U.S. Department of State, Washington, D.C., 1973.

5. There are no generally recognized criteria for differentiating between "strategic" and "nonstrategic" straits. For a discussion of this problem, see Robert W. Smith, "An Analysis of the Concept 'Strategic Quality of International Straits': A Geographical Perspective with Focus on Petroleum Tanker Transit and on the Malacca Strait," unpublished Masters thesis, Department of Geography, University of Rhode Island, Kingston, R.I., 1973. See also, Robert D. Hodgson, "Maritime Commerce in Selected Areas of High Congestion," *Proceedings of the Third Law of the Sea Workshop*, Kingston, R.I., University of Rhode Island, in press.

Notes to Chapter 11

1. Bos Kalis Westminster Dredging Group N.V., *Sea Island Project*, Papendrecht 1972. For a related study, see U.S. Department of Commerce, *Feasibility of a North Atlantic Deep-Water Oil Terminal*, July 1972.

2. See also, "Sea Islands for Waste Disposal," *Shipbuilding and Transport Review* (May 1972), pp. 4-7.

3. The *Draft Ocean Space Treaty*, submitted by Malta to the U.N. Seabed Committee, U.N. Doc. A/AC. 138/53 (August 23, 1971), specifically extends this right to all areas included in "national ocean space."

4. Which reads, in part, "The coastal State must not hamper innocent passage through the territorial sea"; U.N.T.S. 516, p. 214.

5. Article 16, para. 3 of the 1958 Geneva Territorial Sea Convention.

6. See Article 16, para. 4 of the 1958 Geneva Territorial Sea Convention.

7. U.N.T.S. 450, p. 82.

8. U.N.T.S. 499, p. 312.

9. Article 5, para. 2.

10. See Article 2, para. 2 of the 1958 Geneva Continental Shelf Convention.

11. Article 2, 1958 Geneva Convention on the High Seas.

12. See Article 5, paras. 2 and 3, 1958 Geneva Convention on the Continental Shelf.

13. The proposed U.S. *Deepwater Port Facilities Act 1973* makes the granting of a license for the construction and operation of a deepwater port facility, inter alia, conditional upon the requirement that this facility will not " . . . unreasonably interfere with international navigation or other reasonable uses of the high seas. . . .", Sec. 103 (a) (2).

14. See Sec. 103 (a) (3) of the proposed U.S. Deepwater Port Facilities Act 1973.

15. See Article 1 of the 1958 Geneva Territorial Sea Convention; however, there is no international agreement with respect to the breadth of the territorial sea.

16. See H. Gary Knight, "International Legal Aspects of Deep Draft Harbor Facilities," *Journal of Maritime Law of Commerce* 4:389, 1973.

17. This approach was stressed by the representative of Belgium in the U.N. Seabed Committee; see Knight, *ibid.*, p. 387.

18. Sec. 111 of the U.S. *Deepwater Port Facilities Act of 1973* provides that foreign vessels and nationals using such facilities are subject to the jurisdiction of the United States.

19. For an English translation of the act, see H.F. van Panhuys and M.J. van Emde Boas, "Legal Aspects of Pirate Broadcasting. A Dutch Approach," *American Journal of International Law* 60: 340, 1966.

20. See *Report of the Committee on the Peaceful Uses of the Seabed and the Ocean Floor Beyond Limits of National Jurisdiction*, GAOR, 27th session, supplement No. 21 (A/8721), p. 8, item 18.

Notes to Chapter 12

1. *Lloyd's Register of Shipping Statistical Tables 1972*, London, 1973.

2. Because it has been impossible to place all units of measurement into the metric system, 1 metric ton equals 0.984 long ton (2,240 pounds). Deadweight tons are expressed in long tons of cargo, stores, fuel, passengers, and crew when the vessel is loaded to maximum summer loadline. Gross tons of shipping is equal to 100 cubic ft. (0.028 cubic meters) of ship capacity for cargo, stores, and passengers and crew, with certain minor exceptions.

3. *SS McLean* sailed 3,045 nautical miles from Bishop Rock to Ambrose Light in 3 days, 21 hours and 5 minutes for a 32.71 knot average; the return passage was 3 days, 20 hrs. and 30 min. for a 33.005 knot average. The *SS Sealand* sailed 4,424 nautical miles from Seattle to Kobe in 5 days, 23 hours and 38 minutes for a 30.82 knot average.

4. M.W.H. Peebles, "A Forecast of the Liquified Natural Gas Trade in the 1980's," *Proceedings* of the Third International Conference on Liquified Natural Gas, Washington, D.C., 1972.

5. R.R.V. Wiederkehr, "A Forecast of 1970-1985 World Shipping," Tech. Report 199, SACLANT ASW Research Center, La Spezia, Italy, 1972.

6. *British Statistical Review of the World Oil Industry—1972*, British Petroleum, London, England, 1973.

7. "Annual Statistics of Casualties," *Proceedings*, Marine Safety Council, U.S. Coast Guard, Washington, D.C., Vol. 30, No. 1 (January 1973).

8. Unpublished preliminary data derived by Inputs Panel, Ocean Affairs Board Airlie House Conference on "Input, Fates, and Effects of Petroleum in the Marine Environment," May 1973, Washington, D.C.

9. K.G. Brummage, British Petroleum Company, London, England, 1973.

10. S.A. Madsen, F.X. Nicastro, and D.J. Schumacher, "Aviation/ Marine—A Study of Contrast," *Proceedings* 17th Annual Tanker Conference, American Petroleum Institute, Washington, D.C., 1972.

11. V.R.V. Winkelman, "Computer Controlled Automatic Ship Positioning in Rotterdam Harbour," RCTM Meeting, April 1970, San Francisco (Vol. 1, "Electronics in Harbor Operations").

Notes to Chapter 15

1. John A. Knauss, "Factors Influencing a U.S. Position in a Future Law of the Sea Conference," *Occasional Paper No. 10, Law of the Sea Institute* (Kingston: University of Rhode Island, 1971), p. 31.

2. Karl K. Turekian, "Rivers, Tributaries and Estuaries" in Donald W. Hood (ed.), *Impingement of Man on the Oceans*, New York: Wiley-Interscience, 1971, p. 738.

3. A.C. Delaney, Audrey Clair Delaney, D.W. Parkins, J.J. Griffin, E.D. Goldberg and B.E.F. Reimann, "Airborne dust collected at Barbadoes," *Geochimica and Cosmochemica Acta* 31 (1967): 855-909.

4. The ocean is about 3.5% salt; (if you were to take a kilogram of seawater and evaporate it you would be left with about 35 grams of salt). Within the ocean you might expect to find at least traces of every stable chemical element yet discovered; albeit a few elements are there in such small quantities that they yet defy our best analytical techniques.

5. As a result, although there is only ten times more sodium than iron entering the ocean from rivers, sodium is 10 million times more abundant than iron in the ocean. In fact, sea salt is about 85% simple table salt; namely, sodium chloride.

6. J.P. Riley and R. Chester, *Introduction to Marine Chemistry*, London and New York: Academic Press, 1971, p. 465.

7. R.J. Gibbs, "Circulation in the Amazon River Estuary and Adjacent Atlantic Ocean," *Journal of Marine Research* 28 (1970): 113-123.

8. Lloyd Dunlap, "Mercury: anatomy of a pollution problem," *Chemical and Engineering News* (July 5, 1971): 22-34.

9. Along with all the other scientific revolutions of the past quarter of a century, there has been one in analytical chemistry. It is now possible to make measurements with a precision and accuracy that were undreamed of a few years ago. Equally important, these measurements can be made with increasing speed and ease. Fifteen years ago measuring the mercury content of swordfish in parts per million would be a long and arduous task and would be of sufficient difficulty that the best analytical chemical laboratories in the world would require months before they could make such a measurement with any degree of confidence.

10. The amount of mercury in seawater is about 5×10^{-11} grams of mercury per gram of seawater. The FDA ban on swordfish is based on consistently finding mercury levels in excess of their limit of 5×10^{-7} grams of mercury per gram of swordfish flesh.

11. G.E. Miller, P.M. Grant, R. Kishore, F.J. Steinbruger, F.S. Rowland, and V.P. Guinn, "Mercury concentrations in museum specimens of tuna and swordfish," *Science* 175 (1972): 1121-1122.

12. Herbert V. Weiss, Minoru Koide and Edward Goldberg, "Mercury in a Greenland ice sheet: Evidence of recent impact by man," *Science* 174 (1971): 692-694.

13. National Academy of Sciences, *Marine Environmental Quality*, a report of the Ocean Science Committee of the Ocean Affairs Board of the National Academy of Sciences, Washington, D.C.: National Academy of Science, 1971, p. 107.

14. Council on Environmental Quality, *Ocean Dumping, a National Policy*, Washington, D.C.: U.S. Government Printing Office, 1970, p. 45.

15. National Petroleum Council, *Law of the Sea, Particular aspects affecting the Petroleum Industry*, Washington, D.C.: National Petroleum Council, 1973, p. 90.

16. National Petroleum Council, *Petroleum Resources Under the Ocean Floor*, Washington, D.C.: National Petroleum Council, 1969, p. 105.

17. John Albers, "Offshore Petroleum: Its Geography and Technology," in John Gamble and Giulio Pontecorvo (eds.), *Law of the Sea: The Emerging Regime of the Oceans* (Cambridge: Ballinger, 1974).

18. Edward Goldsmith, Robert Allen, Michael Allaby, John Davall, and Sam Lawrence, "A Blueprint for Survival," *The Ecologist* 2 (London, Ecosystems Ltd., 1972): 1-65.

19. Donella H. Meadows, Dennis L. Meadows, Joyen Randers, William W. Bebrens III, *The Limits to Growth*, a report for the Club of Rome's project in the predicament of mankind, London: Earth Island Limited, 1972, p. 205.

20. *Ibid.*

21. See note 18 above.

22. Joel Darmstadter, with Perry D. Teitelbaum and Jaroslav G. Polach, *Energy in the World Economy*, Baltimore: the Johns Hopkins Press for Resources for the Future, 1971, p. 876.

23. According to Darmstadter (*ibid.*) the annual per capita increase in energy consumption in the U.S. for the three year period 1965-68 was 3.8 percent. By comparison it was 0.9 percent in Africa and 12.5 percent in Japan for the same period. A growth rate for the developing world comparable to that of Japan would effectively equalize per capita energy consumption by the year 2000 if all other nations grew at 3 percent per year once they reached the U.S. level.

24. Claire Patterson, "Artifacts of Man: Lead," in Donald W. Hood (ed.), *Impingement of Man on the Oceans*, New York: Wiley-Interscience, 1971, p. 738.

25. Donald W. Hood and C. Peter McRoy, "Uses of the Ocean," in Donald W. Hood (ed.), *Impingement of Man on the Oceans*, New York: Wiley-Interscience, 1971, p. 738.

26. *Ibid.*

27. Mary A. Tiffany and John W. Winchester, "Surface water imports of iodine, bromine, and chlorine to Lake Huron," *Proceedings, Twelfth*

Conference on Great Lakes Research, International Association for Great Lakes Research (1969): 789-800. For comparison the authors estimate the residence time of Lake Huron at about 20 years.

28. The volume of the Mediterranean is about 4 million cubic kilometers. Nearly all of the exchange is with the Atlantic through the Straits of Gibraltar which is estimated to be the order of 150 cubic kilometers per day.

29. There have been a number of efforts in the past few years to estimate the amount of petroleum hydrocarbons entering the ocean. The most recent is a National Academy of Sciences study in preparation which reportedly puts the total input at 6.0 million metric tons per year. Of this, some ten percent comes from natural seeps in the ocean. The remaining 90 percent is from man's activities and is about equally divided between losses related to primary production activities (including tanker transportation) and that related to waste disposal (including atmospheric transport of exhaust emissions).

30. John W. Farrington and James G. Quinn, "Petroleum hydrocarbons and fatty acids in waste water effluents," *Journal Water Pollution Control Federation* 43 (1973): 704-712.

31. James O. Keith, Leon P. Woods, Jr., and Eldridge G. Hunt, "Reproductive failure in brown pelicans on the Pacific Coast," in *Transactions of the 35th North American Wildlife and Natural Resource Conference*, Washington, D.C.: Wildlife Management Institute, 1970, pp. 56-63.

32. Council on Environmental Quality, *Environmental Quality, the first annual report of the Council of Environmental Quality*, Washington, D.C.: U.S. Government Printing Office, 1970, p. 326.

33. National Academy of Sciences, *Chlorinated Hydrocarbons in the marine environment*, Washington D.C.: National Academy of Sciences, 1971, p. 42.

34. The Ocean Science Committee of the National Academy of Sciences, which sponsored the earlier study, is conducting the review and is expected to produce an updated evaluation.

35. George R. Harvey, William G. Steinhauer, and John M. Teal, "Polychlorobiphenyls in North Atlantic Ocean Water," *Science* 180 (1973): 643-644.

36. Study of Critical Environmental Problems (SCEP), *Man's Impact on the Global Environment; Assessment and Recommendation of Action*, Cambridge, Mass., The MIT Press, 1970, p. 319.

37. National Science Foundation, *Baseline Studies of Pollutants in the Marine Environment and Research Recommendations: The International Decade of Ocean Exploration Baseline Conference May 24-26, 1972*. E.D. Goldberg, Convener, Washington, D.C.: National Science Foundation, 1972, p. 54.

38. *Ibid.*

39. Some scientists are hopeful of developing bacterial strains that can be turned loose on an oil spill and break down the oil into harmless byproducts. Although there are periodic newspaper reports of new developments in this area, a practical scheme would appear to be some distance away.

40. H.W. Jannasch, K. Einjellen, C.O. Wirsen, and A. Farmanfarmian, "Microbial degradation of organic matter in the deep sea," *Science* 171 (1971): 672-675.

41. John McN. Sieburth and Allan S. Dietz, "Biodeterioration in the Sea and its Inhibition," in *Proceedings U.S.-Japan Conference Marine Microbiology*, Baltimore: University Park Press, in press.

42. See note 24 above.

43. Theodore R. Folsom and Allyn C. Vine, "On the tagging of water masses for the study of physical processes in the ocean," in *The Effects of Atomic Radiation on Oceanography and Fisheries*, Publication 551, Washington, D.C.: National Academy of Sciences; National Research Council, 1957, p. 137.

44. Redwood Wright, "Deep water movement in the Western Atlantic as determined by use of a box model," *Deep Sea Research*, Supplement to Vol. 16 (1969): 433-446.

45. Byron F. Morris, "Petroleum: Tar quantities floating in the Northwestern Atlantic taken with a new quantitative neustron net," *Science* 173 (1971): 430-432.

46. Christen E. Junge, *Air chemistry and radioactivity*, New York: Academic Press, 1963, p. 382.

47. Wallace S. Broecker, "Man's oxygen reserves," *Science* 168 (1970): 1537-1538. See also note 35 above.

48. See note 36 above.

49. *Ibid.*

50. Maurice Ewing and William L. Donn, "A theory of ice ages," *Science* 123 (1956): 1061-1066. Although the mechanism proposed by Ewing and Donn some 17 years ago appears not to be correct, the puzzle remains. As yet no one has developed a satisfactory hypothesis that quantitatively explains the large climatic fluctuations between ice ages and interglacial periods such as the present.

51. See note 33 above.

52. Margaret Merlini, "Heavy-metal contamination," in Donald W. Hood (ed.), *Impingement of Man on the Oceans*, New York: Wiley-Interscience, 1971, p. 738.

53. Stig H. Fonselius, "Hydrography of the Baltic Deep Sea Basins III," *Fisheries Board of Sweden Series Hydrography*, Report No. 23 (1969): 95.

54. U.S. National Marine Fisheries Service, "The effects of waste disposal in New York Bight," Summary final report of the NMFS Middle Atlantic Coastal Fisheries Center, Sandy Hook Laboratory, New Jersey, Informal Report No. 2 (1972): 70.

55. Max Blumer and Jeremy Sass, "Oil Pollution: persistence and degradation of spilled fuel oil," *Science* 176 (1972): 1120-1122. The authors report that some components of the oil a few centimeters into the bottom sediments remain as "fresh" after two years in the marine environment as the time of the initial spill.

Notes to Chapter 16

1. U.N. Doc. ST/ECE/ENV/1, New York, 1971.

2. U.N. Gen. Ass. A/Conf. 48/14, July 3, 1972 /Report.

3. U.N. Doc. A/Conf. 48/PC, IWGPM I/WP4.

4. See article in *FAIRPLAY Shipping Journal*, "Perspective on Pollution," London, April 26, 1973, p. 6.

5. U.N. Doc. A/Conf. 48/PC, IWGPM I/5 Prov.

6. Many technical, geographical, biological, oceanographic, and national legal data related to the Mediterranean and its people can be found in the papers of the "Pacem in Maribus" Conference held in Split, Yugoslavia, April 28-30, 1972, devoted to the Mediterranean development and its impact on the marine environment.

7. J. René Dupuy, National legislation relating to water pollution in four Mediterranean countries, p. 18 of the paper delivered during "Pacem in Maribus" Conference (see Note 6).

8. IMCO, "Prevention and Control of Marine Pollution Emanating from Ships," paper prepared by the IMCO Secretariat, Misc/72/14, p. 9.

9. U.N. Doc. A/ o. f. 13/38, Vol. II: Plenary Meetings, Geneva 1958, p. 138.

10. *Ibid.*, p. 142.

11. See *New Directions in the Law of the Sea*, Documents, Vols. I and II, compiled and edited by Lay, Churcil, and Nordquist, The British Institute, London.

12. Conventions on Maritime Law (Texts), Bruxelles 1968, p. 67.

13. *Ibid.*, p. 62.

14. U.N. Treaty Series, vol. 480, p. 43.

15. See cited documents in Note 11, pp. 592 ff.

16. *Ibid.*, p. 602.

17. See cited documents under Note 11, p. 611.

18. See Note 11, p. 670.

19. U.N. Doc. A/Conf. 48/14/Report, p. 4 and Annex III.

20. U.N. Doc. A/AC. 138/25/3 August 1970.

About the Editors

Giulio Pontecorvo received his A.B. and M.A. degrees from Dartmouth College and his Ph.D. (economics) from the University of California at Berkeley. He has taught at the University of California, the University of Colorado, the University of Washington, Bowdoin College and the University of Buenos Aires. Since 1963 he has been at Columbia University where he is Professor of Economics in the Graduate School of Business. Currently he serves on the International Marine Science Affairs Policy Committee of the Ocean Affairs Board, the National Academy of Science and on the Executive Board of the Law of the Sea Institute.

John King Gamble, Jr., received his B.A. degree (political science and mathematics) from the College of Wooster and his M.A. and Ph.D. degrees (political science) from the University of Washington. Presently, he is Executive Director of the Law of the Sea Institute and Assistant Professor of Marine Affairs at the University of Rhode Island. His major academic interests are law of the sea, international law, treaties and quantitative methodologies including computerized information retrieval systems.